LANGUAGE AND CULT
IN THE GROWTH
OF IMPERIALISM

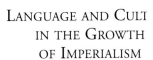

LANGUAGE AND CULTURE IN THE GROWTH OF IMPERIALISM

Sharron Gu

McFarland & Company, Inc., Publishers

Jefferson, North Carolina, and London

LIBRARY OF CONGRESS CATALOGUING-IN-PUBLICATION DATA

Gu, Sharron.
    Language and culture in the growth of imperialism / Sharron
Gu.
        p.   cm.
    Includes bibliographical references and index.

    ISBN 978-0-7864-6848-5
    softcover : acid free paper ∞

    1. Imperialism — History.   2. Language and culture —
History.   3. Imperialism — Social aspects — History.
4. World history.   5. Civilization — History.   I. Title.
JV61.G8 2012
325'.32014 — dc23   2012029663

BRITISH LIBRARY CATALOGUING DATA ARE AVAILABLE

Front cover art: American cartoon of John Bull as an
Imperial Octupus (wikimedia commons); cover design
by David K. Landis (Shake It Loose Graphics)

Manufactured in the United States of America

McFarland & Company, Inc., Publishers
Box 611, Jefferson, North Carolina 28640
www.mcfarlandpub.com

Table of Contents

Acknowledgment

There are no words in any of the languages that I know that can express my gratitude to my editor, Norman Christie, who has supported my research and writing for more than a decade. His good sense of language and poetic instinct can be felt in every chapter of this book.

Preface

This is a cultural history of imperialism from ancient to modern times. It attempts to approach this important issue of international relations from a non-political perspective. Instead of seeing global expansion in terms of economic interest, political control, and ideological influence, it considers global aggression as a cultural and linguistic phenomenon — a common phenomenon that is shared by many cultures in the history of Western Europe, Eastern Europe, the Middle East, and North America.

Like people, language and culture (or civilization) have a natural life which begins with childhood and progresses through predictable stages: infancy, puberty, maturity, and finally old age. Like individual people, language and culture have never been created equal regardless of how much we might wish otherwise. The strengths and weaknesses of a culture are pre-determined (rather than chosen) by a natural inheritance that shapes its future potentials and limitations. This genetic-like composition of a culture is manifested in its forms of expression (including linguistic and non-linguistic expression), and the characteristics and degrees of maturity and refinement of these expressive forms during various stages of its life. The evolution of these forms in each stage, derived from its cultural base, inspires as well as restrains the capacity of seeing, reasoning and understanding that are shared by its speakers.

This work establishes the connection between imperialism and young and emerging language. It ventures to link aggressive attitude, policies, and action in global politics with specific linguistic and cultural types rather than ethnical or ideological origins. Specific culture here does not mean cultural stereotypical differentiation such as English v. Latin or Greek, Christian v. Islam, or socialism v. capitalism. It refers to a specific spectrum of expression, attitude and worldview that developed during certain periods of time in different cultures. For example, the unshakable faith in God and his law that developed concurrently with formative English has more in common with the expression in formative Latin or even early Islamic Arabic than with that of the English of the twentieth century.

Not every language and culture in the world possesses imperial genes. The imperialist cultures are not ordinary members of the global community. They are golden boys who have the good fortune and opportunity not only to survive and grow up but also hold prominent positions on the world stage because they are stronger than their historical contemporaries. World history has witnessed a series of golden boys that have emerged from various places, such as Europe, Asia, and the Middle East during ancient, medieval, and modern times. Each of these dominant cultures, although centuries apart in time, shared a similarly developed self-image and worldview.

This story of the golden boys includes the histories of the ancient Greek and Roman empires, the medieval Islamic Empire, and the British, Russian and American empires of the nineteenth and twentieth centuries. It begins with a comparative narrative of the emergence of these young cultures that focuses on linguistic development. It describes how new literary languages established themselves among a variety of oral traditions and how formative languages sharpened as well as eliminated the worldviews of young cultures and cultivated an adversarial vision and an inflated and fragile nationalistic ego. It demonstrates that the fear and insecurity of the imperial states often constructed an engine of war. It also portrays how cultural maturity was accompanied by an accumulation of descriptive and expressive languages that were enriched through interaction with other languages and cultures. It illustrates how worldviews changed with the maturity of language as these empires passed through puberty and entered adulthood. People began to realize that their world was not as intimidating and isolated as they once felt, and they found their confidence and became more tolerant.

This original reinterpretation of world history is firmly grounded in the latest research of more than a dozen academic disciplines and world languages: history, language, literature, philosophy, arts, music, Ancient Semitic, Greek, Latin, Arabic, Russian and English. The body of references and notes of this book amount to a mass that is much larger than the main text; therefore, only a small part of the references can be listed here. Endnotes are limited to references in English; those of foreign languages are used only if there are not adequate English materials available.

Introduction

The concepts of political science tend to portray and interpret international relations in the abstract and insensitive terms of economic interest, domination, rights and justice. Trapped within a limited horizon, political science alone fails to explain why nations of similar economic structure would have variant ideas and attitudes for their foreign policies, and why nations with different economic structures and ideologies could develop similar global postures during certain periods of their histories. Instead, this is a history of language and worldview of imperialism in the context of cultural evolution and interaction.

Global aggression did not come from the genes of a nation's blood; as a historical episode in many civilizations, it is a cultural and linguistic as well as a political phenomenon. The way that a nation sees its place in the world and the way in which it conducts its international affairs varies with its growth and transformation as a cultural entity. The expression, attitude, and worldview that motivate an aggressive policy toward others do not evolve only from social or commercial interests. These emerge from a certain cultural and linguistic environment that has less to do with types of economic development than with a collective self-image created by regulated language and activated emotion fueled by poetic fantasy and political rhetoric.

This book studies global expansionism from the perspective of cultural dynamic, especially the dynamic of a new or rejuvenated culture. New culture here means a culture that is born and generated by an emerging language and literature. The rejuvenated culture is an old culture that has reinvented itself by assimilating foreign expressions and ideas. This new language and literature often cultivates brand new cultural identities, self-images, and social organizations.

Emerging language and literature has created many dynamic civilizations. Aggressive empires such as Greek, Roman, Islamic, British, Russian, and American each began with a unique cultural identity that encompassed a diversity of cultural forms. Some were born as a written language that codified their oral traditions. Some were redefined by the injection of a brand new ideology into their inherited literary language, which in turn revitalized the existing society. Some were simply transplanted into a barren cultural environment where they had complete freedom to redefine their identities and create new visions of world order. Like adolescents, new cultures, regardless of their ideological tendencies, developed an inflated sense of self and a desperate need for verification, gratification, and glorification.

Every young culture has an oversimplified and polarized vision of the world: good/evil, right/wrong, strong/weak, love/hate, powerful/powerless, and conquer/conquered. To verify its existence and get its way, it is important to be on the correct side and to support the righteous course, whether that course pursues a god, a universal justice, or a type of social order. Since a young culture recognizes only its own language, global issues must be defined and addressed within a narrow range of self-proclaimed universal concepts. Under the name of a one and only God, or a one and only righteous social order (such as capitalism or communism), the young nation assumes a mission to convert the rest of the world in accordance with its beliefs. This act verifies, gratifies and glorifies a new imperial image and subordinates others to its wishes. This imposition of will is a means to impress and convince itself as much as to influence others. Winning means to collect as large a territory as possible, as many colonies as possible — trophies that adorn the fragile cabinet that contains the national ego.

On the other side of this young and inflated persona is an exaggerated fear. Through the eyes of a polarized mind, winners come with losers, believers exist with non-believers (sinners in a religious language), and to love, one must know how to hate. If a god or a moral ideal forms a focal point for love, then an alien god or an alien moral becomes a flashpoint for hatred and fear. People who believe in different gods and practice different morals could be an enemy. The uncompromising adolescent clearly sees that outsiders must think exactly the same way. In order to defend against this potential bad influence, walls and barriers are built which must be defended by a show of military strength.

This exaggerated fear is the engine of war.

This fear was fostered by a low level of confidence due to a combination of many shortcomings: ignorance, lack of knowledge and experience, lack of deeper understanding of human nature, and lack of diplomacy. Most times, a new imperial regime emerged as a bully just as its predecessor had outgrown the game and started to mellow. That is why history has seen a succession of empires come and go consecutively. On most occasions, the mellowing cultures did not die with the decline of their empires, they simply learned to accept their own limits and found ways to make peace with themselves and others. By then, a tolerance and respect for outsiders had replaced expansionist notions.

History has noted only a few times when there was more than one bully reaching puberty and becoming more aggressive at exactly the same time. During these periods, history witnessed lengthy phases of military aggression and war. The first half of the twentieth century is a good example. Many new cultures were reborn or redefined. Many new nations emerged and tried to prove themselves. Through two world wars, the global community punished and disarmed the bad boys ... boys who wouldn't hesitate to murder millions in order to reach their goal of worldwide supremacy. However, the fear and distrust continued. Russians and Americans convinced the world and themselves that the existence and lifestyle of the smaller and weaker nations (under the premise of capitalism and socialism) needed protection, a protection from a big brother. The legacy of the golden boy continued this time in front of an imagined rather than a real danger.

The dynamic energy of a youthful culture, fueled by a vision of global expansion, forced it to grow and mature rapidly. Military expansion opened the door for cultural interaction, an interaction which had a prolonged cultural influence on the new empire. On one hand, the exotic and glamorous older culture seduced the boy. It made him see, feel and think in a way that he had never experienced before. On the other hand, his young language, which had been transplanted (by war or peace) into new soils and was spoken by the seductress, became more enriched, versatile and sophisticated by an absorption and assimilation of alien forms of languages and expressions. With this newly found cultural and spiritual maturity, the boy found himself and his place in the community of nations. History has recorded that these boys either survived their puberty to become cultural giants or died as short-lived military super powers.

In Part One, "The Birth of the Golden Boys," global interaction and mutation of various expressions — such as oral poetry, literature, music, visual images, scientific discovery and original ideas — often give birth to brand new cultures. This part analyzes and compares the cultural diversity that created the Greek, Roman, Islamic, British, Russian, and American empires. Cultural hybrids of this type can develop in different historical periods and various circumstances as long as a complex and large-scale co-existence of different languages and various expressions occurs.

In human history, cultural interaction created dynamic newborns, referred to as the golden boys. These civilizations had distinctive identities and a vibrant energy that destined them to greatly influence not only their contemporary world, but also the world as we now know it. As the specific cultural mosaic often played important roles in the formation and future development of these emerging cultures and their relationship with the rest of the world, their formative history is described here in comparison with another culture that was at least partly its contemporary.

Chapter 1, "Oral and Written Language: Greek and Roman Empires," traces the evolution of languages in these cultures and how they influenced the growth of civilization.

Before it became written, Ancient Greek was a mature poetic tradition that developed rich and diverse local variations as each city and region had its unique language/dialect and political and legal establishment. It took Greeks many centuries of conflict to build a unified nation. Greek unity evolved and finally was found in a classical literature that canonized Greek poetic traditions, streamlined Greek writing and reasoning, and reorganized Greek political administration under the leadership of the Macedonian kings. It was this literary tradition that turned a chaotic and fragmented Greece into a military and cultural empire. Although the glory of Greek global military expansion was short-lived compared to that of the Romans, the influence of Greek literature and philosophy outlived its state. This classical tradition became the cradle of Western high learning for centuries to come.

Latin, as an emerging regional language among many languages and dialects in the Italian Peninsula, became written without centuries of poetic accumulation and articulation, as has occurred in the ancient Greek. The Roman Empire grew up with a young and vigorous written language which had much higher degrees of precision and binding power. The exceptional linguistic efficiency of Latin, which was alien to the more fluid Greek, formed the foundation for Roman legal and administrative structure. However, the influences of Latin literature had much less sustaining power than that of Greek. Latin declined after the fall of the Roman Empire because of its shallow oral expression. An established root of oral expression helps to keep a language alive and allows it to further refine. Latin gradually retreated from its status as a universal language except in religious and high learning and was eventually replaced by European vernaculars. However, Roman law, legal administration and jurisprudence were retained by the emerging European states, and Latin high learning was reborn within modern European languages centuries later. Chapter 2, "God's Words Written and Spoken: The Roman and Islamic Empires," is a comparative study of the formation of the Roman and Islamic empires in terms of cultural expression. Latin and Arabic inherited opposite linguistic characteristics as they evolved into written form. Latin was a relatively young language and grew under the shadow of ancient Greek. It possessed a limited vocabulary with a narrow range of connotation and translated expressions. However, it had an exceptional capacity of clarity, precision and terseness.

Arabic was much more similar to Greek. It was a well-developed poetic language with vivid imageries, metaphors, and multileveled connotations. However, as poetic fluidity contradicted solid boundaries of legal language and administrative efficiency, Arabs also had to learn its advanced philosophical expression from Greek. After military expansion, Romans ruled their empire with silent words of written law, administrative strategy, and unified worldview, while Arabs ruled their empire with the words of a God who was speaking loudly in rhythm, and who revealed different faces to his people who spoke many different languages.

Chapter 3 addresses "The Words of Law: Islamic and British Empires." With an emerging literary form (Arabic rhythmic prose), Muslim writers transplanted the Hebrew idea of a speaking god and Greek philosophy into their ancient poetic. Arabic, a mature poetic language with limited vocabularies, expanded rapidly into a universal language that cultivated a brand new religion, a sophisticated legal system and a powerful empire.

Like the Islamic Empire, the British Empire owed its sustaining power to its highly diverse, adoptive and poetic language. Latin, French, and Italian influences provided English with a degree of diversity that was impossible to achieve for a culture based on a single language. Latin clarified Old English vision and logic by creating a level of abstract meaning. French offered a rich repertoire of precise and technical vocabularies. Italian enhanced the flexibility and innovation of Middle English.

Modern English, incorporating these influences, further refined its poetics and became a language that was able to sing as the Greeks and Arabs, paint as the French, gesture as the Italian, and reason as the Germans. The secret of its success as a universal language is reflected in this versatility and adaptability, and for this reason the influence of English language has survived the British Empire and continues to prevail.

Chapter 4, "Letters and Voices of English: British and American Empires," examines how one language created two different cultures. It emphasizes the degrees of diversity in expression and the timing in which these diverse elements became assimilated into mainstream English. First, it compares the specific developmental stages of English through which each culture took its roots. Secondly, it analyzes the cultural environment in which the particular English at a particular time emerged, evolved or was transplanted. Unlike in Medieval England, American English was transplanted into the cultural vacuum of North America, a place where no unified or established sub-verbal and literary culture existed. In the place of English music and visual arts, which had been the resources of imagination for earlier development, American English was born within a collage of diverse cultural inspirations — including African, Jewish, Italian, Irish, German, Slavic, and Spanish. In this melting pot a new civilization emerged. This cultural stew released an incredible energy that had never been seen before. This multitude of diverse traditions reinvented and took root in America and created a dynamic cultural force.

Chapter 5, "Old and New Songs: Russian and American Empires," is a depiction of the cultural foundation of the Cold War that developed in the middle of the twentieth century. Although with apparently opposite ideologies, Russian and American empires emerged from a similar cultural soil where national identity, sentiment and emotion were heightened by borrowed ideologies. Russia evolved into a global superpower with the spread of ideological rhetoric of Marxism, which failed to prevail in Germany, a land of abstract thinking and learning. Marxist ideals that were isolated in academia in the West found rich soil in ancient poetry of Russia. Russia became the leader of a world of social utopia that caught the imaginations of peasants and working poor. Communism managed to sing in tune with the Russian tongue and activated the same passion once felt for the tsar and the Orthodox Church.

The same pride and passion were felt and demonstrated by the Americans of the twentieth century for different reasons. As the vast land of America opened its arms to seeds from all corners of the world, every soul arrived with a bit of the Old World. Each came to make a new beginning and each hoped to achieve his dreams. Unlike the ancient land of Old Russia where old songs had been sung for centuries, the American garden, wild and un-kept at first glance, had become a cultural mosaic bound together by a singular vision of democracy and equal opportunity. It created new songs to raise a brand new collective soul.

Two large and powerful nations had reached puberty at the same time. Both egos were highly inflated and pumped up with vivid images, stirring songs and slogans and self-righteous ideology. Each claimed to be the champion of human destiny and each was determined to become the best, most just and most powerful nation in the world. Each was willing to fight against anyone who challenged this claim and had the audacity to stand in his way.

Part Two, "Growing Up and Puberty," acknowledges that not every emerging imperial power was equipped to deal with the challenge of cultural interaction. Most imperial states quickly disappeared from world stage as soon as they ran out of ammunition or the last great warrior passed on. Only the golden boys, those with enough education and knowledge cultivated by a mature literary tradition, were able to determine their own identity and formulate a worldview that placed them in a preeminent imperial position for centuries. Their reign of leadership was determined by two basic elements: the literary and intellectual capacities based on the evolution and refinement of its expression, and its ability to evolve, diversify, absorb, and assimilate from alien, older and conquered cultures.

Chapter 6, "Black/White Vision of the World," addresses the evolution of language beyond a simplistic worldview. Just like a child, a new civilization sees a banal, polarized world of black and white. In a brand new language, vocabularies are accumulated first by pairing opposite words: the sky and the earth, moon and sun, ocean and land, mother and father, life and death, and male and female. The initial purpose was to describe a distinction. The relationship between the two poles was perceived as opposite and absolutely exclusive. This limitation of vocabulary created an adversarial vision that did not allow for any shading.

The vision of black and white was also the worldview that revived older cultures. Established societies have, over time, shaded and then colored their vision. Extreme positions were seen as undesirable. The outline of ideas and their expressions are blurred. The babble created by this diversity of thought overwhelmed creativity. Only the artists, writers and scholars dared to present new ideas and expression. And most of these were considered to be outside general acceptance and thus ignored.

To introduce change, the society needed a cultural shock. It needed to clarify its vision and to classify the overlapping vocabularies to reorganize and reinitiate thinking. This was accomplished by the injection of a God, a new ideology or a language from another part of the world. The ensuing polarization motivated a general discussion that invigorated the collective to consider all sorts of new thought, internally as well as from the outside.

The moralization and polarization of worldview are a phenomenon of both young and revived cultures. For the cultures of a brand new language, whether it be the young with its new language, or the old culture aggressively embracing an alien language, rigid polarization is the only describable, imaginable, and finally, the only thinkable course of action. Just as there is only one God, as there is only one sun, there is one universal social system. In this context, the world is always divided between godliness/ungodliness, good/evil, right/wrong, light/darkness, or socialism/capitalism.

Chapter 7, "Inflated Self and Playing God," examines the polarized vision of a new culture that also created a self-image as idealized and as rigid as its worldview. Seeing only in black and white, good and evil, believers and non-believers, the imperial boy imagined himself to be in the world alone carrying the weight of humanity on his shoulders with only his god as companion.

His god was the most perfect being that his mind could conceive. He was perfect and his words were absolute. In old cultures, religion set man upon a tormented and never-ending journey toward an idealized model in which man mimicked his god to lift himself up to divine perfection. The new imperial culture borrowed an alien god who spoke a different (divine and non-human) language. This God was remote and accessible only by repeating his words. As to worship God was to worship his words, a conversation with God and interpretation of his words were a super human act. To act upon his words created a pathway between mankind and his divinity.

As culture evolved the gap between man's words and those of God became blurred and shrank. By writing about and interpreting God's words, man eventually developed the ability to put words into his God's mouth. He felt closer to his God, and came to associate the wishes of man with those of the deity and became convinced that his issues were God's issues as well. As this point, man would use the name of his God to morally justify any action that he considered. He had successfully created God in his own image.

On the other side of the inflated ego was an exaggerated fear, as described in Chapter 8, "Exaggerated Fear and Insecurity." New cultures were obsessed with territories and boundaries; borders had to be drawn, walls had to be built, and barriers had to be set up to defend against outsiders. In a world full of barbarians, the imperial boys could not feel safe unless there was a clear division in land (physical), on paper (document), and most importantly in the mind (moral). They could not feel safe unless there was a clear division, real or psychological, that separated them from outsiders.

The best defense was always an offense. The imperial boys had to push their borders as far as they could to collect as much land and bounty as they could. Their ability to occupy, to expand and to be gloriously victorious was the only way that they knew how to combat the fear in their minds: the fear for God, evil, some "isms" or anything imaginable that fueled this insecurity. Their comfort was determined by their ability to expand, first to neighboring land, then across the continents, across the oceans and more recently, into space.

Part Three, "Marriage and Maturity," is an examination of a more advanced phase of development. Boys remain boys until they fall in love. An imperial boy was on a journey to conquer exotic older people. When he got there, he was amazed and then seduced by the refined and artistic variety of the lands he saw. He realized that they were conquered people who had already surrendered their souls. He found alien spirits, laid back yet confident, who could teach him the ways of life without deflating his ego.

This marriage with other cultures enriched the boy's spirit and helped him to mature. The exchange of words, images, gestures, rhythms, and ideas expanded his vision. He learned how to speak other languages without barriers and without fear until the different languages became one. The boy learned that the true power was communication ... words rather than swords. It was the ability to negotiate and convince or compromise. He had learned that any lasting influence was an influence of the mind.

Chapter 9 is titled "Expending Worldview and Sharing Self." The boys who matured were the ones who outgrew fear and insecurity. They learned to be confident enough to open themselves up. This process began with the accumulation of cultural forms, especially those which enabled them to have personal and individual visions. Songs, artistic music, and lyrical poetry are examples that encouraged individual expression and cultivated a personal level of meaning in communication. At this stage, an individual self-perception emerged and this replaced the old self, which had been defined by someone else: a collective, God, social class, or ethnical community. It allowed the individual to conceive a personal way to relate to the established form of his culture and discover his language and place.

Through individual expression, personal (rather than national) boundaries could redefine themselves. Therefore, the identity of a person became a mental and spiritual choice rather than simply a geographic location, functional language, or social designation. With this newly found confidence, an understanding and tolerance for others could flourish.

Maturity is the topic of Chapter 10, "Confidence and Tolerance." To mature is to recognize and accept one's limits and shed the pretense of playing God or putting words in God's mouth. The imperial boy began to learn different languages, and as they became able to communicate with outsiders' (the barbarians') knowledge, understanding and tolerance emerged. Imperial boys began to exchange ideas and make connections. They were then ready to become the real leaders of the world as they employed their newly found tools of negotiation and persuasion rather than relying solely on military and financial clout.

Many imperial boys survived into adulthood. They became fathers and grandfathers. They finally found peace with themselves and with others; they became convinced that they had secured a place in this world for themselves and for their children. They have learned to be comfortable around other nations and to be a part of the global community.

PART ONE
THE BIRTH OF GOLDEN BOYS

This is the story of how new cultures were born from a mutation of expressions: oral, written words, visual images, rhythms of music, scientific discovery, and original ideology. It analyzes the mixture of cultural genes that created the Greek, Roman, Islamic, British, Russian, and American empires. Although in entirely different periods and circumstances of history, the cultural hybrid always created dynamic new babies — golden boys, who had brand new identity and vibrant energy.

Since the genetic makeup of these cultures often determined their future development and their relationship with others, their formation is described in conjunction with another culture that was at least partly its contemporary.

1. Oral and Written Language: Greek and Roman Empires

This chapter describes the emergence of the Greek and Roman Empires as cultural movements. With an ancient oral tradition, it took the ancient Greeks many centuries to build a unified state. They had been held back until a written language was adopted. After borrowing the Phoenician alphabets, Greece developed a literary tradition. With the power of the Macedonian kings, it finally became a military as well as a cultural empire. Although the glory of military expansion and administration was short-lived, the cultural influence of its classical literature sustained for thousands of years. The Roman Empire grew up with its written language, which made it possible to build a political and legal structure in an amazingly short period of time. As a much younger language, Latin, with its clarity and binding power, created an administrative efficiency that the ancient Greek could never achieve. However, the influence of Latin literature declined because the various expressions that transplanted from Greek could not take root without an equally rich oral foundation, a foundation that kept language alive and refined. Latin as a dominant cultural force eventually died after its empire. The Latin ideas of law and universal God were reborn within the new languages (Modern languages of Europe) in later centuries.

This story of cultural interaction does not participate in the decades long academic debate about the "original color" of Greek culture. It illustrates that, in cultural history, who borrows from whom or who influences whom is not as important as how a culture filters, adapts, and assimilates various external influences, and how it formulates, expends, and transforms its identity in the process. It focuses on Greek creative energy, which reacted, absorbed, and transformed foreign images, motifs, and ideas, and then wove them into its own cultural idioms. The basic fabric of the Greek cultural tapestry was its literary language, poetry and prose. In its formative stage, epic poetic inherited, transmitted, and recreated stories ... stories that had been invented and refined by other languages for a long time. Prose writing cultivated another kind imagination: to depict, to specify, and to analyze in increasingly general and abstract terms. This combined and accumulated diversity created a rich repertoire that the ancient Greek could assimilate into a unique integrated culture.

Latin culture was based on a language with a relatively shallow oral foundation. Growing up among much more sophisticated cultures and languages, formative Latin began by creating an artificial identity based upon translation from classic Greek, in form, vocabulary, expression, and thought. As Greek literature was transplanted into Roman soil, it lost its music, pitch, rhythm, and its theatrics. It lost the Greek audience whose minds, eyes, and ears had been cultivated by its poetics for centuries. After translation to Latin, Greek poetry was silenced. It became statues of words that were envisaged, admired, and superficially imitated. As a new language, Latin had not yet developed the poetic flow to carry Greek imagination. It lacked the inner dynamic and ability to absorb, adopt, and transform alien forms of communication.

Latin created a different kind of dynamic: conceptual precision and efficiency. With a naive and yet vigorous and uncompromising clarity, Latin successfully established a deep and unbridgeable conceptual gap between opposite notions of man and god, order and disorder, and law and outlaw. Latin became the language of a universal God and Christianity, and it completed the ancient unfulfilled dream of Hebrew (Judaism). Latin became the first language that could efficiently distinguish and override many pagan gods and spirits. Latin precision and efficiency established a formidable authority ... words of law.

———

Greek culture emerged from the rich soil of the ancient Mediterranean, where multi-lingual and cultural traditions had coexisted and interacted, through war and peace, throughout the millennia. During the tenth and ninth century B.C., compared to the older Mediterranean civilizations, Greek was the infant. Ancient Egypt had been through many ups and downs, and lived into its forth millennia. The Sumerians had settled in Mesopotamia during the middle of fifth millennium B.C. Babylon emerged as the new center of Mesopotamian civilization during the middle of the second millennium and carried its own legacy for another thousand years. These mature civilizations produced a vast repertoire of idioms, motifs, and ideas. The emerging Greek had access to an overwhelmingly rich resource of expression that could be used to mould their own identity.

From this cultural resource, Greeks took the most important elements and built their own tradition, the idea of language (alphabet, as written language), the idea of one God rather than various gods and goddesses, and the idea of community (state and the world). However, these ideas had been around for thousands of years. Why did they flourish, mature, and sustain only in Greek? It began with Greek epic poetry.

Homeric Greeks grew up with monumental and vivid images as well as chanting stories. During the seventh century B.C., they went to Egypt, as traders as well as visitors. They had seen and admired the pyramids and tomb paintings. They had traded Assyrian jewelry, gems, seals, and bronze sculpture. They were familiar with the story line of Semitic epics that had been articulated in the ancient Near East.[1] The pre-imperial Greeks, who had lived in a multi-cultural and mixed racial environment for centuries, were not as racially conscious as the modern men and women.[2] Amazed by the cultural achievement and material wealth of Egypt, they wished and believed that their own civilization had originated from the Nile Valley.[3]

Large number of Greeks went to Egypt to learn the skills and craftsmanship of stone carving. Years later, Greeks invented their own tradition of building in stone. By the middle of the sixth century, Greeks had built vast temples for their own gods. The sanctuary of the goddess Hera, at Olympia, was a temple stretching 100 meters by 50 meters, and was centered by a monumental gateway. It included double colonnade and twenty-one columns along each side. It had a deep porch, which led to the cellar, where the statue of the goddess stood. The temple of Artemis at Ephesus had double rows of columns like the Egyptian column hall, while the famous row of marble lions at Delos reminds one of the traditional sacred processional routes of the Egyptian temples.[4]

Daedalic, a Greek artist, transformed Egyptian sculpture into a popular style. Statues with wigged hair, triangular faces, and small flat skulls became common during the seventh century. They were first created in small terracotta and bronze and grew into life-size figures of marble. The best example was the statue of Nikandre from Naxos. She exemplified the mixture of numerous styles. She came from the Greek tradition of large-scale wood sculpture, she was styled in an oriental fashion, and she exhibited an Egyptian proportion.[5] During the fifth century, statues became natural and more relaxed in their pose. The sculptures of the great temple of Zeus, at Olympia, showed a real understanding of the mood and feelings of the participants. This marked a beginning of a new age.

A similar change occurred in pottery painting.[6] During the seventh century, a Corinthian theme of animal life was admired and adopted as the best of Greek pottery decoration. It replaced the Athenian Geometric style completely by the sixth century. Even Athenian artists allowed their animals to run around in disorder on their vases. However, by the last thirty years of the sixth century, animals had retreated to the background. Epic and mythical figures emerged and began to be the center of visual depiction. On the Francois vase, there were two hundred figures depicting the myth of Achilles' life. The painting portrayed the marriage of his parents, and the games held in honor of his dead friend Patroclus. Mythical themes became the underlying principle of the organization of painting.[7]

Commercial trade between Greece and the East had significantly increased. Archaeological finds offered a solid foundation for tracing Egyptian, Late Hittite, Urartian, and Assyrian cultural influences.[8] Also found were oriental artifacts and their Greek imitations. There were ivory carvings, ostrich eggs, tridacna shells, gold jewelry, faience and glass beads, gems and seals. Metalwork such as bronze tympanon and shields and silver bowls were more appealing and impressive.

Painting and architecture alone could not have supported a lasting civilization without reproduction and assimilation. Greeks quickly developed their own domestic craftsmanship. They reinterpreted and recreated their own motifs. They not only kept the visual images alive, they also transformed the borrowed images and reproduced them in a refined form, thus making them their own.

The reproduction of Asian and Egyptian images transformed the Greek perception of humanity, visually and in the mind. It transformed the stiff, artificial, and moral into images that came alive with their nature, freedom, and beauty.[9] Although this transition was observed in many ancient and modern cultures, this combination of Greek mixed with alien cultures had accelerated the transition process. It might have taken much longer in an isolated environment. The Greek mind could pick up a previously refined and polished image or motif and simply declare that it belonged to them. This instant conversion made it possible for the Greeks to skip many evolutionary stages and allowed them access to idioms that were not available to them otherwise.

The Greeks benefited from this mixed cultural repertoire, and they outlived their older neighbors. Many contemporary languages went through centuries of idiomatic and technical accumulation in order to find a balance between visual and oral imageries. Language often had great difficulty in upgrading its expression to satisfy its expanding imagination. Words, especially bigger and more general words, "bolder" assumptions, as Professor Gutherie put it, were the necessary stepping stones for new levels of communication and reasoning.[10] Without words, imagery remained dependent on pictures, and imagination was grounded and imprisoned by the senses, its physical vision. Linguistic evolution was blocked, even terminated. With borrowed and reproduced images and visual expressions, the ancient Greek found a shortcut and became a successful cultural mutant. The poetic narrative was inspired and refined by visual images, and verbal imagery flourished.[11]

To verbalize visual images, and to enable the mind's eye to see, was a great challenge for many ancient languages. If a language failed to envisage, it could not branch out and reach general and abstract levels of description and imagination. The language of verbal imagery was crucial in creating abstract meanings, while keeping pace with oral language. All ancient languages lost their oral roots as soon as they elevated into the realm of mathematics, engineering, and higher learning. They began to decline after they lost their speaking voice and became the prisoners of the tower of their own written words. Although these written languages were kept in circulation for centuries after their oral forms died (by inventing new oral vernaculars), none of them survived the test of time.

The idea of an alphabet was the best example of this constant effort to balance voice and script. The mind could fly while keeping root within everyday speech. To make the connection between the sound of language and its script, ancient Semitic was the first to invent a functional alphabetic system. Egyptians and Phoenicians had developed partial phonetic signs representing only consonants. The nature of Semitic language, which could communicate without a specific sign for vowels, made it the first language to build a structural connection between written and oral communication.[12] However, the idea of phonic language did not reach its potential because ancient Semitic script, unlike Arabic, was not fully phonic. It's omission of vowels made it difficult to translate sound to script in a precise manner. The inconsistency of the signs of language and its sound led to a repeated recycling of oral language. This cut off or delayed the accumulation of cultural idioms. It took much longer for Semitic to achieve the formal integration between its spoken and written forms.

Ancient Greek was the first language that successfully adopted the idea of alphabet and created a language whose phonetics provided a solid foundation for the evolution of literary languages.[13] The Phoenician alphabet, improved by the invention of symbols for vowels, provided a power of unity that oral Greek never had. Without a central state and written language, each region in Greece developed its own way to communicate and to absorb foreign images and vocabularies. These various degrees of mixture produced unique forms of expression. As each region developed unique forms of imagery, dialogue, and language, ancient Greek accumulated its own repertoire of highly diverse cultural idioms.

Unlike the silent script of older languages, Greek texts, during the fifth century, were read aloud in public, a literary performance. Teachers performed rhapsodies of epic, students sung lyric in chorus, tragedy and comedy were acted in festivals. Herodotus recited portions of his *History* in public, and the Sophists gained their fame from their speech.[14]

Music played an important role in the oral transmission of Greek. It carried and accompanied words whenever and wherever they were uttered. Music was played as the gods were honored in public festivals, and when heroes were praised after their victory in the games. It accompanied every public performance of poetry or drama whether it was weddings or funerals, or the praising of gods or men. The words of Pindar were choral lyrics, which were properly composed in order to harmonize the voice, musical instrument and the shout of oboes. The monodic lyric of Sappho was accompanied by the lyre.[15]

Written Greek gradually integrated various dialects and expressions from different regions and wove them into one language. This linguistic integration did not only ease the emerging parallel development of written and oral expression, but also significantly increased the adaptability of all expressions developed within Greek culture at large. Any innovative expression of the Greek would be inevitably understood, imitated, and transformed in many other types of expressions. The ways and forms in which each Greek region responded, absorbed, and reinterpreted foreign expressions would eventually consolidate into a culture as a whole.

This unified diversity provided a rich soil for the further development of Greek literature. Unlike ancient Semitic, which repeatedly outgrew its poetics and uprooted from it after they became written, ancient Greek flourished in various forms simultaneously in various regions with their different dialects. For example, Ionic prose evolved as a simple and yet more precise form of expression. It became the vehicle for philosophical speculation. Attic became the vehicle for oratory, aimed at moving men's minds. Lyric emerged from Lydia.

This was the reason why Greek became the only language in which cultural and scientific expression of the ancient Mediterranean was kept alive, reinvented, and flourished. Egyptians and Babylonians had developed a number of mathematical procedures to deal with practical problems involving building and calculation of ratios. Without general and abstract concepts, these ideas and knowledge remained at the level of skills and technique, which could be learned and thought without elevating into general worldviews and abstract thinking.[16]

Before the fifth century B.C., the interaction of cultural images took the form of the exchange of finished products and skill and technique of craftsmanship. Without abstract words, mathematics failed to make the leap into science and philosophy because it remained too concrete and particular to be applied to the equally concrete non-mathematical matters. Without words, especially general and abstract vocabularies, concrete knowledge about nature and the human body remained perceived and understood as magic or skills, rather than religion or science. During the fifth century, only a small minority of Athenian citizens were able to read in more than a rudimentary way. Written word was considered an inferior substitute for the art of memory.

No skill or technology could evolve directly into rational thinking without invention and intervention by language. Language, general vocabularies and expression that conceptualized grander assumptions made abstract reasoning possible. It often took centuries of oral communication, negotiation, and meditation to create a verbal and mediating field between abstract principle and a compelling package of concrete proof and adversarial reasoning.

The best example for the intervention of language was Hesiod's *Theogony*, the forerunner of Greek cosmogony. Every ancient civilization created its own collection of natural gods and goddesses, which were inspired and derived from various natural phenomena. It was the first step that connected between concrete images and the logic behind them. Both Egyptian and Mesopotamian literature had reached the point where a primitive connection, the connection of human relations as metaphor, was established by storytelling. However, there was a gap between personal and cosmological connections that would not allow them to merge and create a coherent whole. The Greek epic was the only language that was fluid enough to tell convincing stories after the Sumerian-Babylonian epic.[17]

Hesiod put Eros, a relatively new god, between the genuine goddess Gaea (the earth) and Uranus (the heaven) in a way that made sense for the ordinary mind. Before Hesiod, gods and goddesses were primal (or general) gods who included all levels of the cosmos within themselves. They mediated between the upper and lower worlds, between light and darkness, and between life and death. Hesiod told the story of a forcible separation which made gods more specific and responsive to man, yet related to the primal gods. Although the story lines in Greek myth resembled the Egyptian and Babylonian myth, Greek re-creation was much more fluid, dramatic, and even emotional. When Uranus and Gaea mated to create the Titans, a new generation of abnormal gods emerged. Cyclopes was one-eyed, and the giant Hecatoncheires had three hundred hands. Uranus was ashamed of their children and hid them in Gaea's body. To allow her progeny to be born, Gaea had to coach her son, Cronus, to cut off Uranus' genitals, an act that separated heaven and earth. Greek myth reduced the crudity of the story by allowing Uranus and Gaea to collaborate after divorce in a plan to save Zeus from Cronus.

Greek was the first language of the ancient Mediterranean languages that was able to make the leap to philosophy.[18] Many ancient civilizations tried, yet none of them succeeded, because they failed to create abstract words. Natural gods and goddesses, often believed to be associated with principle powers (or elements) of nature, failed to uproot themselves from the concrete natural phenomena and the specific names of the tangible. As language failed to abstract, the mind could not imagine something that was shapeless, timeless, and impossible to be seen, touched or felt.

With its God, a person with a name, but not a face, Biblical Hebrew was the first language that attempted to imagine a subject without abstract vocabularies. The only possible way to describe something that was literally indescribable in a primitive language was by negative description. To create a finite subject without a concrete image was to invent a verbal hole or space, vague and yet definite. This empty space, which was later interpreted into a mysterious godhead, was the original Hebrew God. It successfully defined a concept of God the best way possible in its own terms, in contrast to the Canaanite mass of idols. It took Hebrew many centuries to refine this mystic God and to specify His boundary with and path towards man. The Old Testament marked a revolution in human cultural expression and imagination.[19]

By creating a universal God, the Bible opened the eyes of the mind. It proved to man not only that there was a God, but also, that there was something (or someone) beyond the horizon of man's physical vision. This finite point, which could be reached by words and imagination, had changed (or substituted in Guthrie's term) its name many times in many languages throughout history. It inspired many gods of various shape and form, many grand assumptions such as nature, will, or reason, while its distance, and its relation with man was reshaped and redefined ... but, its existence and accessibility remained. In this specific sense, God did not create human mind, but he was a mystic inspiration, like the sun and the moon, for the ancients. He inspired man to climb, to fly, to search, and have the desire to see more and know more than simply the readily apparent.

The Bible invented a brand new way to imagine, to liberate one's mind from the prison of his body and stretch the limits of his physical vision. To imagine in words rather than lines, colors, gestures, or rhythm was to see with one's eyes shut, mouth closed, and hands frozen. This vision of the mind marked the new beginning in human communication and imagination. It also was the beginning of a journey towards the disposal of a mediator — a ladder, a sanctuary, or a church — in order to reach for God. One could bring him closer with words. Words, even words in a primitive language, could reach God by talking to him directly. From that point on, each time that man decided to consult his God directly, he had an opportunity to modify his God without the permission of the established mediator (the religious and political establishment). This idea lived on and inspired many revolutions in human history: cultural, ideological, and political.

General and abstract imagination came to each culture in different ways at different times depending on the degree of its linguistic evolution. The language that evolved in an isolated environment, such as ancient Chinese and

Sanskrit, invented their abstract vocabularies for the intangible by stretching and elevating concrete words. It took Chinese thousands of years to complete this step. Sanskrit created a separate level of language specializing in religious learning and philosophy, while inventing new oral languages to replace its oral function.

Among the ancient Mediterranean civilizations, Greek was the only language that evolved abstract vocabularies while maintaining a lively oral tradition. Most ancient cultures failed to establish this integration of cultural expression because their oral language could not make the leap to abstract expression, or only a section of its language made this jump, and left the common tongue behind. Biblical Hebrew became highly abstract after centuries of theological speculation, but it eventually lost its oral form.

Ancient Egyptian tried to develop a language capable of general speculation that envisaged a world beyond vision. It succeeded only partially. The Egyptian obsession with their gods and afterlife illustrated that the language had the capacity to push the boundary of the human physical being. It did create a world beyond life, but not beyond vision. It was the world living on the walls of tombs. Like the Greek epic kingdom of gods, Egyptian gods were also grouped as a mass. Some gods had more than one name and some gods shared their names. When a god was associated with the sun, he had many names for various forms. The most important were *Khepri* (the morning), *Re-Harakhty*, and *Atum* (the old and evening form). Regional associations formed according to major cult activities and holy places. For example, the main cult location of *Khnum*, the creator god, who created man from clay, was Elephantine, and he was the lord of the nearby First Cataract. The sun god's cult place was *Heliopolis* (a Greek word for the city of Sun God), *Ptah's* was Memphis, and *Amon's* was *Thebes*. Gods had principle manifestations, and most were associated with one or more species of animal. For male gods the most important forms were the falcon and bull; for goddesses the cow, cobra, vulture, and lioness. One still can see these images on the relief of Egyptian temples today. The Egyptian gods needed to have many different animal and natural associations, because there were not enough words (descriptive words or adjectives) at the time to describe their characters. It always took several centuries of story telling to coin a group of relatively abstract words that described these characters. Before the word "masculine" was invented, ancient Egyptians would put a bullhead on their gods to show the masculine personality. To show an ambivalent or mixed personality, they would assign two or three animals to the same god. Some goddesses were lionesses in their fiercer aspect but were cats when docile.

Egyptians were very good at classifying meanings and cultivated a good sense of form. They did not only specify aspects of the characters of their gods that corresponded to animals, but also specified the relationship between nature and its various forms. There were many ancient deities such as the fertility god *Min* and the creator and craftsman *Ptah*. There were also cosmic gods, *Shu*, of the air and sky, and *Geb*, of the earth. Some gods had only human form. Others had both cosmic and human, especially those who provided a model for human society. In temple relief, gods were depicted in human form, which was central to decorum. Gods having animal manifestations were shown with human body and the head of their animal. The opposite creation, a human head and an animal body, was used for the king, thus, a Sphinx with a lion's body. Sphinx could receive other heads, notably those of rams and falcons.[20]

Egyptians were not as good at organizing meanings and various forms, especially organizing meanings in a flexible, verbal and non-mathematical way. Without a poetic narrative as fluid as that of Greek, they could not build a hierarchy of gods as precise as their pyramids. They were constantly reorganizing their population of gods in the only way they could comprehend, by grouping their gods in a numerical manner. The most ancient grouping was the *ennead*, which is probably attested from the 3rd dynasty (2650–2575 B.C.). Enneads were groups of nine gods.[21] In ancient Egyptian the number three symbolized plurals in general, so nine was the plural of "plurality." The principal ennead was the Great Ennead of Heliopolis. This was headed by the sun god and creator *Re* or *Re-Atum*, followed by *Shu* and *Tefnut*, gods of air and moisture, *Geb* and *Nut*, who represented earth and sky, and *Osiris, Isis, Seth*, and *Nephthys*. This ordering incorporated a myth of creation, to which was joined the myth of *Osiris*, whose deeds and attributes ranged from the founding of civilization to kinship, kingship and succession to office. The ennead excluded the appearance of a grouping that brought together existing religious conceptions and was rather arbitrary and inflexible.

Egyptians invented several ways to organize their gods numerically. The *Ogdoad* (group of eight gods) of Hermopolis, embodied the inchoate world before creation and consisted of four pairs of male and female gods with abstract names such as Darkness, Absence, and Endlessness. The common grouping in the New Kingdom (1500–1070 B.C.) and later was the triad. The archetypal triad of Osiris, *Isis*, and Horus exhibited the normal pattern of a god and goddess with a junior god, usually male. Most local centers came to have triads, the second and third members of which might be devised for the sake of form. One triad which worshiped in the Greco-Roman period temple at *Kawm Umbu (Kom Ombo)* consisted of *Haroeris* (older Horus), the goddess *Tsenetnofret* [the perfect companion], and the youthful god *Pnebtawy* (the lord of the two lands). The last name, which was an epithet of kings, is revealing, because young gods had many attributes of the kings. Combining gods was another way to organize divines, such as *Amon-Re*, or even *Amon-Re-Harakhte*. *Akhenaton*'s attempt to promote *Aton* (sun god, the disk of sun) into a universal god ended with his reign.[22]

This primitive verbal structuring and exaction did not lead to a realm of abstract concepts. Egyptians, with their visualized and classified language, developed highly technical and meticulous, even profound, knowledge.[23] For example, they recorded extremely detailed descriptions of bodily injuries and their treatments; they performed highly specialized surgeries. However, without abstract vocabularies, they failed to describe let alone grasp the inner dynamics of the body. Even after they found a word that tried to capture the essence of bodily function, they could not find in their language a word (like *qi* in ancient Chinese) that defined both the way the body worked as a whole and the specific biological mechanics that one could see, feel, and touch. So, their medical knowledge was recorded, treated, and utilized in an extremely specific and yet rigid manner, much like a homeowner following plans and blueprints to effect household repairs. Egyptian medicine, through highly advanced for its time, remained a technology rather than a science because it still lacked the abstract concepts needed to theorize.

Like Sumerian cuneiform writing, ancient Egyptian was highly structured. It began with hieroglyphs.[24] This form of writing was not only laborious to learn and imposed a burden on the memory, but it also could not continue to develop without an equally elaborate sound system. Egyptians left giant, well-designed monuments and vivid paintings; however, those images without sound and pictures without popular narrative could not survive the test of time. Several thousand years of Egyptian civilization left us with only ideas of gods without mythology that was told and retold in common tongue, and pictures without commentary. No oral tradition was established and the hegemony disappeared.

As oral form was the life force of a language, Greek became the first ancient language in Western Europe to survive until present time. Greek cultural images lived and grew into a rich repertoire of varied expression. The stories of gods and heroes were composed, told, dramatized, written, meditated on, and retold. Inspired by visual images, both sensual and imaginary, ancient Greek created a most vivid and fluid mythology. This rich soil of song and poetry guaranteed that ancient written Greek did not detach itself from oral expression as its written vocabularies were climbing the summit of speculative abstraction.

Like Egyptian, the ancient cultures of the Near and the Middle East survived only as ideas, story lines, and fragmented images because they had difficulty integrating the oral and written forms of expression. Like ancient Egyptian, cuneiform writing had always been too difficult to grasp because of its complicated and rigid form. When it became a language of administration and higher learning, it separated from its oral language and eventually left it behind.[25] As the new oral language emerged, it repeated the same process until the seventh century, when Arabic, with its God, swept through the Middle East and harvested all of the cultural expressions and images of that region that had evolved and accumulated for thousands of years.

The Old Sumerian was an agglutinative and highly complicated language which used prefixes, infixes, and suffixes. It had a very simple sound system, with only 4 vowels (each has long and short variants) and 16 (or 15, due to varying opinion among linguists) consonants.[26] About 2310 B.C., Akkadian, which was said to be a spoken language, is believed to be brought into Mesopotamia by Semitic conqueror. The Akkadian, which had 8 vowels and 20 consonants, took Sumerian cuneiform script as its written form. It was this marriage that saved the Sumerian epic of its gods, whose stories continued to be told in Semitic. Sumerian had ceased to be spoken during the Old Babylonian period, but, its vocabularies, idioms, expression, gods, and goddesses were brought back to life in Babylonian literature.[27]

Akkadian, as a dominant oral and later written language, spread across an area extending from the Mediterranean Sea to the Persian Gulf.[28] Like the ancient Sumerian, Akkadian, which had six hundred words and syllable signs, needed a new oral vehicle to further evolve. It found its dialects in Assyrian and Babylonian, while written Akkadian separated from its oral form and evolved into a language of mathematics, astronomy and other learned subjects. The evolution of language, from graphic based on logograms to phonic based on syllables, had begun before the Sargon conquest. By 2300 B.C., more than two thousand words of logograms had been reduced to only six hundred, while the general expressive capacity had widened.[29] The evolution continued in Akkadian as the Semitic spoken in Canaan, and invented the first set of alphabetic characters (single symbols representing each of the basic twenty consonantal sounds) about the middle of the second millennium.[30] Phoenicians took the idea and developed their own alphabet, which was passed to Greek.

During the eleventh century B.C. the Assyrian Empire provided an opportunity to establish a linguistic integration in Semitic. Alphabets established a formal link between the sounds and signs of language and kept the oral and written expressions in step with one another. It took at least a few hundred years for a written language to develop a new oral language to replace the old, which had declined. Oral Akkadian was gradually replaced by Aramaic during the seventh and sixth centuries B.C.

The use of alphabets flourished in Greece because its language had the only mature and well-developed oral poetic at the time. The best illustration of how different degrees of maturity in poetic form influenced or even determined narrative forms lies in an investigation of the degree of diversity and coherence of mythology in different languages. With a much smoother flow of story telling, Greek myth was more systematic and specific than either Egyptian or Semitic myth. Greek gods had long graduated from the primitive stage of natural gods. They were much more like man, while keeping some characteristics of primal function. Greek gods had specific responsibilities and relationships with one another, and each of them had a complicated role.

Different forms of linguistic evolution manifested in the way in which each language depicted its god(s). In order to make gods imaginable, language had to create concrete images to carry the imagination and story lines. Before the primitive cultures became mature enough to develop abstract words, they had to use natural and human images. Egyptians used pictures. Their gods had human bodies with animal parts, which symbolized extra human capacities attributable to lions, falcons, or bulls. Their sun and moon gods had bodies as vast as the universe.

On the other hand, Greek gods were portrayed as idealized super humans. They were bigger, stronger, more beautiful, and more powerful. Most of all, they were immortal. They could transcend physical human limitations and reshape themselves at ease. Otherwise, they were "normal" beings who interacted and enjoyed personal relationships with mortals. Unlike the Hebrew and Latin gods, who were always right and righteous, Greek gods had many flaws. They were moody, unfair, self-serving, manipulative, and lived as a very dysfunctional family — just like their human counterparts. But this was, perhaps, the reason why they lived in the collective memory of their followers for centuries.

The Gods of ancient Greek did not only live on the walls of monuments or sculptures in huge tombs, they also lived in the imaginations of the Greek story tellers who were living with those mythological images every day in their sanctuaries, on the street corners, and on the stage. In the kingdom of gods, with its now familiar clash of values and emotions, each god had his or her own special job. Some of them took care of the ocean, others the sky or the world of the dead. Some managed the affairs of war, others, the matters of heart. They were much more interesting characters than the Hebrew and Latin gods. They had strong emotions and fragile egos. Sometimes they had difficulty separating divine and personal issues. They loved or hated each other and fought contentedly among themselves. They had no morals and expressed opinions whenever they wanted to. They sided with different cities for material and personal favors; they granted all kinds of human wishes and supported different morals for non-divine or non-moral reasons. Emotionally, they were a mirror image of their subjects.

Another example of the non-abstract fluidity of Greek mythology was its easy transition from a matriarchal to a patriarchal system.[31] Greek myth created the most sophisticated gender relationships in human mythology. Matriarchal authority, which began with maternal worship, was evident in many cultures in the world. Goddesses were defined differently in different languages, and associated with nature and the human cycle of life. However, no language had ever developed an extensive mythological narrative as complicated and yet as smooth as that of Greek. The only mythological tradition that was close to the diversity and complexity of Greek was Indian literature. However, with its constant change in oral and written languages, Indian tradition was much more diversified and lacked the same structural framework as that of the Greek.

After their exploits had been told and retold for centuries, Greek goddesses had acquired more complicated personalities and psychological tendencies than those in other languages had. Instead of having different animal heads, *Gaea (Ge, Gaia)*, the primal Great Goddess, divided into three aspects of herself into three separate goddesses, each of which represented at least one part of her totality. *Athena* (virgin), *Hera* (wife), and *Aphrodite* (love) all individually retained some of Gaea's characteristics and symbols. Athena retained the role of the Gaea as a source of wisdom. But unlike Gaea, she had both female and male qualities. Born from the head of Zeus, Athena appeared fully-grown and fully armed with weapons. Guided by wisdom, and enforced with strength, she helped all the important heroes as they defended their families and cities. The statue Athena was originally made of gold, wood, and ivory and stood thirty-seven feet tall. As warrior and defender of cities, she carried the goddess Victory in one hand and held her shield in the other. She also wore the Gorgon's head, a symbol of the terrifying death-giving function of the Great Goddess. The serpents, symbol of the ancient goddess's mysteries, lay coiled behind her shield.[32]

Hera was the most powerful of the Olympian goddesses. She retained *Gaea's* features as patron of childbirth. This function was repeated in her daughter, *Eileithyia*, also a childbirth goddess, with her portrayal as a "cow-eyed" creator whose breasts gave the milk that formed the Milky Way. Hera was the god of marriage and family life. However, she was subject to a double standard of sexual behavior. She remained, as expected, sexually loyal to Zeus, while he constantly betrayed her with other females and males, divine and human alike. Hera's rage went beyond that of a human nagging, jealousy, and vindictiveness. She had the power to change her rivals into animals. She could drive heroes, like *Heracles*, insane. Unhappy and frustrated about her life, Hera focused all her intelligence and energy on the persecution of Zeus' mistresses and their illegitimate children. Zeus, who gave birth of Athena without her, was infuriated when Hera conceived and gave birth to Hephaestus without his help.[33]

The power game between Hera and Zeus was similar to that of the Egyptian cow goddess Nut (or Hathor) and the Egyptian sun god Amon-Ra. In his form as a bull, Amon-Ra descended in into the womb of the goddess, sailed all night through her belly, and was born again each morning as a golden calf. The bull calf of the sun, which then grew into a powerful bull, repeated the journey each night. The cow goddess, who, in earlier myths, sacrificed the bull god to ensure renewal, was now depicted as his mother. The goddess was clearly essential to give birth to the god. But the calf she carried each morning ruled her world, and she was still subordinated. Hera had a similar complex relationship with Zeus. The Greek gender-relationship of gods was depicted in a much more complicated context as the game went beyond functions of birth and reproduction.

Hera was also the god of the social institution of marriage. After an earlier attempt at rebellion (a failed coup, with Poseidon attempting to overthrow Zeus), Hera settled down into an uneasy but permanent relationship with her husband, reserving her anger for his many children conceived by other women. At the same time, her marriage transformed Zeus from an expendable source of conception (as were Uranus and Cronus) to a god of family love who maintained positive relationships with his children. The social aspect of Greek mythology portrayed a longer and deeper reflection of mankind and its own social order.

As a late comer, Greek mythology had the opportunity to learn from African and Asian myth, and it adopted some of these to complete its kingdom of gods. Aphrodite was originally related to various Near Eastern goddesses, such as the Sumerian Goddess Inanna and the Egyptian Isis. Aphrodite was born from the foam surrounding the severed genitals of Uranus, which Cronus had tossed into the sea. Floating to shore on a clamshell, Aphrodite emerged from the sea as the last gasp of the primeval god's creative energies. However, Aphrodite had much more emotional energy than the early fertility goddesses. Like the Babylonian Goddess Ishtar (Astarte), she represented the spectrum of passion from love to hate. Greek was the only ancient language whose depiction of sexual relationship completed the transition from a functional act to an emotional one. Both the Egyptian and Sumerian myths perished before they reached this transition. The Babylonians continued the journey that the Sumerians began.[34]

The emotional power of Greek mythology had no parallel in the ancient myths. For example, Aphrodite's love and rage had devastating, sometimes deadly consequences. Aphrodite's affair with Adonis, her famous human lover, cost him his life. When the queen of Cyprus said that her daughter, Smyrna, was more beautiful than Aphrodite, the goddess took her revenge by tricking Smyrna into the seduction of her own father. After the father realized what had happened, he tried to kill Smyrna, who had been turned to a tree by Aphrodite in order to save her. When the father split the tree open with his sword, a beautiful child, Adonis, emerged. Aphrodite hid Adonis in a chest and asked Persephone to keep him until he grew up. When Persephone also fell in love with Adonis, she refused to return him to Aphrodite. The two worked out a compromise. Adonis would spend part of each year in the under-world with Persephone and part in the upper world with Aphrodite. By trick-ing Persephone, Aphrodite kept Adonis longer than the agreed time, on the upper world, which enraged Aphrodite's divine lover Ares. Out of jealousy, Ares disguised himself as a boar and killed Adonis.

Many other major and minor Greek goddesses were further redefined by their colorful personalities.[35] Artemis, the goddess of the hunt, was one of the most beautiful, but she was also very dangerous. She was self-sufficient and independent from men (who only appealed to her as patron of the hunt). As "lady of the Beast," spending much of her time in the fields and woods, she was associated with the power of instinct of nature. However, she was not erotic in the same sense as Aphrodite. While Aphrodite was the only goddess whom Greeks depicted as fully nude, Artemis was traditionally shown with short hair and dressed in loose-fitting hunter's garb and sandals. She often was portrayed as terrifying and deadly to men who found themselves attracted to her beauty. She turned Actaeon, the brother of Dionysus, into a stag and he was torn apart by his own dogs after she caught him spying on her as she was bathing. Hestia (Vesta), on the other hand, represented a constant and fixed center of family life, both human and divine. She was a divine virgin who devoted her entire life guarding the Olympian hearth and its life-sus-taining fire.

Greek myths were very successful in transforming and establishing a relationship between the dominant gods and subordinate goddesses.[36] God-desses of few cultures survived the transition from creator goddess to the wife or, mother of a creator, the high god. Both Sumerian and Egyptian myth developed in a similar fashion. The son of the primal god and goddess killed the father god and became the supreme and sole god. However, they failed to create a coherent story that explained the transition and that made peace and compromise possible, after the violence between the generations of gods. Such flow and smoothness in narrative and expression mirrored the degree of poetic development over a sustained period of time. In the Mesopotamian world, frequent language change (oral or written language which changed alternately or simultaneously) interfered and delayed the historical accumu-lation of various expressions. That is why our stories in Sumerian, Babylonian, and even Assyrian were mainly repetitions of the same story line without evidence of a major breakthrough in terms of narrative and structure. The depiction of Babylonian gods was not personalized and emotional as it was in Greek myth.

Greek was not the only language that created a high god to control its minor gods, who were overlapping, contradicting and fighting with each other all the time. Hebrew, Sanskrit, and ancient Chinese all had their own supreme gods, a new authority, to exclude or supervise the mass of minor gods. Lacking abstract vocabularies, Hebrew could make the attempt only by utilizing its repertoire of concrete words. It used either the plural form of the names of god to generalize the notion of divine, or it renamed them to create a higher god, *Yahweh, Anathoth* (the plural of *Anath*, and "Queen of Heaven.")[37] Greek analyzed and unified its divine world in a way different from that of ancient Egypt.[38] Instead of building a structure of numerology, the early Greek philosophers, who were also poets, expressed their grand and more general view of the gods and cosmos with verbal images.

Like ancient Hebrew, which had woven its poetics into its prose narrative, Greek organized its divine kingdom within a different literary genre, prose: a "simple and economic" writing.[39] Prose in Greek also meant "naked language," "language without clothing (meter)." As distinct form, prose meant to tell the truth about gods, as opposite to poetry, which was believed to lie. Prose was a down-to-earth language, *pedzos logos*, meaning language walking on foot, as opposed to poetry, *psilos logos*, language riding on winged chariot.[40] With this new language, *Theogony* depicted a divine kingdom where the mass of Olympian gods and goddesses became organized in a humanly manner. The kingdom of gods became an extended family (in many cases a dysfunctional family), which was established in an institutionalized relationship (marriage) and its members lived in relative harmony among themselves. They were assigned specific duties to care for natural and human affairs. They would negotiate and compromise when different opinions and interests appeared. If any god misbehaved, he or she would be punished, except of course, the high god himself.[41]

Like many ancient civilizations emerging from a rich anthropomorphic tradition, ancient Greek was challenged to specify, organize, and unify divine pantheon.[42] It could not create a supreme god who had absolute power to override his competitors because its description of gods and goddesses had spun out of control after centuries of the reproduction of epic and ritual gesture. Greeks became suspicious of their gods and goddesses, questioning their predictions and fairness and blaming them for corruption (taking bribes). They began to abandon the gods and started to worship their human heroes.[43] Among all of this confusion, a new supreme god with an absolute power had to be transferred from somewhere else in a different language.

Up to the time of the Old Testament, gods had lived in human minds for thousands of years. Man tried and did "talk" to his gods all of the time; but the gods had not spoken a word in return. The prayers and hymns, intended conversation with gods, remained a monologue, an expression from men who assumed that the gods were listening.[44] The idea of speaking to a silent god was originated by the ancient assumption that words were magical. Words created and called into being what they stated. The more vivid and expressive the words were, the greater their effect. So words (especially words of praise) were used to instill, call up, or activate what was presented in the praise.[45]

In order to please and convince the gods to allow the desired benefit, increasingly elaborate rituals were invented to emphasize the words of prayers. The ancients began offering prized food, valued gifts, and even human or animal flesh. When men were not sure about how God felt, and what he intended, they attempted to read the divine mind, through observation, rather than conversation. They looked for signals and signs. For example, ancient civilizations developed elaborate systems to observe and interpret God's intentions, which were believed to be manifested in the movements of stars and in the remains of sacrificed animals. This imagination was necessary because the gods did not speak in the tongue of man.

After centuries of religious ritual and ceremony, Greek communication with God became highly diversified, ritualized, and yet increasingly vague. As Socrates described: "sacrifice is giving to the gods, prayer is asking of them, holiness then is an art of asking and giving."[46] This mutual transaction became too friendly and fluid, and it lost its power of sanction. As the Greeks of the seventh century believed, gods should have more sense than to trouble their minds with human affairs. From gods, "we know neither good nor evil!"[47] This divine communication did not involve highly specified moral obligations. The Greeks' mild divinity (as opposed to Hebrew's harshness) emerged from its highly polished and slippery language of ritual. How could man ever know what gods intended? It remained a mystery, even after centuries of praying and worshiping. Like the ancient Indus, the Greeks invented interpreters (mediators) and priests who were authorities in divine communication. But as the numerous interpretations accumulated, the specific and original meaning got lost.

If only God could speak to man! The ancients must have thought of it all the time.

But, if God could speak, in what language would it be? God could not speak Greek, simply because language was the only barrier left in the Greek context of man and god. Greek gods and goddesses looked and behaved like men. Making gods speak Greek was like making sculptures of Apollo and Athena jump out of their skin made of stone.

A written language of God became available through the translation of The Old Testament from Hebrew. The Bible created a new level of language alien to Greek. It became the written language of God, his own words without a mediator, words that superceded all human words, those of the priests, poets, and philosophers. With this new authority, God's words reorganized the entire repertoire of cultural idioms. The images, motifs, wisdom, characters, and ideas which had accumulated became more and more crowded and chaotic. The Christian God transformed the form of communication between God and man from a (leveling) platform to a hierarchy. God, whose language was superior over the increasingly slippery and worn out words of man, provided a much clearer and more unified vision. As the Christian God became the new pinnacle of Greek imagination, he inspired Greek writers to reinterpret and re-create Greek history and heritage. He lifted the established concept of God, his earthly jurisdiction, and his influence in the mind of man.

The Christianization of Greek culture took centuries, during which pagan and Christian elements curiously coexisted.[48] Christianity took root in Greek imagination and all of the established ideas, images, rhythms, songs, gestures, and words that used to serve pagan gods. After Christianity began to flourish in the rich soil of mythology, people would not or could not choose to recognize that it was the dead plants of the mythical gods that nourished the new bloom of Christianity.[49] It was not so much the triumph of the Bible over Homer, as many historians have described, but a successful transplantation of a super God by recreating the divine world in the Greek imagination.[50] Christian literary culture lived side by side with classical learning. They inspired and influenced one another. The Christian God interacted with and eventually became supported by the ocean of mythological images which had accumulated for centuries.[51]

As opposed to ancient Greece, there was hardly any pre-literary culture in ancient Italy except the Etruscan, and in the south, the former Greek colonies.[52] Latin was not the first language in Archaic Italy, but it was a language of infancy with relatively little pre-literary activity. The once sophisticated Etruscan culture, like the ancient Minoan and Mycenaean, died with its language and was buried with its artifacts. To 500 B.C., Latin had been a collage of 40 dialogues and a widely spoken tongue. It was only to be heard in Latium, the region between the Appeninge Mountains and the Tyrhenian Sea.[53]

Without the well-articulated oral epic tradition of Greek, Latin grew up with its public spectacles, festivals and street performances. It relied on dramatic gestures and theatrical images to develop its brand new language. Latin actors used masks and costumes to specify characters and roles.[54] Mimes aided in specifying and distinguishing meanings and forms.[55] Before the stage curtain was invented about the second century B.C., the passing of time was presented by emptying the stage.[56] During the middle of the third century B.C., Roman culture experienced an extraordinary expansion of theatrical representations and works for the stage.[57]

With the absence of a *khoreia* chorus, which played an important role in Greek dramatic presentation, Latin writers had to invent alternatives to create intended theatric settings and mood for their plays. To distinguish Latin from Greek comedies, their actors wore different garments: *fabulae togatae* (plays dressed in togas), or *fabulae palliatae* (plays in Greek cloaks). To divide act I from II, they had to invent a verbal interlude or gesture to void the bewilderment caused by repeatedly re-entering the stage.[58] Latin poets, with their young language, did their best to imitate Greek poetics. They overly stretched and exploited perverse Greek images, simile, and allusions to fit their narrative need.[59] If expression in words was similar to painting, Latin writers had a nearly blank canvas on which to exercise their imagination, while Greek writers had to search out every perceivable small space between the monumental works of the established masters in order to express themselves. With the privilege of a vast space, Latin writers could compose their picture of words in an uncluttered fashion. They created broader and multi-dimensional verbal associations. The accumulated expressions and vocabularies of Latin, having much less expression and connotation than those of Greek, allowed writers to readily bend the limits of the Latin language and create a new poetic.

Due to its lack of indefinite articles, Latin enjoyed a greater freedom in word order and juxtaposition.[60] Words could appear deliberately and unexpectedly to slow or quicken the poetic flow. Words were separated from their dependent adjectives extensively and elaborately. Isolated and suspended words classified and reclassified until they re-acquired fresh meanings. This "mosaic of words," as Nietzsche described, made Latin poetry into a picture painted in pigments of words.[61] While the Greek used poetic rhythm to create mood, the Latin poetic did not develop the musical quality that the Greek had cultivated over the centuries.[62]

Latin theater had its historically determined function, a function different from a mature language such as Greek, especially Hellenistic Greek.[63] Greek theater, like Chinese theater of the thirteenth century and Sanskrit classical drama, drew from a rich epic tradition. It reinvented, represented and provided variations. Disengaged from Aristotlian unity of dramatic form, early Latin theater focused on clarifying and specifying meanings by contradiction and polarization. Plautus' stage deliberately created conflict between various values, and between established perceived and assumed moral standards, by threatening to subvert everything that the audience accepted as normal and natural.

In Roman society, it was normal for unmarried sons to court a woman and that the old men remain in their place. It was necessary that a free man not be treated as if he was a slave. A Roman son was expected to demure to the authority of the head of the household. Comedy told stories that clashed with these legitimate values and expectations. A son would not plot against paternal authority while the father abused money and power, as in the *casina*. Comedy also created crisis when fundamental identities, such as personal identity or distinct identities between man and gods, were mixed and confused.[64]

Latin writers demonstrated great originality in transforming sophisticated Greek vision into a very simple language. Initially, written translation and conversation through translated ideas were a mixture of two languages. To translate Greek literature into a language which was never intended, Latin writers had to borrow Greek words in a Latin context and make Latin as sufficient and technical as Greek.[65] Without Greek music in their minds and fluidity on their tongues, Latin writers created an extremely grand and yet unspecific world. As Ovid began his grand imagery — such as "scope of my spirit led me to tell of shapes changed into new bodies," "Gods breathe favorably on my beginning," or "bring down my poem uninterrupted from the first origin" of the world to my time[66] — he intended to write a universal history in a few hundred lines, and explain how things had come about, so far. Modern scholars called it aetiological vision.[67] Only a writer in a new language, like John Milton of seventeenth century English, would have a vision so vast and grand because what he saw in front of him was a canvas on which hardly anyone had ever written.

For the Romans, a book was a monument of words and a display of patterns of the past. As Livy put it: "This in particular is healthy and profitable in the knowledge of history, to behold specimens of every sort of example set forth in a conspicuous monument; thence you may choose which models to imitate for yourself and your *res public*, and which, corrupt in their beginnings and corrupt in their outcomes, to avoid."[68] He imagined that his story of Rome would be put up for the perusal of his readers "to look upon" (*intueri*), as "transparent" and "luminous," (*inlustris*) as a conspicuous monument.

As small children learning to speak in the presence of their parents, the Latin speakers always tried to say more with fewer words, and they pretended to be more than who they were. Their language was an exaggerated performance, and it put up a seemingly sophisticated "face" or mask, to convince themselves and the world that they were better, taller, and more civilized than they really were. After Plautine, Greek rhetorical practice emerged and became highly desirable. It was considered culturally sophisticated to tell Greek jokes and recite Greek poetry during social functions. Romans showed off their borrowed literary and artistic styles as the moderns do with their automobiles, monster properties, and trophy spouses. In capturing and importing cultural souvenirs as the spoils of war, the Romans also acquired various cultural practices from conquered lands. They assimilated new practices as symbols of integration of the defeated enemy, and incorporated them into Rome as a part of state religion.[69] Without formal sensibility and spiritual depth, Romans made their language a social showmanship and their artifacts into decorations of personal vanity.[70] Cato recorded the setting up of statues in private homes and garnishing of domestic surfaces with citron wood, ivory, and marble from lands afar. Private homes included a pretty *lium*, a garden enclosed by a colonnade of Greek fashion. Everyone in the high society was competing to host the best Greek feasts, *epulae,* and parties *convivia*. Smoked fish and pretty boys, the Greek luxuries, were now worth more than Roman farms and slaves.

The transplanted cultural idioms from Greece did not fit well with Latin roughness and vulgarity, especially crude military glory and greed for flamboyant wealth. It brought about a crisis of Latin vocabularies. Latin was a language which was challenged to juxtapose beauty and manliness and combine "aesthetic" and military glory. Even the great poet Livy could not find adverbs in representing the same identity.[71] The uneasy marriage between Greek and Roman culture was also illustrated by a polarization of different styles within the host language, and Latin's difficulty in weaving them into one. At the beginning of the Christian era, Latin literature expanded mainly by absorbing spoken language. The first generation of Latin writers wrote as if they were speaking. Since Latin was a thin spoken language to begin with, it quickly exhausted what it could get from oral expression. By the time of Cicero, all literary composition entailed an artificial use of language.[72] With all its limitations, the oralized literary writing or literary speech writing smoothed Latin expression to a certain extent. The writers after Augustus displayed a far more flexible use of syntax than the earlier Cicero, Caesar, or Nepos, especially in cases and moods. Their writing became more fluid and much less artificial.[73]

Livy, a writer of subtlety and power, played an important role in keeping Latin prose fresh and vibrant. His language was leaner, more incisive, and less colored.[74] After a few centuries of poetic elaboration that had absorbed spoken language into literary expression, Latin exhausted all it could get from downloading, and began its quest for more vocabularies and philosophical inspiration. As Latin became a literary language, it became highly moralized and mystified. Like a plant with shallow roots, as it grew, Latin became more and more abstract. It gradually detached from everyday language, as did the Biblical Hebrew and ancient Sanskrit.

In Latin, even the language of love was abstract, lacking of concrete imagery, a defined subject, and coherent references.[75] Very much like the courtly love images of later medieval and early Renaissance Europe, the Roman version was an ideal of love, beauty, and unrealizable desire. Ancient Latin love did not depict anything or anyone in a real world. It represented an attempt to describe feelings, both non-moral and unconventional. However, the feelings described by formative Latin could only be as abstract as its morality allowed. It was like an artist who was trying to draw a picture with an unsharpened pencil. The picture that he drew was barely recognizable. From page to page, Delia or Cynthia could be seen as a courtesan, an adulterous wife, or a free woman.[76] It took the Romans centuries to learn to sharpen their pencils and to steady their hands so that they could draw clearly recognizable word pictures.

In the same clumsy way, Romans formulated their political and philosophical ideas within the capacity of their primitive language. Having inherited neither god nor hero, they had to choose, and try to make sense between god and emperor. In a formative language, which was pulled towards the opposite tendencies of concrete and abstract meanings, Latin had to build a meditating ground to keep the realm of language from falling apart. Like the idea of love and its reality, Romans had to formulate a perceivable and conceivable connection between God and emperor. Every civilization in every language began with either God (as idealized authority) or ruler (king, head of tribe or community) as concrete authority, and then moved toward their choice. The universal and social idea needed to have earthly and concrete representatives, such as saints, divine rulers, or religious leaders, such as the pope or caliph. Latin's dilemma was that it had neither. As it tried to grow, especially grow at a fast pace, it was afraid to uproot itself and lose its lifeline. This occurred in many ancient civilizations over time. Without a root at one end, any development toward any direction would break its culture's tapestry.

With its unique originality, Latin eventually found its own way to establish a cultural and political hegemony. It was hegemony based on language alone as the superstructure of social relations, state institutions, and the fabric of the human soul. Although this hegemony did not last as long as those of ancient Greek and Chinese, it built the foundation for the cultures of the modern West. With this Latin tradition as root, the vernaculars of the Western Europe soared and eventually created the most original, vibrant, and soon to be sophisticated cultures in world history. A good example of Latin creativity and its contribution to Western civilization was the concept of law as the superstructure and blueprint of the organization of society.

The significance of the words of law, as the foundation of social and political structure, was not completely a Latin creation. Latin invented it first, but the modern languages of Western Europe reinvented the tradition and carried it into a highly abstract realm. This would have been impossible to achieve if Latin had survived and if Roman law had gone through ten more centuries of further refinement, as did the Chinese imperial law. Change of language and multi-lingual environment further stretched (rather than leveled) the conceptual gap created by Roman legal tradition and opened a well-structured field where new oral and written languages could flourish.[77] In other words, without modern European languages, Roman law would well have become dead words, and exhibits in the museums, like Solon's Law in Greek, Hammurabi Law in Babylonian, Torah in Hebrew, or the Chinese law of the First Empire.[78] The Roman idea of order in written words was not as abstract as we think now during the early Republic period.[79] This abstract and intellectual tendency cultivated slowly as the law evolved. Like any young language, Latin was incapable of abstract description and reasoning in its early stages. Unlike medieval Europe, where law was a general notion of order associated with God and king, the Romans had to coin and distill every single word in law to define and specify meanings, yet remain general enough to be applied to similar procedures. The entire realm of legal language, which Western legal tradition had taken for granted, was created gradually during centuries of accumulation, refinement, and transformation.

It took verbs decades and even centuries to become nouns in which general rulings, rather than descriptions of specific cases, could be formulated. Latin described legal cases in the language of verbs, doing and causing an action, rather than nouns that described impersonal rules. Harm-verb in the active voice drove the law into a corner. It created a system that imposed liability for doing something to another and for causing an action, done such as to be damaged, injured, wounded, broken. This kind of wording conveyed a narrow and linear logic, compared with more modern law, such as German and English, which used more general verbs or the nouns. For example, the English verb to harm or the operative verb *verletzen* (injure in German) are more abstract, as in the statement: a person who willingly or negligently injures the life, body, health, freedom, property or the right of another contrary to law is bound to compensate him for any damage.[80] At the formative stage of the law, the fewer the words, the tighter the law, and the less space between intention, action, and consequence. Those who caused damage to another had to pay for it. It was that simple. The only thing that the law needed to do was to prove that a particular person actually caused the specific damage. This was the key to conviction and punishment. In order to ensure consistency between action and consequence, nouns having a more abstract connotation were coined to replace the verbs. There were only a handful of nouns used in *Vocabularium Jurisprudentiae Romanae*.

For example, *dereliguere* in the sense of to abandon a piece of property occurs sixty times; not once does its related noun, *derelictio*. *Acquirere* has more than one thousand entries while *acquisitio* appears only twelve times. When Plautus was writing, there was only *aequare*, a verb. *Aequtio* appeared as a noun during Ceciro's time. *Humare* in Varro, or *cremare*, from Cicero, advanced to *humatio* or *crematio* only during post–Augustan time. Many Latin words remained only as verbs, even during the Renaissance. *Neutralizare*, until the 15th century, had only verbal form. At the beginning of the Renaissance, it was adopted by the French and used as *neutraliser*, a verb. It took another two hundred years for the French to coin a noun, *neutralisatum*. English borrowed it from French at the beginning of nineteenth century.[81]

Like many legal traditions, Roman law emerged from liturgical procedures. The word *jus* was connected with *iurare* (to swear an oath). It was a word that referred to an oral pledge concerning a private matter.[82] There was no written law or regulation during the early Roman Republic. Law and order were "discovered" as needed to resolve a dispute. Basically, it was made up and recorded as needed.[83] It began with a case. The decision about that case was made under the assumption that should the case recur, it would be resolved in the same way.[84] Gradually, more abstract and impersonal words were needed to streamline the rulings and to apply to other cases.

As cases recurred, it became necessary to record the judgment in order to retain the consistency of the decision. As in medieval England and Italy, in the early Roman Republic, deeds and words were one and the same because writing intended to classify, thus streamline, the cases.[85] The first civil law, *iuscivile*, was largely a collection of the decisions made and opinions given in particular cases, such as ownership, possession, will, and succession. They were mainly procedural, and set out how a legal action was begun and how much time was allowed for the restitution. The purpose of writing was to reach the best solution possible.[86] Roman law, first codified in A.D. 438 after the Twelve Tables, was not a code of law in the modern sense. It was a collection of administrative laws that merely supplemented existing private collections. There was no classified constitutional law, civil law, or criminal law.[87] It was a collection of cases, their decisions, and opinions about them. Even the word *lex* did not mean code, in a legal sense. Lex, from *ligare*, meant unit, which binds. It described a form of being together. Lex, meaning that which lies, described a form similar to the first, less tight yet already together. Lex also related to *legere*, a Latin word from the Greek *leyeiv*, and meant to be read out or delivered. The strong writing tendency of Roman law had more to do with Latin environment, where writing was accepted as the means to control spoken words and deeds. It was the same tradition that molded law into a legal science, associated with eternality rather than humanity. Over the centuries, the law evolved into an independent kingdom of language and logic, the high wall of which only began to crumble during the twentieth century when Western Europe finally awakened from its blind faith in its words.

Roman law was a law of statutes, an attempt to seal every hole in the system by constantly reclassifying and redefining the written rules. From the third century, state legislation proliferated in an attempt to regulate the increasingly diversified procedures.[88] Although statutes were created out of necessity to sanction social behavior and solve disputes, they became overbearing and formed a high mind of law. Unlike English common law of the early modern times, whose uncodified customs played an important role in its legal development, Roman law left very little room for customs as it was repeatedly reinforced with more and more specified rulings. *Mucius iuscivil* distinguished private law from other branches of law. Roman law had distanced itself from almost all religious rulings.[89] The influence of Roman law went far beyond its legal script. It was the Roman loyal attitude towards the words of law (cultivated in Latin and reinforced by the emerging vernaculars) that dominated legal scholarship during medieval and early modern times. Faith in words, which were considered to have the capacity to define, measure, and regulate human life and behavior, was inherited by Western Europeans, who grew up with languages as young as that of Rome.[90] This faith, which supported all the cultural and intellectual pursuits of the west for centuries, did not begin to fade away until the late nineteenth and early twentieth centuries, when European vernaculars arrived at their maturity. Only then did they begin to feel as cynical about words of law as the Greeks had several centuries earlier. In the Greek mind, man created law to serve his own purpose while claiming the right to discover new formulas to interpret, modify, change or multiply the words of law.

If law needed abstract language to evolve and to sustain, God and his authority required personalized attention. Unlike the later Western Christianity that developed various extreme forms of gnosticism to build walls around God's words away from the common believers, Roman emperors inevitably became the tangible god in the minds and hearts of their followers.[91] Ancient Romans were different from the ancient Greeks, who did not need the state, especially a centralized state. The Greeks had gods in their minds who lived to protect them. Romans had never had their own gods. Although they owned a gallery of foreign gods crowded in their shrines, those were borrowed gods, completed as images, bodies, even rituals, yet without an original and sophisticated mythological tradition. Those fragmented gods eventually ended up as empty vessels — forms without content that would be filled with whatever Romans wanted to worship. As soon as these foreign gods began to speak Latin, they became subordinated to the Roman gods.

The disintegration between law and God was illustrated first in a language of ideology that became increasingly polarized. The language of the Christian God gradually uprooted itself from the world of everyday life. The emergence of monasticism from the 3rd century symbolized the institutionalized beginning of this cultural stratification. In order to devote and to pursue godliness, one had to divorce earthly life. This became the claim of the Christian church at the time.[92] Many of the best minds of the time, and a considerable number of the traditional governing class, chose to live in the world of God. What had once been a North African interpretation of Christianity (the fatalist insistence on the universal penalty of judgment except for those saved by grace as the prime result of the fall) became the accepted doctrine of Western Christians. Under the influence of this doctrine, many Roman aristocrats preferred to seek perfection in God's world and to withdraw from politics.[93]

The process in which Latin interpretation changed the image, teachings, and doctrine of the Christian God can be illustrated by the painstaking journey of Augustine.[94] The evolution of Augustine's thought illustrates why and how the ideological and spiritual choice of Western Christianity was connected, even determined, by the capacity of its language.

Unlike Greeks, whose language had the flexibility and adaptability to mediate and counsel philosophy and faith, Augustine had great difficulty making the hard choice between the two. In the beginning, Augustine assimilated his platonic conception of knowledge with his newly found Christian God. At the time of writing *The Confessions*, Augustine described the God, whom he learned to discern by reading the Platonists, as a light that illuminated the soul's vision (7.10.16). However, he later found that God was in no sense already present in his memory; he could not learn of the eternal God by direct notice or encounter.[95] In a formative language and the mind cultivated by it, the imagination was imprisoned by physical vision and was incapable of imagining without a concrete image. One had to have a visual anchor in mind in order to recognize and to remember. "I am unmindful of you. How can I find you if I do not remember you?" (10. 17. 26). "How do I recognize the reality if I do not remember it" (10. 16. 24). Augustine could not see in his mind's eye the appearance of the Divine Word within the world, as the Platonists did or claimed to do. What he found missing in the eternal was that "no man hears (God) calling to us" (7. 21. 27). Thus, the Latin solution: "In the Gospel (your word) speaks through flesh, and this world sounded outwardly in the ears of men" (8. 11. 10). Augustine realized that God was present everywhere, not diffused through space, but by being in no place.[96] The only way through which man could receive God was to recognize his calling rather than to see his face.

The contrast of the form and vision of God (seen everywhere or nowhere), which was illustrated in Eastern and Western Christianity at the time of the late antiquity, was deeply rooted in the distinct capacities of their languages.

Greeks described their experience with the Christian God as "light" because their minds had sharper eyes, which had cultivated various forms to reach, to feel, and sense the divine presence. They had inherited diverse imagery, emotional scales and symbolism from their poetic and pagan past. The Christians of Western Europe, being at a blind point in their linguistic development, could only approach their God through their words, words with general meaning without specific image. Having a formative language without rich visual stock, when they looked up, they could not see their God, except "the cloud, thunder, and fog" (as described in Biblical Hebrew). Latin believers were frustrated and tortured by the visual darkness that cloaked their God. They strained to see their God. They exhausted themselves in a grand intellectual effort and ended up weeping in burning emotions, as the search continued.

As a result, early Latin evolved an abstract imagination without visual and concrete reference. Augustine began to hear rather than see his God. "You have called me, and have cried out. And have shattered my deafness. You have blazed forth with light, and have shone upon me, and you have put my blindness to flight. You have sent forth fragrance and I have drawn in my breath, and I pant after you, and I hunger and thirst after you. You have touched me, and I have burned for your peace" (10. 27. 38).

Latin emotion, although blind, was by no means any weaker than that of Greek. This burning desire, as essential as hunger and thirst, had to find an earthly object to satisfy its devotion. The Romans chose their emperor to fill this need.

The first Roman who was given the position of personal cult by the Greeks was Titus Aquinctius Flamininus, who liberated them. His name was praised with the Gods; his portrait was on gold coins, issued by the city-state.[97] However, the Greek notion of divinity at the time of city-states was rather loose. They honored and elevated any man with outstanding achievement because they believed that they must have been given a special gift from God to do so. The Greek association of man to god was never as authoritarian as Latin because Greeks had many gods.[98] When human divinity translated to Latin, it became more centralized and provoked more intensified worship and devotion. The Sulla cult was instituted in his honor with games (*syllaia*) and sacrifice. After Julius Caesar's victory, honors of every kind were showered on him. He became the first Roman ruler to be widely accepted as crowned with his divinity. The Roman Senate welcomed him like a god and called him god. Romans built temples and worshiped him.[99] As Greek notions were translated to Latin, everything became enlarged and abstracted. Since the Romans had no god to associate their emperor with, they invented a whole language for him ... an abstract language about the highest human virtues.[100]

After emperors became associated with God, everything the Romans did had a divine justification. Romans changed their ideas about war and its purpose. In his third book, *De Repulica*, Cicero claimed that Rome, as the ultimate worldly state, should not engage in war except either for honor or for safety. A ruler should have the power of undertaking war if he considered it advisable and the soldiers should perform their military duty on behalf of the peace and safety of the empire. Good men went to war when they found themselves compromised with the conduct of human affairs.

Augustine added God into the Roman mentality of global war. "When war is undertaken in obedience to God, who would rebuke, or humble or crush the pride of man, it must be allowed to be a righteous war."[101]

2. God's Word Written and Spoken: Roman and Islamic Empires

This chapter compares the formation of the Islamic Empire and its Roman counterpart. Latin and Arabic were opposite in form at the time that they transformed into written form. Latin was in its infancy and had very limited vocabularies, expressions, and flat connotations. Arabic was a well-developed poetic language. It had vivid imageries, metaphors, and intricate connotations. After military expansion, the Romans ruled their empire with their silent words of written law and political rhetoric, while the Muslims ruled their empire with the words of a God who was speaking loudly in rhythm.

It analyzes and compares the different kinds of hegemonies that Islam and Western and Eastern Christianity built. It illustrates that the language in which a religion was articulated shaped the type and depth of its ideology. In three different linguistic soils the ancient Hebrew God evolved into three unique deities, each having a distinct personality — the Latin Christian God, the Greek Christian God and the Arabic Islamic God (Allah). In this specific sense, God's language, rather than his origin, determined his image, his teachings, his relationship with mankind, his influence on the society, and of course, the fate of his empire.

The most important difference between Latin and Arabic culture was the age and capacity of their languages at the time that they took written form. As a young language with relatively shallow oral foundation, Latin was a crude, highly visual and abstract language that could barely flow. Because of its youth, Latin had the capacity to classify meanings and clarify reasoning. Arabic, highly rich and fluid, emerged from Semitic, a tradition older than Greek. The difference between Latin and formative Greek was the difference between an oral and written language. The difference between Greek and Arabic was the degree of poetic lyricism and fluidity that was apparent as they became written.

43

Pre-Islamic Arabic was a rich and highly lyrical poetic that had never evolved an epic tradition of its own. The ancient Semitic epic, after thousands of years of reinventing and repeated recycling of its oral languages, had become a sporadic memory of story lines and a highly fragmented poetic vision ... a vision which was much detailed, refined, and penetrated by human emotional vibration and energy. Arabic vision of the world was no longer as enlarged, grand, and sometimes crude as that of any emerging epic tradition. It was no longer about cosmo and nature, not even the sun and the moon. It was about the sunshine at particular moments, the moon at particular hours of the night, and rain from particular shapes of cloud. It was a vision that had distilled from the cosmic whole and was immersed in personal feelings and momentary moods. Pre-Islamic poetic was finer than the best lyrical poetry of any ancient languages, including that of the Hellenic Greek. In lyrical form it was similar to the visions which were created by Chinese poetry of the late Tang and Sung dynasties and the best modern poetry of English and Spanish. However, pre–Islamic Arabic could not be considered modern in any sense of the word, except for its poetic expression. In general, pre–Islamic Arabic was a much less precise and less efficient language than ancient Greek. During the emergence of Islam, Arabic had not yet developed any general and precise vocabularies, or prose writing. It was unable to describe or imagine anything beyond its horizon of endless desert, camels, and oases.

Christianity was an alien God from an alien language for Latin speakers during the first three centuries A.D., as for the Greeks. As the Christian God gained popular approval, he spoke different languages, created different images, and different moral teachings, and cultivated different relationships with his believers.

The original language that Jesus spoke was Aramaic, the oral language of the Jews, who worshiped a different God. By the time that the first gospels were written down, the original voice of Jesus had been silenced for two generations. In the first Christian community distant from Jerusalem and Galilee, gospels appeared to be based on collections of sayings and parable form.[1] In the written Bible, the original words of Jesus in Aramaic had disappeared except for a few phrases that had been recorded and accepted by the Greeks.

Although historians and theologians have not and would never come to agreement as to how and when the original meanings of Jesus' preaching had perished, one can notice the different form in which each language was telling the same story. Unlike the Pharisees, who emphasized the rigid written law of Hebrew, the Aramaic holy man, *Hasid,* was an individual who had the power to cure illnesses, exorcise devils, and forgive sins. The God who spoke Aramaic, a language without hierarchy, was a much more immediate god.

His coming was sooner; his kingdom might even be already on the way.[2] His prophet had special empathy for the poor and the rejected, while his message spread quickly and crowds would gather to listen to him. At this point, Jesus' God was not yet completely detached from the Judaic tradition of messiah, but represented a contra movement initiated from an oral tradition against the Judaic establishment of written and codified Rabbinical Hebrew.[3]

The reorientation of language (Aramaic from Hebrew) allowed this non-orthodox Jewish movement to form a brand new religion which worshiped a different God, much the same way as the Protestant revolution uprooted from Catholic tradition centuries later. The oral teachings of Jesus did not survive in writing. Even if they had survived in Aramaic, they would have encountered and eventually failed to compete with written Hebrew, which was a more sophisticated written language in the same tongue. The brand new God of Christianity could only compose in alien languages, which did not share oral roots with Hebrew. Linguistic reorientation was the most likely to provide an opportunity to create a brand new vision of divinity. This is the same reason that Judaism flourished in Hebrew and not in the other Caanite languages which had assembled a rich collection of idols and rituals of worship. After Christianity started to speak Greek, it broke many rules of Judaism because Greek recording of the gospels amplified the Old Testament, both in concept and vision.[4] The most influential early Christian preachers were Greek speakers.[5] Paul, whose ministries and acts of the Apostles were composed about A.D. 60, insisted that uncircumcised gentiles could become Christians. He argued his case against the restrictive attitudes of the Jerusalem community with vigor. Paul's teaching generalized and transformed the focus of worship from on adherence to rigid moral and ritual rules to an open yet vague concept of faith.

Christianity became even more Greek when Luke wrote his gospel in the historical tradition of Thucydides. This writing carried an even wider and more general message. It placed Christianity within the context of world history, something that had not been done before. He probably had no written sources to research, and it is believed that the speeches of his main characters were like those of Thucydides ... shaped to the personality of the speaker and the occasion on which he was speaking. By describing Paul, the center figure of the Acts, the Greek writing, which had created a colorful kingdom of gods and goddesses, was better suited than the rigid Hebrew to create a history for a solitary God. This injection of Greek fluidity revitalized and integrated the Christian gospel.

Later, when the language of Matthew became the more popular language of prayer and preaching, the language of Christianity moved farther away from the original teaching of Jesus' Aramaic. It became further distilled and more abstract. The shorter version of Luke was neglected until later centuries, when it was expanded in order to bring it into line with Matthew. The following comparison illustrates how the basic language of the Lord's Prayer changed:

Matthew 6: 9–13	Luke 11: 2–4
Pray then like this:	And Jesus said to them:
Our Father who art in heaven	When you pray say: Father
Hallowed be thy name	Hallowed be thy name
Thy kingdom come,	Thy kingdom come.
Thy will be done,	
On earth as it is in heaven.	
Give us today	Keep on giving us each day
Our bread for the coming day	our bread for the coming day
And forgive us our debts,	And forgive us our sins,
As we also have forgiven our	for we ourselves forgive
Debtors	every one who is indebted to us;
And lead us not into temptation	And lead us not into temptation
But deliver us from evil.[6]	

In Matthew, God is addressed in traditional Jewish liturgical phraseology: "Our Father who art in heaven." In contrast Luke has simply "Father," behind which stands the Aramaic Abba, a word not often used at the time as an address to God in prayer. Jesus speaks of God as Father (without being capitalized in the original) simply and directly, without any of the qualifying phrases which were often used to safeguard the transcendence of God. Jesus encourages his disciples to address God as Father.

The same emphasis on "sonship" is found in Paul's writing. The Aramaic word Abba is used twice by Paul (Gal. 4: 6, Rom. 8: 15). In both passages the gift of God's Spirit confirms to Christian believers that they are adopted as sons or children of God and enables them to pray to Abba, Father. Paul has used this Aramaic word in two letters written in Greek to readers who did not know any Aramaic. This suggests that Abba was a particularly important word. In a similar way some Christians today who do not know any Latin or Greek nonetheless use the Latin phrase *Pater Noster* (Our Father) or the Greek words *Kyrie eleison* (Lord, have mercy). Paul's use of Abba suggests that historical Jesus' encouragement to his disciples to address God in prayer as "Father" was understood in the early church to be an important part of his teaching.

Another example of the same distillation of language was the transmission of the word "bread," from a concrete meaning with material substance to a symbolic one. The text of Matthew has been translated as "Give us today our bread for the coming day." The precise meaning of the word *epiousion* (coming day) is uncertain since the word is not found elsewhere. It may refer to bread to be enjoyed in the Kingdom of God. The interpretation could then be, "Give us bread today as an anticipation of the feast of heaven." Not surprisingly, some later church fathers understood it to be eucharistic bread. But *"epiousion"* may well have a quite different meaning — not spiritual bread of any kind, but ordinary bread, which was sorely needed in a very poor rural setting. "Give us today bread to sustain our physical existence..." Luke's petition means "keep on giving us day by day the bread we need to keep us alive."[7]

Greek impersonalized God in the Old Testament, just as Rabbinical Hebrew did, but in a more fundamental and extreme manner. Greek Christian writers refined bold metaphors associated with God in Hebrew: *ruach* and *nephesh* (breathe and wind). They replaced them with the Greek word *pneuma* (spirit), which had departed from concrete physical function and human warmth. Hebrew "light" in the Old Testament referred to the terrible splendor of God's appearance, which even angels dare not behold. Lightning and volcanoes were weapons of divine vengeance. Fire was associated with God's anger. All of these vocabularies described physical reaction, but with strong mental and psychological effect. When they were translated to Greek, they lost their emotional power. Light lost its spark, radiance, and penetrating heat. It became the "eye of the soul," a metaphysical and philosophical notion associated with seeing and understanding.[8] Furthermore, Greek writers replaced love in Hebrew, using the Greek concept of *eros*, which associated passionate admiration and possessiveness in favor of the more dignified *agape* (normal concept of love) in the New Testament.[9]

Christian scholars created a new God radically different from that of Judaism by changing his language. Greek elevated the Jewish God in a realm which was literally indescribable and non-existent in Biblical Hebrew. It was a realm of abstraction, and yet maintained a verbal connection to the concrete and everyday language. This realm was the missing link in Biblical Hebrew, where oral Aramaic and written Rabbinical Hebrew presented opposite and uncompromising versions of Judaism. Greek provided the link that integrated and interacted between the written words and spoken stories. Greek took the concept of a sole and exclusive god from Hebrew, as well as its moral coherence. It inherited the oral tradition of Aramaic, a concrete and immediate language whose tone and form remained even after its words and phrases disappeared. Its stories of God were retold and refined in vivid images and biographies in Greek, which offered a wide spectrum of connotation from the most concrete to the most abstract.

Christianity, especially its universal kingdom, was created by a clash of languages and cultures. This clash formed a very loose Christian union under the name of one God. Various languages went various ways to envisage their own images of the Christian God and his relationship with the community of believers. Each branch of the Christian church, based on its own language and accumulated cultural history, interpreted a unique version of God, his teaching, and institution. As a whole, because of this diversity and flexibility, Christianity became a universal faith, more widely spread and more powerful than any other religion in the world, before and after.

The first Christian communities were spread over the eastern part of the Roman Empire, especially in the cosmopolitan cities of the coast, where pagan religions had cultivated flamboyant languages of worship. One example was the ceremonies involved in the worship of Demeter at Eleusis. Typically, initiates had to go through ritual purification. There was the promise of some form of personal communication with the god or goddess on earth, and a reward after death. In the same language as Ancient Hebrew, then Aramaic and Greek, the imagination of the New Testament, with its light and darkness, and its faith compared to flourishing crops, was very similar to that found within these regional cults. For instance, the "facts" of Jesus' life were presented in a form which was not unique to him. Both of the ancient Egyptian and Greek evolved stories about humans who were conceived by gods. There were stories of Mithras, who was incarnated and visited by shepherds after his birth in a cave.[10]

Like any primitive culture and language, the Romans made religion into a public affair and built a relationship between religion and state.[11] During the first centuries, Rome became a showcase of world religions, especially those of Africa and Asia. In order to create a national Pantheon, Romans Romanized every god that they could grasp.[12] They patronized other people's gods by giving them Latin names.[13] These foreign religions brought with them not only images and idols, but also rhythm, sounds, colors and rituals. Their performance made a great impression on the Romans.... Mad dancing, the sound of rattles, tambours, and shrill pipes, people with their heads tipped back or rolling wildly on their shoulder were accompanied by howls and yells as they whirled about and worked themselves into a frenzy. Nearly all oriental liturgies possessed the ritual and emotional effectiveness and were bound with daily, weekly, monthly, and seasonal festivals.[14] It did not take the Romans long to realize that they did not have the appetite and sensitivity for those high-toned emotions and colorful images. Even with the tolerant attitude of the first century A.D., the idea of religious passion was as foreign to the Latin mind as it was familiar to the Semitic or Greek minds. As Roman officials were facing the early Christian martyrs, they could not help but to express disbelief and distaste for the passion for God ... any god.

"You wretches, if you want to die, you have cliffs to leap from and ropes to hang by..." (Why you are trying to die in front of me?)

The philosophic Emperor Marcus Aurelius had wondered to himself in his meditations why it was that the Christians were so unreasonable and disorderly when it came to religious belief.[15] "The desire not to die in bed, in miscarriages, or soft fevers, but in martyrdom, to glorify Him who suffered for you." This holy spirit as voluntary martyrdom astonished the Roman pagans.[16] Celsus, the author of a highly sophisticated treaty with the Christians came to the conclusion that the Christians were simply "out of their minds-insane-because they "deliberately" rushed forward to arouse the anger of an Emperor in order to bring upon themselves blows, torture, and even death.[17] Without centuries of emotional cultivation and excises through religious rituals, Romans could not be easily excited by all the noises that those foreign gods provoked. For the Latin speakers at the time, to see was to believe. Romans were familiar with public spectacles where words, deeds, and gestures were displayed and admired. In a formative language, conversion could only be executed through seeing and thinking rather than feeling. As Augustine described: "No one believes anything unless one first thought it believable.... Every thing that is believed is believed after being preceded by thought.... But everyone who believes thinks, thinks in believing and believes in thinking."[18] Roman Christians needed to imagine God's face. Latin became the next language (like Hebrew) to ride on words in order to see its god. Churches and monasteries produced more and more detailed verbal images of God. During the third century, Christianity began to speak Latin as it told and upgraded the stories of Mary.[19]

Opposite to Aramaic, or even Greek traditions, which emphasized the spiritual and personal aspects of religion, Latin forged Christianity into an intellectual quest. The Christian writings in Latin, as Greek did during the early Christianity, further expanded Christian vision from woolly emotion and credulity to philosophical meditation. Like everything else in Latin, Christian Platonism had a Greek root. However, Latin turned Greek philosophy and theology adversarial. It made the Christian God more abstract and remote.

The Latin rationalization of Christianity was a historical necessity for a young language, just as it was for the Rabbinical Hebrew. Without highly formal, emotional, and spiritual languages to inherit from the past, the Christian ideology of the West became more and more abstract. By marrying Greek philosophy with God, Latin further stripped the Christian God of every human element and the concrete images, which had been cultivated by pagan rituals, and imagery of the east. It created a conceptual gap between man and God, world and spirit, as well as body and soul.

Virgin Mary was a Western Christian creation, an attempt to deepen the unbridgeable gap between conceptual opposites. Demeter, Athena (Minerva), and Artemis (Diana in Rome) who came from Greek and Eastern tradition, were virgins but not mothers. From the traditional goddesses, Isis was the closest to Mary, a devoted wife and mother. However, Isis had a bad reputation, as she was associated with sexual promiscuity derived from the activities at the Isiac Temples.[20] It was told during the first century B.C., that the Temples were used as a trysting place. During the second century, Martial suggested that even walking by the Temple of Isis could provide a man with sexual temptation.[21]

Mary did not exist in the Old Testament. She was mentioned only a few times in the Gospels.[22] During the second century, Christian leaders began to retell the story of the Virgin Mary, in order to testify to the divinity of Christ. The story of Mary was important but only as a vehicle of defense for the theological position, which presented Christ's full humanity, on one hand, and his divinity, on the other. The argument was aimed at distinguishing Gnosticism and Judaism by asserting the seemingly impossible contradiction of the virgin birth ... a miracle.

Mary's virginity became further emphasized in Western Europe because its emerging languages (Latin and later vernaculars) required a conceptual clarity to define godhead. The devotion of Virgin Mary, initiated during the fifth century, became an increasingly important part of Western Christianity. It took an insignificant figure from the established text and made it into an idealized object of worship. This was a part of the new forms of Christian asceticism and monasticism, which began to emerge during the fourth and fifth centuries.[23] As a part of this movement toward abstraction, Mary was completely disassociated from sexuality. At this time, she was not only a virgin when Christ was conceived, she became a perpetual virgin who represented the complete opposite to man and his humanly behavior. The representation emphasized her voluntary vow of virginity.[24]

While the Ancient Greeks took centuries to find a written language which could inscribe and codify their oral expression, it took Semitic speakers thousands of years to find theirs. Pre-Islamic poetry was much more refined and lyrical than the Greek epic at the eighth century B.C. This is an important fact that has been overlooked by most historians of literature and literary theorists. Poetry was never created equal. Its distinct characteristics should be perceived as important as the distinction between oral and written language. Without written record, it is very difficult to pin down the date when Arabic began to articulate. However, its highly refined form reflected its rich heritage.

Pre-Islamic Arabic poetry emerged from rich linguistic soil, from which many plants had grown, been harvested, and returned to the earth. This humus fertilized the soil and nurtured the forthcoming new growth. Semitic idioms, motifs, and expressions, like their epic story lines, transmitted orally for thousands of years. Although many ancient Semitic speakers had failed to scribe their languages or failed to keep its oral form alive after inscription, it did not mean that the oral language stopped growing and refining itself. The best examples of this unwritten tradition were the cultivation of the most important ideas of human civilization ... the idea of a universal god, the idea of state, the idea of an alphabet system. Since none of the ancient Semitic languages could develop a writing system while keeping an oral form alive, they lost the copyright on all the original ideas, which were taken and adopted by other languages. Pre-Islamic Arabic was the indirect heir of an ancient Semitic civilization whose heritage persisted strongly in the new world.[25]

The first Semitic, Akkadian, inherited the rich literary tradition of Sumerian, which had a very simple sound system, yet a very complicated grammar. After its written form became extremely complicated, Sumerian uprooted from its oral language and was used only for religious and administrative purposes. By 2000 B.C., Akkadian supplanted Sumerian as the spoken language of southern Mesopotamia, although the latter remained in use as written language of sacred literature, as evidenced in ancient Sanskrit and Latin. About the same time, Akkadian was further divided into the Assyrian dialect, spoken in northern Mesopotamia, and the Babylonian dialect, spoken in southern Mesopotamia. Under the shadow of written Sumerian, Babylon adopted the cuneiform writing system and inscribed its rich canon of literature and epic.

Assyrian gradually lost its oral form, as had its Semitic ancestors. Assyrian dialect was replaced by Babylonian dialect, which became the lingua franca of the Middle East by the 9th century. Two centuries later, Amaraic emerged and replaced Babylonian as oral language but kept Babylonian as the language of mathematics, astronomy, and other learned subjects.

The Assyrian Empire was the second military superpower that the Semites created. They also created the first fully developed writing system, which became the official language of the state (Assyrian language and culture). The Persian Empire (559–330 B.C.) was another empire that Semites created after Aramaic spread and supplanted Akkadian. All of the early Semitic empires ran out of steam in relatively short periods of time. They declined and disappeared from history as short-lived military superpowers. Without written languages to record their oral expression, the Semitic people lost their empires and their gods, again and again, but not their stories and their poetry, which continued to refine and embrace their spoken words.

Like in ancient Greece, gods and goddesses were an important part of the life of ancient Middle East. Since the third millennium B.C., stories of gods and goddesses had been retold, reinvented, and recited in at least half a dozen languages and dialects.

Hebrew was the first Semitic language that developed and accumulated a highly sophisticated literary canon, including poetry, prose narrative, religious teaching, and wisdom.[26] After Hebrew lost its oral form, like its Semitic ancestors, it was its God who kept it alive, and revived it again and again.

When the Israelites began to pray to God, they did so in the midst of peoples whose arms had long been raised and whose heads had been bowed to the gods for thousands of years. They inherited the language of prayer and ritual gesture from their Semitic ancestors. Israelites were not the first to invent a high God that created and supervised a world of minor gods.[27] The Ancient Egyptians, Chinese, Indus, and Mesopotamians, had done that. However, the Israelites were the first who made God speak their language and opened a channel of a direct communication with him.

When Hebrew speakers began to re-imagine their inherited gods, the language of prayer (from both Egyptian and Semitic sides) had begun to mature, and outgrow its gestures and icons. Oral prayer was believed to be inadequate, ("mouth is inadequate for dialogue" to gods); mediators and interpreters (oral or written) became more common. While the Greeks chose a ritual interpreter (priests and priestess), Israelites preferred writing. Unlike the Egyptians, who wrote letters to their gods, the Israelites decided to write in the name of God. With an inherited, richer epic tradition, Hebrew had no trouble describing and writing the entire history of its God and his world.

Israelites invented a new God, *Yahweh*, by renaming the God of their ancestors. They wrote: "God said to Moses, 'I am Yahweh. I revealed myself to Abraham, to Isaac, and to Jacob as El Sadday, but was not known to them by my name Yahweh.'"[28] Yahweh was a different kind of God. He was created by words alone (uprooted from a particular shrine, sanctuary, or a location). He functioned with the capacity of human expression and imagination. He eventually evolved into something that lived in and was carried by human minds. After thousands of years of dancing, singing, praying, crying, and pleading to God, man finally began to speak to him directly ... in Hebrew.

With its new God, Hebrew was the first Semitic language that developed a cultural and religious hegemony where the language of prayers and that of its God were the same.[29] Although Hebrew created the first dialogue with God, its monarchy did not survive with its God. Following the tradition of many Semitic languages, Hebrew lost its oral form to Aramaic after it created a repertory of religious literature. The Hebrew idea of one god had to reinvent itself in other languages. The Hebrew God became the god of other people because they could make him speak their languages to their own prophets and spread his word. Judaism simply did not possess the vehicle to spread the words of its God beyond its limited community.

Another weakness of the ancient Semitic religion of the time was that its language lacked the ability to establish a moral authority strong, restrictive, and absolute enough to reinforce a cultural integration and social unity. Ancient Greeks faced the same problems and decided to adopt the Hebrew God after being frustrated by their own gods. Greek gods were too many and too human.

Semitic was as fluid and elastic as the ancient Greek languages. Since the Semitic gods emerged from tribes where authority was originally associated with the authority of family, clan, and tribe, authority, including divine authority, had been too close to humanity. Although providing an unusual degree of spiritual intimacy, gods in ancient Semitic cultures, like Greek pagan gods, were too human to impose a strong sanction on the society. The Old Testament was the Semite's first attempt to establish a universal and moral God. This God forced man to listen to him and he expected nothing except words (not visual gestures) in return. However, no religion could flourish without a comprehensive hegemony based on a continued language, both oral and written. Hebrew lost its oral form to Aramaic when the literary canon of Judaism uprooted itself from the language of everyday life. Hebrew, Rabbinical Hebrew this time, which focused on religious speculation, was never spoken. This was the main reason why Judaism, having emerged from the oldest culture and language, did not become a broadly followed religion like Christianity and Islam. Hebrew became an obsolete language after the ninth century and was used only in religious function. At times, it adapted and assimilated various local languages, such as Greek, Medieval Spanish and modern European languages, and this initiated a short-lived Renaissance at times. But it was never able to root deeply enough to survive independently until Israel emerged centuries later.

Although it shared the same Semitic roots, Arabic evolved completely opposite from Hebrew. After committing to religious writing for centuries, Hebrew became increasingly abstract. Like its ancestors, Akkadian and Babylonian, it began to uproot itself from spoken language, until by the third century B.C., it was replaced by Aramaic. The Mishnaic, or Rabbinical, Hebrew, like the later Latin and Sanskrit, became a liturgical and literary language that had never been spoken.[30] Ancient Arabic, among other branches of Semitic, kept growing and accumulating without a script. As a result, it was constantly refined and became increasingly poetic. It became highly sophisticated in form and connotation, and yet remained deficient in verbal clarity and logical coherence.

Semitic oral traditions interacted with and were influenced by many younger languages, but none of these had the diversity and richness to assimilate its host. For example, the Hellenistic impact on Syrian cities was always a bit artificial, and Hellenistic culture was always something imposed on Syria from outside. Through ten centuries of exposure to Greek language and culture, the great mass of the Syrian populace remained thoroughly Semitic. Syrians never embraced the Greek tongue or Greek culture to the same extent that some groups of the diverse people of Asia Minor had.

Syriac, a dialect of Aramaic, the language of Jesus, was one of the first languages of Christian literature. Although Syriac literature was deeply indebted to Hellenism, the Syrian mode of Christianity remained Semitic in its heart. Under the cover of Greek religious and philosophical terminology, Syriac tradition was devoted to ascetic ideals and was passionate about the didactic value of the lives of the Eastern Saints. Against Byzantine orthodoxy, which attempted to keep God and man from mingling too closely by confining each to a separate nature in Christ, most Syrian Christians were monophysites.[31]

For the majority of illiterate Syrians, Hellenism had set down only very shallow roots before striking the solid Semitic bedrock. They saw Christ as having but a single nature. He was not merely man and God, as the Greek theologians insisted, but a Man-God.

The Syrian nomadic and semi-nomadic population that spoke Arabic was even less touched by Hellenism. However, Syriac played an important role in the development of Arabic literature. At the beginning of Islamic civilization, Syriac or Aramaic provided crucial vocabularies for Qur'an writing, such as *furqan, sifr, zakah, salah, kahin,* and *qissis.*[32]

Qur'an was the second attempt that the Semites made to integrate the voice and script of the language through the voice of God. This attempt was much more successful than that of the Hebrew because Arabic, in the seventh century, had a strong and powerful voice after many centuries of poetic reinvention and articulation. The Arabic voice was not only well presented in the rhyming language of Qur'an, but also loudly broadcast for all to hear many times a day in all Muslim areas. It was a voice living in the ears of the mind, and carried immediacy and power. It was engraved in the memories of the masses and stuck on the tip of their tongues. Qur'an initiated a cultural revolution, which not only integrated and reformed ancient cultural expression, but also released tremendous creative energies. It was the same energy that generated the cultural Renaissance of Western Europe during the later medieval time, and Chinese culture during the Tang (618–907) and Sung (960–1279) dynasties.[33]

Like any book of religion, mainly focused on the written words of God and accepted interpretation of those words, Islamic tradition began not only with one book, but the only book in the language. The Islamic God spread His words by clarifying and correcting the sound of spoken Arabic. Muhammad and his early companions took painstaking care to ensure that the words of God were remembered verbatim, read and recited in precise pronunciation and rhythm. There was no marking for short vowels, or for â in the middle of a word in all of the earliest Qur'an codices, and in inscriptions, coins and papyri. By the early eighth century, some Qur'an codices used colored dots as indications of vowels, though only to a limited extent, where misreading was particularly likely. But this use of multicolored inks was obviously inconvenient for more general purposes; so too would have been black dots of the Syriac type, since dotting was coming into use for diacritic differentiation between consonants, far more of which needed such differentiation in Quranic than in Syriac. This system, which ultimately prevailed, was to replace the Syriact dots by small obliquely placed lines. This permitted a complete phonetic representation of the word; yet it was virtually never used to its full extent, except in copies of the Qur'an, and to some limited fashion, in writing down verse. Normal usage was, and is still today, either no short vowel marking at all or used extremely sparingly, and only at points of maximum ambiguity.

Arabic was the only language whose written form exclusively began with a single book. Before Islam, there was nothing written in Arabic. Whence Qur'an was written, Allah's words had the absolute control of all the words in Arabic, spoken and written. It was a linguistic vacancy that no religion in history had ever had the opportunity to have.

Qur'an, which was believed to be the bible of Islam, was not intended as a book in the modern sense. It was intended to be something written that had to be read aloud. The Islamic "verses" (*ayat*) of the revelation were compiled into *surahs* in Muhammad's lifetime. It was not until some time after his death that the *surahs* were complied into a systematic arrangement.[34] For nearly a century, these Qur'anic codices remained the only books in Arabic.

Within this unique structure of unity of words, voice, and ideas, Islam triumphed, not by God's words from a literary canon like Christianity, but rather by God's voice recited and memorized from a single book. Until the introduction of printing into the Arabic-speaking world in the early nineteenth century, written words had never achieved the dominance which had occurred in European and Eastern cultures. In other words, God's words, like oral poetry, had been articulated during the centuries by chain memory and recitation.

Qur'anic Arabic, unlike its Semitic ancestors, retained its inherited recital rhyme. Rhyme was a characteristic of many languages, especially in their primitive stages. Rhyme in language originally came from music when words were young and vocabulary was small. Words needed music to help memory, to convey connotations, and to specify graded emotions. As vocabulary and intonation grew, it often left music behind by stepping away from the influence of musical sound, while retaining the ear pleasing pitch and rhyme. For example, ancient Greek and Chinese sounded much more musical than they do now. As they became able to convey emotional shades and distinct levels of meanings with words, they gradually abandoned their musical sound. Arabic was a language that was reborn, as the Italians reinvented Latin. It was a language young in its sound (still musical), yet mature in vocabularies and syntax, when it transformed into a written language.

The musicality of Arabic played an important role in its religious and emotional appeal and persists today. The power of God's rhythmic words, recited five times a day, was a major factor in the continuing growth of Islam as a popular religion while many other religions declined.

Allah was the first God who spoke Arabic, but not the first God in the northern Arabian Peninsula. Arabian queens were created and worshiped by the ancient Semites. These queens were high priestesses of goddesses rather than goddesses themselves. Queen Te'elhunu was the priestess of the goddess Dilbat (Ishtar), who was worshiped locally under the name of Atarsamain. Queens possessed more than religious powers, however, for both Tiglath-pileser iii (744–27 B.C.) and Sargon ii (721–705 B.C.), in referring to the tribute received from foreign rulers, put Queen Samsi on a par with Pir'u of Musru ("Pharaoh of Egypt") and It'amar the Sabaean. The exalted position held by these North Arabian queens can only be justified by the assumption that the cult of Ishtar-'Atarsamain enjoyed tremendous prestige and popularity in North Arabia at that time.[35]

The old Semitic religion — which had evolved sophisticated rituals of gestures and artifacts, social structure, and political hierarchy — had vanished with the death of its language. The goddesses, the priestesses, and the entire idea of God died and were buried with the language.

Since then, there was neither religion nor state institution in north and central Arabia. The southern kingdoms, which were established by a dominant tribe, kept their Old Semitic tradition based on a pantheon of the moon goddess Astral and the fertility goddess Venus. Subordinate to these goddesses was a hierarchy of lesser deities that varied from kingdom to kingdom and obscured a basic uniformity. There was a common course of evolution throughout the whole region, passing from a theocracy of priest-kings called "mukaribs," through secular kingships advised by representative councils, to a decentralized independence of tribal groups within the kingdom. The region shared a social order in which *ashraf* from the noble tribes controlled the lesser tribes.

Iraq was a land divided by barriers of language, religion, social class, and way of life. Like in Syria, most of the population spoke Aramaic. Centuries of Persian rule had left behind an enormous linguistic and religious influence.

Ancient languages like Babylonian survived as local dialects. Jewish communities that had been settled since Babylonian times kept their rabbinical schools. Class and occupational distinctions were also reflected in languages. Most of the high-level administrators, court attendants, and soldiers were Zoroastrians and Persian speaking, while most of the free or slave peasants were Jewish, or Christians speaking Aramaic. The nomadic tribes spoke Arabic.[36]

Changing a language seemed to be a way to start all over again, even when it came to God. With a brand new language, the pre–Islam Arabic society had no signs of a literary hierarchy because within the clan, everyone's spoken words were considered equal to those of another. Like in pagan Greece, the pre–Islamic Arabs developed a language to directly communicate with their gods and nurtured a businesslike relationship with them. It was a negotiation ... for this offering I give you, lord, you will give me that favor for return.[37] They believed in minor spirits (*jinn*) and divines to protect their tribes. The spirits and divines were living in shrines located at a tree, a grove, or a strangely formed rock or stone. Arabs made regular pilgrimages to worship their gods. The pagan Arabic world was merely what the eyes could see. Not much was hidden, just a world of desert and tribes. There were some high gods, but there were no cults, having elaborate rituals like those of the Greek. Without an epic tradition, which accumulated in a continued poetic narration, Arabic did not have a well-connected kingdom of gods and goddesses. Without general vocabularies and prose that made speculative and abstract reasoning possible, there was no hidden meaning about life or higher moral value in the minds of pre–Islamic Arabs before the seventh century.

Like Judaism, Islam emerged through the renaming of an existing tribal god through prose writing. Like the Old Testament, the Qur'an was written in the name of a high God. The Quraysh, Muhammad's tribe, had been worshiping Allah, but had no formal cult for the worship.[38] It was the same as the Hebrew idea of a God who spoke in human language, but, when this idea was transcribed in Arabic, it created a different God. He had a different shape, different attitude, and different relationship with man. Like Biblical Hebrew and formative Latin, pre–Islamic Arabic was a concrete language without a verbal hierarchy. The only way to create an absolute deity with an unquestioned authority was to put words into his mouth. By the seventh century, man had been speaking to his gods for some centuries. The Arabic version of it, in principle, was not much different from that of Hebrew. However, when the revelation was described in Arabic, it took the form of *kahin*, an outburst of rhyming prose from a soothsayer. Pre-Islamic soothsayers were men who were believed to be possessed by jinn, a spirit that carried them to speak. On a higher level of literacy, Arabic poets would utter a similar and yet a far more polished poetic form because poets were believed to possess hidden powers.

This ritual connection between the words uttered by spirits and those of man was the formal foundation of prophecy, the same foundation from which Hebrew and Christianity emerged. Now was the time for Muhammad. However, Muhammad was facing a dilemma that the Latin west world had not yet seen ... the formal connection between words of God and those of the prophetic poets. Islam was the first religion that emerged through a mature poetic. Muhammad's task was to convince his audience that what possessed him was not simply irresponsible jinn or poetic talent, but a *Gabriel,* the real representative of God himself. Muslims have ever since constantly denied that the Qur'an was *shi'r,* pre–Islamic poetry.[39]

By writing down the words of God, Islam consolidated the pagan gods of tribal Arabs into a moral God. However, the difference between the Christian God and the Islamic God lay less in the meaning of moral purity and conduct, than in the form in which these conducts were described. While the Hebrew and Christian Gods had to struggle to establish the authority of their words as divine over human words, the words of Allah had no competitors, at least during the initial period of Islam. In this linguistic context, Allah was a positive God, described and spoken in a positive language. He was the first and only God that written Arabic created. He spoke in a unique language, rhyming prose, which was the first recorded Arabic at the time. His moral rules and regulations were clearly and positively defined.

Like the early Christianity, which spread by word of mouth, the Qur'an was not a discursive book for abstract information or even, in the first instance, for inspiration. The Qur'an was assembled in bits and pieces. It notoriously lacked a sequence of development and a clear logical order. The stories came as reminders of episodes rather than as a linear and fluid story line. A seemingly jumbled and incoherent mass, it was meant to be recited, in parts or in whole. It meant to infuse everyday life with a powerful sense of transcendently divine requirements.

Opposite to any formative written language like Latin, Hebrew, and other early vernaculars, which focused on simply transcription of the oral language, the scholarship of the early Qur'anic Arabic concentrated more on the spoken rather than the written words of God. Muslims normally became acquainted with a text by hearing it read aloud by a teacher and did not have to rely solely on the written text for their understanding of how a passage was to be recited. So, there was hardly any punctuation. Medieval manuscripts usually had no punctuation at all, except occasionally for clarity. The written text did not even show where a new sentence began, nor how the sentence was structured.[40]

While Christianity, following the tradition of Judaism, stated its moral rules in negative terms — commandments — the Qur'an provided two equally prescribed moral options and offered man to choose with free will. There was little trace of fear or threat. Qur'anic Arabic portrayed human conditions in vivid images. God offered to the heavens the trust of keeping faith first, and they refused. He offered it to the mountains, and they said they were not strong enough. Mankind took it willingly. Each man was facing a fundamental choice in life: to believe or disbelieve God. If man chose to stand in awe of his God, He would make him upright and pure. If man decided to turn away from God, God turned away from man as well, and let him be wicked and petty.[41] The unwillingness of man to follow God's direction was interpreted as forgetfulness rather than sinful. Man, by nature, was expected to obey God and assume his moral responsibility. Sometimes, man could forget about his moral duties. Unlike Christians, who were told that they were born sinful and guilty and they had to work hard and live a Christian life to prove otherwise, the Islamic God was a reminder rather than supervisor of human moralities. This mild (or non-adversarial) rather than harsh attitude of Islam was rooted in pre–Islamic Arabic, a language that did not have the biting edge of Latin.

During the 'Abbasid period, Arabic writers rapidly evolved a new style using elaborate and involved paragraph structure, with abundant hypotaxis and precise indications of the logical links between the parts of the paragraph. This was achieved not so much by developing new syntactic tools as by giving a greater degree of functional precision to indicators, which had previously been imprecise and ambivalent.[42]

From the end of the fourth century the histories of East and West were very different. The decline of traditional secular education based on classical and pagan authors began in the West long before it did in the East. The full range of instruction ... elementary, grammatical, and rhetorical ... was offered in fewer and fewer places. During the fifth century, rhetorical education ceased north of Loire.[43]

The Western Christendom was a world built on the written words of Latin. The Latin Christian God was silent, harsh, and remote. This form of religion was not so much by choice than a cultural and linguistic necessity. It presented an idea, a beautiful and glittering monument in the sky, a real spiritual and emotional connection, an approachable road, between God and his believers. When Latin died, the tower of Babel reaching to God collapsed. While churches busied themselves building another, many people left out of impatience. Over the centuries, as the new tower was built by the emerging vernaculars, many decided to stay away because Christianity was no longer the only monument in the sky. Many had chosen another.

The Islamic kingdom was also a monument in the sky. However, with its diversity and flexibility, Arabic created magic carpets on which Muslims could fly to their God whenever and however they pleased. Religion released or restrained man's spirit to the limit of his language and imagination.

The Christian God died in the modern West for the same reason that many ancient gods died. He lost his language. No God could have survived the silence for long. The triumph of Western Christianity, which sustained for over two thousand of years, was a miracle of history. The Christian God in the West was the only God in human history which survived the language of his birth.

Religious vision did not necessarily lead to conflict, but its extreme passion did. It took many centuries for a language to develop intense emotional expressions. This was the reason why it took Christianity more than a thousand years to turn to violence while it took Islam only two centuries.

3. The Words of Law:
Islamic and British Empires

The Islamic Empire was a hybrid of a highly poetic language, a borrowed God, and an alien philosophy (Greek). If the main task of Latin was to produce diverse and rich expressions without losing precision, Arabic's battle (as a poetic and fluid language) had been for precision, logical coherence, expressive efficiency, and systematic reasoning, while retaining its oral idioms.

The Islamic revolution, beginning with a prophetic vision and poetic faith, was carried by a radical transformation in its language, Arabic. By codification and classification of Islamic law, Arabic substantially increased its precision and efficiency. Through translating Greek philosophical literature, it learned to build and defend conceptual boundaries. Out of necessity, it had grown up very quickly, and it created a commonwealth based on religious law of ethical rulings, interpretive legislation, and juristic authorities.

Medieval English went through a similar classification process in another multi-lingual environment made up of Latin, French, and Old and Middle English. A much younger poetic, English interaction with Christianity and Roman legal tradition fundamentally changed the course of its culture. Latin clarified the Old English vision and logic by creating a level of abstract meanings. French offered a rich repertoire of technical vocabularies. English took the Latin clarity, precision, and structural coherence as important parts of its foundation. By the time of the Renaissance, when English poetry and prose flourished, its concept of law, as externally imposed by the Christian God, was firmly in place. The ability to specify and defend verbal boundaries, an ability that Arabic had never had and Latin had for a while but was unable to maintain, determined the characteristics of the British Empire and its policy.

Since the Renaissance, English further elaborated and refined its poetics. It became a creative and adopting host language which absorbed and wove foreign influence into its own fabric. It finally became a language that was able to sing as the Greeks and Arabs, to paint as the French, to gesture as the Italians, and to reason as the Germans. The continuing expansion of English vision, with its cultural idioms, made the English Commonwealth a cultural empire.

Within their own scopes, the Islamic and English empires achieved the same result. They built long lasting and influential empires based on a successful cultural hegemony. However, English and Arabic hegemonies were built on different kinds of law based on different linguistic grounds. The power of English law was a hierarchy of rules, each level of which separated from another. The English order, like that of Romans, created an well-organized system of movements driven by separate orbit, whose direction, speed, and movement was pre-determined. Arabic law was a combination of external and internal (ethical) laws. It was confusing as a system because levels kept penetrating each other. However, the submission to the law of God was as solidly planted in Arab minds as in English minds.

For decades, historians have been writing and rewriting about Islamic conquests. This chapter emphasizes the inner dynamic of Islamic culture, the interaction of its language, its faith, its self-image, and reasoning. This dynamic energized the growth and transformation of Arabic and expanded its vision, expressive capacity, and self-knowledge. It transformed Arabic from a tribal civilization into a universal culture, and a political as well as military power.

When Islamic vision took its form, Arabic was mainly expressed in poetry, composed by the nomadic tribes of the Arabian Peninsula. It demonstrated all the features of a highly conventional lyrical language.[1] In pre–Islamic Arabic, there were no general and abstract vocabularies, no prose composition, no narrative structure (storytelling in a non-lyrical sense), let alone language of law. The Arabic poet was less a narrator than a master of fluid imagery and descriptive brevity. He was a magician of rhythm and parallel wording. For the poetic Arabic, story line and precise meaning were not as important as the form in which the story was told and the shade of meaning that was conveyed. Without a notion of authorship, the Arab poet would let his transmitter, *rawi,* supply detail and elucidate meanings. The commentators/transmitters, often the admirers and diffusers of his verses, learned the poems by heart and performed them in the poet's manner. Since the listeners knew the background of the subjects in most cases, they expected distinct artistic forms in delivering the familiar pattern. They wanted to see how (rather than what) emotion was expressed and how rhyming words and rhythmic devices were used.[2]

Since the ancient Arabic evolved into a language of form as well as meaning, pre–Islamic moral code was far less absolute than that of Latin. Arabic values and ethical behavior had more individual shades and personal color.[3] For example, the social control was exercised less by moral judgment than by well-calculated verbal communication. As the language was able to convey well-measured conceptual shades and intentional understatement, it was used to suggest, rather than define, the boundaries of personal territories. The following example illustrates how words and wording that were notably concerned with one's honor (a matter of life and death sometimes) were so carefully weighed that they could illustrate the point in strength while saving the other party's face:

"'To horse!' they challenged. 'Such is our way,' we replied. 'Unless you dismount: our welcome, always, is warm.'" The second line, in Arabic, expressly conveys: "We are as gallant as you with the lance, but the real test is with the sword at close quarters." This is a provocation, yet is so worded that it also carries the implication 'unless you dismount as our guests.' There were many such well-measured statements such as: "If you come as friend, we shall come the same; if not, you shall find us the harder to meet."[4]

This suggestive language clearly set the boundary between a friendly meeting and the harder one yet made it fluid, relative, and transmutable. A choice was offered and consequences of the choice were inferred. The shading space between the two opposite poles of the spectrum was created and emphasized by a shrewd understatement. Such linguistic consciousness and capacities of Arabic made moral judgment less absolute. It was possible to share moral values and to express, understand, and utilize them as if they were private meanings.

This suggestive language cultivated a different kind of authority and social relationship. Each Bedouin ruled himself and was free to rebuke preassumption in others: "If you are our lord" (if you act discreetly as a *sayyid* [gentleman] should "you will lord over us, but if you are a prey to pride, go and be proud!" (We will have nothing to do with you.)[5] In this sense, respect and royalty were related less to the institutional position than to the quality of the personality and attitude perceived, conceived, and understood by communication.

Unlike institutionalized Latin rights and well defined Christian virtue, Arabic self-reliant justice took the form of a voluntary imposition as a solemn vow sworn to different kinds of gods. Through the form and content of vows, gods were individually defined and personally shaped. They were used as self-discipline bound to sanction one's own action. In this sense, gods or idols of the pre–Islamic period were merely a witness to an oath that judged the truthful from the liar.[6] The verbal function of the gods and idols appear in the following verse of al-Mutalammis, a well-known pre–Islamic poet: "You expelled me for fear of my satire? No, by al-Allat and by the altar-stones, you will never escape."[7] Al-Allat, Manah, and al-'Uzza were goddesses that formed the principal deities of the pagan Arabs, whose images were installed in the valley of "Nakhlat al-Shamiyah."[8] The pagan Arabs often swore in their names: "An oath, truthful and just, I swear by Manah, at the sacred place of the Khazraj."[9] Like other subjects of oath, such as stone (the stones upon which victims were slaughtered, were called 'ansab and blood of sacrifice), pre-Islamic gods served as witnesses of words whose materialization served as determinants for right and wrong.[10]

Vows functioned not only as moral judgment and penalty, but also as a negotiation or bargain with the supernatural. Pagan Arabs took vows that, if the number of their sheep reached one hundred, they would sacrifice one of them in the name of a certain deity. Consequently, they fulfilled their vows once the condition had been met. Their vows became a contract with the deity. Sometimes they tried to escape from their committed obligation, but they feared that the deity might take revenge against them. These responsive ideas of the pagan Arabs remain an essential part of Islamic legal thought, though the content of language, and name of the deity, have changed.

The Qur'an consolidated this loosely defined moral sanction by establishing a new level of authority ... the words of Allah. The Qur'an established its new authority by unifying the sound, vocabulary, and the memory of its language. It was read, recited, and engraved in the mind of Muslims of different regions.[11] While Latin, and later English, established the authority of law by creating a separate level of words (legal language) to sanction speech, Islam established this by streamlining the whole language, written and spoken. The period of the first century of Islam was the age in which the cultural movements for correct speaking, writing, eloquence, and writing styles were one and the same.[12] The Qur'an readers and scholars were the forerunners of the professional grammarians, linguistics, literary writers, and even calligraphers.

Intensive coping, writing, and publishing during the Umayyad period (661–680) became a cultural and linguistic movement. It codified the Arabic language, its pronunciation, its grammar, and its law.[13] While Qur'anic reading was increasingly standardized, various styles of Qur'anic scriptures flourished. With the effort of both private and commercial copyists, who functioned as booksellers, Arabic handwriting became a business as well as an art. "Good penmanship for all general purposes of the literary fields involved careful execution of each consonant, adequate but not excessive orthography, uniformity in the style of scripts and in any use of colors, and abbreviations to indicate source and correctness."[14] While the production of books in the fields of Arabic language and literature kept pace with that of Qur'anic studies, the overlapping of literary and legal languages made it impossible to separate the boundary between legal concepts and literary wording of shade and color. Thus, the command for the knowledge of the standard Arabic became a "sine qua non" in other fields.[15]

The Islamic Revolution, in this particular sense, was a reorientation of language as well as spirit. It was a transformation of culture and society as radical as occurred in Europe during the Renaissance. The Islamic law, like Roman and later English law, created a higher level of language, a language overriding all secular concepts that had been accepted and followed in different regions and cultural environments. The new conceptual level, divine will, created a supreme realm of sanction to clarify or exclude ill-defined meanings.

For example, the word "Islam," designed to mean defiance of death, self-sacrifice or ready to die (for the sake of God) in the Islamic tradition, was the result of reconsideration by exclusion. The word *'aslama*, from which Islam was derived, once meant many different kinds of sacrifice and death for various causes.[16] "When they (my fellow-tribesmen) throw me into 'the mouth' of an enemy attack, the manner in which I fight, *makani*, takes care of them in the hour when the one who denies what is most sacred, is wont to give away, *'aslama*, his life."[17] The notion of "to defy death" was derived from the primary sense of the word *'aslama* as "hand over someone or something" or deliver up a person to someone, to his enemy, his pursuer." The notion of "to defy death" was in fact an elliptic expression for *'aslama nafsahu* (deliver himself).[18] Gradually, *'aslama* was used in conjunction with the idea of defying death in the battle, and further, as a sacrifice for a glorious or sacred cause. For instance, Ibn Hisam wrote: "They exerted themselves in striking the heroes and sacrificed the blood of their souls (*'aslamu muhgati 'anfusihim*) for the Lord of the World (*lirabbi, l-masriqi*)."[19] After *'aslama muhgati 'anfusihim* developed into a self-contained expression, *'aslama* became a linguistic cliché in a popular Islamic sense.

Like Judaism, which created a new God by divine written speech, Islam created Allah and his language, Arabic, all together. By writing down the divine words, the Qur'an enlarged and generalized the concept of God in pre–Islam Arabic and transformed it from a concrete and tribal deity to a universal God, a divine judge of human conduct and behavior.[20] It lifted God up as an ultimate supreme judge knowing and examining everything of men. Allah was a larger and higher God who imposed himself on man and the world. God was no longer a tribal deity with whom man could negotiate and exchange favors.

The Qur'an, as God's words in writing, redefined the relationship between God and man. Instead of being committed by one's own words (oath and pledge), man became sanctioned by the Words of God, a language he had no a part of. This changed the very nature of his relationship with God. Men would be judged, rewarded or punished, according to the written words of God. Men had no choice but to believe or disbelieve and to worship or not to worship. With an Islamic God who heard all and knew all, the law of worship was externally imposed and everyone would be judged at last day, believers or unbelievers:

> And it is God who brought you forth from your mothers' wombs, and he appointed for you hearing, and sight, and heats, that haply so you will be thankful.... And it is God who has appointed a place of rest for you of your houses, and He has appointed for you of the skins of cattle houses you find light on the day that you journey, and on the day you abide, and of their wool, and of their fur, and of their hair furnishing and an enjoyment for a while.... Those who disbelieve and far from the way of God — them We shall give increase of chastisement upon chastisement, for that they were doing corruption. And the day we shall raise up from every nation to a witness against them from amongst them and we shall bring thee (believer) as a witness against those.[21]

Since the Qur'an was the only book in the language, Allah immediately became a lawgiver, a legislator, as well as a judge. Allah's absolute authority would have been easy to maintain if the Qur'an had remained the only book written in Arabic. Like Christianity and Judaism before it, Islam faced the same challenge. To make the idea of a divine empire a reality, its God needed to say (or write) more, to lead the community of the faithful. An industry of the words of God in Arabic emerged out of necessity, as it did for Hebrew, Greek, and Latin after the Old and New Testaments.

Qur'an successfully established a new and unified authority by its persuasive and general language. But, it faced serious uncertainty when it was applied to legal and administrative practice. Muhammad, the Prophet, had to interpret and explain the ruling of the Qur'an when diversified interpretation took place. Gradually his words and deeds were compiled into new books, *Sunna* and *Hadith*, which added to the Islamic canon.[22] These extra–Qur'anic writings provided guidelines for interpretation of Islamic law. Muhammad became the judge supreme of Islamic law and his interpretations became a part of Islamic canon.[23]

To create a divine Islamic ideal, which was only generally outlined in the Qur'an, Muhammad had to specify the vague and fluid concepts in order to resolve dispute.[24] Like the Jewish rabbi and Christian priests, Muhammad and his companions had to explain many Qur'anic injunctions concerning prayer, such as "zakat," "hajj," and some commercial transactions.

These extra Qur'anic provisions and their interaction with Qur'an texts created a new dynamic that drove the development of the Arabic language and Islamic law. For the first time, Arabic was challenged to be clear and precise and evolve a logical consistency. Like the Latin of the Roman law, Arabic was under tremendous pressure by the legislative, juristic, political, and administrative need to be more and more specific and efficient. Originally, Muhammad insisted that he would not put his words into writing for fear of contradicting the written law of Allah.[25] Early Muslim leaders also postponed the writing process of the *Hadith* and *Sunna* for the same reason.[26] However, the accumulation of the writings, revision, and their validations about the prophet eventually created an extra–Qur'anic canon of law.

This conceptual transmutability stimulated the development of the Arabic language and Islamic law until the classical period.[27] Without an immutable set of rules, the early Muslim judges, lawyers, and caliphs cited both the Qur'an and *Sunna* to justify their legal decisions.[28] With levels of connotations and understatements, judges and lawyers had to analyze, compare, and juxtapose seemingly contradictory rules to justify their legal juristic positions. Legal and literary elaboration, in turn, made conceptual boundaries more flexible and elastic. More rulings became needed to close worn out boundaries again.

Moral, legal, and administrative practice of the Islamic Empire pushed Arabic to grow very quickly. The sayings and deeds of Muhammad were cited and implied as an authentic source of Islamic law. After the Muhammadian interpretations expanded and got out of hand, the *Sunna* had to be put in writing. It became a separate legal document and discipline that closed the door on "illegal" and unauthorized writings. The written sayings of Muhammad, his personal juristic and judicial opinions, became an authentic source of law.[29]

The *Sunna* complement further diversified the wording and ideas of Islamic law because writers had different motives, political as well as personal. When the uncertainty of the meanings of law became a deep concern for scholars, judges, and rulers, they took charge of the compilation of the *Sunna*. Like the enactment of the English common law, Arabic writing became a means to gain certainty, whether it was legal, institutional, cultural, or religious. However, the law could only be as defined and certain as the language allowed. With a different nature of conceptual boundary, Arabic enactment took a different form from that of Latin and English. Unlike the common law of the formative English, whose written words became the ultimate arbitrator of legal disputes, Islamic legitimacy was constantly redistributed in a continued debate about the meaning of the legal connotation. Since the same Arabic words could convey various levels of meanings and connotations, the legitimate meaning would be decided by the loudest voices: those of Muhammad, his companions, judges, and Islamic scholars.[30]

As *Sunna* began to be recorded, it added forms of extreme diversity, each of which expanded new meanings and new provisions to the legal Arabic language as well as ambiguous shading.[31] *Hadith* literature represented a new literary trend that was concrete, simple, and elegant at the same time. Its strong legal and moral meaning, expressed in an intimate, personal manner, moved its way into the actual legal vocabulary.[32] Rules and conduct were told and illustrated in the detailed examples of Muhammad's own actions, as well as his personality.[33]

The way in which *Sunna* could instantly elaborate both inclusive and exclusive meanings and stand and move between the two was the result of a constant conceptual redefinition and juxtaposition. For example, in early *Hadith* literature, *Sunna* meant the activities of the Prophet, of other companions, of the community, or of an ordinary person.[34] To distinguish and specify the distinct meaning in each context, conceptual associations, exclusion, and juxtaposition were used. The simplest association was to juxtapose *Sunna* with a particular mode of behavior. "The *Sunna* is that the first *rak'a* (a bending of the torso from an upright position, followed by two prostractions in prayer) is longer than the second"). Or "it is in a well-known *Sunna* that in *ihram* (performing pilgrim) one should not wear the shirt."[35] To precisely classify a particular provision in a different degree of sanction, a distinct yet related conceptual juxtaposition was adopted. As Malik said: "To sacrifice an animal (on the eve of 'Id) is *Sunna* and not obligation (*wajib*)."[36] Different doctrines, in turn, emerged from the distinct juxtapositions. While some of the scholars juxtaposed prayer with *Sunna*, others juxtaposed it to obligation (*wajib*)."[37]

The significance of such conceptual juxtaposition lay less in the particular way in which legal words were associated than in the increasingly widened conceptual ground that it provided for juristic reasoning. Unlike the linear reasoning of legal English (rules applying to cases), without an absolute bond of rule and deed, Islamic law would go in whatever direction the conceptual juxtaposition led. In instance, the *Sunna* of the prophet could be either rules that sanctioned deeds or deeds (of Muhammad) that justified rules (by *Hadith* scholars in the name of Muhammad).

The following example shows how far that conceptual re-juxtaposition could carry a rule away from its original practice and acquire entirely different meanings. Ibn Shihab said: "One who is able to join just one rak'a (bending torso in praying of jum'a [Friday] pray (because he is late and missed one rak'a) should pray one additional rak'a (after if) it *is sunna*." He said again: "I found the scholars of our city holding the same opinion. It was so, the Prophet said: 'Whoever pray a *rak'a* of the prayer with the Imam in congregation has not missed the prayer.'"[38] The *sunna* of the prophet, in this passage, which was used as the justified source of the rule (of *sunna*), was not an action of Muhammad because being an Imam, he never missed a *rak'a*. Thus, the passage was deduced from a saying of Muhammad (that he who prayered a *rak'a* without missing the prayer) about a doctrine applicable to a different situation (one who missed a *rak'a*). In this sense, a jurist when deducing a law or doctrine by using the process of analogy only expounded upon the law rather than laying it down. Thus was establishing rules through, not according to, *sunna*."[39]

The lack of boundaries between Muhammad's practice and his sayings and between his practice and that of others allowed legal rulings to be transmutable. The multi-levels of meanings provided the conceptual ground for inflated and conflicting rulings. Legal texts became never ending books. Each scholar produced legal ideas from his own understanding of Islamic conduct and his ideal of Muslim community. This created broad diversity, as scholars and their beliefs were cultivated and formalized in different regional cultural environments. The elaboration of diverse legal arguments accelerated the codification and recitation of *sunna* and the flourishing *Hadith* literature, which in turn, triggered more diverse juristic variations. In this fluid and adaptive language, both intentional and unintentional exercise of personal opinion and individual reasoning were taken into the body of the law, through rewriting and reinterpretation.

The most influential personal discretion (*ra'y*) was from those who had judicial power. The Muslim judges of early Islam enjoyed the most judicial freedom in Islamic history.[40] The possibility of their discretion lay less in their personal knowledge of and involvement in *Sunna* compilation than in the very extra-textuality of the language of law at a time when it was possible to interpret and even fabricate rules. Lacking a well clarified and specified code with strong binding power, they could easily and simply enacted their own rules (in the name of *Sunna*, of course) whenever judicial decisions needed to be made.

Without a clear boundary between original meaning of ruling and its interpretation, the legal role of caliph, like that of English kings, expanded from judgment to legislation through the recording and writing of *sunna*. The caliphate office was originally formed according to the explicit ruling of the Qur'an: "David, We have appointed you a *khalifa* (caliph) on the earth; so judge between men with justice [*bi'l-haqq*] and do not follow desire that lead you astray from the path of God."[41] However, the distinction between God as lawgiver and caliph as judge who reinforced the law was gradually blurred and even flattened out in both the Umayyad legal practice and the recorded *sunna*.[42] The authority of the caliphate law (as juxtaposed with the law of God) was derived from an Umayyad conceptual confusion between the caliph, who could formulate legal rules for the extrinsic reason that they were also companions of the prophet or exceptionally pious, and later ones, who had no right to interfere with the contents of the law at all.[43]

In early *Hadith* and contemporary poetry, the word *caliph* stood *for khalifat Allah.* Thus, all caliphs were named as deputies of God, *khalifat Allah, a'immat al-huda, mahdiyun* and *rashidun.* The titles implied both judge and legislator in a completely matter-of-fact way. The *sunna* of caliphs was understood to have the same authority as those of previous caliphs and even that of Muhammad.[44] With this legitimate title, caliphs were free to make and unmake *sunna* as they pleased. They issued edicts or mandates to their governors and judges, laying down the legal rules which the latter were to apply.[45] 'Umar II committed himself to restoring a just administration that would deal impartially with all. With an ideal vision of the practice of the rightly guided caliphs, especially Abu Bakr and 'Umr I, he attempted to revive and enforce their model practice. On the one hand, he constantly sought advice from Islamic scholars and commissioned them to record a large part of *sunna* dealing with commercial relationships and economic life of the *Hadith.* On the other hand, he was personally involved in his court and kept close correspondence concerning legal matters with his judges and governors.[46]

However, the legislative power of the Muslim caliph had never become as exclusive and absolute as that of the English kings, because the Islamic jurists constantly clarified and established a conceptual boundary between the judicial and legislative functions. This boundary was created by an intellectual hierarchy, which classified different levels of rulings and various authorities of sanction. The names of the hierarchical levels were redefined from time to time, as were the relationships among them. The structure of hierarchy served as a continuous barrier that separated and restricted the legal power of each of the levels. This structure also prevented the legal power of the caliph from becoming exclusive, and protected the caliph from the competition of other rulings. The immutable arbitrary hierarchy and its transmutability were maintained by a constant re-juxtaposition of rulings that assigned distinct degrees of legitimacy to different provisions.

For example, after *Sunna* outgrew Qur'an, became an independent source of law, and produced overburdened texts of its own, a legal boundary, *sanad* or *isnad* (transmitter or a chain of transmitters) was introduced into the system of textual evidence to distinguish the legitimate provisions from the false ones. As a touchstone of legitimacy, *isnad* created a conceptual authority, authenticity, and reliability of rulings based on a continuous written transmission that traced back to the companions of Muhammad and carried by their family members.[47] With this new measurement, the written *Sunna,* that collected the statements of the companions and prophet, was recompiled as *musnad,* a *Sunna* proper attributed to the prophet himself and subservient to legal discretion.[48]

From this point on, the *Sunna* writing aimed less at the discovery of new materials than at recovery of old materials of varying degrees of acceptability. It classified rulings into categories such as *al-'Ilal* (defects), *al-Du'afa* (weak narrators), and *al-Rija"* (trustworthy authorities) according to the degree of reliability of the transmitters and the authenticity of the texts.[49] This classification provided the conceptual foundation for a systematic criticism of *Sunna* texts, a practical tool for the elimination of mass materials, and an authoritative evaluator of rulings.[50] The movement was called *'ilm al-jarh wa-'l-ta'dil* (science of impugning or confirming of the credibility of the transmitters). To evaluate the authenticity and quality of each rule, *Sunna* authors scrutinized the trustworthiness of each of the transmitters, and the degree of completeness of the isnad as a unit, as well as the precision of the transmission terminology.[51] They undertook a systematic critical study of the *muhaddiths* (transmitters) and their materials. They classified the transmitters as *thiqab* (trustworthy), *thabt* (firm), *hujjah* (evidence), *hayyin* (of little consideration), *layyin* (lax), *matruk* (preferably left out), *munkar* (objectionable), and *kadhahab* (lying). These categories gradually became specific classifications of the quality of *Sunna* rulings according to the juristic opinions about the credibility and authority of texts. With a thorough knowledge of the narrators of a large number of *Hadith* texts, the critics became the authorities to determine the value and binding power of legal rules. This was the first step of the transformation of legislative mode, from authority of words (divine and juridical origins as textual based judgment) to that of legal interpretation (juristic opinions as knowledge based judgment).[52]

By critical examination and exclusion, *Sunna* rulings were defined and recompiled as an authentic code of law that was accepted as universally authoritative. The new versions of *sunna* were written in carefully weighted legal terms and classified into volumes and chapters according to major topics, such as legal, ethical, doctrinal, Qur'anic and eschatological issues. In cases where there was more than one transmitted authority, various versions of text were specifically footnoted by well-classified narrators. In the version compiled by Muhammad b. 'Isa al-Timidhi, each rule was followed by a note about its degree of authenticity and juristic use.[53]

However, the knowledge based judgment that was initiated by the system of *isnad*, could only standardize and justify the origins of the legal texts, not their meanings and implications. Even with relatively authenticated texts, the diverse interpretations of their meaning remained a source of uncertainty in Islamic law. Unlike the restrictions of early Latin and English legal interpretation, Arabic interpretation was almost boundless. As Hanafi once claimed: "This (legal) knowledge of ours is opinion; it is the best we have been able to achieve. He who is able to arrive at different conclusions is entitled to his opinion and we are entitled to our own."[54] The Arabic imagery in law seemed as free as its opinion in politics and its fluidity in literature. The lack of boundaries is also expressed in Ibn Mas'ud's well-known statement: "What the Moslems see good, surely it is good in the eyes of God and what the faithful think is ugly, it is also ugly in the eyes of God."[55] According to this opinion, law could be anything one believed and it would be justified. Thus, the earliest legal interpretation was really an interpretation without text, rooted in an oral mentality that held no sense of textural boundary.

After legal imagery had uprooted from the text of written law, the juristic lost control. To set new boundaries for the interpretive efforts, a new concept, *ijma*, (consensus) was introduced. When legal imagery was removed from the texts, its juristic sanction disappeared, which extended the standard of juristic judgment from merely authorship, to comprehension and negotiation. It transformed an exclusive authority of authenticity (true or false) to an inclusive authority of collective agreement (a spectrum of various opinions).[56] Although different juristic schools had different definitions and standards for consensus, the agreeable opinions of Muslims (Companions, jurists, or others) were established as an extra-textual source of law. As Prof. Mahmassani pointed out, consensus made a great contribution to Islamic law. It made it possible to assimilate the legal opinions of Muslim jurists into the body of the law.[57] At the same time, it controlled personal legal interpretations, and channeled them into a localized negotiation of the law.

The introduction of *qiyas* (analogy) transformed the source of legal interpretation from literal to logical juxtaposition. This transformation created both certainty and uncertainty within the legal system. As the implication of certain rules expanded, they finally went beyond the conceptual bound, eventually erasing the binding power of the legal meaning. The spectrum of logical juxtaposition was much wider and harder to control than that of conceptual juxtaposition. This finally signified the total collapse of the "legal" language, as opposed to political and ethical language. No Western law had ever experienced this until the later twentieth century.

At the same time, analogy substantially expanded the conceptual repertoire of the law. It juxtaposed ideas that originally had no conceptual connection to legal texts. Its interpretation was much looser than the textual interpretation. The analogical interpretation expanded the spectrum of implication for established rulings. Like the basic principles of English common law, that became the ever-lasting foundation for legal speculation, the moral language of Islam remained an inspiration for the legal practice for centuries. While the consistency of English law lay in the unwritteness that made it possible to enact the law differently for different circumstances, the consistency of Islamic law was derived from its loose interpretation, an unexhaustible source of new law.

While numerous levels of the source of law expanded and clarified the conceptual divisions of legal Arabic, jurisprudential reasoning juxtaposed the apparently contrary concepts into a hierarchy of law. The new certainty was established by a logical consistency of the relationships within a mass of legal texts and levels of interpretation. For example, the legal ideas of al-Shafi'i represented a systematic innovation. They transformed the absolute (or linear) reasoning of conceptual clarification and exclusion into a correlative reasoning, which integrated oppositions and blurred divisions. In a language of fluid and penetrating meaning, al-Shafi'i created a different kind of binding power: the formalized and definite relation between different legislative and interpretative authorities.[58]

Al-Shafi'i transformed the dimension of juristic reasoning from locating conceptual boundaries to defining the relationship between the fluid boundaries. The juxtaposition of various juristic opinions became inclusive rather than exclusive. He was aware that the various authorities of Islamic law could never agree on a single point. Although they all relied on *Sunna*, there was a wide divergence in doctrine due to the use of personal opinion, rather than on a strict adherence to a set of rules. As long as there was no well-authenticated *Sunna*, there was no unanimous common guide.[59] Instead of setting conceptual boundaries, al-Shafi'i developed a set of principles to classify, scrutinize, rank, and integrate these different interpretations. To establish a logical consistency out of an inconsistent (fluid and ambiguous) language, he had to impose new boundaries and rules.

First, al-Shafi'i established the authority of the prophet as a lawgiver.[60] He insisted that no words could override the authority of those of the prophet. Further, all well-authenticated words going back to the prophet had precedence over those of his companions, their successors, and later authorities.[61] As he stated in the beginning of *Ikhtilaf Malic wal-Shafi'i*:

> Every tradition related by reliable persons as going back to the Prophet, is authoritative and can be rejected only of another authoritative tradition from the Prophet contradicts it. If it is a case of repeal of a former ordinance by a later, the later is accepted. If nothing is known about a repeal, the more reliable of the two traditions is to be followed. If both are equally reliable, the one more in keeping with the Qur'an is to chosen; traditions from other person are of no account in the face of a tradition from the Prophet, whether they confirm of contradict it. If the other persons had been aware of the tradition from the Prophet, they would have followed it.[62]

Al-Shafi'i distinguished the words of the prophet from those of others by scrutinizing the traditional foundation of legal doctrine.

Second, when more than one version of *Sunna* of the prophet were found contradictory, al-Shafi'i suggested harmonizing them by distinguishing between their respective circumstances. Since al-Shafi'i never had considered that two traditions from the prophet would be fundamentally contradictory, he would not invalidate one against another if he could manage to accept both.[63] To harmonize the conceptually contradictory previsions, al-Shafi'i formulated a series of interpretive rules to build a logical consistency. He reclassified each provision of the Qur'an and *Sunna* rulings on their own merit, and yet he ranked legal connotation according to its source. He reconstructed the conceptually contradictory provisions into logical consistency by using three words of the same root: abrogation, abrogated and abrogating. Thus, Qur'anic rulings could not be abrogated except by other Qur'anic rulings; *Sunna* provision could not be abrogated except by another *Sunna* provision. If God abrogated any of his rules, the prophet would have to abrogate his *Sunna* by another (in conformity with God's new rule). The process of abrogation was further classified into various categories, according to the nature of the texts that had been used to abrogate them.[64]

For the third, when one version of tradition could not be applied without rejecting another version, al-Shafi'i preferred to choose the one that was in accordance with the Qur'an or the undisputed parts of the *Sunna* of the Prophet. He claimed in *al-Risala*: "If two traditions are contradictory, the choice between them must be made for a valid reason. One should choose the tradition that is consistent with Qur'an. One should choose the more authorities in preference to a single authority. One should chose the one that is more consistent with the tendency of the Qur'an, or with the other *Sunna* of the Prophet. One should choose the one that keeps with the other doctrine of the scholars, and the one that is easier with respect to analogy. Finally one should choose the one that is followed by the majority of the Companions."[65] These juxtaposed and yet contradictory principles were a revision of the analogical interpretations. Since the choice between these different dimensions of analogy led to various interpretative consequences, it did not provide a consistent guidance. With an ill-defined distinction of the reliable and the unreliable, of the authenticated and the unauthenticated, interpretation remained loosely sanctioned.

To clarify the confusion of levels of authority, al-Shafi'i further redefined the relationship between Qur'an and *Sunna*. He said the Qur'an did not contradict *Sunna*, nor did the *Sunna* of the prophet go against the Qur'an. *Sunna* of the prophet explained the Qur'an by specifying its meanings.[66] As Qur'an was to be interpreted in the light of the *Sunna*, *Sunna* was to provide an explanatory commentary on the Qur'an. To avoid the conflict of authorities, al-Shafi'i set out rules of repeal or abrogation (*naskh*). The words of Qur'an could only be abrogated by those of the Qur'an, *and Sunna*, only *Sunna*. Since the twin sources of Islamic law were defined as interpretive and interpreted, they could not abrogate one another. The apparently contradictory rules could be smoothly harmonized by dividing them into two basic conceptual categories: general (*'amm, jumla, mujmal*) and particular or explanatory (*khass, mufassir*) statements. A general rule stated in general terms (*jumla makhrajuha 'amm*) could still envisage a special case (*yurad biha al-khass*).[67]

All of these interpretative methods represented a systematic effort to unify and integrate overlapping legal texts and the diverse juristic tendencies. They created a constructive framework in which contradictory legal rulings and interpretations could coexist. To a certain extent, it limited the arbitrary, personal, and disagreeable judgment by regulating the source of law.

The source of law became a magic repertoire of reference in which no disagreement was allowed. But Islamic scholars could still exert their own judgment in search of an indication (*shubha*) that justified their intent.[68] This correlative logic provided the foundation for Islamic jurisprudence, although the particular categories of the law became increasingly technical and concrete. It determined the general tendency of Islamic jurisprudence: to produce compromise between broad classifications rather than exclusive extremes. This two-dimensional logic constantly blurred and flattened out conceptual division and juristic opposition.

As a young language, English was completely different from Arabic, although it also had to transplant an alien God and as well as an alien language, Latin. Arabic invented God and its written language at the same time. Its God had one all encompassing language, including the language of God, that of the state, and that of prayers. Old English emerged from a mixture of many languages. Therefore, English had to interact and struggle with Latin and French, and expand its own level of literacy and keep its own coherence.[69]

Unlike Islamic law, which emerged from a single vision of a single language, English legislation, from the thirteenth to sixteenth century, built its cultural unity by maintaining boundaries and keeping balance between the rights of the state (the king then the parliament), the church, and those of the civil society. It was a process opposite from that of Arabic. While Arabic expanded its vision by juxtaposing and including variations, English kept its classified and abstract vision by constantly redefining and re-specifying the boundaries of various levels of language — legal, poetic, and religious. In other words, English expanded its vision by collecting variations and ended up with a well-organized sum, because until the twentieth century, English had yet to completely outgrow its Latin structure. It was a historical coalition between law and God, yet each of which had its defined and limited realms. The very idea that made the boundary possible and functional was the environment where the English identity emerged.[70]

The vision of the British Empire took root from Latin, Roman law, and its historical association with Christianity. The abstract nature of Latin law and its view of God created the basic structure of English thought during its formative years. This structure, maintained and reinforced by English's constant reshaping of conceptual boundaries, was married with the Roman conviction of externally imposed and inalienable legal rights. This was a very strong union, and became an integral part of English identity. The Romanized legal English transformed legislative power from the common court to the king and to the parliament. It was a language that not only created and retained the authority of law (although the content of law had radically changed), but also provided conceptual possibilities for legislative transformation and its adaptability to legal practice.

English common law developed in three periods: Old English, Anglicized Latin, and Romanized English. In each period, the legal ideas and legislative forms took different turns within the changing conceptual framework. These variations produced many new lines of thought, which were incorporated into the established legal language. During the first period, law was a general and fluid concept. The legal reasoning was characterized by simplicity and lacked of legislative power (in a modern sense). In the second period, after law developed a spectrum of concrete rights, the legislative power emerged from an institutional hierarchy that controlled and stabilized the formal boundaries of law and their interaction. During the third period, law became redefined as a conceptual gap or tension between an abstract and yet unwritten legality (beyond the political institution) and legislation of concrete rulings. This tension became the dynamic of a legal creativity that could adapt to the ever-changing practice.

The Anglo-Saxon law was based on principles combining both divine and moral judgment. It was a language that had wide ranges of connotation, yet only single and opposite scales of judgment: words and deeds, right and wrong, and offense and compensation. This simple logic was expressed in a primitive language, rigid in both meaning and form. The majority of the ninety articles of Ethelbert's Dooms used conditional clauses.[71] "If a freeman robs the king, he shall pay back a nine fold amount.... If a man lies with a maiden belonging to the king, he shall pay 50 shillings compensation.... If she is a grinding slave, he shall pay 25 shillings compensation.... If one man slays another, he shall pay 20 shillings before the grave is closed, and the whole of the wergeld within 40 days."[72] At this point, language could only describe particular cases, such as what should be done when a man did something wrong. This form was primitive compared to an advanced form of law writing, using relative clauses: "Whoever robs the king..." and asks a more impersonal question: "What should be done to a certain type of person who...?"

The conditional clause illustrates a legal reasoning different from that of the relative clause. The former emphasize a linear logic, a judgment based on an actual situation and rules of law. If this or that happened, certain rules would be applied automatically; therefore, there was hardly any space between pronouncing abstract principles of general law and making a particular decision in concrete cases.[73] The latter emphasized the relationship between a certain type of person and certain rules applicable to him. The legal judgment was focused on the application of abstract type or class (or persons) to the particular cases. Thus, the extent of abstraction, which the legal language used, determined various kinds of judicial judgments. In this case, to judge was to compose the stated situation to an actual situation, and to seek an identity between the stated type of person and stated type of actual behavior.[74]

In Old English, the language of Anglo-Saxon law had never developed a concept of abstract person to whom impersonal rules of law could be applied. The personal types always had concrete origins of occupation, or social or economic status. In the laws of Hlothhere (king of Kent, 673 to 685) and Wihtred (690 or 691–725), more personal types by which rules were applied were developed: a "servant," "slave," "a ceorl," "bishop," "king," "priest," and "husband."[75] In the laws of Ine (King Wessex, 688 to 726), phrases of impersonal type were used. "He who is accused of a band is to clear himself by [an oath of] 120 hides;" "he who finds stolen and hidden meat;" "whoever begets an illegitimate child;" "whoever was present on the expedition made of the purpose of killing."[76] However, these abstract and impersonal types were mixed with concrete and personal types. The laws of Alfred (king of West Wessex, 871–899) were written in a personal, sometimes conversational tone: "do not thou heed the word of the false man"; "Do not thou turn thyself to the folly and unjust will;" "I Alfred, king of the West Saxons, showed these to all my councilors and they then said that they were all pleased to observe them."[77]

Only in the later Anglo-Saxon laws did Old English begin to develop impersonal and legal concepts separated from concrete vocabularies.[78] The code of the Ethelred kings (866–871) used words "every," "each," and "all" to indicate the unexceptional application of the law by redefining the concrete person into an abstract one.[79] In *Cnut Law*, God's law (1018) and the secular law of kings were stated side by side as two concerns of equal importance. They were designed and written separately but they were conceptually confused. In Old English, "right" (as justice) and "righteousness" were applied to both religious and secular law. The law of God and that of lord were one and the same. Those who broke the law became outlaw on both accounts.[80]

Without an abstract concept of law, the law of the Anglo-Saxons was merely a process of deciding the payments or *bot* (compensation) for the wrongdoings. The concept of *bot,* etymologically connected with better, was first introduced to replace another approach to tribal feuds and social disorder — retaliation. After loss and damage were negotiated in terms of compensation rather than feud, various damages became associated with different types of compensation. The word *bot* became more specific, in that it specified situations where rights were violated and caused damage. A total loss — death, a foot struck off, or genitals destroyed — was defined by another word, *geld.* *Wite,* which meant punishment, fine, torture, misery, or penance, was the term used for the fine that was paid to the king.[81] Thus, the old Anglo-Saxon legislation gradually invented a whole scale of pecuniary penalties suitable to various specific offenses, until the concept of legality became so concrete that there was no law without offense and no right without wrong.[82]

In this particular sense, like pre–Islamic Arabic, Old English developed a simple perception of right and wrong, true and untrue, law and outlaw. Judicial procedure was a "declaratory judgment" rather than a legal decision.[83] Within the scope of this verbal and intellectual linearity, the mind of Old English could not yet imagine competing claims on the same subject. Written words of law were the recognized authority defining the preposition of the judgment that was shared by everyone in the society. They were understood and accepted as one's own judgment, rather than an externally imposed standard. On this cultural and psychological ground, the concepts of law, not yet purely legal judgment, were not invented and imposed from without, but "simply adopted by the kings."[84]

Old English cultivated a simple vision of the social order and a simple means to solve disputes. While there was no concept of individual, the action of every man involved his kinsmen. They shared his responsibility and right to avenge him. It was their duty to make amends for his misdeeds, or else maintain his cause in conflict. If one slayed or injured another, the offender not only brought upon himself the enmity of his victim's kin, but involved his own kin. By the action of individuals, the families of both parties were legally involved in vengeance or committed to taking it, though they might pay the heavy blood-price or "wergeld" to "by off the appear."[85] Since man's whole citizenship depended upon his being backed by adequate kindred, an individual could not act and be treated in isolation by the law. His words would not be considered as trustworthy until they were proved by the words of his kinsmen, who guaranteed that he would behave lawfully, stand to justice if called upon, and fulfill any judgment the court may put upon him. Thus, the man who could find no one to verify his words was considered as outlaw. The kindred were the only source to "domicile its members to folkright."[86]

The written law of Old English reinforced the common law articulated through the networks of the spoken words of the kinsmen. The power of state emerged and gradually replaced the self-centered and self-helping autonomy of the kindred.[87] When the state controlled and regulated the tribal feud, the law not only justified the right (of kinsmen) but also distributed rights as particular compensations. It verbalized increasingly complex forms of conflicts and disputes, and invented distinct rules for them. The law was hardly concerned with general principles or judgment. It aimed at proclaiming the scale of pecuniary penalties to be paid for specific offenses.[88]

As time went on, the compensation rulings accumulated and became more detailed. The application of rules cultivated an absolute association and logical connection between wrongdoing (offense), consequence (injury), and punishment (penalty). The emphasis of legal procedure, at this time, focused on proving the actual offense of certain person who would be unmistakenly liable for the codified remedy.

Gradually, the linear logic of offense and penalty lost ground after legal procedure invented various forms of language to describe the same offense and gain various remedies. The language that described the wrongs became increasingly varied. Since there was no intrinsic link between the nature of the complaint and the method of proof, and between the formula of wrong and penal judgment, an offense (when used to evoke a specific penalty) might obtain a different judgment during different procedures. To obtain a more favorable judgment, a writ, which "pins the plaintiff down to a specific issue," became a strong initiator of legal action. It replaced the hazy vagueness of the old pleas by insisting on an essential issue, which clearly formulated and demanded a straight forward negative or positive verdict.[89] In the chaotic battle of spoken words, written documents emerged and transformed the initiator of legal action from an indiscriminate description of the offense into a legal claim of right, a particular right of particular person in particular circumstance.[90]

If there was no writ, there was no right (law was procedure). The legal right pursued in a particular procedure was now no more than a claim for remedy.[91] To gain remedy, the language of the writ had to sufficiently define a specific wrong doing, so that the court would know how to proceed. Thus, the court procedure was determined by the claim for which the writ had been devised, and the complaint had to be stated in the formulaic terms of the writ. As Prof. Plucknett pointed out: "the court of Common Pleas was historically and in legal theory a court that had no powers beyond those conferred by the original writ and could not go beyond those the four corners of that document."[92] In this sense, the language of the writ not only created the law at the time, but the form of legal procedure as well.

The orientation procedure of the legal English confined its concept of right inside of a spectrum of concrete and precise meanings. Since to choose a writ was to choose a legal action, language had to precisely specify the types of injuries and remedies. To keep up with the changing procedural practice, legal language became increasingly specified and rigid in two ways. It came to clarify what tenure was in question, by that service it was held, who held it, who from, who complained, what of, who owed a debt, who had taken some land as a gage, his reason and so on. It also specified a pool of distinct and yet "uncouth names" (writs of right): Praecipe, Novel Disseisin, the Assize of Mort d'ancestor (*assisa de morte antecessoris*) or Assize Utrum (*Writ Juris Utrum*), last presentation (*de ultima presentatione*) etc., to classify different legal claims and titles. As the two levels (offense and claim) were integrated into the language of procedure, the meanings of both levels became more specific. This firmly established an absolute association of the language of legal title and that of legal action.

The procedural character of legal English determined the vision of the common law. Unlike the modern law of abstract categories and titles, the formative law of England was nothing but codes of procedure.[93] The lack of any philosophical or oratorical declaration of the rights of man was determined less by a conscious choice than by a linguistic limitation. English law had not yet felt a need to go beyond the rigid boundary of concrete words and to search for philosophical intent of the law.[94] Until then, the system of writs had been the measure of law, and the language of writs formed and sanctioned the form of legal practice. When there were as many writs as there were causes of legal action, the argument from right to remedy was reversed. While the forms of action were given, the causes of action needed to be deduced there from; *Tot erunt actiones quot sunt formulae brevium*, in Bracton's words.[95]

Linguistic evolution rather than choice transformed the legal function of the English kings. Although the Anglo-Saxon legislation provided the king a position of personal preeminence, the legal treatment of the king remained quantitatively distinct from that of the lords.[96] In the laws of Alfred, the relationship between king and his subjects was redefined as that between lord and dependent. If anyone plotted against the king's life, directly or by harboring his exiles or his men, he was liable to forfeit his life and all that he owned. If he wished to clear himself, he was to do it by an oath equivalent to the king's wergild: he who plots against his lord's life is to be liable to forfeit his life and all that he owns, or to clear himself by his lord's wergild.[97] The laws of Edward the Elder contained an exhortation to the witan for the maintenance of the public peace, in which it proposed that they should "be in that fellowship in which the king was, and love that which he loved, and shun that which he shunned, both on sea and land."[98]

The Code of Edmund III (939–946) expressed a similar devotion to the king. The codes of Ethelred kings formulated a higher claim: "He who keeps under his protection God's outlaw beyond the term which the king has set, risks forfeiting himself and all his property to the deputies of Christ, who maintain and control the Christian faith and the kingdom as long as God grants."[99] Finally, the love and loyalty to the king were considered the same as those to God. In the laws of Cnut: "Above all other things they would ever love and honor one God and steadfastly hold one Christian faith, and love King Cnut with due loyalty.... Let us also perform zealously what we wish to enjoin further: let us ever be loyal and true to our lord and never with all our lord and ever with all our might exalt his dignity and do his will."[100]

However, the symbolic function of the king would not have transformed into a jurisdictional power unless the legal language contained enough binding power to control the diverse legal procedures. Royal power emerged during the century and a half between Cnut's codes of law and the legal development and treatises of Henry II's reign. During this time, the legal language suffered through a crisis, as concepts were too simple and rigid to adapt to the new procedural diversity.[101] Kings were called to clarify and specify legal claims, penalties, and procedural rules. As an authority beyond language, the king's legal documents served to establish the framework for various rights and interests. For the first time, royal writs gave the shapeless and fluid common law definite boundaries, not by rewriting the rules but by defining the procedures.

While the legislation of procedure (or legislation from the bottom) created a language of extreme formal rigidity, general principles of the law remained confused and ineffective in both writing and reasoning. The "confused conflict between inconsistent and indefinite principles," in Maitland's words, is best demonstrated in the *Leges Henrici*.[102] The *Leges* illustrates a conceptual transformation in which the old and new concepts clashed and combined. Since it mainly used *Quadripartitus*, the Latin translation of Anglo-Saxon codes, as its source, legal concepts were confusing and ambiguous.[103] The statement about legal argument reads as follows:

4, I There are three kinds of rhetorical argument — deliberative, that is concerned with what is to be done and what is not to be done; demonstrative, that is concerned with administering praise or censure; judicial, that is relating to punishment or reward.

4, I a There are two kinds of issues to be found in rhetorical argument: those involving reasoning and those involving law....

4, 6 The language of an advocate shall be pure and adorned with explicit conciseness, and by virtue of invention, arrangement, expression, memory, delivery, persuasion, native ability, erudite learning, and constant practice, expert in every style of speaking....[104]

It seems that the author knew what a proper legal language and reasoning should be, "irreproachable, not open to suspicion," but he also realized that it would be impossible in his own language.[105]

While conditional and relative clauses were interchangeably used, the concepts of moral and legal judgment were confused[106]:

> 5, 18 Good people very often remain silent and tolerate evils of which they are aware because they lack proof and they cannot establish these things before the judges; for however true they are, they are not to be believed by a judge unless they can be established by unassailable proof.
>
> 5, 18 a We cannot exclude anyone from the communion of the church ... unless he has either confessed voluntarily or been convicted in a court, for in this case such a person can be called a transgressor, as the apostle says who confesses or is convicted by judicial process.
>
> 5, 18b But if a person cannot be excluded as the result of a judgment he is rather to be tolerated lest anyone, through wrongly avoiding evilgoers, should forsake the church and precede them into Gehenna.[107]

As Maitland pointed out, this language conveyed less a "franchisal" justice than a seigniorial one. Certain persons had a certain "soke," or jurisdiction, apart from any legality which may have been expressly conceded to them by the king. However, it was not clear where the legal basis of this soke was located.[108] It distinctly emphasized that people who had a rank of personal status — especially those of archbishops, bishops, and earls — enjoyed certain jurisdictional powers. But, the king had soke as well over all lands which were in his demesne; had granted manors out of some of his lands together with soke, which was exclusive to the grantee or shared with the king; or out of other lands he had granted manors, but kept the soke for himself. The freeholders of land, *vavassores,* were also said to have a certain jurisdictional power. They had the pleas "where the punishment is payment of the white or of the wergeld in respect of their own men and on their own land, and in respect of the men of other lords if they are seized in the act of committing the offense and are charged with."[109] These levels of power and rights were described with indistinctive terms and had no clear boundaries or logical relationships.[110]

At the time, distinction between legal situations and sources of power were conveyed in vague words. The boundaries of different levels of justices (of the king, church, lord, and common land holder) could never be better defined in phrases like "in cases of the more serious matters" and "certain kinds of cases." These words could mean everything yet nothing.[111] The source of jurisdictional power was so generalized that it surmounted all difficulties: "every lord has a certain civil justice over his tenants; whatsoever powers go beyond this are franchises," or "the king must act as kinsman and protector to all persons in holy orders, strangers, poor people, and those who have been cast out."[112] Christian faith and good intention were used as final alternatives when all of the legal concepts had been exhausted or failed. With worship of God and the practice of lawful behavior, Christian faith and legal rights were so freely transmuted and associated that ecclesiastical content apparently gave a general and singular cohesion to the early English text.

Although the *Leges* failed to create a precise law and clear rules, it made two distinctions evident. First, it distinguished the intentional from the accidental misdoings. It claimed "a person is not to be considered guilty unless he has a guilty intention."[113] Second, it formed a hierarchy of jurisdiction, upon which a formidable authority of the royal majesty was based. Although it took several centuries to define the precise legal boundaries between the levels within the hierarchy, a vertical tendency of jurisdictional structure was roughly visualized. This vision shaped the conceptual ground upon which a royal jurisdiction began to take form, and became reality during the age of Henry II.[114]

The scope for the rights and the boundaries of power in each level of the institution were gradually reclassified and redefined in the process of legal practice. During this period, many Latin legal words were introduced.[115] To distinguish different levels of jurisdiction, the Latin word *iuscia* was first associated with the location or the institution in which the judicial practice occurred. For instance, there were various justices in legal writs: *iusticiis et custodibus episcopatus Baiocensis, iustitie et vicecomiti Archarum, iusticiis et ministris de Sancto Marculfo et de Varrevilla, iusticiis Constantini,* and *Algaro de Sancte Marie Ecclesia ceterisque iusticiis Constantini.*[116] Thus, the word of justice was no longer used as only an abstract noun, but with descriptive connotations. After a precise title *justitiarius* was introduced, the conceptual association of the words changed, as well as the imposed relationship: "Henry, king of the English and duke of the Normans and count of the Angevines, to his justiciars, sheriffs, and ministers of England..."[117] The new concept specified a distinct jurisdictional level that later became the "alter ego" of the king.[118]

While Latin multiplied the levels of legal meaning, it took more than two centuries to reorient the logical structure of English law. During the process of reorientation, royal justice was the institution that organized and localized ill-defined and associated rights.[119] In other words, the emergence of the legal power of English kings was carried by a conceptual transmission of the common law, from the law of writs to that of statutes. When the legal function of the English kings moved from a judicial authority into a legislative power, the focus of English legislation began to transfer from rules of procedure to those of the basic principles of legal right.

The following analysis shows how the legal language of royal writs grew formulaic and abstract with the growth of legal writing. It also illustrates how the concept of legal right became so well articulated and established that it finally disappeared from legal texts. After an abstract legality became the underlying assumption (rather than stated rules) of legal argument, the jurisdictional power of the kings (that was beyond legal language) became dispensable.

The language of *viscontiel* writs, which became standard during the reign of Henry II, reveals that transitional characteristics as they moved from communicative, particular, and personal to a more formalistic, general, and impersonal language.[120] *Facias* writs, the earliest *viscontiel* writs, used "facias" (cause) as the main verb and directive to the writ. While the same verb, cause, indicated the procedural emphasis of the texts, various other common clauses were utilized, as Prof. Palmer shows:

> The king to the sheriff, greeting. (1) We command you that, justly and without delay, you cause (*facias*) to be replieved to A. his beasts which B. had taken and is holding unjustly, as he says: (2) and afterwards, that you cause the said A. To be dealt with justly in the matter (3) that we may not further hear outcry thereof for want of justice. Witness etc.[121]

While the *facias* writs ordered the sheriff to intervene in what was essentially a standoff between the parties, the language varied according to the particular litigious contexts. Such wording variations gradually disappeared in the "justices writs," the largest class of *viscontiel* writs, because the connotations of the word "justice" expanded. Justice could be used to order the sheriff to give justice to the plaintiff or the defendant, as well as to demand for an action of execution:[122] "The king to the sheriff of Hertfordshire. We command you to justice [justicies] Richard de argenton by his lands and chattels that without delay he render to Hugh de Nevill 100 marks to our use for the forest..."[123] and "We command you to justice (*justicies*) B. that justly and without delay he render to A. twenty shillings which he owes him, as he says, as he shall reasonably be able to show (*sicut rationabiliter monstrare poterit*) that he ought to render to him, that we may not further hear outcry thereof for want of justice. Witness etc."[124]

The more standardized form implied standard content. While the justicies writs concerned the enforcement of rights and obligations, they were no longer a writ that initiated litigation, but rather a writ that merely ordered execution. Now, the connotation of justice expanded, from particular rights of particular persons to a general right, protected by the particular legal procedure. It follows that the right (a concrete right concerning a concrete dispute), which had been the initial concept of the early legal procedure, had become a pre-assumption (a general right assumed to be protected by the royal justice.)

This conceptual abstraction evolved into an identification of royal rights and legal justice. It became the basic juxtaposition underlying the formation of early statutes.[125] Royal legislation began with the administrative documents of the king ... a few written or even spoken words communicated to his justices, whom he was constantly sending to perambulate the country. These ordinances, *assizes*, were not seen at the time as a new law. They were temporary instruction which might be easily altered as time went on. The departure from concrete instruction to rules of law, accelerated by the royal writs (which used to have the power to create right and make law), gradually lost their absolute authority. As this accumulated and became crowded with variations, royal writs transformed from a voice of supreme right into a pool (a bank, in Maitland's term) of formulae to be selected and utilized for various legal purposes.[126] When the formal control over the legal procedure became loose, the importance of oral representation revived, and so did the use of evidential performance.[127] The procedural variations broke the formal bond of royal writs. The king, whose name was still used for the formulaic writs, had no actual control of how the formula might be modified and commended to suit new cases. Therefore, the words of the particular right lost their value and binding power in a mass of reproduced documents.

Another form of textual certainty emerged in the English common law: Statute, which became recognized as a second source of law, besides the customary law. Statutory law was written to solidify or increase the binding power of English law, which at the time began to lose ground. Wording like "We will not have the laws of England changed" and the nature of clauses pertaining to abuses or evasions of the law revealed an eager intention to establish tightly bound written law.[128] However, both the intention and consequences of the enactment were as diverse as the formal variations of the common law and political positions at the time.

The king needed a form tighter than writs to enforce his words, while the enemies of the king desired to bind him by the existing words of law. As a fertile source of political power and control, the words of law poured out and became increasingly specific in meaning. The law in English politics took different forms according to the degrees of binding power of the legal language. In the early stage, the maker of a statute was also the interpreter. Only gradually did this power migrate to the courts of law, which by this time had separated from the legislature. In either case, the authority of statute law was obviously felt, and interpretation tended to be increasingly restricted. In Edward II's reign, a statute could not be interpreted. It meant exactly what it said. As a statement from the bench put it: "the law that applies ... is statute law, and we shall therefore accept no averment contrary to the statute which is our authority."[129]

The absolute adherence to the royal statutes was further reinforced during the reign of Edward III. The application of the statutes was confined to a strict reading of the words and their explicit meanings. The rigidity of textual reading went as far as to maintain what the written words had said even if there were obvious errors.

The English loyalty and submission to the words of law were less derived from a static "legal tradition," indigenous or imported, than from its particular linguistic history. While the concept of law as an authority survived different kinds of legislation, the meaning and foundation of the legal authority had been radically transmitted and reconstructed. The cornerstones of this foundation were:

- the authority of the law-giver and his words that required obedience,
- the absolute binding force of the law embodied in its precise and specific meanings, and
- the concept of abstract right that was assumed to be protected by the legal institution.

All three principles were based on the same authority — the authority of the words of law.

However, with the expansion of the boundaries of language, the law itself changed and transformed. When the law was based only on the first principle, its authority was strong yet vague. The power of law lay in the supreme position of the lawgiver rather than the law itself. When the law expanded its foundation to the latter two principles (after the legal language became more specific), its authority became grounded on a submission to the meanings and the framework (legislation). After the assumption of law came to include an abstract concept of right that could be concretized variously, the law became a self-contained system which constantly reconsidered its rulings. Thus, the legislator could be replaced while the law sustained.

No matter what the law meant and who enacted it, the principle of the supremacy of the law, as an externally imposed order, underaid the constant transition of legislative power: from God to the king, and to the parliament. Although the definitions of the legal sovereignty changed over time, the authority of a supreme lawgiver (from within or without) remained a cornerstone for the theory and practice of the English common law. This deep conviction was derived from a verbal and intellectual association between law and justice. It was a cultural rather than a political or social phenomenon, rooted less in the particular content or the name of the law than in the assumption of definability, measurability, and manageability of the disputed rights by legal language.

The cultivation of the law-binding mind began with Old English when the law was associated with king and God. While the language was fluid and ambiguous, the law of God, of the king, and of custom was one and the same.[130] A divine/secular penetration and non-legal characteristic of Anglo-Saxon law emerged, due in part from the consistency of its pagan tradition, but mostly from the concrete and precise nature of its specific consequences. The elliptical, unrefined method of recording the legal rules that had been set out in procedure also contributed to this "holy" law. In its ambiguous and confused language, the words of the king, as incontravenable, had the authority to compel people to obey the order.[131]

While the English law was Romanized, the authority of its words remained. To adopt the Latin word *lege* for common law, English lawyers were meticulous in explaining that, although enacted by the king on the advice of his councilors, English Common law was not ius scriptum; it was the rule of law identical to Latin *lege*. Glanvill argued that "if from the mere want of writing only, they [the *leges*] should not be considered as laws, then, unquestionably, writing would seem to confer more authority upon laws themselves, than either the equity of the persons constituting, or the reason of those framing them."[132] He reduced "more generally occurred" legal principles and customs of common law into writing. His treatise was a written collection of those unwritten leges and *consuetudines* which had worked their way into custom of the king's court.

Bracton made a similar yet clearer statement:

> Though in almost all lands use is made of the *leges* and the *jus scriptum*, England alone uses unwritten law and custom. There law drives from nothing written [but] from what usage has approved. Nevertheless, it will not be absured to call English laws *leges*, though they are unwritten, since whatever has been rightly decided and approved with the counsel and consent of the magnates and the general agreement of the "*republica*," the authority of the king or prince having first been added they do not have by law, as in the various counties, cities, bouroughs and vills, where it will always be necessary to learn what the custom of the place is the how those who allege it use it.... We must see what law is. Law is a general command, the decision of judicious men, the restraint of offences knowingly or unwittingly committed, the general agreement of the *res public*. Justice proceeds from God, assuming that justice lies in the Creator, (jus from man), and thus "*jus*" and "*lex*" are synonymous. And though law (*lex*) may in the broadest sense be said to be everything that is read (*legitur*) its special meaning is a just sanction, ordering virtue and prohibiting its opposite. Custom, in truth, in regions where it is proved by the practice of those who use it, is sometimes observed as and takes the place of lex. For the authority of custom and long use is not slight.[133]

These passages indicate a middle ground between the Roman law and the law of Old English. This resolution was created by a conspiracy of the two languages. First, the conceptualization was Latin in the sense that it distinguished and classified the confused or ambiguous English legal concepts. It divided the legal practice into law and custom. Second, the reasoning that juxtaposed the classified concepts remained English. It not only blurred the Latin distinction of written and unwritten law, but also transferred the source of law from writing (an absolute relationship as codification of the unwritten) to trans-conceptualization (a relative relationship as dynamic movement between the law and its practice).

By redefining *lex* from what was read (legitur) to what was just sanction (*sanctionem iustam*), Latin absolute reasoning was modified and replaced by the English relative assumption and logic. Therefore, the English concept of law as "just sanction" was Romanized only in terms of concept. It transplanted the indiscriminate common law into a clear-cut conceptual tension, or space, between law and its practical implication. The underlying logic that juxtaposed the Romanized concepts was Anglicized because it created a structure whose legality of law was transmutable.[134] The (Romanized) distinction and (English) juxtaposition of the levels of law remained the main character of common law throughout its history.[135] The distinction of law (*leges* and *consuetudines*) and custom was grounded on different sources of legislation. As Coke later put it: "The main triangles of the laws of England [are] those laws being divided into Common Law, statute law, and custom."[136] Before parliamentary statute law replaced *consuetude* as the legislative authority, legislative law and customary and judge-made common law stood opposite each other as the main tension as well as the main dynamic of English legal tradition. As the common law had never been codified, justice remained assumed rather than stated and textured. This lack of texture created distinctions between the layers of law and made them mutable. And the lack of a unified jurisprudence allowed the lines between the layers of the law to be constantly re-mapped, sharpened or blurred at different times.

Now, common law had stronger binding power because of the verbal and intellectual classification, in which justice was transmitted from a general assumption embodied in procedure into a legal concept that conveyed precise meanings.[137] Royal justice constituted a linguistic as well as an institutional transition form, from which a new legal system emerged. The writs played an important role in the constant classification and re-ranked the rights and duties of particular persons and judicial institutions. Although they were intentionally formulated to meet the particular needs of judicial discretion and administration, diverse meanings and connotations were expanded, clarified, and accumulated in the process.[138] The accumulated connotations shaped the later development of legal reasoning.

The language of the royal justice produced two different senses of justice: abstract and concrete. The standardization and formalization of the writ stripped concrete meaning from the words of law and justice. When justice was used as a common formula initiating writs of different procedure, it expanded to a spectrum of different kinds of rights. So, justice became associated with the rights of particular action, the right to have pasture, to run bulls, to draw water, to water sheep, to mill free of multure, to have a right-of-way, to have free fishery, or to have closed a customarily closed courtyard. Justice was also seen to set the boundaries between the right of a lord and that of his tenants, and to enforce the rights and obligation between them.[139] Gradually, the formularized justice, which was associated with legal disputes and administration, lost its concrete meaning and became an abstract symbol of legality. Concrete rulings concerning particular rights under the title of justice grew more and more specific and precise after the diverse forms of writs emerged.[140] New writs were constantly produced as new wrongs were perpetrated, until there was a remedy for every wrong.

This conceptual polarization of legal right and justice led to radical changes in legal practice and theory. In the legal practice, the abstraction of the concept of right made the centralization of judicial power possible. Royal power, used to enforce the inherited law, became the ultimate source of legislation. After the concept of law created a realm of abstract meaning and detached from concrete legal practice, justice became the totality of the legal system rather than a particular legal title granted to particular party. Unlike the Latin tradition, whose abstract notion of law had a web of visual and verbal attribution, English law, whose various rights were mainly undefined and vague, emerged with one concrete symbol of legal power and certainty ... the king. Before the abstract concept of law developed into an independent legal realm, the authority of the words of law emerged, operated, and was finally established through the judicial and jurisdictional authorities of the English court.

The early dependency of common law on the political power of the English kings was rooted in a formative language that needed a definable certainty to rely on when legal practice went beyond the established words of law. Instead of an independent body of law, represented by prerogative power opposite to another legal body called the common law (as many historians portrayed), royal justice was the first of many levels of English law that began to be definitely discriminated. In the medieval England, where law meant everything, thus nothing specific in definite language, the Common Law became an instrument of political conflict which could be used to establish, as well as to abrogate, legal rules. Without an absolute division between the enacted and unenacted rules of law, any definable justice was associated with a general concept of legality. During the fourteenth century, the wide discretionary powers of the king created the first well-defined version of English law. The English king symbolized an ultimate source of law — judicial, juris-dictional and legislative.

After the abstract legality was well established, the king became a neutral operator who mediated and restricted political disputes. During the process, in which English legality outgrew and departed from its political institutions and the royal power, the source of legislation shifted from the king and his coun-cilors to parliament. Thus, the legislation transformed from an exercise of per-sonal power into negotiation and compromise of various rights and interests.[141]

This transformation (the legalization of politics rather than politicization of the law, as had occurred in the Islamic sphere and occurs presently in the contemporary West) came about through a particular form of legal commu-nication. In a young language whose conceptual boundaries were just begin-ning to take form, the more interests, rights, and disputes were specified, negotiated, and settled, the more precisely rights were defined. And a deeper conviction and faith for the defineability (or abstract rights) emerged. It was a faith in language and its ability to define rights. When the abstract legality became taken for granted by all concerned, democratic institution emerged — no one person or group could dominate the law.[142]

The legalization of English politics did not mean the de-politicization of the law. Rather, it only transformed the way in which legal and political issues and positions were presented and argued. As every particular right was assumed as entitled and protected by an abstract law, legal argument came to focus on pinpointing that right by the language of law. Thus, the source of the redistribution of rights expanded from political and legislative power to legal knowledge. Legal knowledge, an ability to make particular positions coherent to the law, in turn, expanded the scope of legal interpretation and implication. While law represented a unified vision of justice, legislators monopolized the source of legal interpretation. After the law acquired levels of meanings, the spectrum of legal interpretation expanded from defining a legal ideal of general justice to mediating the principles and particular cases.

The transformation of English law from ideal to knowledge, and from the end of social justice to its means, was also carried by another level of thinking: searching the philosophical consistency beyond both abstract and concrete laws. This philosophical level of the law was created by legal theories that originally emerged during the fifteenth century.[143] Common law borrowed Latin principles of jurisprudence and rethought them in English terms. For example, John Fortescue brought forward his theory of law on some confused abstract concepts, such as law of God, of nature, and of reason. Like previous English writers of Latin (Glanvill and Bracton), Fortescue redefined and recon-structed the Latin concepts with an English reasoning. He began his systematic approach to law with the Latin legal divisions. "Jus is to lex as genus to species.

All law is Jus, but it is not convenient to call all Jus Lex; for every man who seeks to have back what is his own possesses the jus, but not the lex, to claim it. The law resides in the judge, whereby he decrees the restitution to the plaintiff, and in so doing renders him both Jus and Lex." Law, Fortescue repeats, is the bond of right by which a man is constrained to do or suffer what is just. But though law be a species of right, it is itself a genus in relation to the law of nature, law of custom and of statute, and to all special and private laws, "the number of which is like that of the stones in the heap or the trees in the forest." [144]

By juxtaposing jus/lex and genus/species, Fortescue reformalized the structure of Latin jus and lex and established an English attitude toward law. The conceptual distinction of genus and species was much broader than that of Jus and Lex in two ways. First, it could be applied to any conceptual relationship between abstract and concrete or general and particular meaning, regardless of their forms (written or unwritten). Second, the same concept could be both genus and species (thus, jus and lex) according to the nature of the other noun to which the concept was associated. For instance, law, as species of right, was also a genus in relation to the law of nature. This fluid conceptual boundary and association reconstructed the Latin legal reasoning. Instead of a complete supremacy of one law (or legislator, be it God, nature or emperor) over all the other, levels of laws were correlatively defined and their binding power was conditional upon one another. Mutable concept of natural law was the cornerstone of Fortescue's jurisprudence. [145]

Although he borrowed the exposition of canon law, his argument and reasoning confused the Latin concept of natural law by blurring the division of the law of God and that of man. He claimed that all human law was classifiable as a law of nature, or as custom, or as statutes. The law of nature, which had governed the human race from the time of Paradise to the time of Moses, expelled other human laws. On the other hand, he quoted S. Thomas to confirm that the origins of natural law sprang from God alone. [146] Yet, he failed to define what he meant by human law. Was it a law based upon human assumptions and beliefs (according to its content) or a law that governed human activities (according to its function)? With such ambiguous and loose language, he attempted to clarify his idea by juxtaposing the word "nature" to other equally abstract concepts, such as truth, justice, right, and reason. He classified that the divine law came from divine providence, while the law of nature was the truth of justice, which was capable of being revealed by right reason. Although he was inconsistent in the meanings of these words, he successfully redefined the law of nature as an independent level of law, beyond both custom and statute. The detachment of natural law and the law of reason from the enacted law later became an important source of legal theory.

This reproduction of legal theory created a conceptual level which made all definable laws and legislative powers relative, as well as restricted. Fortescue associated English law with a set of abstract concepts and untethered their absolute boundaries by juxtaposing them to an English logic. For example, he created a conceptual middle ground between two established Latin forms of legal authorities: "dominium regale et politicum" between "dominium regale" and "ominium politicum."[147] This new juxtaposition uprooted the royal legislative power from the right of heredity, and yet preserved its right of legislation and its role as supreme judge. As Fortescue pointed out, the twofold nature of the imperial legislation held that the king was the supreme lawgiver, and the succession was not ordered by hereditary rule.

The two-dimensional argument of Fortescue was derived from the Anglicizing of Latin concepts, which redirected reasoning. Instead of the static dualism of Latin, Fortescue's concept of *dominium regale et politicum* was changing as it was used in different texts and contexts. In *De natura legis naturae*, the *dominium regale* and *dominium politicum* were well defined and clearly discriminated. The features of a "dominium politicum" defined a law made by the people and taxes that needed their consent. In the *De laudibus legum Angliae* and *The Governance of England*, the same features were described as those of the *dominium regal et politicum*.[148] After the concepts were used separately or in a combination, their meanings were blurred and flattened out. In *De natura*, there were three possible forms of government. In *The Governance of England*, he only referred to two kinds of government.

The mutability and inter-changeability of these concepts created a different kind of legal reasoning. The horizontal movement of opposite concepts made it possible to juxtapose two originally exclusive legislative sources, not as absolutely opposing, but as restricting and yet completing one another. As Fortescue claimed:

> A king of England can not, at his pleasure, make any alterations in the laws of the land, for the nature of this government is not only regal, but political.... He can neither make any alteration, or change in the laws of the realm without the consent of the subject, nor burden them, against their wills, with strange impositions, so that a people governed by such laws as are made by their own consent and approbation enjoy their properties securely, and without the hazard of being deprived of them.[149]

This compromise of royal and political legislative powers produced a hierarchy of law whose levels so restricted one another that none of them was made absolute. After stripping the king's law of absolute connotation, the law had several faces and various degrees of legitimacy.

With several faces and various degrees of legitimacy, the absolute association of law and justice, which had been the conceptual base for royal legislation, was broken. Law began to be juxtaposed into different directions according to its origin and nature. The following passage seems confusing to a modern reader, yet it shows a genuine effort to discriminate the levels of rights and laws in a language that was not discriminative enough yet to do so:

> The right of the king is the power of the king, which when it hath done aught contrary to the Law of Nature, hath never escaped punishment. The law of the king [ius regis] ... relatively to the king is nothing but the king's power, which a prince governing royally can exert over his people; but when that law is referred to the people, to them it is always a law, though sometimes good and sometime bad.... As a piece of land which is given to me is called my right [ius], so the power which is given to the king is rightly named the king's right; under which mode of speaking the laws say, that a man compelled by force to do anything was then not "sui jris," that is, in his own power, and that a woman united in marriage to a man is not "sui juris," because, being subject to the power of her husband, she is not governed by her own power. Wherefore to say, tell this people the law of the king, was the same as saying, tell them the power which the king when set over them will be able to assume. And although an unjust king may unjustly use that power, the power itself is always good, nor can it be defiled by the use made of it by the ruler, since all power, even as all good, cometh from God ... for the fault is not he power, but in the mind of him who abuses it. Thus we often abuse free will, which is good; and the kingly power, which is most excellent and is called "ius regis," many most iniquitous kings, if kings they ought to be called, abuse to the ruin of their subject. Far be it, then, from us to intend that a king tyrannizing over his subjects acts legitimately, although he hath received of the Lord the power of the thus venting his fury upon them; ... yet ... no edict or action of a king, even if it hath arisen politickly, hath ever escaped the vengeance of Divine punishment, if it hath proceeded from him against the rule of nature's law.[150]

With nature (and God) as an abstract level of law, Fortescue localized the laws of the English kings and opened a new realm of legal and philosophical argument beyond the words of law. This debate of the law became two-dimensional because the conceptual fluidity provided a basis for viewing law. On one hand, the law (or right) had its divine origins and good nature; on the other hand, it could be good or bad, used or abused, and justly or unjustly applied according to the mind of the ruler and legislator. The divinity of the law, in Fortescue's vocabularies, was not equivalent to an insertion of justice as in the thirteenth and fourteenth century England.

Although Fortescue succeeded in discriminating multi-levels of the law and those of legal application, he failed to formulate a consistent relationship between philosophical law (or nature, God, or reason), abstract law (as total legality), and concrete laws. His multi-leveled sources of law (or levels of law) were lost in a mass of confused concepts and the ill-defined relationship between them. However, this conceptual and juxtapositional uncertainty made it possible for the common law to exist among diverse theories in the next centuries.

The attempt to clarify various levels of law was carried on by the English thinkers of the later centuries. First, the certainty of the law, after it went beyond the political institution, was refined by a juxtaposition of abstract concepts as to the origins of law, such as reason, nature, (as non-human), and human nature (as will and desire). With different meanings and forms of juxtaposition expounded by various scholars, law was always conceived as universally coherent and applicable.[151] When right and obligation were juxtaposed, legality found its certainty in political power, especially that of sovereignty. After right became abstract enough to override obligation and deviate from the legal practice, law found its certainty in the ideal right of the individual. During this process, both the meanings of right and law expanded and transmitted, but not their abstraction and absolute juxtaposition to each other.

Second, the fluid boundary of the abstract concepts made legal interpretation and reasoning multi-dimensional. The more that legal concepts were clarified and specified, the more that legal ideas became diversified and sophisticated. If Edward Coke's argument clarified and specified the levels of law, Hobbes' and Locke's reasoning was built on levels of meaning that had freely juxtaposed into each level of law. From the vague concepts of the fifteenth century, law/nature/reason developed into several better defined and more systematic ideas of law. Each was focused not on a single concept, but on its various levels of meanings.[152]

This conceptual spectrum rapidly expanded, particularly in the areas of human philosophy. Although the ill-defined vocabulary of the time could not quite hold the diversity of legal argumentation, the certainty of law began to transform from the vertical juxtaposition of law (as abstract legality) and law as concrete rules, toward two horizontal juxtapositions ... two separate kingdoms of law. The first allowed scholars to comprehend law in terms of abstract and universal categories, which framed the philosophy of law. The second focused on legal rulings and representations. As time went on, each kingdom cultivated its own language, scholarly circle, and society.

The definable boundary between the two kingdoms, which was kept consolidated by elaboration and arguments from both sides, became the foundation of the British legal, political, and social system. It had served as the cornerstone of hegemony for its mighty empire until the time when it was overcome by the development of its own words.

4. Letters and Voices of English: British and American Empires

This chapter is a study of how English, one language, created two different cultures. First, it compares the cultural environment in which Medieval English emerged, and that in which Modern English was transplanted into North America.

English literature emerged with its music and theater during the Renaissance. At its formative stage, between Latin abstract ideas and later medieval artistic expression, English developed defined and polarized worldviews and self-images. It was much like that of the Romans, a vision with the simple colors of law and outlaw, Christian and non–Christian, and cultural self and others. This conceptual gap, which was inherited from its historic and unbalanced cultural expression, nurtured its cultural enlightenment and philosophical rationalism.

Like the Roman Empire, the British Empire was built on powerful written words that could define, judge, triumph, and defeat. Unlike Latin, English was the second language of their Christian faith. By reinterpreting God in a formative language English Protestants sharpened their worldview and strengthened their faith. The faith placed on those words and their moral implication ensured British self-righteousness and sense of mission to "correct" the wrongs of the world by bringing it under British rule.

English faith was rooted in the clear boundary of written words. American English developed a much more pragmatic attitude towards language. Americans began with a mature language, which had already established its shapes of meanings and connotations. Americans had to find their particular shapes suitable to their colonial experience and find their unique English speaking voice.

The American voice emerged from its own songs, images, and gestures, which determined the way that the language was spoken, but not the language itself. American artistic expression, regardless of diverse forms, added variations to literary language rather than shaping it from scratch. When English was first transplanted in North America, there was no unified or established sub-verbal culture. In the place of English music and visual arts, which had been the resources of imagination for earlier development, American English was born within a collage of diverse cultural inspirations such as African, Jewish, Italian, Irish, German, Slavic, and Spanish. In this melting pot, a new culture emerged. This new culture released an incredible energy that had never been seen before. This multitude of diverse traditions reinvented and took root in America and created a dynamic cultural force.

Unlike the formative English, whose form was shaped and defined by its various expressive media, American English had the fluidity and flexibility to collect, combine, and weave its cultural diversity into a unique hegemony. This hegemony, with all of its seemingly contradictory variations, was based on an increasingly unified and centralized adversarial reasoning that aggressively portrayed itself as different from anyone else.

As illustrated in the last chapter, English was a culture that grew under heavy influence of Christianity and its Latin media. It all began with Word, Word of a foreign language spoken by a foreign God, and a foreign law. Like Greek and Arabic, English absorbed and transformed this influence into its own idioms, and became a culture of its own. With a much younger and less sophisticated poetic tradition (compared with oral Greek and Arabic), English faced a much greater challenge to imitate, re-imagine, and recreate, in order not to follow the passage of Latin, which declined after a few centuries of creative activity. English voice was the only linguistic advantage over Latin tradition at the time, and it triumphed. Growing into an outstanding literary language, English not only transplanted the God, the law, and philosophy, it also made them speak English with the necessary precision, efficiency, fluidity, and flexibility. It was in this way that English gradually outgrew Latin tradition and became a culture of its own.

The Renaissance was the cradle of English as a literary language. It began with music, dramatic gestures, and eventually visual images.

Compared to Greek and Arabic, Old English, as poetic, was in a much more primitive condition. However, it was the least primitive among the languages of the British Isles at the time of the Norman Conquest. The Celts and Saxons brought oral literature with them to England, and so did the Normans, Danes, and Vikings.[1] The reason that English survived and outgrew these other languages was that it created its own idiomatic repertoire of songs, gestures, and imageries during an exceptionally short period of time. This repertoire became the rich soil from which literature began to flourish. English evolved into a mature language capable of assimilating foreign expressions and outgrew many European languages, that were originally much richer and more diverse.

Like many oral traditions, English poetry began with the accompaniment of a harp. Poetry was almost a branch of music. The author of the poem would give the first performance. It was sung in the king's hall after banquets and recited at social gatherings.[2] By the time of the Norman Conquest, Old English lyrics had begun to leave their music companion behind. It was called *singan ond secgan*—to sing and say. A much younger language compared with the ancient Homeric epics, English emphasis was marked by the strum of the harp, and music governed the verbal composition. Old English began to lose its melody, after its poets could memorize their songs and became skillful in composition. English music developed more complicated expressions: plain songs, binary rhythms and the polyphonic.[3] After music became too complicated for an amateur to master, poets left musicians to compose. However, since poetry and music remained side by side, they inspired and influenced one another. Each of them, in its own ways, grew more and more sophisticated in form and connotation.[4]

English inherited Roman church music through the Frankish musicians. The reinvention of Gregorian chant prolonged the marriage between English words and music. The troubadours of Provence offered brilliant expressive variations that the English had never heard before from its Germanic heritage.[5] The culture of South France expanded the English scope of melodic convention, which in turn increased the formal variety of English poetry.[6]

The musical setting of Mass movements flourished in England at the beginning of the fifteenth century. Mass was attempted, for the first time, to fuse the succession of individual movements to a body of musical unity. English musicians centered all the movements on the same melodic motive and specified the entrance of upper voice in the same melodic fashion. In his composition, John Dunstable realized a natural flow of language through free, prosodic rhythm and a melody based on the psalmody.[7]

While English words and their structure remained in a formative stage, the unity between words and music was based on melody rather than words. The accumulation of musical forms, in fact, carried the transformation of religious music from simple liturgical chant to Mass. While music was only a loose, almost accidental arrangement of tones, it was used as an aid for expression of the words. After music evolved rich variations, such as trope and polyphony, it transformed into the structural foundation of the sound of Mass. It became capable of mirroring the syntactic coherence of the language.[8] It was time for music and words to separate again.

During the formative years of English, music served as a vehicle carrying the flow of language. Language, especially poetry, borrowed its patterns and forms of expression from music. Stanza is a good example. As soon as poetry assimilated and verbalized musical form, it outgrew music, which distilled it into a metrical form of language. After the formative years, English language continued a close relationship with music, but the nature of this relationship changed. Words took control while music took a back seat to the expression of language (as explanation rather than formulation of meaning). English poetic, from this point on, graduated from the use of music as transmitter of presentation. It began another kind relationship with music, as inspiration to verbal imagery.[9] As English found its own voice in music, it created its own vision through dramatic expression and performance. This became an important part of English cultural identity. While English prose was not yet sufficiently developed to allow many stylistic effects, or even much precision of meaning, Latin remained a dominant language for the educated. English stage emerged as the theater that represented examples of the established ideas — the morality play. At the time, there was hardly any individual characterization in the moralities and their interludes. There was no personality except as a moral instance. The speech and action on the stage were highly predictable in terms of moral philosophy, rather than character.

During the sixteenth century, English stage gradually became an important laboratory for a new language of realistic representation.[10] The language of drama increased in scale and complicity. More details were added on the stage, and scenes of real life were presented. Shakespeare stroked his audience with many "unnecessary" details in *King John* (1590–1) and *Richard III* (a. 1592). He presented his scenes and events integrated with characters and their variations. In *Henry IV* (1597), Shakespeare provided a fully detailed action. His *Henry VIII* (1613) was presented in first person and displayed complex and contradictory characteristic traits.[11]

To represent real life, language needed to become more complex in structure. Simply repeating and enlarging things or adding to them was not enough. While the morality play followed simple themes, such as "youth, led by plausible vices, is redeemed by grace," later Renaissance plays introduced much more intriging plots and interaction of ideas and stories. By the end of the sixteenth century, English drama was able to produce whole scenes on the stage, as if they were transcribed from life.[12] At this point, English drama went beyond any classical inventions that it had ever inherited, Greek or Latin.

The total involvement of the audience in the Shakespearean stage made English language an experience of the ears, eyes, and mind. Theater became an "imaginary vault" of languages — languages of lights, color, shape, movement, and gesture — that framed the spoken words. This visual re-creation of words expanded verbal language beyond its apparent capacity. Dramatic expression made English speak volumes and created a rich spectrum of possibilities for its words.[13] Theater that provided a total assault on the mind and senses of the patrons fostered a communication that was extremely efficient, effective, and immediate.

Dramatic expression gradually internalized English. It was able to create complex characters, demonstrate a fine range of texture and emotions, and illustrate gradated details of a change of mind.[14] Theater was the best place to present distinct perspectives and multi-pointed views. It all began with a secret, which triggered gaps in awareness. To exploit these levels of awareness, stage plays created diversified viewpoints (as in *Romeo and Juliet*). The deep, central, and enduring secret, which used to be exploited to enhance the dramatic force of each play, became the play itself.[15] To specify the degree of awareness and movement of ideas in each character's mind, the play opened the character up for the audience to see and feel. From this point on, what was displayed was not only a story unfolding, but also an "inner" world of the character, who had life intentions, ignorance, fear, passion, partial knowledge, self-deception, self-doubt, and conviction. This inner journey was led by various styles of language: smooth poetry, golden expressions, raptures of passion, ugly and brutish images, hollow impressive morals. Masks portraying vivid dramatic imagery slipped away, and disclosed the naked personality.

English drama eventually outgrew its single-minded moral prison through formal and stylistic development. After the language became refined enough to depict multi-levels of emotional texture and cultivate a clash of alternative viewpoints, it liberated itself from moral analysis. Poetic expression of sentiment, or mood and descriptive details, which were used to exemplify the moral analysis, moved the center stage.[16]

By the seventeenth century, English had discarded its visual and gestural aids and became able to describe a world of the mind with words alone. It began to move away from the flowing amplitude of the Elizabethans to a style that was compressed and concise. It began to compact its expression while continuing to accumulate novel expressions and connotations. It began to drive towards a closeness of texture and economy of expression. It began to build diversities of material into meditative structures that satisfied the larger reason, this time based on experience rather than empty labels.[17] English literature left theater with an important improvement in expressive capacity, a capacity that Latin classical literature had never developed. It could now describe ideas, even large and abstract ones, in intimate and even passionate language.

Poetry, which could imitate Latin forms with newfound English poetic ease, began to outgrow its borrowed structure in terms of both ideas and literary form.[18]

English prose developed even more compressed meditative forms. It could advance ideas less by argument than by persuasive lateral means, such as paraphrase, parallel expression, association, or undulating movement between opposites. It allowed verbal inescapable paradoxes to stretch rather than fill up with ideological reasoning.[19] By the time the new form of prose, biography and history, developed, English became totally detached from Latin form and content. The characters described in English biographies broke free from their formal Latin characters who represented an illustration of the explicit moral formulations.[20] English writers wrote vivid personal memoirs and created a new consciousness of individual identity.[21] History began to be written in historically real times and "plain" style.[22]

During the battle against figurative language, the first scientific writing and natural philosophy emerged. The earliest scientific writers fought vociferously against both literary and philosophical languages, which they accused of focusing on words rather than real things. They promoted a style of "mathematical plainness" and a separate language for the "secretary of nature."[23] Although their initial languages were full of Latin metaphors and ornaments, they initiated a movement of classification which made it possible to branch out into various levels of functional language such as the cultural, literary, administrative, legal, and scientific sub-languages. This classification made it possible for English to develop various tendencies simultaneously and independently. Instead of swinging back and forth and clashing with each other, the literary, philosophical, and technical languages began to define their own territories and expand without interference from the others.

The classification of English language and its solid conceptual boundaries paved the way for a rationalist revolution ... the Enlightenment. Science began to challenge religious establishment and rational thinking replaced superstition. For the first time, English became self-conscious of its own mission, rather than that of God.

Poetry and theater made English heard and understood. The prose movement made it more coherent and readable as a written language. English was on its way to becoming a comprehensive and functional literary language.

———

The first generation of American settlers was not any less musical than their English cousins. However, their musical sense was different. Their music was not the only song and voice of the new land.

When the European colonial settlers came to America, they brought with them the music of their native countries — England, Germany, France, Spain, Italy, Ireland, and Austria.[24] The English, who came in successive migratory waves, brought with them their hymnals, their songs, their virginals and other keyboard instruments, and their chests of viols, a rich European musical heritage.[25] At the beginning of the seventeenth century, England was the global center of choral music. It created the best choral schools in Europe. Renaissance England was a land of song, where popular ballads were sung on the streets and metrical psalmody swept the court.[26]

The Puritans brought with them the Anglican psalm book of 1563, the "Old Version," or Sternhold and Hopkins' *Whole Book of Psalms*, which they replaced with the *Bay Psalm Book* in the 1640. One hundred and fifty psalms were sung to forty-six tunes. Away from religious establishment, colonists had the freedom to creating their own texts, and set about composing metrical versions of the psalms with boundless ambition. However, they kept their Puritan tradition and its rigid attitude toward music. They felt that they must "regulate all recreations and pastimes, all that is delightful to man..." "No music should be heard, no song be set or sung, except what was considered grave and 'Doric.'" All the dancers should be licensed to make sure that no gesture, motion, or deportment would be taught to Puritan youth except what was considered correct and proper. All music instruments in every house, all the lutes, the violins and the ghitterns were examined in order to produce perfect music.[27] Under the same Puritan tyranny, which tightly regulated and controlled musical expression, American music was liberated from its verbal prison much earlier than that of the Europeans.

American music started to move out of church and into the chambers and concert halls after 1731. In successive migrations of Moravians and other Germans, polyphonic and homophonic music was seeded in North America. The music of Bach (1685–1750), relatively unknown in Europe except in some northern German cities at the time, was played in Boston and New York. Handel's (1685–1759) music was played in North America extensively and William Tuckey brought to New York a performance of the *Messiah* in 1770, a few years earlier than the Germans themselves. Mozart's (1756–1791) string quartets made immediate transference to America by Wissahickon German Pietists and the Moravians at Bethlehem. They were played when Mozart's music was only in the form of manuscript.[28] Boston became a music center where German musicians came to live and perform. They gave the first public concert in the country. Americans, before Germans, had the opportunity to be familiar with Bach's music, especially his harpsichord music, most of which remained unpublished during his lifetime. Sacred music, on the other hand, went through a great transformation. Organs were installed and singing crept back into church music. William Billings (1746–1800), the "fuguing composer," created melodies "twenty times as powerful as the old ones."

During the eighteenth and nineteenth centuries, New York, Boston, and Philadelphia became a part of the European music sphere. Americans were enjoying foreign music and operas. They were performed in America, but composed by Europeans.

By the nineteenth century, America became a world leader in providing the best innovative music. It opened its arms to the greatest musicians and performers from every corner of the globe: Norway, Sweden, Germany, Italy, and Austria.[29] New York witnessed a steady invasion of musical prodigies from Europe, and the most famous musicians of the day sooner or later came to America. During the middle of the nineteenth century, the United States became a mecca for more than a million and a quarter Germans who immigrated to the middle West. The "Germania," the first all German orchestra, appeared in America. Its performance of Beethoven, Mendelssohn, and Wagner played an important role in cultivating an interest and taste for chamber music and symphonies.

The American music of the early centuries was an imitation of European music. No music could be called purely American until after its European music became combined with African rhythms. The African rhythms came to America with the slaves. African songs and music were a part of the American experience from day one. As the least willing participants of the cultural mixture, African were everything Europeans were not. They were intensively emotional, spontaneous, and dramatic. They could be heard when they were humming while working, when they were singing in church, when they preached, moaned, and gave "gravery" in their sermons.

The English of the first generation of Americans was a language of God. Language was a means to imitate and hopefully reach God. By the accumulation of religious literature during the centuries, God's image, quality, and ability radically expanded. Biblical English, after Latin tradition, produced diverse presentations combined with the local colloquial in England, Wales, Scotland, and Ireland. Each region developed its own distinct vision, doctrine, and interpretation of the Christian God. For instance, Scots developed their ingenuity and passion for the divine elect described in the "language of saints," "an improbable amalgam of biblical English and colloquial Scots."

America did not possess a unified oral tradition which provided specified and diversified visions of the divine to distribute God's grace and glory to its people. It took America centuries to find its voice of God and the ways to approach him.

However, it was going to be more than one voice.

The Protestant Revolution initiated in Europe from changing the voice of God and transforming the way people communicated with him.[30] With psalm-singing congregations began to communicate with God in a different language: from Latin to Hebrew, and from unmeasured to measured music. Just ten years after their arrival, the American Puritans published their first volume, the *Bay Psalm Book*, which recorded psalm verses to be sung.[31]

America did not have its own Milton, who justified and rationalized God in poetry. Unlike that of Hebrew prophets, Milton's voice of God was not the voice of mysterious power proclaiming the inconceivable wonders of creation and its indifference to the needs of individual men. He brought God into the light to be seen, looked upon, and talked to. His God was just, responsible, and communicative. He was trying to answer human inquiries and answer them with irrefutable logic. He explained and demonstrated God's ways to men. He told them that they suffered deservedly for their abuse of free will in Adam's original disobedience. America did not have Tennyson or Wordsworth, who worshiped God as if he walked in the country and who made a tour through Westmorland a pilgrimage to Jerusalem...

Music, visual, and performing arts are the resources of literary language. The different times in which the English language assimilated its artistic inspirations in Great Britain and the United States allowed these two branches of English to establish unique relationships with their art forms and unique verbal expressions for them. This cultural environment, not the choice of an individual, group, or even a generation, was the starting point from which each culture evolved and matured. England had been evolving for centuries, but the primary host language of America was rapidly maturing and an increasing belligerence appeared.

British English evolved with its rich repertoire of images; images that were created by painters and sculptors, dramatic performance, and eventually, the writers who painted with their words. American English was bathed, saturated, and molded in tones, rhythms, and eventually the symphony of moving pictures.

Songs enhanced the power and suggestiveness of literary language, especially its capacity to evoke and stir up emotion. This power to move and possess without understanding and distinction through verbal classification made literary language intense, yet unyielding, extreme, and occasionally dangerous. (The best example of this combination can be found in the conspiracy of extreme ideology, hate-motivated political rhetoric, and musical vitality in German during the first half of the twentieth century.[32])

As New England Puritanism declined, it gave way first to Unitarianism, which Emerson called the "corpse-cold Unitarianism of Brattle Street and Harvard College," and then, to the more luxuriant appeal of transcendentalism. Resembling in some ways the Moderates in Scotland, the Unitarians revolted against the New England Puritan tradition and liberalized and rationalized Christianity to the point that it became a genteel creed. A new theology by "belles-lettres" and religious enthusiasm by a cultured urbanity took root.

But, just as the polite deism of eighteenth-century England had opened the way to the Wesleyan counter-attack, and the polite conservatism of the Scottish Moderates was challenged by the Disruption, so the elegance and literality (by the 1830s hardened into a deep conservatism) of the Unitarians forced those who thirsted after a more immediate kind of religious experience into new habits of thought. The Calvinists of Princeton, who upheld to the old orthodoxy, could only rub their hands with an "I-told-you-so" attitude when the Unitarians found transcendentalism flourishing on their left wing. It was inevitable, when one abandoned orthodox theology. It was all very paradoxical, because, having rescued religion from Calvinist grimness and wildness, the Unitarians now found that the transcendentalists were reintroducing the very emotionalism and mysticism which they had fought so hard to eliminate.

New England during the nineteenth century developed what might be called post–Puritan sensibility, as portrayed in the poetry of Emily Dickinson. Dickinson's inheritance of New England Puritanism, with its stern Calvinist logic, furnished her with images of suffering, redemption, death, soul, immortality, and eternity, which she used in her own way. Through the language of her poetry one can see the legalism of the Calvinist theological concept of covenant, and ironically, association with the legalism that she knew from her lawyer father. She did not embrace the great New England philosophy of her day, transcendentalism, but something of its mystic power, though without the optimistic grandness of Romantic acceptance, managed to co-exist with her post–Puritan heritage. She totally rejected the notion of original sin, and indeed lacked the Puritan concept of sin altogether. She could refer to God, ironically, as burglar, banker, father, and she could ask ironic questions about the Calvinist notion of Heaven, "If Heaven was a physician or an exchequer?" She also refused to be a part of this negotiation. For Emily Dickinson all significant life marched towards death and immortality, which were associated, if not identified, with the ultimate unmoved mover, God.

Grand concepts and imageries of God had not lost out. They reappeared in the poetry of New England, but with fresh associations. They were associated with matter-of-fact daily experience. The familiar emotions ... comfort, fear, even terror ... were depicted and mixed in a new way. The noise heard by a dying man was referred to as a fly buzzing, and the desire for the divine was described as hunger.

Dickinson's poems show how American Puritan tradition was shaking off its God, its religion (institutionalized or theology) and its philosophy (as any system of thought to oppose the doctrine). The poems of Wallace Stevens further shook off what little sense of eternality that was left in Dickinson and created a precise poetic language that represented the only redemption of humanity. He was not Matthew Arnold, who preserved a God in poetry by moving from literary to poetic interpretation. Stevens' position was much more radical. He thought that "in an age of disbelief when the gods have come to an end, when we think of them as the aesthetic projections of a time that has passed, men turn to a fundamental glory of their own and from that create a style of bearing themselves in reality."[33]

Therefore, America began with poetry and artistic creativity without concrete verbal images as models. The task of creating of a self-image without face, voice, or color was extremely difficult and yet exciting.

The marriage of European melody and African rhythm bred a new generation of music, which was fresh, and very un–European and un–African. This embryonic form was the most dynamic hybrid from the widest variations. Like other ethnic groups of the melting pot, African Americans brought with them their own language, music and dance. In the new environment, they relearned and recreated the rhythms of their African ancestors.[34] African rhythms opened up a completely new horizon for American as well as all Western music, which had stagnated at the pinnacle of its refinement of melody and harmony.[35]

Jazz was the newborn of American music. It began with groups of improvising, blues-oriented players. They played in a style that was spontaneous yet deliberate, passionate, yet controlled — controlled in ways that made their passion all the more convincing. Jazz did not create a template for emotion, or even its intensity. Rather, it was a language capable of delivering well-controlled passions and expressing them in an acutely, reflexively attuned and responsive manner. It was the first time that Western music was able to have a dialogue with an individual listener or fellow musician, rather than being an ensemble of musicians playing to a captive audience. From the very beginning, the blues was personal music, or a diary of conversation, as opposite to grand painting or symphony.[36] By the time that jazz emerged as an art form, its language had been polished by a brilliant collection of musicians into a sophisticated art of soloists who performed together.

Jazz renewed and refined the musical language, from melodic and harmonic variations, from a commune into a personal language.[37] As African music opened new horizons of emotional expression in melody and rhythm, African poetry substantially increased the spectrum of emotional expression in American English.

The culture of the African Americans was a reverent religious one.[38] The reason was that God was the only thing they were allowed to have and imagine for centuries. Christian preaching was the grandest vocabulary of their language; God was the most brilliant image they could hang their spirit on. God comforted them when slavery became too hard to bear. God was the judge they would appeal to when their lives seemed unfair and unjust. God was their salvation, their dreams, and their hopes. God and his words had tremendous emotional and psychological appeal to them.

There was a thin line between black religious and secular worlds. It came from the sensual and concrete characteristics of language. The English that African Americans spoke was a language without abstraction. God, in their language, was much closer to their lives and hearts than the God in Puritan tradition, which established a rigid and logical line between human and divine. The motifs and idioms of African American expression in words, ideas, and songs often were interchangeable.[39] It is universal that human imagination always finds a way to express itself regardless of its form. (Germany, whose language was the youngest and least poetic among the European vernaculars, produced the most brilliant philosophers and composers.) The sub-verbal cultural resources of African Americans nurtured many of the most original musicians and lyricists in America.

The self-definition of African Americans began from their personal relationships with God, and the European Americans initiated theirs from nature, a much more impersonal god. As Walt Whitman celebrated himself, he used a direct, familiar, and even slangy tone. Whitman's self did not collapse in on itself, as did the Victorians, who brooded in an introspective cadence, reduced nature to personal moonlight, and communed with a very lonely self. Whitman's self glowed in comparison. It was isolated, yet communicated with others; it was able to separate, establish its uniqueness, yet participate with the collective.[40]

5. Old and New Songs: Russian and American Empires

This chapter illustrates the cultural foundation of the cold war, which developed in the middle of the twentieth century. Russia emerged as a superpower after the new ideology of Marx was successfully transplanted into the rich cultural soil of Russian people. Communism could sing in the Russian tongue and touch the soul of its people. It had created an emotional appeal that replaced the passion once felt for the tzar and the church.

Americans were very proud of their achievements. The seeds of their souls had blown in from all corners of the world. And with each seed, a little bit of the Old World arrived, each with an expectation of making a new beginning. The American garden, wild and unkept at first glance, had become a cultural mosaic bound together by a singular vision of opportunity.

Two large and powerful boys had reached puberty at exactly the same time. Each was flush with the success of his role in ending the worldwide military challenge from the German and Japanese boys. The old men of China, India and the Middle East posed no threat to them, as they spent most of their time sleeping. The sometimes tiresome and cranky Britain was mellowing, and seemed content with the loose ties that it promoted within its widely scattered commonwealth.

So, there they stood ... an American and a Russian.... And as they turned to face each other, their eyes locked in a cold icy stare ... the stare of challenge.

Identity crisis was a way of life for Russia. Russia was always obsessed with himself and his history. For centuries he had convinced himself, and the world, that Russia was unique. Russia was neither West nor East, and he had never been touched by the education of mankind (education of the West or East, European or Asian). He was able to leap out of human history and time with his burning desire and pure energy.[1]

107

This Russian sense of rootlessness was not entirely without merit. Like formative America, Russia imported everything from somewhere else, even its written language (Greek alphabet) and God (Orthodox Christianity). Also like America, Russia had a hungry soil for cultural product and Russians were talented and fast learners. As one of the youngest European literary traditions, Russia borrowed literary and artistic forms that had been cultivated and developed in pre- and early modern Europe and adopted them as his own. It took only a century for the Russian literature to grow from a clumsy imitator of half-understood models to a master of European cultural idiom. During the middle of the 18th century, European literature, music and arts flourished in Russia; by the early 19th century, Russia began to produce original literary and musical giants comparable to its counterparts in Western Europe.[2]

The source of this cultural energy was Russian oral poetry, sung everywhere, in every occasion, and for many centuries. As Gogol whence put it: every pine logs of every Russian peasant hut are cut with a song, bricks are tossed from hand to hand with a song as villages and cities sprout like mushrooms. Every Russian baby is diapered with a song and Russians marry and are buried with a song. There isn't a nation on earth is as steeped in singing words as Russia is.[3]

This old oral tradition, which was constantly re-imagined, reversed, and re-written, cultivated a sense of togetherness and belonging. However, like any oral tradition without written definition (as evidenced by Old English and pre–Islamic Arabic), it fostered a fluid sense of identity, like sand that could blow anywhere on the whim of the wind. Russia was constantly redefined into different persona through its written words and the influence of alien ideologies. The Americans, whose ancestors chose to uproot themselves from their own cultures (with African Americans as an exception), came to North America to resettle and start again. The first generation of Americans were seeds that flew from every corner of the world, looking for a place to grow, because their homeland, somehow, was barren for them. On the contrary, the Russian people fell in love with their own land. They would search the world for exotic seeds to grow at home. Russians were excellent farmers. They made everything that they transplanted grow and flourish — Greek speaking God, German philosophy and abstract music, French art and music, English literature.... However, realizing the foreign origins of those plants on their land, the Russians needed to constantly declare, demonstrate, and validate that they were home grown.

This sense of cultural insecurity had become an incredible engine that drove extraordinary artistic and literary creativity in Russia. Having too little and starting too late, Russia became a restless teenager, eager to start all over again whenever there were new words, new ideas, and expression about a new age.... He was the professional revolutionary in mind and attitude. He could very quickly embrace new and foreign ideas and reinvent himself accordingly. Each time, he redefined himself with a new identity and new ideas about his country, and his country's new god (or evil depending on the language one speaks).[4]

The conviction that Russia was unique reached its zenith in the Stalin period. It looked upon itself as a post-apocalyptic culture. The final verdict on all human culture had already passed, and all that was once temporally distinct had become forever simultaneous in the blinding light of the final judgment and the ultimate truth revealed in Stalin's *Short Course* of party history. Socialist realism regarded historical time as ended and therefore occupied no particular place in it.[5]

In order to keep up with this apocalyptic image, Russia had been vigorously writing and rewriting its history all the way along. In the formative America, where new images and voices, regardless of their origin, constantly inspired and generated new poetry and prose, literature created various styles and explored diverse directions. In Russia, words, especially written words, always played God. While words were the god, images and voices were created as the symbols for divine worship and sacrifice. So, contrary to formative American culture that had emerged from the bottom and out of its diversity, Russian culture always began from the top where a tiny group of elite writers defined the cultural agenda. While American culture was made of prime colors, a clash of hues of original ideas, and fresh images derived from sub-verbal languages, Russian culture was made from a single word ... *Russia. Russia* was the same lyric for various old songs, words that were sung in different tunes.

Russia was a vibrant kaleidoscope with written words as its center. It changed color as its axis spun about its focal point. Each time, according to the speed and the direction of light, it changed. However, in each moment, it had only one color at the top, which controlled and filtered the cultural image of the light. Unlike the early Americans, who were satisfied in buying talents from around the world, and embracing everyone who was willing to jump into its melting pot, the Russians built their cultural foundation through their words, Russian words ... one language of one voice, dominating and controlling dialogues, images, tones, and gestures. The patriotization of outside influence and reinventing it as Russian was the proud responsibility of writers who translated everything that they had, learned, and borrowed. In an incredibly short period of time, this translation built a monument of literature, arts, science, and philosophy. By writing and rewriting, it also built a unique Russian temple that worshiped all of the creation of its literature.

Russians were worshipers like the Americans. However, from the very beginning, they worshiped a different kind of God and worshiped him in a different formal context. The Russian notion of God was much broader and more complex than that of Protestant and Puritan America. Rooted in Orthodox Christianity, the Russian God had more concrete, diversified, refined images, and more sophisticated rituals than the Western Christian tradition (which was an important part of the American belief system). For instance, the Puritan God and his kingdom existed within a very restricted, rigid, and abstract realm. God, in Russian, carried more refined and variant literary and artistic forms. The Russian vision of Christianity included heaven and hell, demons and anti-heroes, as well as God, saints, and angels. Russian literature, with all of its shortcomings due to its short history, was the first European language to develop a vivid vision of faith, the widest and the deepest Christian vision of modern time.[6] It was the same vision that English began to depict at least a century later.

The first cultural characteristic of the Russian persona emerged from an oral tradition that went back to ancient times. As Russian formed its written language, it did not come into a barren wasteland like that of America. Unlike America, whose culture took root in a clash of highly diverse and imported languages and idioms, Russian culture grew from the native soil of Slavonic.[7] Like Homeric Greek and pre–Islamic Arabic, Russian oral poetry had been articulated for centuries. By the time that Russian took its written form, its oral poetics had already matured enough to shake off its music. Musical instruments were no longer in use in *byliny,* a poetic narrative. The monotonous tunes that Russian singers used to recite their epics were only a limited few, with very little variation. Musical forms had already been verbalized by repetitive recitation and performance. The tension and emotional energy which the singer/performers generated proved that their songs had power to carry every listener to the place where the story occurred. The eagerness and anticipation of the epic listener confirmed that Russian singers and performers could stir the hearts and minds of their audience in the same way that American television could do with viewers.[8]

Old Rus of the tenth century was a land of songs, the songs of Old Slavonic heroes. The *byliny* or heroic narrative and poems covered a period of nearly a thousand years. They supplied a popular supplement to the more scholarly forms of historical record, such as the chronicles kept by religious houses, the memoirs of the lettered classes, and the royal archives. The byliny gave us the history of Russia as seen through the eyes of the illiterate — an aspect of history, which, despite its paramount importance, would otherwise pass unrecorded. They brought a new factor into history by supplying what Sir Bernard Pares called "the running chorus, so intelligent and so suggestive, of the best wisdom of the Russian peasantry."[9]

Unlike other oral traditions that evolved in ancient times, becoming a piece of the historical puzzle, the Russian popular epic was a living tradition. It did not disappear or die, even after it became inspired and recorded as a written language. It did not retreat into the rural life of peasantry, as had other oral traditions. Russian oral poetry, time and again, revived, renewed, and recreated as it closely interacted with its written form. It constantly reinvented itself according to the need of its cultural, national, and political history. This cultural and linguistic integration, rarely seen except in Islamic Arabic, determined the speed, direction, and form of the Russian cultural evolution. This integration ensured that words dominated, directed, and controlled artistic expression. This uninterrupted tyranny of words consistently consolidated the boundary between itself and literature and the arts. The verbal hierarchy would never be overwhelmed.

The earliest cycle of byliny told stories of its oldest heroes. It represented the remains of ancient Slavonic mythology. Volga was a military prince who fought successfully with *druzhina* and repelled invasions, and carried his aggressions into the heart of Tsargard. He, very much like the Greek gods, had superhuman strength and wisdom. Mikula and Svyatogor were mere human heroes. Their weapon was a steel club.

The largest byliny emerged in and around Kiev. It was about the earliest Russian hero, Prince Vladimir of Kiev, the founder of the Russian Empire.[10] The byliny of the period between the twelfth and the sixteenth centuries was about heroes of the older principalities, a legend of knights. These stories contained more real historical elements. The occurrences of marvelous and superhuman acts were very much less pronounced and were quite subordinate to the heroic narrative of adventure.

The third cycle related to heroes of a different political milieu — the citizens of the wealthy city-state of Novgorod. This *byliny* offered a relatively large range of episodes, increasing the number of incidents and narrating them into summary form. While retaining many of the characteristics of heroic narrative, the framework of the story began to draw closer to the style of the medieval metrical romances.

Written Russian was a language as young as English, but it grew up in an entirely different cultural environment. Instead of the multi-lingual influence in which Old and Middle English emerged, Russian prose arrived to the world of Rus as a unified sign of the Christian God.[11] The imported language, in which the Christian God spoke was, at first, Greek (commonly known as Old Church Slavonic). This language was initially based on the dialect spoken by the Slav population of Thessaloniki, but it was strongly influenced by Greek models in vocabulary, phraseology, syntax and style. It grew within an accumulation of translations from Byzantine writings.[12]

Unlike the Latin translation and adaptation of Greek as a total package of literary and philosophical tradition, Russian translation from Greek began with the very narrowly defined purpose of providing reinforcement for Christian preaching and liturgy. There were no classics of ancient Greek literature and philosophy. Not even humanist histories such as *Tale of Troy* or *Romance of Alexander* were translated into Russian. The hierarchy of translated writings included *Leitourgikon (Sluzhebnik)* and *Horologion (Chasoslov)*, containing the prayers and hymns for the fixed yearly cycle, and the *Triod katanyktion (Triod postnaya)*, the *Pentekostarion (Triod tsvetnaya)* and the *Oktoechos (Oktoikh)*, with their prayers and hymns for the moveable cycle. They were also Lectionaries, drawn from the Gospels, from the Acts and Epistles of the Apostles, and from the Old Testament, and the Psalter (Psaltyr) and the Synaxarion (Prolog), a collection of short exegetical sermons and stories about the lives of saints.[13]

The second type of literature that was translated into Russian was the extended *Lives* of the saints and writings of church fathers. For instance, Russians received the works of John Chrysostom, Basil the Great, his brother Gregory of Nyssa, and Gregory Nazianaen, the classics of Greek patristic literature. It was Russian tradition that written words and their scope were completed under the arbitrary control from God, church or the state. In the eyes of the Byzantine church, this small portion of Greek literature was all the Russians needed to read.

Russians were told: If you want great stories, you may read the Books of Kings. If you crave exciting and edifying reading, you have the Prophets, the Book of Job, or Jesus Sirach. But if, finally, your demand is for song books, you may read the Psalter. The body of translated literature accumulated in Kievan Rus during the first century after Vladimir's conversion corresponds fairly accurately to the selection of books found in monastic libraries throughout the Orthodox world.[14] Upon this transplanted hierarchy of words, Russian princes strove to emulate the splendor of Byzantine art in Kiev.[15]

However, this artificial culture transplanted from Greece and imitated according to its model (as the Romans attempted centuries before) surprisingly survived and flourished in Russia. The words of the Christian God in the Slavic Church, unlike the words of the Old Testament, did not encounter a local dialogue as primitive and cruel as the Latin of the first centuries AD. Russia was a land of epic poetry and pagan rituals.[16]

Greek, this time, had been transplanted into a thick and rich soil of Old Eastern Slavonic. As Pushkin realized, centuries later, it was a lucky hybrid for the Russian language and culture. Greek gave the "sonorous and expressive" Slavonic what it needed — regularity and flexibility, thus the ability to fly as a literary language. This marriage of Greek and Russian was a rare example of high level compatibility within two languages, which had independently developed similar grammar, majestic poetic flow, and theatrical expression.[17] This compatibility manifested itself in the way in which the host culture, Russian, selected and transformed the alien language, literature, and religion.

When Christianity arrived, pagan Russia — like pagan Greece, England, and pre–Islamic Arabia — was a polytheist society. It was assumed, in a matter of common sense, that there were many gods, and that these gods demanded worship through concrete, publicly visible gestures of reverence and gratitude. The gods were there. They were invisible and ageless neighbors of the human race. Gods were not abstractions. They were vibrant beings whose lower order shared the same physical space as mankind. They could be seen, touched, smelled, and heard in all natural and human aspects. Unlike Jews and early Christians, Slavs built neither tombs nor temples. They worshiped rivers, land, and trees. They went to holy places like forest groves and the shores of rivers and lakes; they invoked vampires or werewolves, called Upirs.

Russian goddesses had been around at least as long as Greek goddesses. Like ancient Greece, Slavic culture absorbed many foreign images and idioms in its formative age from their Greek, Sarmatian, and Iranian neighbors.[18]

Like pagan Greeks, Russians did not see foreign gods as competition. They could always extend their divinity to include them by inventing a relationship. In bowing to the myths and ethos of the patriarchal and warrior ruling classes, the peasantry tried to temper these with their own concerns and values. But over the centuries, the gradual process of partriarchalization also affected the themes of folklore and rite. Masculine rituals and supernatural figures became assimilated by feminine prototypes. As elements of the archaic folklore tradition were incorporated into the newer epic one, the ancient divinities of the pagan Slavs and their predecessors, the bereginy, the rozhanitsy, and the earth mothers, were paralleled by masculine counterparts. Christianity played a vital role in this process by imposing, as had the pagan Varangian rulers before it, the cult of male gods and a priesthood over the indigenous population.[19]

The formal compatibility of Russian pagan gods and the Orthodox Christian God was bonded in the language in which Gods were described, worshiped, preached, and understood. Russian worship had always been concrete, visual, and emotional rather than abstract, remote, and hard to imagine. Russians believed in and worshiped saints as well as God. Russian Christianity was rooted in the way in which its God was articulated in songs, dance, words, and images. Unlike early Western Christianity, which was based on blind faith and rigid doctrine, Russian Christianity was more concrete and actually spiritual. Through the life stories and the teaching of its saints, Christian doctrine, morals, and values in Russia were not only listened to and prayed for, but also visualized through rituals and demonstrated by the teachings and deeds of the monastery saints. Even in the late nineteenth and twentieth centuries, when God had died in Western Europe, he kept being imagined, narrated, and argued about in completely secularized novels.[20]

The best example of this smooth transition was that Slavic pagan culture was one of the few traditions, other than Greek, that successfully established a divine system in which its mother goddess established a consistent relationship with other gods. Orthodox Mary, with an urban and historical origin, entered Kiev with triumph during the tenth century, following a long tradition of great Rus goddesses. She became the principal vehicle of the popular conversion to Christianity, an alien and essentially masculine faith, which was rooted not in the fertility of the soil or the forest, but in the principles of paternal authority, punishment, and filial love.

Unlike the Greeks, who wrote stories to justify the transformation of divine power from goddesses to gods, Russians simply turned their fertility worship and maternal love to the empress. The Grand Prince Vladimir of Kiev imposed Byzantine Christianity upon his subjects in 988–989. The Byzantine linkage of church and state appealed to the ambitious trader-prince as a means to convince the Kievan urban elite, as well as the peasantry, that his rule was supported by divine sanction. What Vladimir attempted to impose had been embraced with love and enthusiasm much earlier by his grandmother, Olga, hailed by the monk-chroniclers as the "grandmother of the Russian Land."[21]

This smooth transformation was made possible by the ancient tradition of Russian epic. Heroes often obeyed not the law of God, as described in Western epic, but the law of their mothers, or mother figures such as enchantresses, temptresses, witches, wives or priestesses. The Russian hero's powerful guide, and yet most feared antagonist, was his own mother or mother figure, who could appear in any of these forms. Russian epic portrayed the mother (figure) as the source of power and wisdom that provided the hero's victories, and decided fate as well as decreed defeats.[22]

The adaptability and creative energy of Russian culture existed though its creative integration of different levels of cultural expression.[23] Unlike Western cultures where every form of expression evolved in highly classified and rigidly guarded fields, in Russian, there was a constant dialogue among different forms of expression. They described, visualized, celebrated, and praised their images and ideas. This constant repetition and reinvention in various cultural forms made it possible for Russian, the youngest language in Europe, to produce literature and scientific learning of top quality in the shortest period of time.

Compared to Latin, Russian transplantation and transmission of Greek culture was much more active, and creative at times; it was more like the

English translation and assimilation of Latin tradition centuries earlier. This well directed, selective, and controlled process made it possible for Russian literature to quickly reach its impressive expressive and artistic level. During the eighteenth and nineteenth centuries, Russian became able to produce masterpieces of literature that were comparable to those of the Western vernaculars.[24]

Compared to formative English, the early Russian reaction and assimilation of Greek culture was much shallower. Russia was exposed to only a very narrow spectrum of Greek culture, primarily the Greek phonic system and Orthodox Christian theology. Greek literary and dramatic forms, political ideology, and humanist philosophy were not included. In other words, the Greek influence did not create a linguistic and mental gap in the Russian mind, as did Latin tradition in the English mind. On the contrary, Greek alphabets and phonics revolutionized oral Russian. The new written Russian narrowed and focused the meaning of various expressions, thus, integrated its verbal and sub-verbal languages.

Another unforeseen result of the Russian adoption of Greek alphabets was that it opened Russian eyes, ears, and minds to the cultures of Western Europe, a new ocean of communicative and expressive idioms for Russian language. From this repertoire, Russians of the seventeenth century could select and transplant whatever they needed to reinvent and create their own canon of literature. Russian literature of the nineteenth and twentieth centuries, a mere teenager in the European literary scene, produced masterpieces comparable with the English and the French.

Like the mature American culture, formative Russian culture was very much driven by its artistic expressions. While in contemporary American society, communication was largely illiterate — oral and visual (on big and small screens) — Medieval Russians lived surrounded by song, dance, and liturgical music. Religious processions, parades and theatrical performances were regular features at various times of the year. They involved the majority of citizens, as both participants and spectators. God had always been associated with the images, displayed in the church, in architecture, market places, sanctuaries, cemeteries, and theaters.[25]

These imaginative and expressive variations quickly verbalized as soon as written Russian emerged and began to accumulate literary canon. Like pre–Islamic Arabic, whose high level of poetic elaboration turned to rich variations of literature very quickly, Russian poetic and prose narrative erected a sophisticated high cultural form in a few decades.

The best example of this high-speed development was Russian lyrical poetry. Russian poetry was the youngest among the Slavic languages.[26] It emerged only during the seventeenth century, when it had not separated from the musicality of its sound and tended to be theatrical rather than metaphysical. Emotion was described more in pitch and color than in verbal imageries. Perhaps the most possessive and most self-reflective of the writer–Pushkinists is Vladimir Nabokov. His commentary to *Euene Onegin*, while claiming to be no more than a modest point to the original text, outgrows its source several fold, with every bit of Pushkinian text serving as a pretext for a veritable orgy of cultural free association in four or five languages. It is a vivid confirmation of the notion that Pushkin's texts are essentially metonymic and refer to an array of mutually coexisting possibilities, from which the reader picks and chooses. The problem, as we see Nobokiov's commentary, is that what is perceived as an open structure can breed an infinity of complements. The only principle of selection is the taste and discretion of the reader, a guarantee of which was haughtily asserted by most of the elistist poets. Of all readers, the poet addressee regarded himself as best equipped to trace the oblique logic of those "strange affinities," which was called the "law of the syntagmatics of the artistic text."[27] Pushkin's poetry, with his astonishing ability to transport himself easily and freely into the most contradictory spheres of life, is reminiscent of Shakespeare. The more Pushkin perfected his creativity, the more his own identity concealed itself and disappeared behind the wonderful, sumptuous world of his poetic visions.

The Russian artist's ability to impersonate and incorporate any European nationality is testified by Pushkin's divine capacity for disappearing behind the heterogeneous array of his creations.[28]

This verbal fluidity and flexibility was the reason why Russian literature could expand at a much higher rate than other languages. It was the difference between interaction of various forms of expression within the same culture and between those from various languages. In other words, the richer and more varied the host cultural repertoire, the easier it was to find a point of communicability with foreign expressions, and the sooner it could evolve with a complete canon of literature. Americans spent centuries collecting various languages and cultures to make their stew of cultures. It took much less time for the Russians to collect various spices and simply add flavors to the previously prepared Russian stew. As a result, from the very beginning, the fabric of Russian cultural idioms had a much higher degree of consistency and unity. Americans could not achieve this until the twentieth century.

Russian cultural unity manifested itself not only in diversity and variation, but also in the established form in which those variations related to each other. In Russian, words (rather than images, visual or theatrical) were the leading dynamic for the evolution of literary imagination. The Russian artistic renaissance could only be assimilated by words, rather than by creating a gap or rupture within the literary scene, as had occurred in English and American history. As a new and singular written language, Russian had a much easier time maturing. While dealing and struggling with three different written languages, formal English took a few centuries to fill the gap between abstract and concrete, and between grand ideas and miniature images. As an emerging single written language, Russian did not create a similar gap in its vocabulary. The formal swing between opposite tendencies which drove the evolution of English literature took a much shorter time in Russian. As a result, Russia enjoyed a much greater capacity to absorb and assimilate various expressions and weave them into its own idioms.

The Russian arts, especially the popular ones, did not have the same trendsetting power and influence that was occasionally possible for the Americans. While the American popular arts became the rich soil and inspiring repertoire for literature, Russian arts, for centuries, remained controlled and directed by words. They followed rather than led literature. Russian artists could imitate and bring any foreign expression to its best use and yet, could only serve and symbolize what the words chose to do. With the control and discipline that their words exercised over their arts, Russian arts were always swiftly streamlined by literature, which in turn channeled their energy into the power of words. This swift and forced assimilation made it possible for the poetic and narrative capacity of Russian literary imagination to arrive a century earlier than the same stage of American theater and film. The variety of imageries that American films and theater were trying to convey during the twentieth century had already developed and matured in Russian poetry during the nineteenth century.

Russian culture was a scene of well-ranked hierarchy in which various expressions were classified and positioned within containers. All these layers existed and functioned according to ancient rules. Words needed to be worshiped. Boundaries between different kinds of words — cultural and philosophical categories — needed to be respected. Like stars traveling across the sky, it was not only the sun, the moon, or the planets that kept them in line, it was also the habitual orbit. It was not a loyalty to any specific person or specific idea. Russian art held absolutely no loyalty to anything because it had been programmed in its history to support the "high" culture and to assimilate the "low" culture. Within Russia's well-ranked repertoire of artistic expressions, there was no freedom or competition in a unified art.

In its language, its canon of languages, Russia eventually discovered God within himself. Language, even an oral one, had made them poets and artists. They could borrow, adopt, and invent God whenever needed. They made him change into robes of different colors — black, red, or gold — as need arose.

America discovered its own God during the later twentieth century after they eventually created and accumulated a canon of cultural idioms as diversified and yet highly unified as that of Russia. Very much like Arabic, Russian culture emerged from a single and ancient oral tradition. It spent most of its effort in diversification, in order to survive the turbulence of cultural inter-action. It learned this skill and survived as a chameleon, by constantly changing its color. America spent centuries in creating a God in its own image, a God in many forms and colors. It was an idea shared and lived by generations of immigrants. It crystallized their best hopes, dreams, and expectations, not only for themselves, but for their children as well. It was the image of a col-lective soul that was brought, transplanted, and reinvented in the new land. America emerged as a reincarnation of diversified religions, various forms of the same God, and various shapes of belief systems, religious and secular.

In the beginning, America, a piece of wild land, was a god who had no face, no name, and no shape. Every American and his group — divided by ethnic background, cultural heritage, political view, and business interest — promoted his own name, face, and view in an effort to outshine his opponents. The competition was to win and to be the idol of America. Those who suc-ceeded did not last for long. It took Americans more than two hundred years (including a hundred years of bloodshed) to realize that America could not be one color. It had to be multi-colored. American culture could not be any-thing except a mixed, melted diversity. Everyone within the collective became convinced that the name "America" was much more than his or her name, or his or her own ethnical origin, and more than his individual vision.

Color was the most primitive way to make someone distinct. However, because of its simplicity, it was the most versatile and mutable ... very much like the cultural mold of the formative America, where various idioms started to compete. They began to take their basic hue and become ready to mix with others. The American God emerged in many forms and clashes of colors (like Indian gods) but with a unified God supervising the mass of minor gods and goddesses, like Zeus. However, without a common history of storytelling long enough to articulate communicable images and voices, the new divine remained vague in vision and unclear in definition.

Music, like color, was another simple way to define unity in a literary vacuum. Instead of hot debate and elaborate rhetoric in England and later America, politics of nationalism between the late eighteenth and nineteenth century America began with a solitary song. "Yankee Doodle" was originally a European tune; "God Save the King" was changed to "God Save the Thirteen States" and eventually "God Save America."[29] The tune, rather than the lyrics, at the time, was universally America.

In spite of ambiguity, one thing was certain. America was grander, more imaginative, and more powerful than any one of its ingredients. This enlarged vision, the vision of the melting pot, changed the political and racial game of America. Instead of fighting for their own identity, as signified by their original culture, Americans began to fight for a larger slice from the American whole. The more they fought against each other, the more complicated the rules of the game became, and more they worshiped the game. In a pot where ingredients had already melted, the fight was no longer about ingredients; it was about the definition of spices and flavors.

When America created its collective identity by verbalizing all of its artistic inspiration, it began to narrow the gap between itself and Russia.

PART TWO
GROWING UP AND PUBERTY

Not every boy was equipped to face the challenge of cultural interaction. Only the golden boys, those who had enough education and knowledge, were able to define their own identity and create a worldview that placed themselves in a preeminent imperial position. Their ability to lead was determined by their ability to evolve, diversify, absorb, and assimilate.

Unlike the mature cultures that already possessed a framework of mind, for the young, to learn was to name, to classify, and to accumulate piecemeal knowledge. It took them awhile to figure out how and what to do with this increasing pile of information. At this stage of learning, there were only two categories apparent — black or white, then, black and white. As they learned, they found it harder and harder to decide and to choose one extreme or the other. They noticed that more and more items seemed to be somewhere in between. This was the time that they began to question their primitive definitions and the definability of their language as their thinking began to evolve. They were now beginning to leave their childhood behind.

In order to evolve, imperial boys had to learn more words and develop a more sophisticated language, one that was rich and flexible enough to diversify and expand. Their language had to be able to multiply in vocabularies, verbal patterns, and styles in order to backtrack, to re-qualify and modify their previously accepted ideas. Their logic needed to bend, recognize plurality, and expand in order to consider the contrary. A new flexibility and open mindedness emerged. Their imagination had to be able to envisage and understand the world, which was now much larger and complex. Their language needed to catch up with their expanding vision in order to find their place in the world and establish their relationship with others.

Although all of the imperial boys shared this common search for knowledge, the variant size of the repertoires of cultural idioms which each of them inherited, conquered, and drew from led them on different journeys as they matured.

6. Black/White Vision of the World

To create a worldview and a general way to look at life, the first step for any culture was to establish verbal distinctions, which built the boundary of meanings. All young cultures began by seeing the world in rigid oppositions: black/white, day/night, good/bad, and light/darkness ... because of their limited vocabularies. The vocabularies, which were based only on sensory distinctions, opened the eyes of man, and yet imprisoned his mind to only that which he could see, hear, touch, smell, or taste. Without general and abstract words, the eyes of his mind remained closed as if he was asleep. Most young cultures died in their sleep.

Over the past seven thousand years, many civilizations were born. They either outgrew this primitive stage or died prematurely. The death rate for young civilizations was very high before the Christian era. Among many ancient cultures of the Mediterranean, Greek was the only survivor. Most of these decaying civilizations left their voices and visions behind for newcomers to carry on and rebuild.

Only the civilizations whose imagination went beyond primitive vision survived their childhood. It took generations of communication and accumulation of cultural expression to cultivate the vision and sensibility to describe the world, both its visual phenomena and its rhythm beyond the visible. How each culture developed its worldview depended on the characteristics and the degree of maturity of its language. The relationship between its oral and written languages, and between its native tongue and borrowed vocabularies, often determined the timing and developmental tendency of its ideas. It could be a vision of the eyes as well as the mind: to polarize or to centralize, to diversify or to consolidate; to become more abstract ... more concrete, or shadings in between.

Ancient Greek was the only language among the languages of the imperialist boys that coined its own abstract, moral, and philosophical concepts. The general and abstract concepts of Greek evolved naturally (without translation) from the concrete words used and accumulated in its poetic and prose narrative, dramatic dialogue, and oral rhetoric. The earliest Greek philosophers were poets: Xenophanes, Parmenides, and Empedocles.[1] They used hexameter to make social, moral, and cosmological comments and to express opinions about issues of general significance. All these poets developed their own ways of emphasizing their insights and wisdom using direct narrative, reinterpreting the history of goddesses, or retelling mythical tales. Their works represent an expansion of writing, and thus thinking, from particular to general and from concrete to abstract.[2]

Prose writing that flourished during the Ionian Enlightenment did not invent theological and cosmological speculation. It provided a form, a distinct language, through which philosophy could take off and separate itself from the language of sense (poetic, at the time).[3] Generations of philosophers who lived and wrote during a five or six century period filtered and exacted a level of abstract concepts on which the Greek systems of philosophy germinated.[4]

The process of cultivating verbal imagery began by painting a picture of the world with words, a description of the vision of the eyes, then a vision beyond the eyes — a wordplay.[5] Like the small sketches that landscape painters create when they go on a field trip, these new images did not only imprint or imitate the vision of the eyes, but they also portrayed what the writer chose to see and where he focused the naked vision. The word-sketches were visions of the mind which were selected, reflected, and penetrated by contemporary thought. Wordplay eventually re-projected the visual image and internalized the vision from concrete phenomena to a sense of order and logic behind vision. The early Greek philosophers began to see the world as a continuous cycle of change, in which the oppositions expressed by such pairs of words as "up/down," "day/night," and "war/peace" formed a cohesive unity. This train of words and thought transformed the focus of writing from a scattered imitation of the world to a unity between external vision and invisible logic.

Wordplay, paradox, and juxtapositional imagery helped writers to organize their ideas and to explore the underlying logic of the world. The early philosophers used ordinary language and promoted common sense before a special level of abstract concepts was established: "nature is accustomed to hide herself;" "sea-water purest and most polluted, for fish drinkable and healthful, for men undrinkable and destructive;" "a road, upwards downwards, one and the same.[6] Sophists distilled wordplay into more abstract verbal oppositions: *logos-ergon,* or word-deed, and *nomos-physis* or the apparent and the real.[7] The conceptual classification and separation paved the way to a sharper fundamental division: seeing and being, language and world, mind and nature. This division made it possible to further polarize abstract language and concrete knowledge into something else, later called philosophy and science.

The first generation of "pure" (abstract) philosophy (as opposed to poetic or wisdom philosophy and technical knowledge) emerged from dialogue writing.[8] By writing dialogue, Plato transformed the language of drama into that of philosophical inquiry.[9] From his earliest to his latest dialogue, Plato gradually uprooted conversation and monologue from personal voice, performance, and gesture. He created a branch of language which was later further separated and isolated (by writing in capital letters as in European vernaculars) to describe something intangible, immeasurable, and infinite.

The plain and simple speeches, without dramatic overtone, empowered the language with clarity and precision. Using dialogue in prose initiated a new direction for Greek literary language. It provided a vehicle to specify and restrain meanings. This was opposite to the established mainstream poetry in Greek epic and drama. Prose dialogue sought out, redefined, and tightened moral, theological and cosmological concepts. Discussion, carried back and forth by questions and answers, represented contrary positions and clarified argument and its logic. After establishing dialogue as the means to carry philosophical deliberation, the voice of interlocutors began to disappear. Speeches became longer and longer, and eventually became a narration of ideas without a conversational framework.[10] In the hands of Plato, philosophy began to create its own language, a language that escaped the senses and pursued a pure and untainted activity of the mind.

Plato's work substantially expanded the verbal horizon of ancient Greek. He abstracted, clarified, and rationalized thinking by separating knowledge from art, truth from poetry, and sanity from madness. By pointing out the limitations of literary imagination and creativity, he established new goals for words, images, morals, and spirits to which human creativity could ascend.[11] This conceptual space later became the rich soil of philosophical and literary meditation on which the creation of many languages was based.

The battle of words, inspired and reinvented by Plato, became a literary genre in its own right during the second half of the fifth century B.C.[12] Legal oratory and public speeches, which were an important part of Athenian democracy, gave abstract words clearer definition. The slippery logic and vague sense of order, expressed by poetry, were further sharpened and tightened, eventually becoming more adversarial. After two centuries, during which the art of verbal persuasion was cultivated, exercised, and polished, philosophy finally took off and became an art of its own ... an art of mind illustrated in a written dialogue with oneself.[13]

As a result of this literary elaboration, a new and more absolute reasoning emerged in ancient Greek. In a number of his dialogues, and particularly in the *Republic*, Plato presented a contrast of two worlds: the world of absolute qualities ("Forms" or "Ideas") and the everyday world of particular phenomena accessible to sensual perception.[14] This contrast was only one of many conceptual distinctions that a philosopher used to forward his argument. Like many verbal distinctions in an actively evolving language, like the ancient Greek of the fourth and fifth centuries B.C., this gap did not remain deep and permanent. Unlike a multi-lingual environment (such as European vernaculars) where conceptual gaps took centuries to resolve, the Greek conceptual gap almost immediately began to narrow and was gradually filled up by rhetoric and philosophical rewriting and re-imagining.

Aristotle was the first influential philosopher who put forward a whole system of classified knowledge, sciences ... theoretical, practical and productive ... into the conceptual gap that Plato created.[15] Aristotle wrote many logic treatises, not as parts of any one science, but as a method or argument that could be applied to all science.

Aristotle's writing, which redefined the methods and classified the categories of knowledge, became a bridge between the language of philosophy and that of science.[16] The largest part of Aristotle's writing was theoretical knowledge. This included empirical investigation of nature at the level of general principle, as well as particular movements, changes, and biology. There was also what he called "first philosophy" or "theology" (metaphysics), the subject matter of which covered principles of reality or the primary objects of scientific knowledge. He categorized his writings on ethics and politics as "practical knowledge." For him, poetics and rhetoric were a part of productive knowledge. He had fathered a language, in which one could frequently find an expression to deliver the most abstract thought clearly and coherently.

Aristotle's stylistic writing also softened the highly polarized and rigid boundaries of Platonic concepts. He often elucidated and defined central concepts by illustrating different uses for the same concept. For example, he began his *Physic 2* with an analysis of "physis nature," which he believed to have two fundamental considerations: the "matter" of something or its "form." After having defined the subject, Aristotle would discuss specific details, which not only clarified the definition but also modified it. He also repeatedly interrupted his main exposition of a subject to consider an "aporia," a special problem which a modern writer might place in a footnote, and which he himself may leave unresolved. Sometimes it was difficult to tell if a particular aporia was part of his original text or something added on.

By focusing on various forms and details in the "demonstration" of logic, Aristotle further diversified Platonic language and its styles of expression.

Through this formal approach, he turned oration from a philosophical pursuit into an artistic one which moved the mind and manipulated emotion.[17] Through his work, philosophical language expanded its scope from a pure mind game expressed in unconceivable vocabularies into a system of knowledge — a skeleton for the human mind. It recognized plurality in description as well as reasoning.[18] Aristotle's writing opened Plato's philosophy up and expanded it by allowing contradiction and plurality. It was this plurality and open-endedness, supported by its fluid language, that allowed Greek philosophy the capacity to backtrack, reinterpret, and requalify over the next two thousand years.

Greek philosophical concepts remained the inspiration of the Western worldview because Greek language was much richer than European vernaculars. Until the twentieth century, none of the Western languages had accumulated enough literary variations to go beyond the Greek mind because the formative stage of their languages was constantly compared to the mature Greek. There were two major linguistic re-orientations, Latin and the European vernaculars. In each case, new languages developed with and according to the borrowed Greek concepts, as a plant that grows and blossoms by climbing an established frame — a structure of ideas and a hollow system of knowledge. It had been a restrained and controlled living until the new literary language reached the level of abstract frame imposed by translation. The gap between the two remained so constant and revealing that it became accepted as a natural course of cultural evolution. In fact, this was a normal course only for culture, which had experienced a continued speculative tradition, religious or secular, and a discontinued literary language. This normal pattern began to change during the later half of the twentieth century, when the European vernaculars matured and overgrew the established and borrowed frame.

It took many centuries for modern European languages to fill up the conceptual gap between the ideal and the real world, and between particulars and their universal form. But this process was initiated by transplanting Greek concepts. It was not Plato's intent to have lasting influence. Words, like currency, belonged to the market and began a life of their own as soon as they were uttered or written. The original intent of the first uttering became irrelevant. What the words meant to other readers, and how they were going to be interpreted, was determined by the comprehensive capacity of the interpreter whose imagination was defined by his native language. The constant reorientation of language in Western Europe, where Plato's ideas were rethought, rewritten, and reinterpreted, kept Greek philosophy alive. The verbal gap could only be filled with words which were not simply isolated vocabularies. Language was a well-woven tapestry. Its threads were knitted into each other. As a new language emerged, it could only borrow a few threads from the piece of old tapestry. Every time a new language emerged, it began to pull the same threads. It often took centuries to knit another piece of tapestry because the new culture still needed to weave and color its own yarn.

As the only old tapestry existing in Europe, Greek philosophy became a rich and seemingly unexhausted mine of thought. The gap between ideal and reality, a passing distinction and temporary polarity created by the Greeks, was substantially widened as it was translated into Latin and European vernaculars. During the eighteenth and nineteenth century, Western philosophers, with their formative languages, kept redefining the polarity over and over again, and turned it into a deep and unbridgeable canyon. When Greek philosophy spoke formative Latin, English or German, it lost its conceptual fluidity and logical flexibility ... especially in German, the most abstract language among the Western vernaculars. For the last two thousand years, the best minds of Europe cultivated and maintained this abstract world as the pinnacle of their imagination, and with it, they built their divine or earthly kingdoms, their societies, nations, commonwealths, and their empires. During the last two hundred years, Western philosophy created a world divided by this classical canyon, half of which was expressed in capitalized words such as God, Logo, Word, Nature, Reason, Law, Beauty, Love, Justice, Rights, and Spirit. The other a half was the world of the tangible phenomena, called nature, and its cultivated form, science.

Until the middle of the twentieth century, the history of Western philosophy had been both inspired and imprisoned by this conceptual gap. The poverty of words, caused by a repeated miscarriage of literary language, secured the power of the abstract mind and delayed the accumulation of concrete expression and imagination. In Greek, literary language had never left philosophy or theology very far behind. The language of Greek philosophy made it possible to transform the Jewish God, rooted in the language of the anthropomorphic world, into an immaterial being, the Christian God.[19] The rich soil of Greek literary tradition also provided the colorful language, which had accumulated to describe pagan gods and goddesses for centuries, to describe and connect the invisible Christian God and his visible and concrete world. This literary rooting of Greek was one of the reasons why the hegemony of Orthodox Christianity survived much longer than its counterpart in the West.

Plato was the first Greek philosopher whose work was translated into Latin. During the first century of the Christian area, Latin began to receive the imprint of the Greek philosophy. However, imitating Greek was merely a fashionable idea rather than an intellectual inspiration. There was hardly any translation of Greek texts. For centuries, the major part of Plato's *Timaeus*, was the only Greek philosophical writing that was translated into Latin.[20]

In Latin, which had just began to formulate as a literature, life and its language, cultural images, and ideas mingled and were inseparable. There was not any conceptual foundation for abstract ideas. There was not any abstract word, such as philosophy, religion, or even literature, as we know it today.[21]

However, worldview did not have to be abstract. It could be general and yet concrete. As in the Homeric Greek, the world could well be a scattered, fragmented, and multi-cultural place that invited contradiction and competition.[22] Without a separate level of abstract language, the Roman worldview was cultivated and articulated through dramatic gesture and ritual performance.[23]

Although armed with hundreds of model plays from the ancient Greek, the Latin audience did not have the poetic, thematic, and mythological memory upon which Greek drama depended. Without an epic tradition behind it, Latin theater had to work harder to confer solemnity and intensity upon its language. It imitated, borrowed, and adopted Greek models and yet freely re-imagined and reinvented them to deliver meaning and to dramatize linguistic pursuit of sympathetic response.[24]

Like the early Greeks, Latin character building had to begin with masks, whose stereotyped features of face and color were more efficient than their primitive words for depiction, and allowed an instinctive identification of characters and their intended traits.[25] Gradually, the audience expected soldiers to be loud, boastful and low witted, and slave dealers to be sleazy, greedy, and cowardly. Plautus was never obliged to spend time on the exposition of character because one glance at the masks conveyed these stereotypes.

Unlike the early Greek drama, which added new and various connotations to the well-articulated themes and characters, the dramatic presentation of young Latin was created from scratch. It used gesture to convey new and fresh meanings. This historically determined intention explained the choices and emphasis of Latin authors when imitating and reinventing Greek tragedies and comedies. Latin drama was an enlarged and orchestrated affair between the play and audience.[26] Instead of pretending to be real or natural, Plautus intended to draw the attention of the audience to the fact that they were watching theater.... Characters revealed their thought to the audience aloud. Latin dramatists had to write their plays down to the their audience's low taste (perhaps like daytime soap operas on contemporary TV) to achieve the desirable reaction from them. They had to render Menander's smooth monologue as a choppy, salty exchange.[27]

Unlike the Greek drama whose presentation became increasingly artistic and refined, the early Latin drama provided a stage where the audience could participate very concretely in crises that it portrayed.[28] The audience was often passionately involved with the matters on the stage without being sermonized or lectured. However, there were lessons to be learned about proper order, which was defined and played against by its opposite, disorder. The sense of order and disorder were repeatedly illustrated in a very narrowly defined basic scheme, to which the deceptively numerous varieties of individual plots could be reduced. There always seemed to be a situation where a property, which could be a woman or the money needed to purchase her, was in a crisis. It was a moral situation where social values were challenged, violated, and tested. A freeman was treated like a slave, fathers attempted to take advantage of their sons' love interests, or a married man pursued an adulterous relationship. The narrator of these morality plays, such as Plautus, would subvert everything that the audience accepted as normal and natural. The conflict created a suspension of order and promoted abnormality. Then, comedies would always return to the original way that things were before the conflict.[29]

At this point, the dramatic exercise of order and disorder was not a mere repetition or imitation of Greek moral conflict, which had accumulated endless colorful connotations through centuries of poetic and philosophical meditation. Rather, Latin, as an emerging literary language, was struggling with its own concepts to describe and comprehend the conflict and even chaos that the people were facing in their civil life.

Another way to give an order to life was to regulate language, its sound and rhythm, then eventually transform it from oral to written expression, which carried a more unified and regular mode. Since Latin originated from a very simple oral tradition, its verses were naïve and moving because it was metrically free and contained infinitely possible forms. The Latin style of alliteration was typical of the earliest "carmina." It was found in proverbs, laws, and sacral formulas. It passed into Naevius's Saturnians, and into the comedies of Naevius, Plautus, and Caecilius.[30]

Interaction with Greek literature forced Latin to grow faster, especially when the Roman Empire became a superpower in the Mediterranean region and marched into Greece and Asia Minor. In order to impose its will as conqueror, Latin needed to grow. It needed to stretch itself by creating a cultural identity as lofty as that of Greece. Latin needed to sound, look, and think as the Greeks. To imitate Greece, Latin was willing to give up everything native, anything naïve, raw, coarse, and unsophisticated.

It began with the sound of their language in their poetry. In early Latin, alliteration lent a kind of regularity, a kind of rhythmic armature. The translation, imitation, and influence of Greek poetics interfered with the natural progression of Latin poetic, and imposed the alien structure of hexameter. With Latin alliteration applied to the Greek hexameter, it produced a monotonous and heavily cadenced sound. For this reason, the poets after Ennius would use figures of sound very selectively and with great restraint. Hexameter gradually replaced alliteration. At the highest point of this revolution, Virgil alliterated far less than Ennius. He alliterated only when he chose to give his verses the ring of a poetry more ancient and traditional, but now far away.[31] To replace alliteration with verbal form was a common transformation of poetic in many languages. However, to force the transition (rather than letting poetic form naturally into it) by translation planted the seeds for a later rift between oral poetic and its script. This formal rift took place in Latin during the third century, as Latin began to be replaced by Romantic vernaculars.

The general sense of order (as opposite to disorder) that was portrayed by Ennius was further refined by the comedies of Terence.[32] This time, life and world were displayed and polarized less by different behaviors, attitudes, and opinions, but rather by distinct languages.

The dramatic gap between languages and masks in Latin became refined and smoothed out by poetic elaboration. Rewriting and reinterpreting Greek epics in Latin helped the emerging language to cultivate an intellectual world that mediated between glorious ideas and the earthly struggle to realize them.[33] Although Lucretius could hardly recreate an image of a shamanistic poet-philosopher, like that of Empedocles, he attempted to combine cosmos and nature with man ... physics with ethics ... nature to be studied and described with man to be spiritually healed. With his limited repertoire of Latin, Lucretius' analogy lacked the visual and sensual power of the Greek, which could easily grasp similarity in difference and abolish distinction in favor of continuity. For the Greeks, unity was intimately and intuitively seen, felt, and sensed. In the Greek condensed perception, everything was also the image of something else: "Olives, eggs produced by trees," or the sea as "the sweat of the earth." The analogy here established a seamless juxtaposition that Latin was not able to portray until many centuries later.[34] In the formative Latin, the association was only logical rather than verbal and sensual.

Roman worldview became more and more polarized during the generation of Caesar and Cicero, when political rhetoric flourished. Without abstract vocabularies, Latin speculative thinking took the form of political rhetoric that defined two most important concepts: idealized state institution and idealized ruler. Unlike Plato's dialogue that constructed an abstract and idealized state, Cicero portrayed a concrete mode for Roman constitution from its historical past.[35] He called this model *princeps*, a type of eminent politician who guided the Senate and state. He painted an ascetic ruler who was the representative on earth of the divine will, who was reinforced in his dedication to the service of the state by his disdain for human passion. Even then, Cicero's Latin solution, inspired by Plato's idea of law, had never been as abstract as that of the Greek philosophers. He based exposition of his law not on a philosophical logo, but rather on Roman legislative tradition, a guiding principle which was based in pontifical and sacral law.[36]

Latin writers rethought and reproduced the entire body of methods, ideas, and theories of Hellenistic philosophical schools in order to recompose it to serve the purpose of their own culture. Latin interpretation, selection, and emphasis were far away from what the Greek philosopher had originally intended. This deviation came about less as a choice than as a cultural and linguistic necessity. The Latin mind of the early republic simply could not imagine the abstract of the Greek manner. Their imagination was not as clear as that of the Greeks. They could not imagine a world separated from the real world, and then, later, reconnect it to reality through pure logic.

The Latin pre-imperial worldview hung somewhere in between the earth and the heaven because it did not have enough vocabulary to create either an abstract spirituality of the divine, nor God's visible earthly kingdom. This middle grounded place was comprised of politics and morality. Latin ideas tended to be highly moral and political, rather than philosophical.[37] While Hellenistic philosophy had uprooted itself from literature by creating a separate language and discipline of knowledge, Latin culture applied everything they had learned from Greek philosophers to real life. It brought Greek philosophy down to earth. By moralizing and synthesizing social issues, Romans set their goal as the pursuit of political and imperial power.[38]

After Latin had outgrown the need for oral gesture and became an independent literary culture, it began to shape its own view of the world in verbal imagery. However, unlike Plato, who enjoyed a rich repertoire of words and images, Cicero had to deal with a language of "the poverty of the ancestral vocabularies," and struggle for basic concepts while he was writing. Like Lucretius, Cicero decided not to use Greek words and took pain to build Latin vocabularies, especially abstract ones. He began a constant dogged lexical experimentation with Greek terms, which literally began to formulate an abstract division of Latin. This level of abstract language later became the fountain of Western speculative thinking.[39]

The size and depth of the accumulated repertoire of general and abstract language in Greek and Latin determined the basic characteristics of their worldviews. If vocabularies were pigments of black and white, and poetic vocabularies were colors and shades, Plato's vision was a depiction, a drawing on top of a canvas full of mosaic, while Cicero's vision was a picture painted on a blank canvas. Therefore, Latin vision was far more clear than that of Greek, but also much less colorful.

After Cicero, prose writing expanded Latin's capacity to create images of thought. Unlike Cicero, who pursued fluid intonation and verbal symmetry, perfect balance Sallust's style, *inconcinnitas,* frequently used antithesis, asymmetry, and variation. The balance between this restless dynamism and a vigorous movement to restrain produced an effect of austere, majestic *gravitas*, an image of deliberate thought. Its economic expression, *asyndeta*, and a more general omission of syntactic links, ellipses of auxiliary verbs (thought cut short), brusque interruptions, and concision condensed the discourse and intensified its effect.[40]

This ability to imitate and to coin abstract vocabularies in its cultural infancy made it possible for Latin to maintain a polarized worldview for a much longer period than Greek. Seeing the world as endless opposites created a gap in language, in the description of vision, as well as in logic. While vocabularies, invented in pairs, accumulated on both sides of the gap, the new words piled up and the gap became wider. A more rigid thinking evolved. The best example of this conceptual and ideological gap was the chasm between man and god.

Both Greek and Latin pagan beliefs emerged from a ritualistic system where gods were associated with natural and human attributes. The Romans imported the image of Greek gods through rituals, poetic narrative, and dramatic performance. However, since the Romans could not import the whole of the cultural idioms that accumulated in Greeks myth, epics, and theater, their worldview was not nearly as colorful as that of Greece. The eyes and ears of the Roman minds were not nearly as sensitive as those of Greeks.

By the time of Hellenistic Greek, there was no concept of God without concrete tributes. Like many inventions of anthropomorphic gods, the divine was originally defined and expressed as "other" or "outside" of the visible and human world. After centuries of re-imagination and accumulation of mythology and epic, Greek almost shook off their sense of otherness after they invented a whole kingdom of gods and goddesses, complete with highly humanized characteristics. Greek mythical imagery of gods and half-divine human heroes constantly filled the human-god gap, which was originally created by poetry. In Latin, the situation was opposite. Any concept of divine had to search out for tributes in the world to prove and convince the human mind. Since the divine searching mind was almost blind, the sense of "otherness" attached to god was deeper, because the boundary between man and god, and between visible and invisible, was more absolute.

The Latin ignorance and fear of the unknown world, as in any emerging culture, was as overwhelming as that in the archaic Greek. Cicero used phrases like *nisi quis noss deus respexerit* ("unless some god or other has a care for us," Att. 16.6), *qui illi di irati!* ("many the angry gods blast him!," Att. 77.1), and *sad haec deus aliquis gubernabit* ("but some god or other will guide these matter home," Att. 117.3) to address a mass of unspecified and unrelated gods and their world.[41]

Latin writers also made a connection that Greek writers never achieved before, with their association between gods and goddesses and abstract morality. They portrayed both gods and godly qualities in literary personalities, who acted and were seen on the same stage. For example, towards the beginning of *Bacchides,* when the young man, Pistoclerus, is going indoors for a party, the slave Lydus asks him who lives in there, and gets the reply "Love, Pleasure, Venus, Venusness, Joy, Joke, Fun, Chat, Lusciouskissitude" (*Amor, Voluptas, Venus, Venustas, Gaudium, Jocus, Ludus, Sermo, Suavisaviatio*, 115–6). In this long list of abstracts "Venus" of course stands out as a "real" goddess, but Plautus personifies her quality by juxtaposing her with the cognate word for "charm," *uenustas*, "the quality of being Venus-y." He may also be making us retrospectively wonder whether Amor is a noun or the name of the son of Venus.

This reclassification and re-association, originally out of linguistic necessity rather than ideological choice, had great influence upon the formation of Latin worldview.[42] Latin literature uprooted the Greek gods from their epic narration, cutting off all their divine family and the human infatuation with them, and utilized them as isolated divine persona. While Latin theater represented personified gods side by side with imagined (personified) concepts, the boundary between gods and men became blurred, and diminished into a juxtaposition of a noun (as ideal quality) and a name (of gods). Therefore, the boundary shifted and transformed into another kind: that between a presented (in abstract form) noun and non-presented noun. Idealized and abstract words, in Latin, became another type of divinity. As Plautus brilliantly asked: "Is Lusciouskissitude any god?" (*an deuss est ullus suauisauiatio?*)[43]

Through rewriting and re-imagining the Greek kingdom of gods and giving them a Roman choreography, Latin gradually reinvented its own gods. They were now described in words rather than depicted as images. During the time of early republic Rome, all the artists, painters and sculptors were Greek. It took Latin writers many centuries to be able to paint with words. They were not nearly as good at this as the Greeks, even as their language was being replaced by Italian, French, and Spanish. In early Latin poetry, gods and goddesses were non-speaking and unspeakable, and customarily describable as absent (or separated) from humanity. Without concrete words and images, like the Hebrew God, Latin gods were described as powerful and full of energy yet without a visible face. And unlike Hebrew, which left God in a conceptual hole, Romans, for political reasons, created and consolidated a wall of distinctive images from outside their readers. Latin had a vague concept of divinity because it could not see or touch the divine subject that it had heard and feared for so long. Latin struggled to know where this hole was located, and attempted to find it by making the surrounding visible.

Like the early Greeks, who created gods in the human image, the Romans began to search for their concrete divine by using a most familiar image of father. Father was associated with ruler, and united with god in the ambiguity of Virgil's words on Nisus and Euryalus. Nothing could be more concrete and familiar than a notion of God as father.[44] Father could easily apply to Augustus, Jupiter, and the generic "Roman father" of "patria potestas."

While the Greeks spent centuries trying to find or determine a hierarchy for their mass population of gods and goddesses, the Romans had very little interest in representing, organizing, and rearranging their gods.[45] If literature was the foundation of general and abstract worldview, Latin simply was not mature enough to be able to describe and imagine a world beyond the vision of the eyes.

As Latin speakers began to philosophize, they found that they had neither the abstract concepts to imagine something beyond vision, nor the concrete vocabularies to carry and apply logic to diversified phenomena. They were hindered by their language. The youth and simplicity of formative Latin could not perceive and elaborate logic in the Greek fashion. Although Roman intellectuals undertook a major effort to make Greek philosophical thought available in Latin, without an effective translation, Greek continued to hold a monopoly as the language of learning. An innovative Latin philosophical tradition did not emerge until many centuries later, when Latin had accumulated enough vocabulary and expression to comprehend and to reason.

During this time, Latin evolved as quickly as possible under the shadow of Greek learning. Due to the poverty of its vocabularies, Latin had no capacity to absorb and digest what was received from Greek.[46] For the next five hundred years, philosophy spoke Greek only and continued to flourish in Alexandria.[47] By now, Greek philosophy had grown and become even more diversified by the rewriting, rethinking and re-imagining of the Neoplatonists (philosophers who lived and wrote about six hundred years later than Plato). This time, the Neoplatonists paid very little attention to Plato's political theory. They took Platonic contradiction of forms and particulars into an elaborate metaphysical system, in which each level of the universe reflected and imitated the one above.[48] In other words, when Latin began to build its systematic worldview, Greek was no longer Plato's Greek. It was that of Plotinus.

However, Latin, with its clarity, became the language that successfully combined Christian theology and Greek philosophy, which had developed side by side and yet evolved independently in Greek. After centuries of rewriting and rethinking, Platonic ideas in Greek had many variations, each of which emphasized one of Plato's abstract concepts. For example, Clement's (c.150–213) redefined God as Reason presented the image of "logo" in the human mind. Origen defined God as the Holy Ghost who created in man the capacity to receive Christ and to love as Christ loved.[49] As the language of the Christian God in Greek had to fight the overly crowded repertories of images, abstract and concrete notions, and their associations, God himself got lost inside of mystic and ritual traditions.

The highly eclectic Christianity of Latin could only pick the most important aspects of Neoplatonic thought and let them serve rather than confuse God.[50] When the diversity of ideas reached the point where many concepts competed for authority, and none of them had the power override another, it opened the door for a new and less complex language to impose an arbitrary unity. Latin of the fourth and fifth century A.D. was much closer to the Greek of Plato's time than it was to Hellenistic philosophy. The degree of conceptual clarity in Latin, which was impossible for an old language like Greek, finally heralded the arrival of Christianity and philosophy in the West.

The writing of St. Augustine (A.D. 354–430) exercised a massive influence not only on the Western theological and literary imagination, but also on the development of medieval scholastic philosophy.[51] The reason was the scope of Latin literary repertories upon which Christian thinkers excised their eclectic elaboration, similar to those of the medieval Europe. This was the same reason behind the popularity of Greek philosophers during the high Renaissance, when European vernaculars developed to the point where they were about to outgrow Latin.

St. Augustine's dialogue was a reinvention and continuation of Plato's dialogue in two fundamental ways. Like Plato, he eludicated a dialogue with the self, where the objects of knowledge were the participants, establishing consciousness through speech. Unlike Plato's dialogue, which was merely a means to present and clarify meanings, Augustine's speech and spoken words were believed to be the only path that led to divine truth. Writing in Latin about the Christian God, Augustine modified Plato's theory by creating a new and higher layer of meaning ... the words of God. By creating a higher reality above Plato's abstract and concrete worlds, Augustine placed God on a third level, the pinnacle of the hierarchy. For Augustine, truth (not truth or "logo" in Greek) was not an innate part of man's mind; it had to be learned. This learning was initiated by prayer and reading the words of the scripture. This exercised man's memory and reminded him of the reality of God. By adding this new level of meaning, Augustine simultaneously reversed Platonic logic from reason to God and from knowledge to faith, and also established the authority of divine words overriding any secular pursuit of learning.

As he surrendered his early confidence in the moral and mental capacities of humanity, he finally closed the door which Plato had opened. He created a new picture of the world, as polarized as that of Plato's, but divided in different ways and called different names. Rather than the known and the unknown, the abstract and the concrete, it now consisted of God and the world that he created, complete with believers and non-believers.[52]

It took Latin more than ten centuries to evolve from the conceptual level of Plato to that of Aristotle because the intellectual gap in Greek was widened in the formative Latin. Latin, like any language in its infancy, could envision its world only in sketches of black and white. With its intention to imitate Greek, Latin could only admire rather than embrace all that was Greek, as its relatively shallow imagery and superficial understanding allowed. Latin required many centuries to cultivate its own pigment and to paint more colorful pictures.

Without a literary foundation, early Latin worldview was extremely rigid and highly analytic. It was based on a painstaking analysis of propositions and concepts, of sentences and terms, and was sprinkled with dogged attempts to clarify the relationships between language and world, words and things, signifier and signified. There was an intense interest in the philosophy of language as they hoped that grammatical rules would regulate and streamline thought. The study of logic remained abstract, focusing on analytical tools and procedures. One of the favorite occupations of philosophers was formulating logical rules and exploring how well both new and traditional rules performed in extreme conditions. Philosophers made an extraordinary effort to lay bare the structure, both of their own argumentation and of that of their opponents.

It was imagination of a different kind from that of Greek. Latin writers would compose strange sentences and set up strange thought experiments create hypotheses. While respectful towards the classics, they felt no fear in going beyond the ancients. While they would talk about the ancients as giants on whose shoulders they were sitting, they believed that from that position they could see farther than the great Greek thinkers. From an early date there was a consciousness that philosophy was a different enterprise than theology, even if the difference was not institutionalized until the late twelfth or early thirteenth century. At the same time, however, there was a broad acceptance of the use of philosophical method in theology.

In short, Latin created a simpler vision of the world by superficially translating Platonic philosophy and an abstract idea of the Christian God. Until the late Middle Ages, Latin, as a literary language, had not been ready to embrace plurality. With their highly polarized vision of black and white, too many colors and shades were unrecognizable. The Greek classics disappeared conveniently for centuries until they were rediscovered in the Renaissance.[53]

Islamic philosophical elaboration was rooted in Arabic, a highly developed language of lyrical poetics, yet primitive in its prose. For decades, scholars have been debating the impact of Greek philosophical tradition on Islamic philosophy. My analysis here is to investigate how Islam developed its abstract thinking through increasing the precision and efficiency of its language and how Arabic verbal and speculative elaboration was both similar to and different from those of other languages.[54]

Medieval Arabic scholars spent two centuries translating and compiling the ancient scientific writings of Sanskrit, Greek, and others, such as Syriac and Pahlavi of the Greek tradition. This translation, reinterpretation, and reproduction of mathematics, science, and philosophical literature substantially enriched the Arabic language. It borrowed and invented a wide scale of vocabularies and syntax patterns which had not existed in pre–Islamic Arabic. In the process, Arabic, which was a poetic essentially poor in linguistic means to classify and to subordinate one phrase to the next, learned to deliver an abstract discourse. Arabic became a written language sufficient to carry the whole range of pre–Modern culture.[55]

Like formative Latin, Arabic evolved and expanded its vision by translation from Greek tradition. However, as a much more mature language, Arabic translation and assimilation were much deeper than that of Latin. The Arabic reproduction of knowledge accomplished far more than the Latin type of imitation, which had only a few threads from the Greek heritage to begin its brand new tapestry. Arabic was already a well-woven tapestry, which could use the Greek threads to strengthen and highlight its native textile. The newly found collection of information about medicine, astrology, biology, mathematics, and chemistry inspired the highly verbalized mind of Arabs. They focused on distilling analogical processes and considering the theoretical implications underlying this information, rather than physically attempting to purify it, as did the European alchemists. While the West was interested in material science, numeral procedure, and practical knowledge, Arabic scholars were dedicated to philosophical reasoning and general principles underlying world diversity.[56]

In the pursuit of logic, Arabic had both advantage and disadvantage compared with Judaism and Christianity. This was due primarily to its inherent fluidity. Semitic was a language in which it was structurally impossible to absolutely separate abstract from concrete meanings. This made it difficult to draw solid boundaries between nouns and verbs, especially nouns, which were derived from the same roots. In Arabic, it was very easy to distill an abstract meaning out of a concrete word because every noun had a verbal root to begin with. In other words, Arabic could readily invent a whole universe made of abstract nouns, while it took Latin decades and even centuries to turn their verbs into action nouns. In the same way, the Arabic nouns were so easy to abstract from verbs and would just as easily slip back to their concrete verbal forms in the same swift and effortless manner. The meaning of most Arabic nouns could easily shift as soon as they were coined. They could move back and forth in complete fluidity.

The classical style of philosophical speculation was established in the conceptual clarity of the Greek tradition and later emphasized by Latin, and much later by the German speaking philosophers. This degree of clarity and rigidity was impossible for Arabic to achieve. Conversely, it was equally impossible for Latin and German expressive poetics to match the Arabic fluidity and eloquence. Hebrew, another language of similar structure, became crystallized, gelatinized, and highly abstract only within and after the time that it lost its oral form.

The fluidity of Arabic made the philosophers of classical Islam the best students and the heirs of Greek philosophy during the Middle Ages.[57] The best example to illustrate how Islamic philosophers created a philosophical language in an amazingly short period of time is to compare the writings of Affarabi (870–950) and those of Ibn Sina (Avicenna, d. 1037) and Ibn Rushd (Averroës, d. 1198).[58]

During the first a half of the tenth century, only two hundred years after the first prose was written, Arabic philosophers were trying to translate Greek, a philosophical language that had evolved over more than ten centuries of writing and polishing. Affarabi had great difficulty underpinning and nailing down his Arabic concepts into the Greek container. His imitating mutant, as primitive as that of Latin, was partway between philosophy, jurisprudence, and politics.[59] Exactly as the Romans had done to Greek philosophy during the early republic period, Affarabi mixed politics with philosophy, social salvation with divine realization, and law with cosmology. He turned Greek philosophical and metaphysical truth into a political truth. In his eyes, the cosmos, the city, and the soul shared the same structure provided by Allah.[60] Unlike Augustine, who tried to separate God's kingdom from the world, Affarabi incorporated jurisprudence and theology into political philosophy. In the loose concept of science in his *Enumeration of the science*, he repeatedly departed from his subject. Almost one-third of the book consisted of discussion of subject outside of science in the Greek sense.[63]

With the growth of Arabic prose writing, Affarabi's confusion was substantially reduced by the work of later classical Islamic thinkers such as Averroës and Ibn Rushd (1126–1198).[62] By the time of the early Middle Ages, Arabic became a reasonably functional philosophical language, complete with all of its conceptual and logical fluidity.

The conceptual stability, which was essential to philosophical elaboration, was fostered by repeated meditation on key concepts of language, its reinterpretation, and logic. The best example of this was the concept of speech (*kalam*). Apparently, there was no difference between the English *word* and the Arabic *word*; they both mean that which is spoken. In English, what was spoken and written was indistinctly called word. Different persons who made the speech would give word different meaning and distinct power and significance, but not the word itself. Thus, the word of God was written as Word because it was associated with God. In the English mind, until the twentieth century, word had to be believed in order to confirm a constant and absolute meaning. The Arabic word, *kalam,* was different from the English word in two fundamental ways. It was not just word; it was the spoken word. Unlike written words, spoken words were uttered once and immediately silenced. They were words that could not and were not expected to be repeated exactly the same way. Words changed every time they were spoken.

With this specific respect for the spoken word, *kalam,* when referring to the speech of God, logically became associated with silence rather than meaning, as it did in Western languages.[63] The meanings of spoken words were untraceable once spoken. It follows that the Western obsession with original meaning and textual genealogy, especially the genealogy of the divine words, would have never occurred to Arabic speakers. Like Christians, who debated about the meaning of the Bible, Muslims argued and fought for many centuries about what exactly the Qur'an was saying. However, no Muslim, regardless of his scholarship, could claim that he knew enough to know the meaning of God's words. In the Muslim mind, to worship God was not to worship his words, but rather, to remember, recite, and apply his words to corporal matters. Therefore, in the discussion of God, silence was the best.[64]

This basic and distinct understanding about language set the Arab philosopher apart from his Western counterparts. Muslim scholars began with the same dialogue that Plato started centuries before. They performed rhetoric (words of battle) to prove and disprove their ideas about logic and grammar. However, it did not take them long to realize that speech was only an instrument of argument. One speaker could not prove or disprove (right or wrong) another speaker. While each language was a conventional rather than natural system and each had its own interpretive perspective, the matter of speaking could not be judged under moral or even grammatical rules. It was about proper (or improper) speech, an esthetic rather than moral or political choice.[65]

In rethinking Greek logic, Islamic thinkers uprooted language from moral and philosophical judgment, and turned it into a procedure through which ideas were carried out, specified, and clarified. The best example of this movement could be seen in the way in which *kalam* evolved. After *kalam* became isolated as a topic about God, it stopped being used in any other matters. As it was redefined, *kalam* became a verbal structure that consisted of question and response, which belonged to a science of word game. In this specific sense, *kalam*, like the Word of God in English, became a fountainhead for the ongoing discourse of theology and literary interpretation. However, while English discourse was about the content (meaning) of the Word, Arabic discourse was about its form of presentation. For the Arabs, language was a means to attain truth rather than truth itself. For them, the logic that was described in Greek was Greek rather than universal.[66]

With this linguistic and logical fluidity, Islamic philosophy quickly deviated from the path of Greek philosophy, which was based on a constant classification of language and knowledge. The influence of classical tendencies, which was represented by Shi'it Muslims, who tried to bring some sense of order into Islamic law and philosophy during the 'Abbasid dynasty (9th century), died away.[67]

Arabic refused to be bound in Greek categories and moved on with its rapid diversification and juxtaposition. This was the reason why the only sustained conceptual gap in Islamic thinking was religious and ethical rather than legal.[68]

Although the classical tendency of Islam was short lived, it substantially rationalized Arabic culture and improved its expressive efficiency. By translating and rethinking Greek philosophy into Arabic, Islam enabled itself to re-categorize and organize its thinking.[69] The Islamic classicism was cut short by the bloom of Arabic literature from the ninth to the middle of the tenth century. This added color to the Islamic worldview.

The language of the Christian God in formative English was much richer than that of early Latin, yet not as colorful as that of Greek. By the time that England converted to Christianity, Latin had accumulated a substantial repertory of images, motifs, and expressions of Christian imagination. As English was just an infant emerging from its oral form, its version of Christianity was transplanted through a translation from Latin antiquity that persisted until the sixteenth century.

Old English began to translate Latin philosophical text during the late ninth century.[70] Alfred the King of Wessex's translation of Boethius was a reinterpretation, in the light of his experience and obligations as a medieval Christian king. It reflected his own personal quest for an answer to the problems of a world in which evil and sin often seemed to have the upper hand. Even in the central discussions of Fate, Fortune, Freewill and Providence, major differences merged between the attitudes. While Alfred shared Boethius' acceptance of Fate as the agent of God, he emphasized a personal God, a Christian God speaking his language.[71]

English worldview, like that of Latin, was created in the same way through rewriting and rethinking classical texts by translation. Both Latin and English transplanted worldview presented by borrowed languages and cultivated their own spiritual authority by describing borrowed ideas in their native languages. Latin established its hegemony of the Christian God away from anthropomorphic and ritualistic deities (in Hebrew and Greek). English, on the other hand, had classical texts in two different languages, each of which inspired a Renaissance at each end of the Middle Ages. The first created a Christian worldview while the second cultivated a new God; a humanity that separated his world between the idealized and the real.

Like the Roman Empire, the British Empire began with very little written history and only a primitive sense of identity cultivated in their tribal society. However, English culture was created by a real and live (not artificial like Latin) oral tradition, which constantly produced original voice. This living voice became a dynamic engine which drove the formation of English culture and created its unique worldview.

English radicalized the worldview that it inherited from Latin (which advertised unity of the Christian God) by widening the gap between man and God. It did not begin by rejecting the Christian God, but rather by changing the *form* of God's words. As the Christian God spoke English, his words became the same words that one used in everyday conversation, heard on street corners, watched in drama, and prayed in the church. During the formative years of the English language, there were no abstract concepts. (For centuries the learned language was Latin. Abstract language in English had not been developed until the late seventeenth century.) God was perceived as high in heaven but as a concrete (if not real) "person," rather than some undefinable and invisible entity. Words of God were concrete, as seen and written in the Bible, read in the church, and taught in school.

The Christian hegemony in sixteenth and seventeenth century England spoke Latin. The orthodox church stressed unity and universality. One nation required one church. The body politic and the body of Christ were to be coterminous, integral, and entire. One reformist tract, called *the Fortresse of Fathers, Ernestlie Defending the Puritie of Religion* (1566), emphatically proclaimed the centrality of church. "There is one word, one scripture, one Baptism, and one death of Christ, one Father, one Religion, and one Charitie, one sacrament of thankes giuing, one laing onne of handes, and one discipline, and one consent of the Ministers ... to concluded, all things that are ordained, to the buylding or profitt of the Chirch, we must haue all those as one thinge." Throughout the subsequent century, this call to unity was taken up by writers of strikingly diverse ecclesiastical perspectives. While those arguing for episcopacy and those advocating presbyterianism, for example, may have differed in their conception of church government, there was no question that there could be only one church.[72] Lurking behind the call for religious unity, there was a multiplication and confusion of religious identity which destabilized systems of order and confounded traditional social and ecclesiastical categories.[73]

The first two English translations of the whole of Ovid's *Metamorphoses*—Arthur Golding's (1567) and George Sandy's (1632)—were landmarks of English perceptions of Ovid. The English imitation of this Latin masterpiece illustrated the similarity in which Latin and English created their worldview under the supervision of a dominant religion. The way in which Nietzsche described the Romans' sense of history and justified self-assertion is accurately used as applied to English: "They did not know the delights of the historical sense; what was past and alien was an embarrassment for them; and being Romans, they saw it as an incentive for a Roman conquest. Indeed, translation was a form of conquest. Not only did one omit that was historical; one also added allusions to the present and, above all, struck out the name of the poet and replaced it with one's own — not with any sense of theft but with the very best conscience of the Imperium Romanum."[74]

The confidence and self-assertion that Nietzsche finds in Roman imitation and translation usurps the past and uses it to bolster the present. In English poetry of the Renaissance period, elements of such a self-promoting form of writing are apparent, but there are also signs of a less dominant culture grappling with a literature that still held the high ground. It is highly relevant to this study that England's imitation is of Rome, which provides a daunting example, having come to represent not only how to learn from others, but also how to stand ruthlessly aloof.[75] Quickly, English rebelled and got rid of "barbarious tongues" and began to build it's "kingdom of its own language," as Spenser long wished.[76] Compared with Latin, English had great advantage. Its voice had been carried by Old and Middle English for centuries. Insisting upon and defending English voice in its rhyme, English writers forged their own identity.[77]

It was a long struggle. A language needed a model to imitate for its growth and yet it was unwilling to be overrun by it. Rewriting and rethinking of the Latin viewpoint began with an inclusion of fragmented Latin text with English translation.

The English translation of *Ovid* initiated a translation that amplified messages with English morality.[78] There were 192 lines of text and 896 lines of moral statement. The mortal attitude and authority were amplified through its marginal notes, which commanded: "Marke thys," "Prid marreth all" and "No man oughte to trust in his owne strength."[79]

By the time that Golding's translation was published (1567), Ovid's text had separated from interpretation, and was recognized as preface and epistle.[82] This subtle change did not signal a radical change of worldview, but rather a formal separation between vision of the past and that of the current. This separation initiated a rift of Latin hegemony based on ideas and literature, which provided the possibility of perception for English. Readers could now search and perceive the Latin classics according to their own need.

The literary repertory, a collection of accumulating verbal images, patterns of juxtaposition, and extensive similes crafted during centuries of poetic consideration, was a multi-colored pigment for the imagination. This colorful collection made a fundamental difference in the evolution of the speculate thinking of each culture. During the enlightenment, this repertory of colors was pushed aside, only to be picked up again after the culture had acquired a verbal perspective where images were organized, sorted out, meditated, and re-imagined in a systematic way. This explained the quick transition of Greek, Arabic, and Russian literature from enlightenment to Romanticism, where rich colors and shadings were rediscovered and re-imagined. This also explained why it took centuries rather than decades for Latin and English to cultivate a vision of colors and shades. Without a pre-existing repertory of colors, these languages had to begin from scratch in accumulating them in their literature ... one color, one image, one word, one sentence, one story, and one idea at a time.

The enlightenment, representing one stage of speculative thinking, was characterized by the verbalizing of visual images, and their mediation and organization. For the first time, each culture became self-conscious about its own language, including its vocabulary, its grammar, and its stylistic and logical possibilities. This process built the foundation of classification and separation between speculate and practical reasoning.[81]

The writing of Plotinus (A.D. 204–270) — the first Neoplatonist, who lived nearly 600 years after Plato — represented the near end of Platonic reasoning in a mature literary language. The Neoplatonists treated Plato's thought as a unity and sought to interpret his works as a coherent whole. Their reinterpretation and rewriting blurred the contradictions between different dialogues.[82] By the third century, after hundreds of years of imagining and re-imagining, writing and rewriting, the Platonic gap between concrete and abstract reasoning had been substantially narrowed and nearly filled up by Greek literary accumulation. This produced endless verbal distinctions and variations to overlap and overflow original conceptual boundaries. (Similar philosophical transformation driven by literary imagination can be observed in ancient Chinese and Sanskrit histories as well.) As a result, abstract speculation began to lose the rigid edge which barricaded itself from other types of expression and thinking. Its worldview began to penetrate into literature and the arts. Greek worldview became more colorful and more personalized.

However, in a multi-lingual environment, where abstract speculation was transplanted rather than home-grown, the gap between abstract and concrete, between philosophy and literature, grew wider. The philosophies of early Latin, English, Arabic, and Russian were philosophy of translation. Describing, thinking, and reasoning in a foreign language were like transplanting an alien organ into a different body which needed time to accept it. It actually widened instead of filled up the gap between abstract and concrete expression ... a reverse process compared to that of Greek. Like the alien organ, it either took over the host language, or was taken over by it, one or the other.

Latin translated an entire stock of philosophical vocabularies into a culture lacking a well-developed literary language. With a literary tradition that was as shallow as the abstract language itself, the Latin worldview was the most rigid and separated from everyday language. Christianity in Latin West, which was articulated in a language based on a quick and shallow marriage of Greek philosophy and pagan ritual devotion, failed to transform into a personal and spiritual force, as did its Eastern counterpart. However, due to its uncompromising clarity and airtight discipline, Romans created the most extensive and powerful state institutions.

Abstract vocabularies which emerged from every formative language often led to a metaphysical tendency in ideas. Ancient Greek, Latin, Middle English, and Arabic shared the same process in which an abstract language emerged and separated from concrete words. This evolution defined and specified meaning as well as thinking. This conceptual polarization turned these cultures into a sphere of moralization. However, the road to abstraction was different for each culture and language, and so was the vision.

The language change from Latin to English represented a rebirth of Greek philosophy in Western Europe. Greek philosophers of the third century had reinterpreted Plato within a new linguistic spectrum as Greek literary language had outgrown abstract philosophy. English and the Western vernaculars rethought and reimagined Plato's original ideas in much younger languages, which had sharper boundaries, and cultivated more clear yet less flexible reasoning. This linguistic reorientation made it possible to widen the gap that the Greek philosophers had initiated.

Philosophy did not stand still between the times of Plato and Aristotle because Greek as a literary and philosophical language kept evolving. The boundaries previously established by Plato became blurred and eventually flattened out. In the third and second centuries B.C., new schools of philosophy arose ... the Hellenistic schools of Stoicism, Epicureanism and Skepticism. By the first century B.C., Plato, Aristotle and the Hellenistic schools all had their adherents. During this period philosophers of different schools were casually borrowing ideas from one another. In the subsequent centuries, Stoicism and Platonism became the dominant philosophies. The works of Plotinus marked a crossroad for philosophy because they developed a complex metaphysical system dependent on the One as its ultimate principle. Plotinus' One was envisaged as the transcendent source of all beings and represented a more lofty supreme principle than any of those postulated by previous philosophers. Plotinus, however, saw himself as an interpreter of Plato, and his successors likewise regarded themselves just as Platonists. Greek Enlightenment of the fifth century centered on a close, meticulous observation of nature, followed by rational analysis and deduction from the observed phenomena.[83]

Just like a child, new civilizations saw a simple, banal, polarized world of black and white. In a brand new language, vocabularies were accumulated first by pairing opposite words: the sky and the earth, moon and sun, ocean and land, mother and father, life and death, and male and female. The initial purpose was to describe a distinction. The relationship between the two poles was perceived as opposite and absolutely exclusive. This limitation of vocabulary created an adversarial vision which did not allow for any shading.

This vision of black and white was also the worldview that revived older cultures. Established societies had, over time, shaded and then colored their vision. Extreme positions were considered as undesirable. The outline of ideas and their expressions became blurred. The babble created by this diversity of thought overwhelmed creativity. Only the artists, writers and scholars dared to present new ideas and expression. And most of these were considered to be outside general acceptance, and thus ignored.

In order to introduce change, the society needed a cultural shock. It needed to clarify its vision and classify the overlapping vocabularies in order to reorganize and reinitiate thinking. This was accomplished by the injection of a new ideology and a language from another part of the world. The ensuing polarization motivated a general discussion that invigorated the collective to consider all sorts of new thought ... internally as well as from the outside.

The moralization and polarization of worldview are a phenomenon of both young and revived cultures. For the cultures of a brand new language, whether it be the young, with its new language, or the old culture aggressively embracing an external language, rigid polarization is the only describable, imaginable, and finally, the only thinkable course of action. Just as there is only one God, as there is only one sun, there is one universal social system. In this context, the world is always divided between godliness/ungodliness, good/evil, right/wrong, light/dark, or socialism/capitalism.

The Greeks had become aware of their own identity as separate from that of the Orient when they succeeded in repelling the attacks of the Persian Empire. Soon after this, during the crusades, the concept and the term "Orient" actually did enter the language of the West.[84]

In the fifth century, Athens invented a means of identity-construction which established the concepts of "Greekness" and "barbarians." This process began as the Athenians mythologized their victories over the Persians at Marathon and Salamis, partly in order to justify their imperial strategy in the Aegean Sea (purportedly a defense force against Persia).[85] Athens had much at stake in representing Greece as a unified territory, since it was attempting to engineer for itself a position as Panhellenic leader.

Any generalization about the knowledge of Greek texts in medieval England is hard to make. However, it would appear that during the first half of this period, any acquaintance with the works of Plato was at least second or even third hand information. It was through the writings of authors such as Macrobius, Martianus Capella, Augustine, Boethius and John Scotus Eriugena, and through Latin and Old English texts drawing on one another, that Plato's ideas were expressed. The most important contribution to the English vernacular was provided by the late ninth century reworking of Boethius' *De Consolatione Philosophiae,* by Alfred, King of Wessex. Platonic or Neoplatonic ideas are also found in Alfred's *Soliloquies,* by way of Augustine and in a few Old English homilies.[86]

Middle English was a language that grew under the shadow of Latin literature and Christian theology. Unlike a language that grew naturally from concrete visual and sensual images, English vocabularies multiplied along the lines of theological logic conceptualized in Latin. Every word came with a twin, its opposite. After English became the first language, its conceptual structure, already established, had accumulated and piled up various logic gaps such as God/human and religious/secular ... everything was allegorical. Even a detail of posture could carry a metaphorical implication.

English eventually broke away from its Latin prison when it discovered theater.[87] It extended its resource of language from a single book (Bible) to real life. It meant that, for the first time, English found a repertory of expression, a language of real life. Beginning at the end of the fifteenth century, drama conveyed meaning through an apparently free-standing, self-contained imitation of life. Drama also provided a stage where a fine texture of emotions could be gestured and expressed. This marked the beginning of literature, as it was still "alive."

Plato never contrasted the two worlds as inner and outer, but Plotinus clearly identified the spiritual world with the inner world: "We are each of us the intelligible world." This phrase illustrated one of his favorite metaphors for the relationship between the One, and all other reality — that of a circle, with the One as the center and the rest of reality reaching out to the circumference. To seek the One was to seek within the circle. Christian thinkers took this emphasis and became an inward religion as opposed to outward display. The idea that the higher world was the inner world became axiomatic for Augustine. For him, God was "*interior intimo meo et superior summo meo* (more inward than my inmost self and higher than the highest part of my being)."[88] The beginning of the search for God was to return within: *in te ipsum redi* (return into yourself).[89]

Equally important as this injunction to inwardness was the exploration of man's inner world. Here, Augustine's influence was unparalleled. The idea that man, or more precisely the human soul, was created in the image of God made the human mind the fulcrum on which the doctrine of the two worlds balanced. The human mind was no longer simply poised between two worlds, it was a world of its own, reflecting in itself the divinity. The word Augustine turned to for this inner world (perhaps hampered by the limitations of Latin which has no word as evocative as the Greek nouns) was *memoria*. More than memory, it recalled the Platonic doctrine of "anamnesis," although by a transposition, in which nothing of the soul's pre-existence remained.

This notion of man's inwardness reflecting the divine took a curious twist in the West during the thirteenth century. The twelfth century had seen an enormous growth in the influence of St. Augustine, but it also saw the introduction of a significant influence of the writing of Denys the Areopagite. Denys had already been translated from Latin in the ninth century, once incomprehensibly by Hilduin.

English transformed Latin worldview by changing its images and metaphors. Poetry and dramatic expression empowered formative English and made it mutable enough to bridge the gap between abstraction and concrete. It could now create an otherworldly sphere and lead the real to the ideal. It was a spiritual power that had occurred in Greek once, and then been exhausted. Latin had attempted it, but never managed to establish this quality through Christianity. The Romans failed to produce enough variations to lead every believer to embrace their God. English imagination was the real engine driving this island nation, which was starving by material limitation and spiritual isolation (after the split with the Catholic world) into becoming a world empire.

It all began with an empire in the mind as described by words, gestures, and images. Like the ancient Greek and Latin, English abstract imagination coincided with the emergence of its prose writing. Unlike Plato's Greek, English abstract vocabularies were borrowed from Latin rather than homegrown. During the middle of the sixteenth century, when Thomas More wrote *Utopia*, English had not yet developed sufficiently to allow for many stylistic effects, or even much precision of meanings. More's writing, in English, seldom reached the same literary highs as did his Latin writing.[90]

It took English more than two centuries to create its abstract world; about half of the time that it took the Greeks. While Greeks had to distill and mold their abstract concepts from concrete narrative, poetry, and dramatic dialogue, English could just pick up and translate the Latin and Greek concepts which had been cultivated and tested by articulation for centuries. However, seeing the world through translation and imitation left a considerable mark on the English worldview, especially during and after the Enlightenment.

In its formative years, English vision was an extremely rigid world of black and white. As the abstract concepts of Latin and Greek were translated into English, they were words taken out of literary context, naturally connected to foreign concrete imageries, story lines, and vivid characters. Until English, as the host language, produced enough expressions to fill this gap, the world became a picture without color and shading, a world without a place (uprooted from its geography), as well as a world that could be anywhere. The formation of these abstract worldviews, which were less an intention of a person, a nation, or a language than an accident in cultural history, generated enormous power to transcend geographical and cultural boundaries.

This primitive picture, painted by various English writers of the sixteenth, seventeenth, and eighteenth centuries, germinated and cultivated two powerful empires — Great Britain and America. The cultural repertories (or pigments) from which each country painted its worldview determined the different path that they chose while constructing their nation and their global policies.

It was not a coincidence that Renaissance England produced Shakespeare and colonized America.[91] During the sixteenth century, the English language began to outgrow its Latin shadow and become its own. When theater, music, and poetry produced vivid imagery and powerful expressions, England evolved into an independent cultural identity, rather than merely a piece of geography. With a living oral tradition and an emerging written literature, Englishmen were ready to rethink their world. This process of rethinking, triggered by literary reorientation during the Renaissance, built the foundation and the key concepts and ideas on which the British Empire was established.

Unlike Latin and later, Spanish and Russian, English did not build its empire on the English crown. Although the royal courts of Britain played an important role in its colonial history, the main idea upon which the British Empire was formulated was not imperial, in the sense of kingdom and its king and queen. It was driven by a much newer, grander, and abstract concept, a highly impersonal idea of law, order, and shared interests ... commonwealth. This new vision, combined with its tradition of common law, survived and outlived English courts and even the Christian God as a new hegemony separate from the institution of religion.

England began the same way as the Romans, Spanish, and later, the Russians, by establishing a cult for the crown. However, at the beginning, England was ruled by a very highly depreciated or even embarrassed queen, who was praised only in very marginal poetry, compared to the more intimidating classics of the Italian, French, and Spanish. This was almost the same situation that Romans experienced as they compared themselves with the grand Greek cultural heritage. England, at the time, was known to be "the desolate isle of pitiful," a kingdom of "wildness or a desert, because the philosophers and wise men did not pass upon it" or passed and decided to leave because of the climate.[92] It had not occurred to the world that the new and the most powerful empires always emerged form the "uncultured" or "low cultured" peripheral.

Englishmen, like the Romans, needed a symbol that represented their island as a nation under the blessing of God. The Romans, who simply converted to an existing universal God, needed only to build a connection between themselves and the Christian God. During the sixteenth century, the Christian God, at least the one that Englishmen worshiped, had built his central kingdom (its institutional hierarchy) somewhere else. The language of God changed as well. So did the connection between the God and his earthly kingdom because Dante, who magically built a monumental ladder between Heaven, earth, and hell, did not speak English. In England, the tower, which was supposed to bridge the two worlds, fell into pieces after the English language overwhelmed Latin.

During the Renaissance, God remained in the English mind because he had been there for centuries. He was, and had been, the center of their imagination, and their verbal and mental universe. Everything that Englishmen knew and comprehended about life and death came from him and under his name. However, the tower to heaven, in Medieval England, was a shaky one. It lacked the consistency of a unified structure that a single language could provide. It was already falling apart when the Roman church built a barrier between its versions of God's Words, and English words of God. In order to keep God alive in their minds, and keep their world in understandable and reasonable terms, Englishmen needed to make their God speak English. And they did so through Protestant reformation.

Protestant reformation re-described (or re-imagined and recreated) a Christian God in English terms.[93] Making God speak English opened a dialogue between the Christian God and his English believers. To the early reformers, the Bible was a central part of Christianity, hidden from the people in the occult language of the Church — Latin. For the sake of their souls and salvation, Englishmen needed a Bible in their own language. So, in the latter part of the fourteenth century, John Wyclif and his followers, the Lollards, translated the Bible from the Latin Vulgate.[94]

The translation of the English Bible was a battle of languages. It began with a highly literal version, which was primarily a guide to the Latin Bible.

It was a pile of English vocabularies pasted together in Latin word order.[95] To provide a truthful and clear rendering of the meaning of original Latin, the quality of English was often sacrificed. It was literally Romanized and imposed a spiritual reading on the text. It was not a piece of literature that could soar in the English mind.

The translators of the English Bible would have been horrified to find their work acclaimed as literature. God's Words were truth. Compared with God's Words, man's words were lies.[96] Literature belonged to man, not God! Wyclif and his later followers, and Tyndale and Coverdale, were all educated as Catholics and did not necessarily set out to be enemies of the Roman Church. They just had different ideas about the source of divine truth. They did not agree with the church, which monopolized the words of God by controlling interpretations that built a barrier between their God and believers. They chose not to challenge the established hierarchy of the words of God, knowledge about divine meanings, and the tower of words that was possessed by (God's institution) the church.

However, God's words were a source of power. Even those that were imagined and composed by the human mind had an impersonal power over believers. To search the original words of God was simply to discredit the established authority and to deconstruct the tower of words built, possessed, and defended by the church.[97] Regardless of its apparent innocence, the translation of the Bible inevitably sought and subsequently invented an alternative power base. To separate God's Words from the interpretations, the Roman church produced and accumulated rituals, festivals, and ceremonies. The English Bible constructed the foundation of another tower of words to reach God ... the English tower.

God's words in English were different. Compared to those of Latin, they were more open and more personal.[98] They gave definite priority to feeling rather than allegorical meanings. The freedom to feel the Words of God, and to understand the spirit, rather than a well defined and controlled interpretive meaning, opened the door for communication between men and God. It enlightened biblical interpretation and transformed the focus of bible study from the technically literal to the emphatically simple. It stripped Christian worship of its festivals, rituals, and ceremonies and cut back to the bone the Words of God.[99]

The English Reformation was a cultural revolution, as well as a religious and political movement. Another important, although unintended, consequence of the English Reformation was that it established a higher level of language that overrode every single English word, oral and written. It was the language of Scripture and of the divine. When God began to speak English, Roman authority declined. As the early Reformation resistance theorem of

Romans 13:1 stated, there is no power but of God and the power that exists everywhere is ordained by God. Unless you were the pope, no one had the temporal jurisdiction over the English church. James I and his religious radicals translated the Bible to authorize their independence from centralized religious authority. When the Christian God spoke English, the world changed in the eyes of Englishmen.

The English world split into two parts. Divine and secular were increasingly described by two imaginative sub-languages of concrete and abstract. Like the ancient Greek, both of these sub-languages emerged from poetry and went their separate ways as literature evolved more mature and diversified styles. The best illustration of this process was the emergence and evolution of the English concept of nationhood. It began with Renaissance poetry. In the English epic poems of the sixteenth and seventeenth centuries, the English queen was depicted as divine.[100] Imagining the state as if it were a person, their world was divided into its divine and secular parts. This separation was reflected first in the poetry that described English monarchs. A good example is Spenser's *Faerie Queene,* in form as well as in content.[101] This attempt to suggest the divinity of the queen was unsuccessful.

The divinization of English rulers represented a period or stepping stone on which the English culture of the Renaissance formulated a language and template to recognize and define itself. It was an invention that personalized England, which had just emerged as a nation. English monarchs, like the Roman emperors, tended to be too human and too common.[102] The royal cult had never been as successful as that in Prussia or Russia. However, as for literary presentation, it served its purpose in history. It did succeed in creating a symbol, a very English symbol which hung and is still hanging between human and divine, common and royal.

English rulers were portrayed in another kind of poetry ... drama. They were depicted in an entirely different light. They were human as opposite to divine. Shakespeare imagined and showed Henry V on the stage as an "amiable monster," "an imperfect man," or "the man placed at a disadvantage in the sphere of personal relations." He appeared to be as human and full of flaws on the stage as the audience.[103] Like in ancient Greek, as the various royal images, divine and secular, were meditated by prose writing, they distilled from their concrete images, dialogues, and gestures. They became abstract ideas about the English nation and its ruler. They described the desirable virtues of the prospective rulers. Virtue included not only the philosophical heights of the governor, but also the local details of how a future ruler should be nurtured, reared, and educated. They insisted that virtue was the first desirable characteristic for the king. They insisted upon the connection between the regimentation of the ruler's body and of his mind. Dancing, for instance, was no mere exercise in deportment and courtship, but a metaphysical experience that provided both recreation and meditation of virtue.[104] It was a highly idealized and abstract way to approach the politics of ruling. It did not mention the art of manipulation and displaying power, which were very common in the same type of writing in the Italian Renaissance.

The religious identity of the nation served to mediate its transformation into the abstract form of the modern nation, an entity independent of particular institutional form. The pregnant language of Spenser and Shakespeare suggested many points of elucidation and jointed similitudes.[105] The new scripture confounded the distinctions between political and religious oppositions. The elaboration of a community, independent of institutional form, could also be traced to the familiar medieval notion of the monarch's two bodies, with its abstraction of the body politic from the body natural. Its notion of a policy independent of the frailties of a particular governor provided an Elizabethan incarnation — the difference between the corporation and its local form. Its embodiment was given an added force, and a symbolic marker, in the monarch's gender.[106] The old Latin division always could still separate or unite. The English choice of the former was determined by its re-rooting in the Hebrew and Greek Bible.

This highly moral tone came from the language of Christianity. The English ideal of nation and good government (although secular in nature) was conceptualized within the words of God. It carried the same flavor as the homological nature of the world. God's work was viewed as coherent, both thematically and structurally — the way in which the household, for instance, resembled the state, and the father, the king.[107] It was a very abstract and yet pregnant language of words such as virtue, nature, body, and soul.

With these newly deregulated and dis-institutionalized divine words, the language of God could initiate chaos. Without a religious hierarchy, verbal or institutional, the language of God became too familiar, frequent, and mutable. It was taken by gentlemen to be circulated from the mouths of babes and barbers to maintain its binding power.[108] The best way to control the common space of meaning was to depersonalize the language and to make it abstract and inaccessible to the common speaker: the law is king.[109] The best way to establish a recognizable notion of nationhood was to personalize the language and place God on one's side.

The British Empire was established on a concept of commonwealth which was derived from a fairly staid image of corporate welfare. It recognized a shared public opinion of universal welfare, potentially contradictory to order, and regulated the degree of distinction. Remote as to actual social possibility, this connotation was, not surprisingly, one that contemporary political theorists wished to rule out. They insisted that commonwealth did not mean that all the wealth should be common, but rather the whole wealth, wit, power, and goodness of every particular person must be conferred and reduced to the common good. This abstract concept of common good created a new collective ideal that was concrete (or common) enough to be understood by all.

By the end of the nineteenth century, imperialist ideology became a part of the language of patriotism. The queen and her empire had become synonymous. For the first time, both English popular and high cultures found their common ground marching to the music of Elgar and the patriotic song of the musical hall.[110] A new language had cultivated a new type of cult for hero worship, a collective hero, the nation. Let's learn to think imperially! Let's think grand and high of ourselves by putting every other European state down, the Englishmen told themselves.

While the imperial rhetoric soared to its highest point, the business of the British Empire became increasingly undermined by deep feelings of insecurity and uncertainty. British pre-eminence in the world had seriously declined. The views of Great Britain on European issues began to account for little. Bismarck's Germany now dominated the continent. America's shadow was stretching across the Atlantic, and Russia was advancing in the Balkans, central Asia and the Far East.

The connection between God and Great Britain was found in the mission that the Empire was supposed to carry. It was Britain's divine destiny to carry light and civilization into dark places of the world, to touch the mind of Asia and of Africa with the ethical ideas of Europe, and offer peace and security which millions would otherwise never know.[111]

God had endowed the British race with a worldwide Empire, an Empire transcending all imperial systems that the world had known.... Fear of God had made England great. Everyone English should cultivate a sense of mission to humanity.[112] The British Empire had been simply blessed by Providence. Her eminence, her strength, her prosperity, her intelligence, her moral and religious advantages, made her, particularly, obey the laws of God who had given this destiny to them. The Empire was chosen to carry civilization, humanity, peace, good government, and knowledge of the true God to the furthest corner of the earth. This empire, commissioned by God, this advocate of heaven on earth, was going to be built, not by saints or angels, but by the work of men's hands ... British hands. With God's pure and splendid purpose, English blood, brains, tears, and sweat would erect this edifice of the divine.[113]

> To complete this divine vision, the English even made themselves brave enough to face their own fears, the fear of being weak and unadventurous, and the fear of facing hell. To keep empire, the poet preaches: "To enlarge your hell; preserve it in repair; only a splendid hell keeps heaven fair! To secure your birthright, face to fate, join the warfare of the times, climb into heaven at, one and stay there!"[114]

English had cultivated its own language and nationhood before its global expansion; America used the reverse process. Americans built their nation first and formulated their nationhood while they went through global expansion. The first step that America had to take was to invent its own culture and language, language distinct from that of British English.

As a cultural infant born with a mother tongue, America inherited more than a tongue. It was a whole package of words, ideas, rhetoric, and viewpoints, the totality of what English had cultivated and established for the past thousand years.

The first generation of Americans was culturally English. Captain John Smith, William Bradford, John Winthrop, Roger Williams, Anne Bradstreet, Michael Wigglesworth, Edward Taylor, and Samuel Sewall spent their formative years in England and arrived in the New World during their early middle ages. They spoke, wrote, and thought like any Englishman who read *Paradise Lost* and *The Pilgrim's Progress*. Most of all, they did not call themselves Americans. That name was for the aboriginals.[115] Naturally, they created their colonial world as an idealized image of English society and culture. The imitation of English forms, values, and institutions created the beginning of this new and unstable society.[116]

However, the imported English culture that the first generation of immigrants brought from the homeland could only last as long as they lived. The Englishness firmly implanted in their souls would be lost when their time came. The culture of their children had to be determined by what they saw, heard, and read in the new country, English or otherwise. The second generation would begin formulating a unique self-image as an independent nation.

Much like its natural environment, early American culture was void of European refinement. The Bible was the only important book of the seventeenth century America. Its meaning was rigidly defined by Calvinism, and its interpretation was controlled by the Calvinist and Puritan Protestant church.[117]

Although English values and ideas provided a place to start and a series of reference points for the colonies, the American experience began with a different and wild land separated by geography from the rest of the world — an island. The new Americans had subjected themselves to all the physical and emotional agony of resettlement because they wanted a different kind of life. They cherished their freedom from the establishment and freedom to make their own way. It took them centuries to realize this goal. The first generation of American Calvinist and Puritan Protestants left England to escape from religious intolerance and persecution. They were refugees from their own country and culture. This anti-establishment attitude carried them in a direction that was opposite from England.

Contrary to England, which became more tolerant after the civil war, Americans became more single-minded in what they believed and how they pursued it. They were very focused on their interpretation of the Bible and their view of the world.[118] This characteristic had little to do with the personal choice of the founding fathers of America and their specific spectrum of English, on which their religious beliefs were based.

American Puritans were not regular Protestants. They were the most militant section, the nonconformists. Because of their radical interpretation of Christianity, they were discriminated against and persecuted in England. They left their homes in "the best island in the universe" (in the words of Cotton Mather) and began a new life in a dark primeval forest, establishing their frontier 3000 miles across the turbulent Atlantic. Just like the ancient Jews of millenniums ago, they came to America singing the praises of the Lord, who helped them to escape religious tyranny. America was their "promised land."[119]

"A holy commonwealth" was the style of government that the seventeenth century Puritans wanted. It was a holy commonwealth governed by God and his representatives, the church. Puritan clergy were men of vigorous intellect, deeply learned in theology, Hebrew and Greek. With church and state being closely united, the clergy guided the magistrates. Together they determined that the welfare of their Christian society was not to be compromised. If they had sacrificed so much to come to America, they chose to keep faith and create a life of their own.

Calvinist and Puritan Protestants were passive believers. Like many passive religions or passive phases or passive branches of other religions, they inherited rigid doctrine and uptight morals. As they saw mankind as totally dependent on God's will, they had to unconditionally wait and be prepared to be elected to receive grace, because there was nothing else that they could do to achieve salvation.[120]

This level of devotion was cultivated by translating ancient Hebrew and Greek to English, where it became much more rigid than that of the original texts. The words of God in ancient Hebrew and Greek, uprooted from their entire literary canons of interpretation and reinterpretation, often became softened and pluralized in their meanings. They were then transplanted into a formative language, which had very poor shade and very few connotations. Through translation into the foster language, the words lost their verbal tapestry, connection, and fluidity. They had lost their verbal soil that allowed them to flourish and diversify, and they were now seeded in a less fertile soil. Since the words of the Bible, which were spoken through the church, were perceived as the voice of Christ himself, they had to rely on spoken words for reference, interpretation, and speculation. As a result, the good preacher became a "living, breathing Bible."[121] This living breathing Bible, therefore, reduced the Christian tradition, which had evolved during centuries of literary elaboration, into an oral Bible. The oral Bible lost its distinctive layers and shades of literary connotations. The Christian God was now speaking American English through the mouths of its ministers to specify distinct moral conducts.

Without a canon of interpretive literature, God's words changed hands, from literary to non-literary meanings, and from the hands of the Christian writers of the past centuries to the performing theologians of the contemporary church. To bridge the gap between the Words written in the Bible and the words spoken to imply Christian teachings, an institutionalized authority for interpretation was established. It is said and believed that God did not tell man everything in the Bible. He told only that which was needful for man to know (declared will). The *untold* part was God's secret will, for which one could only hold blind faith. This radical interpretation of the Bible reduced Christian tradition to moral rules and duties, by which social conduct would be measured and monitored.[122]

Behind this blind faith in God's Words, there was an extremely negative notion of humanity. Man was considered nothing compared to God. Due to this, man became entirely incapable of virtue and could only be saved through the operation of divine grace. Because of his corrupted reason, will, imagination, and affections, man lay open to the perversions of sin. He could be restored to health only by the ministration of grace, "holy sparks of Heavenly fire," which might kindle him at any moment, inflame his higher notion, renew head and heart simultaneously. The sparks might come in various ways: an experience of bereavement, any affliction, any providential deliverance, but most commonly, through the ignitive words of a minister of the Gospel.

Since everyone's salvation was at stake, God's words had to be taken literally and worshiped earnestly and completely. To the Puritans, the Bible was a complete body of laws, bringing the spiritual life into relation with not only theology and ethics, but all knowledge and conduct. Unlike other Christian interpretations that sought to reduce the doctrines required by scripture to a bare minimum, Puritans extended scripture to cover the entire life. Within this rigid literary interpretation, scriptural language penetrated into all the books of theology, science, politics, morality, poetry, and even love letters. One could easily recognize this penetration of religious worldview from American literature of the seventeenth century, which was written primarily by Puritans.[123]

Within this narrow literary spectrum, the direction of the American worldview proceeded opposite to that of England. Unlike England, which was enlightened by science and natural philosophy, American Christian theologians remained the dominant thinkers until the nineteenth century. Like the Islamic thinkers who incorporated Greek philosophy into Islamic theology, American theologians revised English natural philosophy by combining it with Christian spirit. In examining Locke, J. Edward, one of the most influential thinkers of the seventeenth century America, revised the doctrine of sensation and reflection. He insisted that both sensation and reflection entailed the experience of the mind because they were simply different organizations of the same material. Through this argument, Americans closed the conceptual gap between material and spirit, nature and human, rational and irrational, and between science and theology. By associating sensation with grace, he resurrected the life of the Christian God in America for another century, at least.

Theologian philosophers creatively included dualism in religion and made science serve their God. The new Calvinism asserted that the cosmos symbolized the divine, but the symbol was completely indecipherable. The natural world was not a sure transcript of what existed. Unable to adopt an abstract language, which was essential to separate religion and science, America did not develop a "pure" philosophy in a German or English sense during the entire eighteenth century except for the theologians who borrowed and adopted philosophical reasoning. Like Romans of the early Imperialist period, all the best minds of America were primarily interested in politics. In this particular sense, American secular speculative thinking had never taken off as did its English and German counterparts. It married politics as soon as it had divorced theology.[124]

In the same semi-scientific and semi-religious language, America did not embrace nature as their new god as had Englishmen during the eighteenth century. The language of nature in America did not begin to evolve until the twentieth century, when modern poetry and prose flourished. For now, America needed to find a concrete way to define itself. This is the reason why religion was a dominating component of American culture much longer than it was for its Western European counterpart and why it took centuries for Americans to cultivate and invent other idols to replace its God. Americans had to invent their language, the pigment to paint a new image.

Non-abstract language also manifested itself in the form of political rhetoric and oral persuasion. In the eighteenth-century colonies, as in their parent country, religious organizations functioned as political parties. In New England government, power, though exerted by laymen, responded and conformed to what was, in fact, an established church of "nonconformists." In Virginia, the Church of England was also the colonial establishment of power, although dissenters were tolerated. In Rhode Island and the "Middle" colonies, church organizations existed independently of government. In Pennsylvania, Quakers regularly were elected to control the provincial assembly until 1756.

Religious organizations dominated political development during the period of the Revolution. The church rapidly recruited and doubled its size through political affiliations. Church rivalries became political campaigns for the control of governments.[125] Clergies were worshiped as divine bodyguards because the simple minded Protestants were ignorant of the possibility of distortion and manipulation of the words of God by their clerical leaders. In their minds, words of God, as they were spoken, read, and heard, had exactly the same meaning. God's voice was constant behind his words.

The written constitution did not create the American democracy. It simply established the dimension and limitation of its debate ... a debate which was constantly expanding. The Pennsylvania constitution was never submitted for popular approval, and it remained, simply because its opponents had no formal and legal way to change the document.[126] Emerging from a practical document to gain and defend political power, the concept of democracy was focused rather narrowly. At the time, liberty was for Europeans and white men. However, after the concept of liberty was established and articulated, it began to transcend the original boundaries in the same way that the concept of law did in England a few hundred years earlier.[127]

This early pragmatic tendency in American thought and attitude evolved naturally from a new and emerging language, American English. The creation of a new language was not any easier than the creation a new country. Americans invested a great deal of effort to make English sound American. They fought for every single word. During the hot debate over language, they gave their new words the same status as the American nation. For example, the North American Review in 1815 contemplated the future of American literature, given the fact that American English derived from a nation "totally unlike our own." The journal put it crisply: "How tame will his language sound, who would describe Niagara in language fitted for the falls at London bridge, or attempt the majesty of the Mississippi in that which was made for the Thames?"

Henry Adams observed that as Americans as they "must, whether they were fit or unfit, create a world of their own, a science, a society, a philosophy, a universe, where they had not yet created a road or even learned to dig their own iron. They had no time for thought; they saw and could see, nothing beyond their day's work.... Above all, and how to do it, by men who took their ideas and their methods from the abstract theories of history, philosophy, or theology. They knew enough to know that their world was one of energies quite new."[128] The American English was highly goal oriented and pragmatic, opposite from the highly idealized English and abstract German of the eighteenth century. American English was a language of self-fashioning and self-reliance.[129] The merchants and fashionable congregations who made up the American elite were often Unitarians, who believed that God had empowered them to fashion their earthly success.[130]

The creation of earthly success always began with words, spoken words, that consciously — even ostentatiously — side-stepped the use of terms that would even hint at aggression. It was a small set of vocabularies, a parrot-like repetition of the idealized abstractions, religious formulae, and stereotyped notions which produced an emotional reflex that assumed American values were purer and morally better than those of others. The language was used to justify American purposes and deeds.[131]

Late colonial Americans regularly — almost obsessively — voiced their concern with moral character. And this naturally translated, after independence, into a concern with the national character. Congressman James Bayard, in 1806, wrote: "We must learn to insist upon our national rights, or by and by none will belong to us. We must learn to defend our honor as a people, or soon we shall be without national character." "Character" was not neutral in tone. It meant national virtue or self-esteem, a recognized and deserved honor. An Andrew Jackson supporter, in 1828, reflected on the boost that the 1815 Battle of New Orleans gave to American pride: "Our national character was elevated and our citizens secured, perhaps for ages, from injury and insult, by the respect and awe, excited principally by one unparalleled achievement." Here the national character was even more plainly defined, both as unity of parts and global reputation.[132]

National self-image and national ambition had become ever more self-centered, ever more morally secure, with minimal conscious regard for any larger Western intellectual tradition. Clearly the nation governed by "virtue and talent" that inspired John Adams had long since evolved into a hardier, more broadly competitive society of the dollar-worshiping.[133]

The first of these models, an idealized conception of the character and achievements of the several colonial societies during their early years of settlement, was external in the sense that it emerged from the colonial past rather than from the colonial present. The "powerful psychological reality" of this conception in the New England mind of the late seventeenth and early eighteenth centuries has been described at length by Perry Miller.[134] Within a generation of the Great Migration to Massachusetts, the Puritan clergy had begun to indict the people for "declension" from the virtues of their fathers, and called for a return to the "Primitive Zeal, Piety, and Holy Heat found in the Hearts of our Parents."[135]

Like the Romans, Americans' self-idealization began with a deification of their founding fathers. The clergies used the same language to create a gap between the founders and their degenerated contemporaries. To devalue contemporary New Englanders, who were considered to be at odds with the values of their forefathers, the towering "Leaders of the first Generation" (capitalized words were in the original) were portrayed as heroic, exemplary, and almost saintly figures. They were men of extraordinary character, remarkable for their strict piety, simple purity, and brilliant accomplishments. The way in which the "Holy Experience" of the founding fathers was magnified and exaggerated was to contrast the failure and shortcoming of the later generation.

It was a strong and highly emotional language, which evoked guilt, shame, and disgrace as well as a call to worship an idealized and perfected image. "Degeneration" was the word used to make contemporary Americans feel inadequate and inferior. It bothered them to feel a sense of failure and to realize their obvious fall from the "primitive simplicity" of their forefathers. They had to carry the burden of a glorified past, knowing that they would never be able to live up to the original goals of the "Holy Experiment" and "Virtuous Past" envisioned by William Penn and the first leaders of the colony.[136] In Joshua Scottow's words, the "Noble Vine" had obviously decayed into a "Strange Plant." The contrast was so disturbing that it forced people to look upon themselves with amazement, hardly capable of understanding how they had come to be what they were, and what and who exactly they had become.[137]

The creation of American saints emerged from a desperate and practical need to observe the moral and spiritual authority that was slipping away. From all the colonies came complaints about a growing contentiousness in all areas of colonial life, insubordination and declining deference among social inferiors, rankly antisocial individualism, neglect of calling and of public duty, deceit, avarice, extravagance, and pursuit of pleasure. God had given the colonists "Plenty, but Plenty begat Ease, and Ease begat Luxury; and Luxury had introduced a fatal corruption of every good and virtuous principle."[138]

But later, as the transcendentalists Ralph Waldo Emerson and Henry David Thoreau were calling religion a "corpse-cold" institution and the state an "imbecile," Lockeanism was about to experience an ironic twist in America. The American poets saw that government in America was too impotent to command authority and religion was too casual in commanding devotion. What would influence people and govern their lives was not government itself, but society, precisely where Locke had located sovereignty in the democratic will of the majority. People looked, not above to God, but to each other, as they sought the recognition and approbation of their fellows while responding to the vicissitudes of public opinion. As America moved away from its Lockean roots, property and money became separated from labor and work, and with the worship of wealth itself, it entered the modern age of Thorstein Veblen, the first social scientist to analyze the status of leisure and the stigma of labor. Today in the contemporary consumer culture, wherein more and more people spend and borrow on credit in a fever of frivolous luxury, would bring tears to the eyes of the moralist John Locke. Yet it is the premise of his philosophy that constituted many of the foundations of their culture.

America went on its way to self-deification and self-worship.

American cultural narcissism is an indictment of modernity. This phenomenon could be traced to the country's foundations in an interpretation of Lockeanism that made "Man, being the master of himself, [the] proprietor of his own person," the ego sovereign unto itself. At the end of the road of liberalism, where one could not liberate oneself from oneself, Americans became a country without the authority of unified ideas. They tried every conceivable political idea that had been suggested by the English language. They worshiped all sorts of Gods — spiritual, corporeal, and material. They pushed the idea of freedom to its limits and found that there were no boundaries or many boundaries overlapping. They had convinced themselves that they had created a haven for all rebellions. However, they also found that when everyone strove against authority, there was no order to protect their idealized freedom. It took about one hundred and fifty years for people to realize the fear that James Madison felt in 1787: the states might "continually fly out of their proper orbits and destroy the order and harmony in the political system."[139]

The worldview of Imperial Russia had progressed the same way as America, from rootless to self-worshiping, but in a much shorter period of time. Unlike America, which began its journey with a rebellion against authority, Russia had been the homeland of tyrants and was saturated with ideas and philosophies serving and promoting authoritarianism. While America was a country that was ruled by an illiterate public and their unsophisticated opinions, Russia was a country that was crowded by overly educated scholars, engineers, philosophers, writers and artists. America had a government that was too weak to excise hegemony, while Russia had a government that was too strong for the liberty of its people. However, they ended up in the same situation. The only thing that they could reflect upon, negotiate, agree upon, and unite for was their flag. It was an extremely shallow pond, where self-made identity was polluted with shortsighted interests and strategies.

During the third and fourth generations of the Puritans and Calvinists, the American dream transformed from a personalized God or a secularized saint to a collective impersonal dream painted with primal colors and abstract principles, such as freedom, equality, and liberty. These hollow concepts became an umbrella overshadowing diverse and superficial interpretations.

American democracy was a world of battling words. Every issue, every right, and every inch of territory had to be argued and fought over. Like in the early city states of Greece, everyone's voice was equal to that of his neighbors. This equality of voices could not have emerged within an already institutionalized society, monarchy, or aristocracy, in which the voices of individuals spoke different volumes because of their social background, religious beliefs, and class positions. The one who was better connected and established always had the loudest voice. In the America of the nineteenth century, in which the society became a loose collection of variations within a structural vacuum, real democracy was possible.[140] It was not as if no one wanted to have a louder voice than that of the other, or no one wished to extend his right to override that of another. Simply, no one had been able to institutionalize his superior position. Therefore, everyone had to position himself in each battle and on each occasion. Without an established structure, nobody could win all of the time.

"Simply democracy," in the terms of Richard Henry Lee and John Quincy Adams, was an authority that emerged, produced, and functioned in a society where language had yet to build its hierarchy.[141] It was a game of numbers in which a solution was determined by the sheer volumes of its participants. This was the case in early Greek city-states, where public debate and oral rhetoric were the only means to make decisions for the collective. In England, the language and ideas of democracy were cultivated and articulated, but never actually executed, due to the interference of the royal executive and legislative hierarchy. The English concept of individual rights and freedom overachieved on American soil because they, less out of choice than necessity, had the first opportunity to find a space where abstract principles interacted directly and without mediation with the spoken language of the public.

The American dream became a mosaic as its different colors began to compete for shading and toning of the canvas. The boundaries that used to separate these different colors and shadings became increasingly elastic.

Like England, Russia was a language and culture before it became a nation. Unlike England, which cultivated its concept of a nation while it was growing up, Russia was, or was made to believe, that it was a part of a "commonwealth" before its nation or even its written language was adopted.[144] The cultural formation of Russia could best be described as an orphan who was adopted by a wealthy estate. He got used to the lifestyle, but never comprehended it, because he had no words of his own to describe it. Yet this glittering inheritance was all that he knew, and it dyed every thread of the fabric of his personality and shaped every dream that he could imagine.

The emergence of Western European vernaculars radically reoriented

Europe because each new language created an increasing distance from its Latin heritage as it grew into its own. This was especially true in England, which had never felt as comfortable as Italy or France did as a part of the Roman Catholic universe. Russia's Byzantine had adopted the masses before the birth of the nation and played an important role in the formation as a cultural being. It was language which created her identity. The first image of the universal empire that Vladimir saw in Haghia Sophia, where the splendor of the Byzantine civilization was located, left him speechless.[143] From that point on, Russia invested every ounce of energy in an attempt to emulate the Byzantine Empire, complete with its desire to rule the earth.

However, Russian did grow into a distinct language and culture. She gave the Greek tradition a Russian twist. Like the European vernaculars that created their own versions of classical heritage, when Christianity spoke Russian, it ceased to be Greek. One important development of this transplantation was that Russia redefined the Christian emperor, the image of God in Greek, as the God himself. Russia completely eliminated and flattened the conceptual distinction between man and his god. This distinction had been a major engine of Greek creativity and cultural development. Russian did not have a Greek childhood of banal vision and polarization. Unlike the classic image of Greek culture, as represented in English and Western vernaculars, the Russian image of the Greek tradition was the opposite. The Byzantine Greek was an old culture that had lost all of its idealistic creativity, social democracy, and political aggressiveness. It became an extremely refined culture with sophisticated aesthetic values, yet no cultural or social dynamic. Greek tradition as perceived and transplanted into the West (after double translation of Greek and Latin classical scholars) was a hollow structure, a skeleton, which could filled by emerging languages. On the contrary, the Russian vision of the Greek tradition was a tapestry of flowers in full bloom impressive enough to cover all underlying structure. This was the same Greek tradition yet in a different phrase of evolution, projecting different images at different times of its life, which made the imitation of its model into a different task.

Russia inherited a worldview and a concept of universal empire from Byzantium, an old version of Greek civilization. By then, Greek had evolved into a complete nonverbal and verbal universe distinct from the abstract perceived by Latin and the European vernaculars. In classical Greek, God was a clearly distinct realm opposite to the natural and sensual world that contained human languages and institutions. In Byzantine Greek, the Christian God had assimilated every image and every gesture that Greek art and literature had ever created, and penetrated into every sphere of life with very limited political and social intervention. It was an empire that united church and state ... one universe and one power.[144]

Another reason Russian perception of Greek tradition was different from that of the West was the scope of Russian translation from the Greek originals. Russian transplantation of Greek culture was extremely limited compared with that of Latin and English.[145] This hybrid determined the different paths through which English and Russian evolved during the next centuries. The cultural movement of the Enlightenment in the West was ignited by a reorientation of the literary language. The European vernaculars grew under the shadow of established worldviews cultivated by Latin Christianity during the past centuries. While the new vocabularies and expressions accumulated following the old theological and philosophical framework, verbal classification created a division between abstract and concrete meanings. The linguistic reorientation that initiated a verbal simplification rationalized thinking and solidified reasoning. Grand visions were freely imagined, and abstract ideas flourished with new imageries and expressions.

Russian, on the contrary, interacted with a relatively narrow section of Greek literature and culture, Orthodoxy literature.[146] In other words, Russian's Greek lessons were extremely limited and delayed for centuries.[147] The Russian association between the monarch and the Christian God was different from that of Western Europe. Unlike the English monarch, who was associated with God *through* words of God and his universal law, the Russian tsar *was* visualized in the very image of Christ himself. It began with the Byzantine ideal of emperor during the 6th century, which saw combined divine and secular powers as one: "through an emperor in body like a man, yet in power of his office he is like God ... for on earth, he has no peer." Russian pushed this unity a step further: "O pious Tsar, that all the orthodox Christian realms have converged in thy single empire, the only Tsar of the Christians in all universe.... Two Romes have fallen, but the third stands and no fourth can ever be. Thy Christian Empire shall fall to no one."[148] From the very beginning, Russian imagined the Great Prince as a perfect model of Christianity, saintly by nature.

Unlike Western European languages that struggled between at least two languages and between abstract ideas and concrete tributes for centuries, Russian, from the Byzantine Greek, had never formed a conceptual distinction between God and human. In its place, Russian developed a different kind of distinction, representing two kinds of Christian saints within the same royal families. Russian hagiography portrayed St. Vladimir and his grandmother St. Olga, who were the very first Christians in Rus, as the equivalent to that of Constantine and Helen in early Christianity. It depicted the victims of the Russian political power struggle as Christian martyrs who were elevated to sainthood. These included the two young sons of St. Vladimir, Boris and Gleb, who were murdered by their older brother, Prince Igor, in 1147; Andrei

Bugoliubskii, grand prince of Suzdal, and Vladimir, who were murdered in 117;, and even Tsarevich Dimitrii, the young son of Ivan the Terrible, who was murdered in 1591.

By the time that Ivan the Terrible had changed the saintly prince into the tsar, Russian had completely and officially closed the conceptual gap between its secular ruler and its Christian God. This elevated the Russian ruler into a higher apocalyptic level and transformed Christian sainthood from a way of life attainable by every Christian to the sole claim of the imperial ruler of Rome and Constantinople. By dividing king as man/God, it eliminated God altogether by stretching the body of the king. In Russian, the tsar, like Christ, was both God and man; he was man in his being and God in his function. Moving the original Greek external duality from between God and man to an internal duality, the body of the tsar eliminated God altogether. This was a radical reorientation of Christian doctrine, much more radical than any Eastern Christian church had previously considered.

As a result, Russian of the eighteenth century had very limited capacity to describe and separate the abstract from the concrete and to recognize the difference between the ideal and the reality. As Russia's God in Russian could not be separated from monastery saints, images, and rituals, social ideas could not be imagined without referring to the actual political system of the imperial dynasty. For example, there were no precise boundaries among the notions of generic monarchy (*monarkhia*), Russian autocracy (*samoderzhavie*), and European absolutism (*edinovlastie*). Those words were indiscriminately and interchangeably used.[149] In literature and historiography, writers might provide different reasons to support the monarchy or different members of the tsar family, but they unconditionally supported a dynastic autocracy rather than a democratic system.[150] There was no word for abstract rights. Therefore, rights did not exist and were not possible to pursue. Democracy was indefinable, therefore, unimaginable. They believed that the natural and ruinous democracy was not strong enough to uphold and defend the freedom and rights of its citizens. Russians understood that the rule of a single person was both incomparably profitable and useful for society.

The Western version of Greek thinking was abstract and rigid compared to its source. The Russian version was much more fluid. These opposite tendencies in the interpretation of the Greek tradition emerged from their distinct linguistic environments. European vernaculars evolved within a multi-lingual context, in which various languages stretched the formative vernaculars in opposite directions. Russian was the only language that began with a very narrow set of religious vocabulary, already evolved into a divine web composed of God, its saints, its symbols, and its tributes in the natural world.

As the result of this super fluidity, an electrical fluidity perhaps, Russian, like the early Islamic Arabic, evolved rapidly and moved from conceptual distinction to unity at an amazing speed. It took Greeks many centuries to finally penetrate the barrier between man and God; Russians made their tsar the God, not the image of God, taking only a few decades.

This fundamental transformation of divine concept did not take place through political or ideological choice. Rather, it was accomplished by expanding the repertoire of Christian language and imagery. The Russian image of God was grander, more diverse, pluralized, and even contrary. It was grand enough to perceive a humble, merely human Christian God, complete with a dark side. This type of Christian imagery was very important in the early times, as Christianity began to articulate in the Eastern Mediterranean countries. It was an idealized divine image that had two related and interwoven sides that gratified and glorified the divine through suffering and sacrifice. This notion was thousands of years old, and was rooted in pagan ritual. It was a way to be with the divine through an emotional and subconscious experience, rather than through reason or morality. Ancient Greek assimilated this side from Asian culture, but transformed it into a sensual yet emotionally detached experience. Russian restored and reinforced the emotion of worship, which gradually faded in Western Christianity.

Russians did borrow some of the most fashionable ideas from the French Revolution. The Russian empress herself created an image of enlightened monarchy.[151] Catherine II affirmed her belief in the Enlightenment theory of natural law, and promised to turn Russia into a law-abiding state that would respect the natural rights of all men. However, it did not take her long to realize that she could not afford to let her empire be ruled by English or French ideology, whose words would eventually override her crown. She preferred to translate English law of nature into Russian. Only in Russian did rights possess shading and create hierarchies. Only in Russian, could she enact legislation forbidding peasants to make complaints and silence the debate for mitigation of the serfdom. In Russia, law was naturally defined, implicated, and practiced from the top down, because its language imposed its written form on its voices. Any translation could only enrich the written words, which were always in control, rather than change the relationship between the words and voice. This created an enhancement rather than a reorientation of literary language.[152] Like in America, Russian Enlightenment was utilitarian rather than philosophical, as in Western Europe.[153]

Russian was a language whose voice was always unexceptionally directed and tightly controlled by the written words of God or the emperor. Unlike the Western humanism that initiated a radical revolution that overthrew the religious hegemony, Russian Enlightenment simply added another layer of worship, the "enlightened" monarchy. Without the abstract language or philosophy of English or German from which a grassroots democracy emerged,

Russian was enlightened from the top down. Russian law was always defined and implicated in this manner. The brightest star of the Enlightenment was the imperial family.[154]

The unique form of Russian Enlightenment determined the political and social consequences of the reform. Unlike the West, where cultural and philosophical reorientation initiated a profound ideological and social change, reason and rationality, as abstract notions, could not respond from the Russian language. Russia interpreted and utilized German, French, and English concepts in its own way.

Russia was a land of saints, saints who were called different names in different political systems and during different historical times. In Russian, God had never been as abstract and remote as he was in Latin and the Western vernaculars. Neither were ideas. The conceptual gap between general and particular, between abstract and concrete, which took the western European languages centuries to fill, had never been created in Russia. Russians would borrow someone else's written form of expression. But they made it sound Russian and serve Russian purposes. What Russian borrowed was not a philosophy, a new way of life, or a new worldview, but rather just letters ... alphabets. This was the same way that the Greeks borrowed alphabets from the Semitic as a recording and written instrument for a mature poetic.

In Russian, like in ancient Greek, there were no separate languages to worship God and to praise heroes.[155] Unlike the Greeks, Russians had never elaborated an abstract notion of god, philosophical or otherwise. The part of Greek culture that Russia borrowed, the Orthodox Christian concept of God after it assimilated all stock of pagan imageries, was extremely and narrowly eclectic. It was not a faceless and aloof God like that of Latin.

During the reign of Catherine the Great, the imagery of triumphal goddess had remained alive as the conquering monarch. The empress was portrayed as a perpetrator, or the very least, an initiator of transformation. Joined by the leading members of the nobility, Catherine presented her rule as a model of European monarchy ... the Roman Empire reborn. She was able to appear as the successor to Peter the Great, a heroic sovereign who transformed the elite, and the Russian state, into a semblance of Europe.[156]

While European countries began to shift their national symbols from God to people, in Russia, the emergence of the concepts of "nation" and the "people," often uttered with the same word, "*narod*," brought discordant notes into political rhetoric.[157] If the birth of ideas was rooted in language and its imagery, Russia had what it took to revive the divine image of the tzar through its flamboyant army uniforms and coronation rituals.[158] In the persona of the tzar, "the soul of Sacred mother Russia," Russian nationhood was highly concrete, specific, crowned with religious symbols, and worshiped as God.

Catherine had confirmed her myth of being a godlike legislator by representing provincial towns and conquered territories as a piece of paradise. Alexander, as a divinely inspired commander, sought to use the order realized on the drill field to uplift the spiritual life of the empire. This spinning of personal and historical mythology around the monarchs elevated the rulers to a figurative stature revered or worshiped by the nation.[159]

Nicholas remained true to the Petrine myth. National motifs embellished a heroic history of foreign domination. They were invoked to show the distinctive character of that domination. The historian Michael Pogodin presented the tale of the calling of the Varangians as both the primal historical expression and the prototype of the Russian people's acceptance of absolute rule. Therefore, in Russian, orthodoxy and autocracy were an inseparable part of nationality.[160] Russian culture was a highly collective one. So, its concept of nationhood was always interlocked with the state.[161]

The sense of universal mission came from the abstract side of Russian language. This was the same sense expressed in Western ideas, through religion and social science. However, unlike in the West, where ideas were imprisoned in an equally abstract language and articulated by an isolated elite, Russian abstract ideas were often quickly absorbed by the popular literary and artistic languages. This was why Russian, a transplanted written language, evolved into a mature literary and philosophical language in an amazingly short period of time.

As Dostoevsky predicted, Russia would not fall victim to the collapse in Europe. Instead, after Europe's imminent destruction, Russia would emerge to pronounce the word of universal salvation. "Our mission and our role are not at all like those of other nations, for there each separate people lives exclusively for itself and in itself, while we will begin, now that the time has come, precisely by becoming the servants of all for universal peacemaking."[162] This was simply a restatement of Russian conviction cultivated by its orthodox doctrine since the sixteenth century: "The Church of ancient Rome fell because of the Apollinarian heresy, as to the second Rome — the Church of Constantinople — it has been hewn by the axes of the Hagarenes. But this third, new Rome, the Universal Apostolic Church under thy mighty rule radiates forth the Orthodox Tsar, all Christian kingdoms have converged in thine alone. Two Romes have fallen, a third stands, a fourth there shall not be."[163]

7. Inflated Self and Playing God

Every culture grows from a single-minded notion of self, from which it begins to expand. The initial step is to recognize the boundary ... as to define what is self and what is other. Noting that racial difference and racism are two different things, this is where and why modern political theorists and sociologists read Greek incorrectly. They read ancient Greek as if it was English or German. The Greeks' sense of self began before the fifth century B.C. with vision and sound rather than an abstract concept of race or ethnicity. During the epic period of ancient Greece, the word "barbarian" did not once appear in Homer's poetry, either as a noun or an adjective.[1] Homer's archaic world of poetry remained homogeneous. Its inhabitants, Greeks and non–Greeks, shared the same status of heroes. In *Iliad* and *Odyssey*, non–Greeks were only occasionally distinguished and described as the "barbarophones," Carians, people of "another tongue," and "of wild speech."[2]

Conceptual polarity was not a genetic trait. It was a basic phenomenon of cultural infancy. As a new culture with its binary vision of the world, it created a new self-image, as idealized and as rigid as its worldview. However, Greek had a childhood which was different from that of Western vernaculars. It began with a concrete vision and voice rather than a borrowed verbal structure. During the fifth century B.C., when Greeks began to redefine the cultural self and outsiders, they made a formal, rather than a moral distinction. In ancient Greek, the distinction between self and other was not conceived as opposite but as equal or mutually complementary. They were asymmetrical, hierarchically ordered, and antagonistic.[3]

Seeing only in black and white, the boy needed to create verbal as well as physical boundaries to protect himself from the outsiders. If the boy believed in God, this was good. Those who did not believe in his God, the outsiders, were evil. To ensure one's own position next to God, one had to fight the infidels. A young culture did not have the language and vision for compromise. It was just trying to survive.

God was the most perfect being that his mind had ever imagined. God was everything that he had ever dreamed of … perfection. In old cultures, religion set man upon a tormented and never-ending journey toward an idealized model, in which man mimicked his god to lift himself up to its godliness. The boy's new culture borrowed a god who spoke directly to him. For the new culture, god was only words away. All the boy needed to do was to have a conversation with god, and to interpret his god's words.

As a culture evolved, new language and philosophy were put into the mouth of his god. He felt closer to his god. He eventually associated his wishes with those of god. He became convinced that his fight was god's fight. As this point, his god became the justification for him to convert or destroy the infidels. He had successfully created god in his own image.

Every culture created and accumulated a gallery of self-images as it was growing up. Self-imaging did not begin with abstract concepts of ethnical or philosophical self, as the modern scholars believe. Rather, it began with images, waves of images, that were reinvented and repainted over and over again through time. Initially, there were only two images: I and whoever was not I. In order to create an identity, I had to raise myself up to create the distinction. The only way to raise oneself was to push others down. Every culture did this when it was young. The Mesopotamians, ancient Egyptians, Chinese, and Sanskrit speaking Indians were once children who participated in this playground bullying.[4] As the culture grew older, it created more images and painted more varied and diversified pictures of self and others.

Cultural images began with a primitive sense of distinction between familiar and unfamiliar. At this non-moral (non-political) level of distinction and definition, primitive language separated the world with a clear line between the inclusive (familiar) and the exclusive (unfamiliar). Observable differences, such as color of skin, unfamiliar lifestyle, strange habits and mannerisms, incomprehensive language, gestures, or a combination of these factors, formed the basis of distinction. At this stage, differences in people's appearance were noticed and recognized, yet not named. Once named, sometimes they were not always considered as opposites to be polarized and morally judged. They were just different. This is why in Homer's epic the word *barbarian* was not used.[5]

The Greek racial consciousness emerged within the conceptual polarization of ancient Greek of the fifth century B.C., as did the racial consciousness of the modern West during the pre-modern period. Conceptual polarization was not a moral or political movement, but rather a new stage of literary development during which the verbal distinction was emphasized and reorganized. The Greeks' sense of alien and concept of difference started with a reclassification of language. The Greek word *barbaros* was originally an adjective describing the sound of incomprehensible speech.[6] It took many years for language to modify and to crystallize stereotypical expression.

Greek literature of the fifth century B.C., especially its dramatic images, gestures, and visions, produced thousands of barbarian theatrical characters, and an all-embracing concept of barbarian emerged. As an exercise of self-definition, Greeks created an opposite image for barbarian who was often portrayed as inferior compared to the idealized Greeks.

Greeks were not alone in building self-image through the concept of the cultural alien. The ancient Chinese, Mesopotamian, Egyptian, and Sanskrit each created a similar notion of barbaric characters in various ways. However, none of those images matched the degree of precision and rigidity that ancient Greek had created. The depth of this was not seen again until the emergence of modern European languages.[7]

The idea of the barbarian as the generic opponent to Greek civilization emerged during Greek expansionism.[8] Until the fifth century, it had been more important for the ancient Greeks to be Athenian, Spartan, or Theban than to be a Hellenist.[9] A Greek would, at times, identify himself by his patronymic, but in some circumstances (in Athens at least) by his deme, tribe, phratry, or "genos" (as a citizen of a particular polis) or as an Ionian, Dorian, or Aeolian. In *Iliad*'s world, different groups of Greeks were called Aetolians, Cretans, Boeotians, Achaeans, Argives, and Danaans. A Homeric character's home was his "patre," a word that referred to his town or district of province. Strangers were asked who their parents were and what was their town. They answered by naming their town, father, and famous ancestors.

Herodotus provided the first image of non–Greek, "the otherness," after he visited Egypt in 449 B.C. His famous passage said:

> The Egyptians in their manners and customs seem to have reversed the ordinary practices of mankind. For instance, women attend market and are employed in trade, while men stay at home and do the weaving.... Men in Egypt carry loads on their heads, women on their shoulders; women pass water standing up, men sitting down.... Sons are under no compulsion to support their parents if they don't wish to do so, but daughters must.... Elsewhere priests grow their hair long; in Egypt they shave their heads.... When writing or calculating, instead of going like the Greeks, from left to right, the Egyptians go from right to left.[10]

Before the fifth century, the word "barbaros" was never used in the plural as a noun to denote the entire non–Greek world. Greek writers described the outsiders, even invaders, as "Medes" or "Persians," never "barbarians."[11]

Greek tragedy visualized and portrayed the images of Greeks and barbarians creating polarized distinctions. While dramatic presentation made it

possible to create a separate space in imagination, stage invented a distinct
people from a distinct world. Unlike the mythical world of epic, where foreign
experiences and people were visited and described as an extension of Greek
vision, the tragic world became divided and barricaded. (For decades, scholars
of the classics have been debating about the time and origin of the concept
of "barbaro." I am particularly interested in the formal rather than textual or
political origin of the word.[12]) It was a barricade of songs, acoustic effects,
cacophony, gestures, scattered foreign vocabularies, and words. It was an invisible barrier that was heard, gestured, and felt. This literary imagination was
the rich soil from which the later Greek abstract opposition of Hellenism and
barbarism was grounded.[13] The stage presentation made the "scarcely distin-
guishable" barbarians, whom were originally portrayed in archaic poetry, stand
out as a different class of humans. On either side of this barrier, the characters
behaved differently. The barbarians were portrayed to behave in ways which
fell short of the standards of Hellenic virtue. They were emotional, stupid,
cruel, subservient, or cowardly.[14]

As a result, the Greeks began to build monumental walls around themselves. There were walls of words, fortified stockades, that were built not from
bricks, but from fictional characters and heroes. Within this "ethnical" castle,
they imprisoned themselves, and they could observe outsiders only from their
turrets. From behind the walls of the castle, looking out, the Greek vision of
the world was much more focused and yet limited. The horizon existed only
straight ahead. This new point of view, so to speak, fractured the wide and
homogeneous horizon that the ancient epic had created. They could no longer
see places as far north as Scythia, as far east as Babylon, and as far south as
Egypt. From this new viewpoint, those who used to exist within the Homeric
landscape of heroes and their allies became color coded and racially distinguished.[15]

Very few historians have been able, so far, to distinguish between Homer's
originally intended meaning and later interpretations, and between Greek's
racial prejudice and that of German or English interpreters. As during modern
times, the most important area in which Greek and barbarian were polarized
was within classical political rhetoric. In the works of tragedians, historians,
and orators, the democratic Athenian ideal was insistently defined and
applauded in comparison with the tyranny thought to characterize most barbarian societies. Very much like the polarity of democracy and authoritarianism created by the modern West, Greece invented a polarity of freedom
and tyranny (or despotism) based on the political ideal of the city state.[16]

The subtle comparison between Greek and barbarians later developed
into a full-scale rhetoric. This was not a vague model of the generalized Greek
city-state but a specific demonstration from the tragic stage that placed an

overwhelming emphasis on the respective political ideals of Greek and non–Greek. This artistic and literary presentation of opposition between the Athenian invention of democracy and Persian despotism served as propaganda for Greek domination and hegemony in the Aegean. Therefore, the battle against barbarian Persia was perceived as the battle for democracy and freedom.[17]

Greek Orientalism used a powerful new range of effects to characterize a foreign people and culture. Its barbarians were simultaneously anti–Greek and anti–Athenian. A dazzling variety of methods obscured the fact that they were speaking Greek — the use of foreign names and vocabulary, cacophony, repetition, a proliferation of "meaningless" cries and Ionic forms, and especially, epicisms. The presentation of the Persians was predicated on the antithesis of Greek and the barbarian. The barbarian character was powerfully enhanced not only by the elaborate rhetorical style, but by the use of a distinctive new "vocabulary" of words (ploutos, chrusos, habro-compounds, chlide), symbols (the bow, the chariot), significant actions (prostration), possibly rhythm (Ionic a minore), and by emotional excess, especially in the closing scene. Cultural differentiation was expressed primarily in the terms of political psychology and not in religion. This reinforced the position opposite the Athenian political ideals, and supported, through extensive references, the protocol of the court and the administrative apparatus of the empire. The tragedy was not decorated by oriental coloring, but suffused by it. This represented the first unmistakable file in the archive of Orientalism, the discourse through which European imagination has dominated Asia ever since, by conceptualizing its inhabitants as defeated, luxurious, emotional, cruel, and always, dangerous.[18]

Two separate languages were developed in order to describe Greek and barbarian stereotypes. The perceived major Hellenic virtues, defined by Plato, were wisdom or intelligence (sophia or xunesis), manliness or courage (andreia), discipline or restraint (sophrosune), and justice (dikaiosune).[19] These virtues became the basic concepts with which Greek tragedies created their Greek characters.[20] On the other hand, barbarian characters were portrayed according to Plato's other list — a list of vices corresponding to and opposite the virtues. They included ignorance (amathia), cowardice (deilia), abandonment (akolasia), and lawlessness (akikia). Euripides' drama used barbarian characters to interact with the Greeks, who represented the supremacy and perfection of humanity.[21] Along the conceptual and artistic gap between Greeks and barbarians, more and more myth was created. As myth accumulated, the gap between the two became wider.

Another part of self-identity involved self-glorification and gratification. In this aspect, Greece had the easiest job. Ancient Greece was a land of gods and goddesses. Its landscape was crowded with monuments and images of gods. Although the Greek gods were much more humanized than the Hebrew or Christian gods, Greek cultivated great respect for the divine kingdom.

Ancient Greeks were always proud of their democratic tradition, and imagined themselves as anti-tyrannical and anti-authoritarian heroes. The reign of Alexander marked the watershed in the development of the ruler cult in Greece. Alexander became the first Greek monarch to be worshiped as a divine incarnate.[22]

For centuries, Greeks, in their language, images, and ideas, cultivated a soft and yet perceivable distinction between man and god(s). Although Greek gods exhibited many human shortcomings, such as emotional instability, political bias, low self-esteem, and lack of morals, they were gods. In the Greek mind, gods by definition were ageless and deathless, whereas men, by definition, were mortal. Hero cults provided a halfway house between man and god. After death, mortals of acknowledged virtue and achievement might be honored by a sacred precinct and blood offerings, but the cult was essentially a cult of the dead. The ritual was different fundamentally from that observed with the Olympian gods. Before the fourth century B.C., a heroic cult following was the most that any mortal could expect. The cults were largely confined to city founders, such as Battus at Cyrene or Hagnon and Brasidas of Amphipolis.[23]

The heroes were supermen. They were demigods, even the peers of the gods, but they were only associated with the gods by analogy. This analogy, however, occurred from the earliest times and was not confined to heroes. At times, the mortal man could be thought to transcend the limits of his mortality. Pindar, who usually was adamant about the fundamental distinction between mortal and immortal, was prepared to concede that despite the ephemeral character of human life, man did in some way approach the immortals by way of greatness of mind or nature.

The border crossing between superman and god took centuries to form, and the gap between divine and mortal was bridged by mountains of words. The godlike image of man was only transient and fated to be overtaken by adverse fortune, whereas divine felicity was permanent. Heroes of Olympian games and city politics became praised as well as warned. Although they might some day enter the heroic cult, they were reminded to keep their places and not to attempt to cross their own mortal limits.[24]

Until the fourth century, Greek philosophers had the same line of thought. Aristotle, in general, accepted the basic division between god and man. However, his political vision prepared him to visualize a hypothetical perfect ruler who would be so superior to his fellow men as to appear a god among men. In his *Nicomachean Ethics*, he finally recognized that the popular saying might be true; that men became gods and heroes by a surpassing display of excellence.[25]

It was, once again, the poets who finally completed the process of combining gods with ideal rulers. As Isocrates' described King Evagoras of Cyprus: he achieved the greatest of felicity without any admixture of adversity, excelling in mind and body, reaching a healthy old age and leaving numerous progeny, all in positions of power. All the poetic praise for gods, which had accumulated for centuries, began to be used for rulers. All the sacrifices, memorials in prose and verses, and sanctuaries, became theirs to enjoy.[26] By the third century B.C., Lysandreia was honored, as god, by the Greek cities after the battle of Aegospotami. He became the first of the Greeks to have altars erected in his honor and have sacrifices made to him as a god. The Samians actually renamed their national festival the Lysandreia.[27]

By the time Philip acquired power in Greece, there was a climate of thought congenial to the idea that the outstanding ruler was a god among men. To honor Philip, his statue was introduced into the temple of Artemis. The people of Eresus in Lesbos erected altars to Zeus Philippios, which meant that he was worshiped and offered sacrifice as a peer of god.[28] Alexander became convinced that he was more than the distant progeny of Zeus, through some heroic ancestors, and was in some manner the actual son of god. In 323, the god died. But his cult continued tenaciously. The stories soon emerged that he, like Heracles, had been translated to heaven.[29]

Over the history of mankind, very few people have expressed so much passion and lust for glory as did the Romans. As a young and vibrant language, Latin rhetoric fueled and manufactured the emotional engine behind military expansion.[30] While Greek's justification came from its belief in its right for security and equal opportunity for profit and prestige, Romans were led to believe that their empire was willed and ordained by the gods, whose favor Rome had earned by piety and justice.[31]

The blessing of God held entirely different things for Greeks and Romans during their expansions. With various names, forms, and functions that Greek gods and goddesses had developed, keeping a god or two on one's side no longer guaranteed victory on the battlefield. Besides, the meanings of divine words were so hard to read and understand that a mistake in interpretation could create disaster. For Romans, the gods would not only bring fortune in affairs of war, but also ensure conquest. In his public speech, Cicero gave the most eloquent expression to the notion: "It was by our scrupulous attention to religion and by our wise grasp of a single truth, that all things are ruled and directed by the will of gods, that we have overcome all people and nations."[32]

The ceremony of Roman triumph was the best demonstration of its military power and world status. The victory parades took place in Rome, which was a huge world city, decorated at great expense. The offering of thanks to the gods who had brought the conquered world to Rome was demonstrated with an extravagant procession that paraded from the city to the Temple of Jupiter on the capital hill.[33]

The general's cheeks were daubed with red; he was clothed like Jupiter, in a purple cloak over a toga sown with golden stars. In one hand, he carried a scepter crowned with an eagle, and in the other, a laurel branch. Above his head, a slave held a heavy gold crown. The triumphal procession dramatized the splendor of Roman victories, reinforced public pride in the value of conquest, and instantly elevated the successful leader.[34]

Political rhetoric activated and exaggerated this single-mindedness and enshrined the idea that it was *arma virtusque* that guaranteed Rome's perpetuity.[35] There was no limit for Rome's expansion because its notion of security and the security, of its friends and allies involved more and wider territories. Thus the limit of the *orbis terrarum*, within which she claimed dominion in Rome's name, was continually advancing.[36] With the expanding borders and advancing territories, the Roman concept of just war inflated. War occurred not only when self-security was threatened and diplomacy had failed, but also for the protection of allies and friends.[37]

Rome was prepared to police the world with her "love of peace and tranquility, which enable justice and good faith most easily flourish." To respect this just principle, Rome had to abstain from doing wrong herself, and as far as possible, prevent wrongdoing by others.[38] This would demonstrate her respect for the rights of others by punishing unjust demands in the name of god. The Roman vision of the world consisted of only rulers and subjects, conquerors and the conquered. Her reaction to a possible or imagined threat was the same as that of a nervous tiger, disturbed when feeding. Romans began to judge the justness of their own fear, a fear that became exaggerated and inflated with the advancement of their borders.

Romans, with their younger and more coarse language, created a much more vague self-image. They truly believed that virtue, fortune and the will of god made Rome undefeatable. Power, not persuasion, remained the most striking characteristic of the later Roman Empire. The fourth-century empire, described in the work of its principle Latin historian, Ammianus Marcellinus, was, frankly, authoritarian. Ammianus found it unusual and praiseworthy that the emperor, Valentinian I, did not attempt to "bend the necks of his subjects by menacing prohibitions." It was more normal to impose obedience by imperial fist in religious as well as in secular matters. In the words of John Matthews' masterly study, Imperial government in Ammianus's time was unmatched in Graeco-Roman history in its scale and complexity of organization, in its physical incidence upon society, the rhetorical extravagance with which it expressed, and the calculated violence with which it attempted to impose its will.[39]

While the Greeks took centuries to bridge the gap between man and god, Arabic self-divination came much easier and quicker. This difference was determined by the differences between the two languages. Different kinds of gods were created. They were located in different places, and could be reached in different ways.

Until the fifth century B.C., Greek had been a language driven by visual images. Greek epic poetry had spent centuries imagining and portraying a king-dom of Olympian gods, each of which had a distinct character and temperament. They related to each other as an extended, sometimes dysfunctional, family. The "one and only universal image," which Greek had created at the time, was described by philosophers. It was written and articulated in an abstract lan-guage, a language that needed a few more centuries to become concrete and specific enough to establish a world of clear logic and coherent structure.

At this particular moment, to be a god, a person, especially a ruler, needed to travel an endless road, past the endless lines of divine images, glo-rified with marble sculptures, monuments, and pottery that had accumulated over the centuries. He was expected to mimic and compete with each and every one of those images before he finally earned his godliness. Only then could he be placed side by side with the ancient gods and receive sacrifice and offerings.

Even if he managed to take his divine place, he still could be rejected by some of his countrymen. Divine standards were so widely varied in form and content that every city, even every person, had many spiritual choices in wor-ship. Even the established ancient gods had trouble establishing themselves as the superior "one and only" God, and they spent their lives in conflict with each other. A human, a monarch or a scholar, always ran the risk of rejection by the citizens of some cities, who could decide to follow other gods.

This is why ancient Greece developed a political system that was very different from Asian despotism. Its language and political rhetoric did not provide a foundation for a unified and absolute authority. Greek tyrannies and the Greek empire never lasted long enough to obtain strong and unified support. The spectrum of authority had been spread out too thinly to establish a hegemony and unified authority.

Ancient Semitic created a different kind of authority and different kind royalty to support it. Like its Greek counterpart, ancient Semitic had a very loose concept of god; its poetics always had difficulty to create a negative god who upheld a rigid and strict moral code. Semitic gods, before Judaism, were laid back and easy-going. They had patience and tolerance for human mistakes. They did not see the worst of human nature and they were not eager to punish. They established repeated calls of repentance, and deferred punishment while there was hope for amendment. They were sympathetic with right conduct, but not strongly enforcing of it in any manner. There was hardly any human imitation of divine in ancient Semitic.[40]

There was very little mythology left by Semitic, as it was a language much older than Greek. Although fragments of mythological literature from ancient Babylonian writing were discovered, they had died with Babylonian, as its oral language adapted Sumerian writing form and vanished after a few centuries. The story line of the old myth survived by other oral languages; however, mythological literature had never functioned as a written form to which Semitic oral language could return and accumulate as ancient Greek did with its epic tradition[41]

Without a continued literary language, the Semitic gods, until the time of the Hebrew Bible, had neither history nor relationship that connected them to each other. For centuries, Semitic gods had been living with humans as a part of their families. They were much like the Indian gods had been, but without the retold stories and lavish ritual ceremonies.

The Hebrew Bible represented the first attempt by a Semitic language to create a transcendental and abstract god. It was also the first time that a Semitic language tried to create a unified moral authority through writing a script of God.[42]

Without a language of abstraction which could draw a clear line between God and man, Semitic, Hebrew, and later Arabic had to find a linguistic form to pull God away as far as one could imagine from nature and human activities. The Hebrew Bible, a story of God, his history and language, broke the established intimacy, or "primitive" fellowship between man and god, established by ancient Semitic for centuries.

Keeping the history of the Semitic language in mind, it is easier to understand the nature and growth of the Islamic Empire. The Islamic Empire was based on a religious hegemony which was created by a very old oral tradition and its own written form. This beginning set it apart from Judaism and Christianity. Both Judaism and Christianity experienced linguistic discontinuity shortly after the words of their Gods were codified in writing. Hebrew lost its oral form to Babylonian, Armaic, and then to the European languages. Judaism became a religion of a God that needed a translator after it had lost its native voice. The Christian God was a transplanted God with a book of translation. He lost part of his tongue when Latin died in both oral and written forms except for fossilized classical texts. However, he survived in better shape than in the East because Greek and later Slavic had developed rich collection of literary and visual images to keep him alive.

In a continued language, the Islamic God retained his intimate relationship with his believers. Although Islam went through a classical period during which Arabic tried to develop abstract ideas and reasoning similar to those of Greek and Latin, the gap between man and God, in Arabic, had never been as deep as that in Latin or even Greek.

The distinction from man to God, in Arabic, was only words away. One did not have to look like God because there were no divine images in Islam. No one even needed to try. All he needed to do was to speak like him. In a mature poetic language, which had been developed and refined for many centuries, everyone could find a way, his special way, to interpret and understand his God, and create a godhead in his mind, and bend god's words to personally unite with him. This kind of verbal imagination was cultivated in Arabic speaking countries from the day a child could hear the rhythm of Qur'an in the air, and speak and memorize the words of Allah.[43]

The Semitic verbal imagery made it possible to quickly bridge the narrow gap between man and God. For example, in biblical Hebrew, god might be transcendental and rigid, but he was human in many ways. He could be emotional, unfair, or even full of prejudice. Since god was never universal by any stretch of the imagination, he could be as political as a king or tribal chief. When a person moved from one tribe to another, he assumed the god of his new tribe.[44]

Unlike the battling Greek gods who fought for personal favors and interests, Semitic gods fought for territories, tribes, and later national identities. Fighting against someone was the same as fighting against his god.[45] While Greek pagan gods were self-serving and moody, Semitic gods were full of political bias and racial prejudice. Semitic gods participated in every war that their worshippers waged and granted them rights overriding those of their enemies. In other words, for a worshipper to win in a political and military battle was to win his god's support and sympathy. To lose in this battle meant to lose his identity. A person without a god was a person without a face, a name — without life.

In the eyes of a Semitic community, men and their gods formed a social and political as well as a religious whole. Unlike in Christianity, where divine fatherhood had uprooted from the physical basis of natural fatherhood, the ancient Semitic God was the "biological" father of man. This bond of blood had been seen, demonstrated, and reinforced for centuries by sacrificial rituals.[46]

Since Semitic communication with God had been focused on word rather than vision, the imitation of God took a different road. Mimicking the Christian God, especially in the first a few centuries of Christianity, involved visions and visual imitation. That was because Latin, the main language of Christianity, was a very young language, which needed visual images and gestures to express and communicate. The focus of Christian communication did not turn to words and verbal imagery until a few centuries later, when Latin accumulated enough vocabulary and created a verbal repertory of divine images and allusions.

The use and abuse of divine words transformed the nature of divine imitation from a mimicking of God's image to a mimicking of God's will. With its long history and rich vocabularies, Arabic had never developed a desire or need for a visual vehicle to aid meaning because its language was vivid enough to paint with verbal imageries. While visual image for Islam was art, like calligraphy, visual image of early Christianity was illustration of meaning.[47]

As holy words created a world of their own, the image of God and his will became harder and harder to be recognized. Everyone could imitate his words and pretend to be him. This was the time when God lost control of the words that had originally made him powerful. When that happened, God and his words were forced into retirement. His mind, his body sometimes, but not his name. He became a hostage of the will of the men who owned the industry of God's words — religious institutions, states that pretended to be religious, and, every man.

The mutation of God's image began with poetry. The time and speed in which God was personalized was determined by the degree of the maturity of the poetics. The Roman Empire spread Christianity quickly because Latin was a common language.

Christian poetry flourished. The immense output of Latin poems were written primarily for specific feasts on the Church calendar, specific parts of the mass, or for the monastic daily Liturgy of the Hours. They were written to be chanted or sung, to put the dogmas of faith in a pleasing form for a congregation largely unable to read. As liturgical poetry, it was inherently public, meant to express communally held beliefs. And occasioned as so much of it was by Church feast, it was tied less and less to the figures of Jesus. Saints' feast days crowded the Church calendar, and the family of saints was ever-growing, as foundational biblical ones like the Virgin Mary and Peter were joined by scores of figures both legendary and historical, held up by the Church as models of the Christian life.[48]

Christian poetry began to accumulate an increasing family of saints. The medieval stage of Latin poetry was filled with characters whose stories, while gaining meaning only in relation to Christ, upstaged him as the drama's immediate focus.[49]

During the high Middle Ages, Christ became impersonal and abstract through allegorical presentations in poetry, stage, and painting. Everything that Latin had created by then had formed in the street corners and on stage.

The typological figures, the swelling family of saints were all created from a single grain of wheat. The angels were now all patterned into grand allegorical systems that linked every detail of the cosmos in an intricate correlation.

The person Jesus of Nazareth disappeared. However, his body extended into a heavenly body and his spirit gave the universe its meaning. The entire universe was inscribed in Christ. He represented order. Without him, nothing could make sense. On the Christian stage, Christ was personified as the Virtues. The human soul, floating somewhere between the devil and the divine, was torn between the perfection of Christ and its own shortcomings.

Latin died with its divine image frozen in the abstract. European vernaculars brought the human images of Christ back to the forefront. The simple and vivid language was meant to move listeners to tears, to feel his pain, and motivated them to examine their spiritual commitment and their own shortcomings as worshippers. This devotional stage was empty of all but two or three pietistic figures, yet it was filled with feeling. This presentation evoked feelings of identification with Christ.

The devotional appeal to Christ's humble humanity was quite startling. He was addressed tenderly by his personal name, Jesus. He wore not the Triumphant King's glorious crown, but his crown of thorns depicted in the Gospel narrative. His title, taken from one of Isaiah's descriptions of the suffering servant (53:3), was Man of Sorrows. He was also very much the Son of Mary, who became the Mother of Sorrow. In painting and poetic representation, Mary's grief was so intensely portrayed that it became a double passion for both the Son and Mother... The feelings between them and worshippers were shared freely. The same pain was felt by the Mother, the Son and the worshippers, as if their own hearts were pierced and bleeding as their Savior was crucified. The poet became an actor in the scene, where he shared his anguished heard to Jesus for His love.[50]

The non-human and remote side of divinity was also a very strong part of the Christian mind. Before establishing a repertory of literary imagery and expression, the emotional personification of God's images ran the risk of separation from the abstract. Each vernacular had to find its own way to fill the gap within the fragmented world of God's kingdom. The Romance languages, with their closer tie to Latin literature, used the concept of love. Loving and feeling God became the chosen way to unite with him and also keep a sense of connection with him in a highly fragmented and unstable world.[51] Protestant literature took another path in its search for a more concrete unity with God — Words.[52]

Another method used to inflate imperial ego was to orchestrate a grand spectacle to display one's power. During the reign of the Emperor Titus Colosseum, inauguration was used in this manner. Roman dominance was paraded through the vast arena for the world to see, and masses to acknowledge.[53] Gladiators from distinct parts of the empire, lions and elephants from Africa, bears from Dalmatia and tigers from India were brought to Rome and assembled in a reenactment of the Roman conquest.[54] The spectacles provided a sumptuous and awesome demonstration of the extent of Rome's power. The display of colored people in the arena symbolized the empire's global reach. There were Thracians, Sarmatians (from the region of the Danube) Sygambians (a German tribe), Arabs, and Ethiopians ... who exhibited with their exotic clothing, hair arrangements, and their incomprehensible speech. These people embodied the vastness and diversity of Roman territory. Their presence in the heart of the city emphasized Rome's power to rule thrillingly alien cultures and reinforced the vast scope of the empire.[55]

Romans elevated themselves and promoted self-worship in the same manner that Americans do today. They invited the world in and created a realm of superficial diversity. It was a world that appeared as a colorful mosaic, but was in fact a highly uniformed structure, guided by very simplified rules. The Latin concept of the city of God best exemplified this kind of cultural establishment. Romans, from the time of Cicero, liked to play on the idea that Rome was a city that captured the essence of the world.[56] It was like a museum where the world's most valuable treasures, the most beautiful artifacts, the best books, and the best minds and bodies were collected and claimed as the property of Rome.

8. Exaggerated Fear and Insecurity

On the other side of the inflated ego was an exaggerated fear. What the imperial boys wished and looked for was a place in the world where they could feel safe. However, in the language and vision that they inherited, there was no place to hide or rest. Life was a constant struggle, requiring all of their strength because the alternative was unthinkable and unendurable. The picture of Hell became more and more vivid as the language accumulated. The fear was intensified. Like children, young cultures had a unique way to deal with things that scared them. They closed their eyes and hoped that it would go away. They were silent about the negative things in life and repressed the fear by looking to the heavens. They looked up and imagined the beauty and glory. This was the only way that they knew to avoid the ugliness and shame. It was an escape ... a refuge.

This was why new cultures were obsessed with territories and boundaries. They imagined and created borders, walls, lines, and barriers because they could not feel safe unless there was a definite division, real or psychological, that separated them from outsiders. Their sanity lay in their ability to expand as far as they could and collect land and its bounty. This vision expanded first to neighboring land, then across the continents, then to the oceans and more recently, to the stars. Bigger was better and the more the better.

Fear fueled the arms race. Monstrous weapons were built. Huge vessels, to mobilize an army of millions, laden with the latest tools of destruction were constructed. Soldiers with all of their new toys — rifles, tanks, missiles, nuclear warheads and chemical weapons — were marched and demonstrated in a huge show of bravado. The everyday needs of people were eroded, or even worse, ignored as all resources were engaged in the pursuit of the beliefs within the boundaries of the realm — a little boy who was afraid of god, evil, some "isms," or anything he imagined.

The use of political propaganda was another kind of weapon. With it, the boy spread fear and hatred against anyone who did not follow his own god or "ism." He went out of his way to conquer and police the world in order to control and dominate. He wanted everyone to convert to his own ideas, voluntarily or otherwise.

Imperial boys were control freaks. They actually did not mean to be that way. They just could not help it. Being afraid was a normal state of mind when one had just begun to create his personal boundary and formulate his self worth. Boundaries placed limits on the known, and prepared the imperial boy for his first unsteady steps into the world beyond his borders. His fear was a part of growing up.

Every rising culture had a primitive sense of order that emerged from its limited and rigid vocabularies and its simple, linear view of the world around it. It often took centuries for a young culture to realize that the line between order and disorder, like the horizon, moved depending on where and when one looked at it. Initially, the world was described in the terms of basic polar opposites: day/night, brightness/darkness, sun/moon, and man/divine. The way of the world was expressed in the some manner as order/chaos, safety/danger, right/wrong, and good/evil. At this stage, perception was very simple. Things either existed or did not exist. Things interacted with nature in a specific, observable manner. This interaction created either favorable or unfavorable results. Mankind was a mere child, playing in a world that was limited by his sense. However, as language accumulated, variations became evident, conflict emerged, and the clear snapshot of the world became fuzzy. Man began to question his world and himself.

When the well-defined picture of the world was disturbed by disorderly variations, the boy began to feel threatened and afraid. "This should not be happening!" He hated to lose control and feel confused. He struggled to relocate his "horizon" from where he could reorient himself and begin to see, to speak, and again think. He had to know and feel the ground that he stood upon, so that he could carry on and do something to correct the madness of the world. But the world had not slipped into madness. The boy had begun to mature.

This type of panic was very normal for young cultures, or cultures that were young at heart. For the early Greeks, there was fear for "pollution" in both a physical and moral sense. The fear came from the deep rooted religious ritual to maintain "purity." Although the connotations of pollution went through centuries of evolution and diversification, the fear of pollution was constant.[1]

Like many Greek moral and philosophical concepts, purification originated from a verb which depicted an act. *Katharmos* meant division, making distinction.[2] It began to be used as an abstract term in prose writing that was distinct from the word *agos,* as used in epics, tragedies, and comedies at the time. *Agos* made a similar moral and religious distinction between the way in which a behavior pleased gods and the way that it offended them.[3]

Purification, as an action of washing and cleansing, was intended to mark the boundary between the sacred areas and the profane. To show respect to the gods, Hector and other Homeric characters did not merely wash their hands, they also bathed and changed clothes as a preparation for prayer and sacrifice.[4] There was abundant evidence of this from literature, vase paintings, and the excavation of sanctuaries. Gradually this act became symbolic in that it not only cleaned away any pollution, but excluded the disgraced from ritual activities.

After these ritual acts had accumulated many variations in form and expression, the general concepts uprooted from the original intentions of preparation for worship, and public hygiene became symbolic. Historians had difficulty in determining the exact time that the early Greeks stopped washing themselves before they went to the sanctuaries. However, they concurred that the physical act of cleansing pollution and purification became increasingly symbolic — *miasma.*

The best sense of the *mia-* words was that of defilement, the impairment of something's form or integrity. However, unlike the English word "dirty," a common form of order, *miaino* was used to connect the pollution of a reputation through unworthy deeds, or of truth through dishonesty. No English verb had been so freely applied as *miaino,* which could mean to endanger justice, law, and piety.[5] It became a word or a metaphor for any behavior that deviated from the acceptable cultural ideals or symbols such as God, morality, law, piety, and justice.[6] The implied moral judgment became harsher when the noun *miasma* or the adjective *miaros* (except in the sense of "revolting") were used. They almost always referred to someone deemed ritually impure and thus unfit to enter a temple. This impurity was conceived as contagious and dangerous.

Miaino became more and more abstract. It transformed from a physical repugnance into moral and mental deviation, and even abuse. *Miaros,* and its closest synonym, *bdeluros,* were among the strongest and the most common disparaging terms. *Miaino,* as disgusting, was often used in conjunction with the shameless, brazen or bold, and was constantly directed against traitors, law-breakers, or someone who had lost their self-control.[7] The physical cleansing of the body was expressed as *katharmos,* and was restricted to the concrete meaning of cleansing and sacrifice.

After *miasma* further abstracted, it depicted a general character of everything that was believed to be deviant, contradictory, and opposite to the established moral standard. As a result, it intensified feelings of resentment and fear. It cultivated a fear that could be triggered not only by a single instance of "pollution" of morals or degeneration of character, but also extended this fear into many other connotations connected to many other instances of "pollution." In other words, with an abstract moral code, fear of its deviation and violation became organized and highly collective.

There were many examples for this abstract and exaggerated fear and imagined or perceived danger. The fear of pollution was one of the most important motifs of Thucydides' history. During the fifth century, a Greek state might attribute a natural disaster to a pollution it had incurred. The Athenians expelled the Delians from their island to ensure the purity of this religious center. In the fourth century, Aeschines could envisage Demosthenes as the "demon who pollutes all Greece" and brought it to misfortune.[8] Greek states intervened in the internal affairs of others to drive out the pollution, or made war because of that.

The predominant theme of the works composed between the death of Caesar and the Battle of Actium could be called "the great fear." Uncontrollable anxiety no longer pervaded only Rome, which for some time had been unstable and convulsed by political vendettas, but also the once tranquil world of the provinces. The armies of Caesar's murderers and of Antony and Octavian had strewn bloodshed and desolation all about the empire. The civil war had reached inhuman excesses, striking, almost incidentally, harmless populations of farmers who had long lived beyond the reach of any political change. The wounds of the great fear experienced in the years 43–40 B.C. remained painfully portrayed in Augustan literature, a literature frequently praised above all others for its calm, clear balance and the lessening of contrasts. Contrasts and lacerations, however, remained wherever the memory of the civilization was still felt.

European exploration confronted Europe with races and cultures that had to be explained in terms of the assurance, in the Book of Genesis that we all descended from Adam and Eve. As late as the nineteenth century, many ethnologists and anthropologists were content to assume that all human beings indeed descended from Adam and Eve, but that some branches of the human species had been cursed for their sins, and had degenerated from their original noble state. In Galton's Britain, increasing urbanization confronted the middle class with an apparently permanent underclass of poor people — beggars, thieves, and prostitutes — often in poor health, apparently indolent and lazy. This underclass, moreover, was increasing in size relative to the middle class because of the differential birthrate. The frequency of social problems such as murder, pauperism, disease, mental illness, alcoholism, and prostitution was also rising.

As early as 1871, analysis of records of the height, weight, and general health of army recruits throughout the nineteenth century in Britain suggested "a progressive physical degeneracy of race." The early defeats of the British army in the Boer War (1899–1902) confirmed for many that degeneration had become a national problem. In *Degeneration, Culture and the Novel: 1880– 1940*, William Greenslade offered an excellent history of the emergence of belief in degeneration during the last half of the nineteenth century, a view that could explain the growing sense in the last decades of the century of a lack of synchrony between the rhetoric of progress and ... the facts on the ground, the evidence in front of people's eyes, of poverty and degradation at the heart of ever richer empires.[9]

Part Three
Marriage and Maturity

The imperialist boy had just begun to learn who he was. He always had mixed feelings about himself. There was always deep doubt about everything that he had ever done. The young empire was neither ideologically homogeneous nor administratively hegemonic because the nation was just emerging, growing, and experiencing.[1] The world seemed too big a place for the imperial boy. Although he had strong will, enormous power, and endless energy, he had very little direction, or the wisdom needed to bring the whole world under his control. ("Move on, march! With the best ships and weapons, I can go anywhere I want," he told himself, trying to be brave.) He would go to places where he could find things of value for his homeland. He brought home gold, fur, and treasures ... exotic spices and cloth.... "Look! Have you ever seen anything like these?" "I have gone to a lot of trouble to get them." "I only spent two shillings for this piece from a stupid local! He had no idea of its value here!" "This didn't cost me a thing! I just picked it up from the ground!" It was always gratifying to establish the spoils of conquest and control. The imperial boy, proud of his accomplishments and seeking adulation, was on top of the world.

The boy, attempting to verbalize and comprehend this new experience, ran out of words. As he began to encounter alien people, he described them in his own vocabularies. The initial description, which came naturally rather than as a conscious choice, was self-centered and superficial, as he could recognize only the most obvious ... the color of skin, the incomprehensible language, strange custom and gesture. From his own cultural space looking out, racial distinction became the focus of his initial conceptualization, recognition, and imagination of the world. It was a self-inflated and self-righteous vision with mixed degrees of fantasy and truthfulness. It was irrelevant whether his vision was true or false. For the boy, the primary purpose was to define the boundary between self and the outsiders. He needed this distinction to clarify his self-image and to provide him with a place of refuge if he felt threatened.

Racial language was a wall made of words, which was set up to defend a young and insecure soul. It did not take long to exhaust the superficial comparison of self and non-self. Differences were bound to become internalized as cultural interaction became more intense. In order to promote self-image, it became desirable to reinforce the conquests of the battlefield with heroic words. National epics, historical legends, with all of their glorifying stories, were born.

The imagined enemy became a real one, consistent with the imperial boy's make believe world. With his highly idealized self-portrait, everything that he had accomplished needed to be defended and justified. This is why he, who believed in justice and sovereignty, invaded other people's land. This is why he, who claimed to be the most civilized of people, waged the cruelest of wars. This is why he, who championed liberty, took conquered people as slaves. His ideal self-image, which was shaped by staring at his own reflection, became distorted as the imperial boy looked into the eyes of alien faces. The imperialist mission of civilizing the barbarian whispered in his conscience and began to haunt him. A new vision began to take shape. The outside world was not only a place to occupy and exploit, but also a sanctuary of reflection and rediscovery. The killing fields of war and the new arena of international politics became a promised land of a new maturing spirit. The boy had passed into manhood.

Imperialist expansion had a far deeper impact on the boys than they had ever imagined. It became an inner journey as well as an external conquest. As the boys' visions widened, they began to see a different world, a world with unfamiliar landscapes and strange images, and a world with different colors of light and rhythm. As they got closer and more involved, the world became a mirror, reflecting a thousand faces — faces that presented a confused portrait which did not match self-image. This eye-opening experience provided an opportunity to step away from a narrow illusion of self-perception. It encouraged him to explore the interior of his own soul.

The process of enlightenment was gradual and lasted for decades, even centuries. It was painful as well as exciting to find and reshape oneself; one's guard moved up and down as his sense of the world and its boundary changed … it was perhaps as emotional as falling in love. This time, the love subject was no longer a dream or fantasy or a courtly game. She was a flesh and blood person, yet unknown. To know her was to know oneself; to love her was to expand one's horizon. The outside world was real, wild, and limitless. This exotic adventure was attractive and alluring and allowed a more realistic sense of self to emerge.

Boys remain boys until they outgrow their untested illusion of self and learn to look at themselves from different perspectives. Knowing and understanding other cultures enriched the boys' spirit and helped them to mature. They learned to speak other languages without boundary and without fear until various languages became one. The boys realized that the true power was communication ... words rather than swords. It was the ability to negotiate and convince. They had learned that any lasting influence was an influence of the mind which could not be occupied, possessed, bought, or owned.

9. Expanding Worldview and Sharing Self

The boys who matured were the ones who outgrew their rigid worldview and developed a sense of shading and color for their visions. This transformation began with a widening of their horizon and the accumulation of visual idioms. By the end of the expansionist period, the language of most young cultures, like the initial stage of older cultures, started to become capable of describing the grey areas between the two extremes. A shimmering rainbow was discovered between the starkness of dark and light — a new dimension of color and diversity that would reshape the world around them.

From this visual shock and revelation, a new vision began to take form. It crumbled the walls of the adversarial prison that the boy had been locked inside, and allowed him to see and become a part of a New World.

The boys who eventually matured were those who outgrew feelings of insecurity and fear. They became confident enough to open up to the global community. It was confusing, in the beginning, because they were accustomed to admiring that familiar noble, god-like self-portrait. Their only dream was to be as perfect, beautiful, successful, and in control as they thought they were.[1] There was nothing that they could not do to pursue their rivalries. How fiercely they contested! What exultation they felt when they won, and what shame when they were beaten! How they disliked reproach! How they yearned for praise! What labors they would not undertake to stand first among their peers![2] For him the world was a solar system with a single source of light, beyond which there was darkness and nothingness. Perhaps it was like traveling in a tunnel toward the light at the other end. There was no alternative. There was no going back.

Adulthood was a different life in a different environment. The boys discovered a new and grander galaxy where lights came from different directions and in different intensities. They realized that many paths were open to them, and they finally became accustomed to pressure from various forces. Gradually, they became comfortable with the idea of being one voice in the chorus of humanity. They realized and no longer wished that they were the center of the universe. They learned that security did not come from lines on a map, but from an awareness of who they were and where they were positioned in the global community. Coming out of the pigeonhole of self-centeredness and blind narcissism, their eyes opened to face a much wider and more enlightened world.

Imperial boys took different paths to maturity as they inherited different degrees of diversity in their cultural expressions. With more diverse cultural expressions, ancient Greek and Medieval Arabic were the quickest to outgrow the "worrier culture" and had the easiest time achieving tolerance and metropolitanism. Their periods of military expansion, as well as their centralized imperialist administration, were much shorter lived than other imperialist cultures. They developed an attitude of tolerance, and eventually, respect for different cultures and ethnic groups, especially in their occupied territories.

The influence of Greece and Islam, as well as the later European vernaculars, was developed by cultural form and style rather than military and territorial aspirations. With their philosophy, science, and poetry, the Greek and Arabic languages initiated and revived great cultural movements. Latin and the European vernaculars were inspired by and strove to reproduce their Greek heritage, and in so doing they were equipped to surpass the accomplishments of their linguistic ancestors. Arabic philosophy and science became a cultural and intellectual beacon during the time of Medieval Europe, and transformed and delivered Greek antiquity to the rest of the world. Arabic poetry inspired and revived the unprecedented golden ages of cultural development in Iran, Turkey, and Spain. The influence of modern European languages, especially Modern English, has and is going to play a similar role in the contemporary world.

———

Spiritual expansion always began with an expansion of words, which opened up a panoramic horizon for the imagination. Travel literature, which described foreign territory and alien people, opened the eyes of the imperial boys to a world that they had never known to exist. It is not down in any map; true places never are, as genuine explorers and adventurers believed. One had to see it by going there and experiencing it.[3] Travel literature provided a description of foreign lands in familiar terms.

The Greeks' interest in other peoples and other places was apparent long before their imperial expansion. Homer's listing of contingents on both sides of the Trojan War includes Delphi's role as geographic center, Kolaios' discovery of Tartessos, Herodotos' very wide-ranging interests and travels, Pytheas' circumnavigation of Britain and exploration of the Baltic, Alexander's recruitment of the Indian philosopher Caalanus to his court, and Plutarch's speculations on possible inhabitants of the moon.

The earliest Greek travel literature had very practical applications and was not as refined and romantic as those of the later Italian, English, and Spanish. Indika written by Skulax of Karia in the sixth century B.C., the earliest surviving geographical text (mentioned by Herodotos, 4.44), was motivated by a conqueror's interests. Skylax was a Greek mercenary in Darius' service. This Persian king conquered part of the Indus River region c.515 B.C., about two hundred years before Alexander repeated the achievement and more than two thousand years before Great Britain did.

Hecataeus of Miletos wrote *Periodos Ges* which survived only in fragments. This work was novel in two senses. It was the first attempt as a systematic description of the world. Book 1 (Europe) covered the Mediterranean coast and islands and set the paradigm for the periplous as a genre; Book 2 (Asia, which included Africa) gave an outline of the rest of the world as known to Hecataeus and his sources in the early fifth century B.C.[4]

As a young culture among many mature neighbors, Greece held a great admiration for older civilizations. Herodotus had immense respect for the scholarship of the Egyptians, largely because of their practice of keeping records of the past because, at the time, Greece was a land of oral tradition. Some Greeks of the fifth century B.C. thought that Greek civilization developed from the Nile Valley. In matters of religion, for instance, they believed that the Egyptians invented altars, processions, and ceremonial meetings. They even claimed that the Egyptian festival of Osiris resembled that of Dionysus in Greece, and, as further proof of the cultural links, they noted that the Greeks and Egyptians were the only people to forbid sexual intercourse in temples.[5]

Ancient Greece of the archaic period witnessed a considerable degree of interaction between Greeks and those who would later be categorized as barbarian. Greeks were mercenaries of the eastern armies. The brother of the Lesbian poet Alkaios served the king of Babylon; Ionians and Karians served in the army of Psammetickhos I, pharaoh of Egypt between 664–610 B.C. Greek mercenary involvement in Psammetickhos II's expedition to Nubia can be verified by the Greek inscriptions carved on the rock statues at Abu Simbel on the Nile.[6]

The high luxury enjoyed by the Persian emperors, which was to become a central tenet of Greek belief about the Asian way of life, was suggested by the use of certain symbols, items of vocabulary, and even possibly metrical forms, which were to become its standard poetic markers.[7] Their fabulous wealth, ploutos, rather than the decorous prosperity implied by olbos, was established in the opening sentence; the palace was described as rich and golden. Gold was mentioned no fewer than three more times in the parodos alone. Even their race was described as born from gold. As Aeschylus rendered symbolically relevant the genealogy recorded by Herodotus, the Persians were descended from Perseus, who were conceived in a shower of gold. Later the queen left her "golden-doored" palace. When briefly mentioned, the treasure to be found near Athens was the silver from the mines of Laureion. The plentiful supply of precious metals, and the skill in working them, characteristic of the peoples under Xerxes' sway, produced repeated references to their military hardware — the Lydians' chariots, the spears of the men of Tmolus and Mysia, the bows of Babylon, the short swords worn by the hordes of Asia, and Xerxes' own Syrian chariot. It created an impression of the clangor of arms, or brilliance and hardness, almost at odds with the cushioned softness of the palace life believed to be enjoyed by the Persian royal family and imperial staff.[8]

Various terms used in *Persae* to evoke the luxury of the Persian court were to become closely associated with the barbarian characteristics, especially "chlide," "luxury," "pomp" and the concept of "habrosune" (or habrotes), an untranslatable term combining the sense of softness, delicacy, and lack of restraint. The word "habros" was found in a Hesiodic fragment in reference to the delicacy of a young woman. It was a common expression in Lesbian poetry describing women, and goddesses such as Sappho.[9]

The unrestrained emotionalism of these dramatic Persians was a component of their habrosune, and the great dirge which concluded the tragedy was usually advanced as the primary evidence that Aeschylus presented abandonment to grief as an oriental characteristic. The threnos was anticipated by the pictures of Asia's lamentation conjured up by the chorus. The citadel of Cissia, they sing, will echo to the cries of women tearing their robes (120–5, 537–83). The inter-ethnical experience did not directly lead to racial consciousness and insecurity, as the description of ethnical distinction was not a racist act. The archaic literary world of heroes remained largely untouched by racial interest except the barbarophone carians. The *Iliad* mentioned twice the language of the Trojans' allies, who were not Greek speakers. The *Odyssey* used two terms for non–Greek language: allothroos (of other tongue) and agriphnos (of wild speech).[10]

This non-specified consciousness was reflected in a language which was not yet clearly defined. The English words "ethnic" and "ethnicity" were derived from the Greek ethnos (plural, ethne). But ethnos in ancient Greek embraced a much wider variety of meanings than simply "ethnic group," as defined by modern sociologists. In the Greek context, ethnos could be, but was not always, restricted to a group of people who shared an ethnic background.

Even during the fifth century, when the ancient Greek became increasingly more definite and classified, the term remained ambiguous. Herodotus used it to describe the inhabitants of a polis, such as the Athenian and Attic ethne, or the ethnos of the Khalkidians. Alternatively, it could refer to a larger population, consisting of several poleis. For instance, the Boiotians were described as an ethnos. Herodotos, in his description of the peoples of the Peloponnese, wrote that seven ethne live in the Peloponnese. Of these, two — the Arkadians and Kynorians — are autochthonous and are settled in the same territory which they occupied even in the past; one — the Akhaians — did not depart from the Peloponnese but left its own territory and now inhabits a different region. The remaining four of the seven ethne — the Dorians, Aitolians, Dryopes and Lemnians — are newcomers. The cities of the Dorians are many and well known; Elis is the only Aitolian city; Hermione and the Asine, which is situated opposite Lakonian Kardamyle and Dryopean, and all the Parorretai are Lemnians.

None of these terms applied restrictedly to the Greeks as a homogeneous ethnical and racial group. They were applied to the populations ruled by Lydian king Kroisos, or the people within the Caucasus region. The word ethnos could also describe groups of various sizes and origins.[11]

The meaning of *ethnos*, in the days of Herodotos, had already narrowed and tightened a great deal compared to its usage in prior centuries. In Homer, the term was simply designated as a class of men, a group of warriors or young men, living or dead, or even a flock of birds or swarm of bees and flies.

During the fifth century, Greek writers went through great effort to reclassify and streamline their fluid language. They tried to pin down the meaning of ethnos. Unlike the formative Latin and English, which began with clean cut concepts, Herodotos had to clarify established and slippery words by association rather than exclusion. He juxtaposed ethnos with another word *gene*. *Genos* was related to the verb *gignesthai*, which meant "to be born," "to come into being," and so eventually "to become." *Genos*, then, could be seen as both the mechanism by which one's identity was ascribed, and the collective group in which membership was thought to be ascribed through birth. Herodotos employed *genos* to describe the Athenian families of the Gephyraioi or the Alkmeonidai. But *genos* was not reserved exclusively for the family groups. It could be applied to a category of any size that recognized its members as automatically enlisted by birth. Thus, he could describe the population of Attika, not only as an *ethnos* but also as *genos*, since Athenian citizenship was restricted to those of Athenian birth. Similarly, the Hellenes could be described as both an ethnos and a genos, since one of the defining criteria of Greekness — along with language, custom and cult — was, for Herodotos at any rate, shared blood.[12]

With this clarification, a brand new concept of Greekness emerged.

Through the isolation and firm definition of this single word, a unified Greek identity emerged through distinction and exclusion. The process of defining "other" and "barbarian," as opposite to Greek was well under way. Greek writings began to polarize their self-image with their perception of others. Outsiders were redefined as opposites.

However, Greek ethnic distinction had never been as clear cut as that of the early German or English. There were confusions, even in Herodotus' writing. With the intention of further classification, the word *genos*, used as a synonyms of *ethnos*, specified some distinctions yet confused others. As more words brought more classifying power, they also increased the possibility of confusion and overlapping of meaning. As he compared Spartans and Athenians, Herodotus said that the Spartans belonged to the Dorian *genos* and Athenians to the Ionian *genos*. While the Dorian *genos* was an *ethnos* that was Hellenic, the Ionian *genos* was an *ethnos* that was originally Pelasgian, but became more Hellenic over time. In this analysis, the two terms were not quite synonyms, although sometimes, ethnic identity could be substituted by bloodline. As soon as Herodotus wandered into the complexity of blood relations, his conceptual boundaries became even more overlapped. Blood relation (or shared ancestors), whether defined as family unit or a larger collective, had a natural tendency to be segmented and mixed of lineage. What if someone was born between bloodlines, or shared blood with various ethnical groups at various generations? To clarify and bind the emerging distinctions, Herodotos introduced more concepts, such as *syngeneia* (regular notion of family kinship). Yet, the meaning of *syngeneia* evolved quickly beyond the meaning of shared ancestors. It could also portray someone who was recognized as belonging to a specific *genos*, but not necessarily biologically linked.[13]

With their accumulation and cross association of various concepts, ethnic identity became an extending collection of loosely connected, nonexclusive, and overlapping notions of shared family kinship, geographic location, ritual custom, social values, and political ideas. It was very easy for one to claim his Greek heritage. Politicians could direct political rhetoric toward any of these groups to gather allies and troops. Yet no one could create a strong state and efficient unity as strong and sustaining as the early Romans.

This Panhellenic, tolerant notion of identity was deeply rooted in the conceptual fluidity of the Greek language. This fluidity made it impossible for the meaning of any word to stop at its originally intended boundary. Ethnical distinction was only one of many distinctions that ancient Greek invented during this stage of its language development. As a passing distinction, it quickly transformed, relocated, and overlapped with other categories of distinction, such as kinship and classification based on social, ritual, and linguistic practice. The ethnic distinction, like many Greek distinctions such as

real/imagined, world/logo, and man/god, expanded its boundary and connotation. For the Greeks, the boundary of meaning was a constantly moving
thought ... a sand dune that could form one day and be gone overnight, almost
as quickly as it first appeared.

With its high level of literary sensibility, Greece's external expansion and
war quickly internalized. As soon as the winds of war became apparent, Greeks
felt an inner disturbance almost immediately. Thucydides' history illustrated
this internal struggle in both words and actions during the Persian War.[14] Hellenic unity facing a common danger was a main Herodotean theme. In his
history, the awareness of a special Hellenic character was very clear. However,
Herodotus' Hellenic image was not rosy and highly idealized, as were those
of the young English of the eighteenth century and American of the twentieth.
Even with the Persian pressure, Herodoto's Hellenic states and individuals
acted in a selfish and shortsighted manner. This vision was not unique. It
fairly represented the general attitude and feeling of Hellenism in the fifth
century, arising from the great victory over Persia. Archaic "Pan-hellenism"
was much more limited.

The contrast between the idealized self-image and actual behavior under
pressure created constant internal conflict in the mind of the Greek intellectual. Thucydides recounted in his history how the zeal for military victory
and global expansion led to acts of unusual brutality and cruelty and the des-
ecration of religious customs, codes of morality and civic loyalty. Moderation
disappeared, and the essentially psychological justification for going to war
made negotiated peace impossible. The war could not end as conventional
wars did. Thucydides' language illustrated how Greek moral codes were
stretched through historical writing and rhetoric. He explained the wartime
Greek actions, such as "to satisfy their lust to dominate by seizing power
through either an unjust vote of condemnation or brute force," in terms of
an instinctive reaction to the situation. War made Greeks commit unthinkable
acts as their passion overwhelmed their rational judgment and brought them
down to a crude level. This war mentality changed Greeks and made them
capable of brutality and violence.[15]

Thucydides gave ample examples of this moral transformation by describing and analyzing words and their associations. "People exchanged the conventional value of words in relation to the facts, according to their own
perception of what was justified. For reckless daring was now considered courage true to the party, whereas prudent hesitation was considered specious
cowardice, moderation and discretion a cover for unmanliness, and intelligence
which comprehended the whole an unwillingness to act in anything. Impulsive
rashness was attributed to the part of a real man, while careful planning was
written off as a nice-sounding excuse for evasion."[16]

The boundaries of established morality and judgment were shifting and flipping before one's eyes through the use of unconventional or innovational conceptual juxtapositions. Thucydides and his most modern commentators viewed this change of language and values as abnormal and contradictory because they had been accustomed to a language of clear-cut oppositions and rigid moral judgment. They failed to see that it was natural for a language to become more flexible and tamed for human intent. So instead of broken down language and failing communication, it was a historical transformation of expression that transcended value by verbal disjunction rather than moral opposition.[17]

The best example of this concept was the demoralization of the meaning of justice. The key for this transformation was a combination, and then exchange, of justice and expedience. In the Corcyreans' rhetorical contest with the Corinthians, they argued not over the meaning of justice and expediency or whether one took precedence over the other, but how the two concepts both applied to the situation. Both states presented their claims to Athens, based on a perfect combination of justice and expediency. The Corcyreans argued that forming a naval alliance with them would both ensure Athens' supremacy on the sea (expediency) and demonstrate openly their willingness to help a wronged party (justice). The Corinthians argued on the wrongs of Corcyra and the blame any new ally would share (justice), and hinted at the long-term danger of Corinth's enmity. Athens was presented with a choice between action and inaction as the best, most just and most advantageous course to take.

Corcyra's main consideration was the advantage of immediately attaching its strong navy to Athens' forces. Yet this was also the most serious potential pitfall of their position. The alliance would provoke an immediate, uninvited war with Corinth. The Corcyreans accordingly placed most of the weight of their argument on the expediency and practical advantage of a naval alliance, while using unclear and scattered arguments about justice to try to smooth over the concern of an impending sea battle.

This combination of expediency with justice can be seen in the first sentence, where the Corcyreans tell their Athenian audience that it is right for them to prove the advantage of the alliance they offer. Here the word "right" could only mean proper or fit. It certainly implied none of the moral or legal compunction with which the Corinthians would presently endow the word. The precedence of practical advantage over moral or legal sanction in the Corcyreans' use of the word "right" emerged from their somewhat presumptuous warning, "you will be allowing them to acquire military power from your own empire, which it is not just to have; rather [it is right] either to prevent them from hiring away mercenaries from within your empire or to send us as much aid as you may be persuaded is necessary, to receive us openly as allies and help us."

Here justice was defined in accordance with Athens' perceived military interests. The substitution of the word "expedient" for "justice" would not significantly change the meaning of the sentence.[18]

The rhetorical quarrel between the Corcyreans and Corinthians pertained not to the precise meaning of justice, but to its implication in the given situation and its relation with expediency. The antithetical speeches invoked justice to legitimize contrary courses of action, each aimed at hurting the other. Their evaluations of justice were at odds. The Corinthians advocated a more conventional application, in which colonies must honor their mother-cities even at the expense of their immediate interests and safety. They claimed that treaties must be honored and virtue and morality practiced, but, they refused arbitration. They maintained that justice may exceed those traditional claims to meet the challenges and exigencies at hand.

The Athenians said that while the Spartans always calculated and acted according to their interest, it was only recently that they started calling their interests justice. The Athenians further asserted that the moderation and fairness they themselves exhibited in the judicial procedures of the empire proved them to be more just than circumstances required. This arrogant remark would only infuriate the audience, but that was not the Athenians' aim. They addressed their remarks not to the assembled Peloponnesians, but to the Spartans, whom they expected, as a great power, to implicitly understand their view that justice was a perquisite of the strong and a favorite appeal of the weak. These words revealed a certain disappointment, as if the Spartans used to understand but had now joined the rest of humankind in misunderstanding the nature of power and its relation to justice. Pericles in his last speech acknowledged the general view that the Athenian acquisition of power was "unjust," but he rejected both the validity of the notion and any influence it should have over Athenian policy. The Athenians should think only about the safest course, he said. He did use a concept of justice, conventional or otherwise, in his speeches. For the most part, he used the Greek word fair or right, in a neutral or technical sense, without any philosophical or moral implications.[19]

It was the sophistication of Greek political language and its levels of connotations that made the Hellenistic notion of Greekness less ethnical and more moderate. It was not about the boundary of a single word, but rather the relationship between levels of meaning and their implication in rhetoric. Identity in Greek was more characteristic rather than ethnical in the modern sense.

As Aristotle put it: Hellenic people, as situated between Asia and Europe, were intermediate in character. If it could be formed into one state (*politeia*), it would be able to rule the world. Europe was cold, spirited, but unintelligent, whereas Asia was hot, languid but intelligent; Greek was moderate warmth, as a combination of spirit and intelligence. The focus of self-definition transformed from ethnical to intellectual and cultural. Self-worship, in turn, occurred as worship of one's history, and Greeks began to worship perfection of the Greek past, an early paradise of human ideal of grace, now lost.[20]

Rome gradually created its worldview, distinctive from that of Greek, through the evolution and maturity of its own literary expression. With a narrative much less fluid than Greek, Latin produced a clear and more grand vision with more visible layers. Latin literature evolved a different kind of sophistication. Its highly structured vision and complex perspectives did not occur in the much older and more fluid languages.

While other imperial boys needed to go out of their world to find fresh inspiration, Romans inherited a world full of classical images, motifs, expressions, and ideas, which were confusing for their eyes to absorb and their language to grasp. Latin was born within and grew up surrounded by a gallery of ancient portraits that constantly cultivated its taste, vision, and self-image. While other imperial boys struggled to establish their self-images as they encountered alien cultures, all the Latin boy had ever wanted was to imitate the maturity and sophistication of his Greek model.

However, different language always portrayed unique visions of the mind, regardless of the intention of the painter. With its limited vocabulary and expression, Latin vision was extremely abstract. Virgil displayed an abstract theme with a geometrical simplicity. It took several centuries for this hollow vision to be filled with details and images. However, this initial emptiness and simplicity made it easier for Latin to develop clear and precise images and distinct perspectives in literary narrative. It took Latin less time to attain visual diversity than Greek or any of the other European vernaculars, except German.

Latin was the first young language to develop discrepancy in narrative vision, and levels of verbal persona, each of which had distinct perspective, voice, and ideas. It cultivated a literary narrative capable of presenting a dialogue between various perspectives and characters. This was similar to the effect created by theater, but used words rather than a stage. Horace was the first to write narrative that created different postures and personae in different tones.

At this stage of separation, poetic voice had multi-layered connotations that were addressed to various audiences and performed various functions.[21] For example, Horace had several audiences, any of which could be in attendance for any one particular performance.

Gradually, the author disappeared. The secret of all this narrative architecture was the linear simplicity of a tale, in which Encolpius was set up front-stage as a "homodiegetic" narrator. He told his story, he saw everything, and every character moved within his field of vision. He could look on the surface of his narrative, and present with the greatest possible openness all of the ideas, judgments, and associations in his own mind. He saw everything, but could not see himself. Only the author, situated outside the narrative, like his accomplice the reader, could see the narrator as a divine (and ironic) spectator.[22]

On one side there was a narrator who continually fell victim to his desires of heroic self-promotion, and, on the other, an author who fed him situations that could be elevated to the sublime. Here, Latin became sophisticated enough to have a mythomaniac narrator and an ironic author, a novel form which only appeared in a much older literary language.

Latin, now, had developed a narrative structure that was almost as sophisticated as that of Greek, although with far less imaginative fluidity. Instead of an independent novel as in Greek, Latin had fragmented, flawed, and barely functional sequences, "a parasitic, unimaginative parody," in Conte's words.[23] In the midst of these fragments, episodes, and sequences, the author (and his unity of narration) disappeared. The literary repertoire from which Latin writers constantly drew was instead of a continued text mostly a translated collection of pieces, passages, famous recognized scenes, emotional stereotypes, and fine examples from anthologies.[24]

With all the space between and among levels of images, Latin separated from them as persona and as characters behind them. In the Neronian culture, literature became an exhibition, a declamation of speech. Artistic emotion became the desire to gratify the audience. Popular literary words were those of shock, sensationalism, vogue passion, pretension, and disturbing place. Many poets, like Eumolpus tried to reformulate the old Horatian dichotomy, but the distinctions were blurred beneath the pressure of the sublime driven to excess; the furor of *enthousiasmos* got the upper hand. He still wanted his poetic voice to sound like a prophecy, and his spirit remained neglectful in grooming, tormented in expression.[25]

This separation gave writers a tremendous freedom to multiply imagery and to juxtapose seemingly diverse images. Without a visual structure, verbal imageries had a more powerful capacity to create than ever before. For example, it was possible and yet would disturb a pair of eyes if a painter wished to join a human head to a horse's neck or a beautiful female head on a black fish. It seemed easy and natural for poetry to make these connections. It was normal for Horace to present different faces to different audiences as circumstance required. He wore one face, we may presume, in the presence of Augustus, and a quite different face when he was giving orders to his slaves. With multi-personae in his poetic repertoire, the tone of poetry changed. It came to address the direct audience as well as the audience who happened to overhear it.[26]

Since the time of Plato, Greek philosophers noticed that words were a dangerous gift. Rhetoric could empower itself rather than the original context that it was meant to deliver. Words could make black seem white, and old seem young. For Isocrates, rhetoric was something higher. It was a part of practical wisdom, and when combined with general culture, became philosophy.

Latin, without a figurative art as rich as that of Greek, began to evolve its verbal imagery and illustrating power from Petronius' art of deception. The realistic effect of the Cena was derived from the dense weave of the narrative, which was full of details.[27] This verbal imagery deviated from the visual continuity of a participating eye, which reminded of bits of illusion rather than a whole picture. (More like fragmented imageries created by Medieval Chinese and Modern English.) He represented things from inside various partial spheres of life. This explains why the Petronian realm offered a collection of vignettes but did not become a totality.

Modern literary critics have exhibited a tendency to read more into Latin poetry and less of Greek poetry. From the perspective of their own language, they could not believe how confusing Latin poems were. They have been trying for centuries to reduce fluid Greek into the well structured and clean expression of modern vernaculars, while at the same time convincing themselves that Latin poets knew what they were doing, although they sounded absolutely chaotic.[28] The idealized image, borrowed and imitated from Greek classic, and a poorly constructed cultural infrastructure made Latin self-image segregated and multi-layered. Romans were not the only people who had multi personae, but they were clumsy as they switched their masks. They were obvious to the extreme in their portrayal and had the greatest difficulty in delivering a convincing performance. This clumsiness could be seen and heard in Latin poetry.

Latin never had the opportunity to mature before it declined and was eventually replaced by European vernaculars. The abstract and fragmented Latin worldview became the foundation from which the cultures of Western Europe germinated and grew. For the new languages, the hollowness and fragmentation of Latin vision was as essential and important as the sophisticated Greek heritage was to Rome. This made it possible for the European vernaculars to start from different points and stretch in different directions.

During the 18th century, the entanglement between the English self and the world became a central concern. Travel knowledge was defined as a necessary stimulus for understanding and self-improvement. The curiosity of the adventurer and the imagination of the scholar combined and penetrated one another. Unlike Portuguese and Spanish pirates who plundered and exploited in the name of the crown, English travelers were less motivated by sense of duty than a desire to experience and discover.[29]

As the vision of travel literature began to internalize, the entire idea of travel began to transform. It elevated from writing about new surroundings, to an idea. It represented a search for an idealized world, a heaven on earth. Good examples were William Bartram's *Travel Through North and South Carolina, Georgia, East and West Florida*, 1791, and Rossean's concept of nobility and happiness of simple people.[30]

The influence of English travel literature went far beyond the intention of its writers, who wrote within a well framed literary cycle of departure, adventure, and return. As soon as the reader's eyes had opened, the brilliant light of imagination would take over ... there was nothing that could stop the enlightenment. The literary journey become one of self-discovery, as the mental and spiritual expansion that it encouraged allowed a means to step away from one's established self-image and look at the inside from a distance. (In this sense, I agree more with the most recent critics than I do with the conventional critics of travel literature, who see the vision of the reader as one who follows the words and steps where they are led. I believe that the opening of the eyes and mind was more important than what was seen initially.[31])

English self-image, unlike those of Greek and Latin, had clearly defined boundaries after the Enlightenment and scientific revolution. It took great effort to flatten those boundaries and resolve its own image into the portrait of God. The initial English self-image had to be temporarily abstract and faceless, although not any less idealized and glorified.

In the opening years of the eighteenth century the strange distant East was brought vividly and imaginatively before the eyes of English readers through the *Arabian Nights*. English men were amazed by the "store house of ingenious fiction and of splendid imagery."[32] By the end of eighteenth century, *Arabian Nights* had attained its eighteenth "edition." During the next forty years, the rate of its publication was to double.

The British image of self actually evolved and formulated gradually within a collection of images that were complex, variable, and self-contradictory. There were always questions about where the reader could and would go and the location of boundaries. It was a dialogue in one language that attempted to speak for exotic outsiders who spoke different languages and who had different perspectives. Without a medium of translation, the other languages and hence, the other people's images, were distorted, untrue, and sometimes even ridiculous. However, this dialogue broke the silence that had made cultural boundaries unbridgeable. It was the first step in the demolition of the walls of race, culture, and geography.

Romanticist writing pioneered this dialogue, although in the beginning, it was very limited. Romanticism made it possible for a culture to have a dialogue with itself. And as the dialogue began, so did the capacity to speak for others.

Cultural growth began when the imperial boys' language and mind started to wander outside of the prison of their previously declared boundaries. They outgrew their childish and rigid glorification and worship of self. They began to fantasize about others. In the fantasyland, they embraced others and began to question themselves. They came out of the shell of the old language and began a search of their soul. Interaction with other cultures did not begin here, but it was seen and pursued in a different light from this point on.

In Russian, Pushkin's description of the foreign landscape was most poetic, and it was so imaginative that his contemporaries never sufficiently recognized that he invented rather than recorded the Caucasian landscape.[33] Like the French and other Western Europeans, Russian writers did not recapitulate to the English "discovery" of mountain gloom and glory, until the end of the eighteenth century. Unlike Byron, who associated landscape and feelings directly by declaring: "to me high mountains are a feeling," Pushkin dramatized his landscape with sound, smell, and gesture to enhance feelings.[34] During the nineteenth century, Russian imagination, carried by a much more fluid poetic, always traveled faster than English did. Russian poetic imagery quickly moved on and turned landscape into a temple of worship. "I bowed before the Almighty at the foot of the Besh-Tau mountains and equated myself to earth and dust. Indeed I am no more than dust set in motion by passions; and yet by taking wing, this animated dust can ascend to talk to the Creator of the magnificent Caucasus, the Creator of nature."[35]

Unlike English imagination that eventually created a new world to contrast with the old, Russian imagery swiftly reduced the alien world into a distinct gender within the old. Alexander Shishkov's Ketevana, for example, turned Georgia into an erotically enticing female. During his first trip to the sunny verdant country, the place assumed, in his eyes, delightful form of a "beautiful woman, lying luxuriantly on a multi-colored carpet, her head resting on the snowy Caucasus as on a white pillow, while the fragrant roses of Gilan bloom at her foot!"[36]

Unlike in England, where the image of others struggled with the moral side of self-image, the longstanding and ongoing Russian curiosity toward Asia did not turn to academic research until the nineteenth century, when the state became convinced that the oriental knowledge served the purpose of national interest and prestige. Oriental studies became a trophy to win, collect, and decorate the imperial ego. Unlike the French and Germans, who were claiming a young culture's self-promotion as the modern era's poetically superior race (most akin to the East), Russians upgraded themselves in relation to Asia with greater ammunition, since they could boast much more genuine geographical, historical and cultural connections to the East.

Russian feminization of the orient came easily because of Russia's confused identity. The early writings created a mythology of Muslim tribes as shadows, endowed with heroic machismo, a love of liberty, instinctual authenticity, simplicity and an aura of Homeric song. This masculine side of the "other" reflected a more complex self-image compared with that of Western Europe.

The Russian recreation of Georgia (of an age-old Christian culture) was a Muslim female who was the beauty in a chadra, the long veil customarily worn in public by the women of Tiflis. There were hardly any male figures in the perceived land of Georgia. The captive Muslim heroine often was powerless, abused and summarily eliminated, sometimes even executed by her master when he learned that she had a lover.[37] However, unlike the absolute stereotype that Western literature had created, Russian images of the Muslim female carried a double identity. As seen by a cool headed culturally refined Russian, the Asian black eyes were too fiery. A flame burned in them but did not warm the heart. Pushkin's Zarema appeared to be a dark and sensual concubine who determined to preserve her place of preeminence in the seraglio. The oriental thirst for vengeance, ferocity, and killing instinct were portrayed side by side with its attractive moral purity.[38]

This pattern of portraying a cross-cultural erotic alliance reached its zenith in Alexander Odoevsky's "The Marriage of Georgia and the Russian Kingdom." The allegory personified Georgia as a fiery dark "maiden," while Russia was a bold, light brown-haired giant who guided the axis of the world with an iron hand. Afire with passion for her bridegroom, the woman refused all "other suitors" by referring to defeated rivals who failed to win Georgia.[39]

Like Americans of the twentieth century, Russians had a tendency to confuse ethnical and cultural diversity. They did not need to go outside of their own border to peek at the East ... at least, what they thought was the East. Even during the Tsarist times, they could travel just five hundred miles from Moscow to see Eastern faces of all kinds: exotic, charming, bothersome, and distasteful. The East looked far away, yet it was right next door.[40]

The Russian method of corralling various ethnical groups into the empire was far more difficult than that of the Americans. Russians were trying to convert non–Russians who occupied their land to Russian culture and religion. Americans only faced the challenge once, at the very beginning, when they landed on North America and faced aboriginal Indians. In other words, Russians had to fight Indians many times over. They accomplished integration mainly through military ventures, but also used political and administrative integration and cultural assimilation.[41]

Russification of the nineteenth century actually had much more depth than Americafication of the twentieth century. Very much like the emerging trends of the West, which began to understand the other cultures, Russians' assimilation of an alien religion began with education and psychological conversion rather than social isolation.[42]

There were actually two battles across the boundary — military and cultural. The first one seemed much easier than the second. The imperial boy did not always have to deal with the second one. He just came in, got what he came for, and left. But what if he was forced or chose to stay in a foreign land? Of course, he could earn more money than he could in his homeland. One could make a fortune that was absolutely impossible to make anywhere else. One could live incredibly well with an incredibly small amount of money in a country where everything, including slaves, cost next to nothing. It was satisfying to feel like a member of the higher class of society or even like royalty when one was served, waited on, and even worshiped by the locals. The sparks of longing and smiles of gratitude from the Negro, the Chinese, and the Indians left great memories in one's mind of his own importance, as he threw a few loaves of stale bread to these that he oppressed. Kicking someone to the ground always made one feel taller. It was only human to feel good when one was strong and dominant. This exhilarating feeling of being lifted and gratified was shared by the majority of the imperial soldiers and officers who had never felt this way in their own country.[43]

The language of the early English, like the medieval Russian, came with the message of the Christian God. The English speaking Bible gave England a language which penetrated into the levels of a society that had never possessed a language before, even the language of the Renaissance and that of Shakespeare.[44] The English Bible played an extremely important role in educating Englishmen about who they were and who they would like to be. Its influence, as literary inspiration as well as oral rhetoric, was the backbone of English culture until the eighteenth century.[45]

However, God would remain in the people's minds only as long as his language evolved and constantly reproduced new meanings and fresh imageries. The language of Christianity was failing after a few centuries, as English began to evolve into a literary culture.

With the expansion of English literature, the language of God appeared to be more and more inadequate, especially when English poetry was trying to widen its horizon of imagination. The best example of this linguistic blocking was the metaphysical poetry. English suffered poverty of imagery, especially concrete images that could fill the gap between Latin theological and philosophical vision and English vocabularies capable of describing images perceived by visual senses. This was similar to Latin, after the Cicero period, when Latin absorbed all it could from contemporary oral expression and began to verbalize visual images.

The major difference between English and Latin was that the English Renaissance created a much larger and richer repertoire of oral and written idioms. The Renaissance theater, when compared to Latin drama, invigorated oral English and lifted it to an incredibly sophisticated artistic level. It became an inexhaustible fortress of forms, images, motifs, and ideas that became the inspiration for the next centuries of literary elaboration and accumulation. This was the reason that literary English was able to surpass the accomplishments of its Latin heritage.

The English poets of the later Romantic period were the last generation to create poetic imagery against the tyranny of ideas. (I associated Romanticism with universalism rather than racism because I view English literature from a perspective that differs from those of sociologists or researchers of literature, who construct their scholarship within the framework of sociology. As I see literature as form which carries and transforms ideology, Romanticism becomes a forerunner of the cultural renaissance of the twentieth century.) From the beginning of the nineteenth century, the national vision of English poetry became darker, and more abstract. At this time, English was looking for new and grander imageries to carry its imagination.

The frustration of the poets demonstrated how difficult it was to imagine without a verbal latitude as wide as that of Arabic and Greek. English had difficulty describing a broad vision without losing its emotional and visual contact with sensual feelings. When the vision of eighteenth century English expanded, it became stretched too thinly to be impregnated with concrete connotation.

English poetry had a blackout, but it was not the fault of any of Byron, Coleridge, or Wordsworth. When imagination expanded and tried to reach higher altitude, (like a kite, snapping its thread, and disappearing) it lost its perspective of the land below, where it had started its journey, and where its universal vision was anchored. For example, in the years after Coleridge's return from Malta, the wholeness of his vision, which he described in "The Eolian Harp" (1795) was lost.[46] It became "all is blank on high, No constellations alphabet the Sky—/ The heavens one large black letter only shews." In this new, darker vision, the universe, as manifested by the black sky, was unreadable, indecipherable. Nature, once seen as a universal book of English poetry for the past decades, had turned blank and silent. This nullification of the literary symbolism did not occur as a turn of heart or personal ascendance, but it as a conscious choice made by English poets. They decided to cease looking and seeking something behind natural phenomena. As Coleridge put it: "in looking at objects of Nature while I am thinking, as at yonder noon dimglimmering thro' the dewy window-pane, I seem rather to be seeking, as it were, asking, a symbolical language for something within me that already and forever exists, than observing any thing new. Even when that latter is the case, yet still I have always an obscure feeling as if that new phenomenon were the dim Awaking of a forgotten or hidden Truth of my inner nature."[47] It was still the same word, a symbol, logo and the God himself, but it was now found in a different place ... within.

The new vision in "Coeli Enarrant" was poetry of simile rather than metaphor. It was a personification calling attention to its own fictiveness rather than evoking something other than what it was saying. It intended to bring together object of desire and personified abstraction in one self-allusive quotation.[48] Looking into the soul and hoping to find "light," Coleridge was simply asking too much of the formative English to perform a miracle: "A light, a glory, a fair luminous cloud —; Enveloping the Earth...." Or, "A lovely and beautiful Woman, a Woman capable of gazing, in that inward communion of Silence, on Vale, Lake, and Mountain Forest, in the richness of a rising or a setting Sun ... the Angel of Vision."[49]

Coleridge was well aware of the danger of losing the sense of sight. He made it concrete in the image of the blind old man. Without sight, Coleridge asked the English poet to have the ears of an Arab. He needed to be able to "listen in the silent desert ... the touch of a blind man feeling the face of a darling child." His "anti-visual" image successfully projected the feelings of unimage: "The dragon foul and fell —/ The unreveable, / And Hidden one, Whose breath / Give wind and fuel to the fires of Hall!"[50]

Coleridge chose to sail into his own mind looking for a new Heaven and a new Earth. Byron's enlightenment took the form of "sailing beyond horizon," a pilgrimage in the ocean. He turned his back on the worn out and repeated images and set sail for the edge of the world.

In his pilgrim journey, Byron insisted that nature was supremely ambiguous. Her stormy sea could reflect either an all powerful divinity, or the absence of any controlling power at all. This image is projected in his notorious shipwreck passage in Don Juan through a harrowing narrative of panic, madness, cannibalism, and death. The Eternal Sea of Byron changed the perception of nature from truth to uncertainty, and from harmony to chaos.[51]

In different degrees and various means, Romantic poets were trying to expand the language of God through the stretching of both abstract and concrete imageries. Although they had difficulty convincing their contemporaries that they were simply helping to make the Christian God more powerful and compelling, their contribution to English poetics influenced literature for many centuries.[52]

In creating a different mind-set, the mind that is its own place, variations occurred in language as well as vision. As the mind of its own place turned Hell to Heaven, the whole perception of the world transformed.[53] Romantic poetry contributed to the English culture in a fundamental way. It expanded the horizon of English literary language and made it less rigid and more tolerant, and therefore more flexible. It transformed English from a moral language, constructed by adversarial logic, into a formal language, capable of presenting balanced discourse. From this point, language, as form, began to detach from moral judgment.

Unlike any other culture whose development evolved from an expansion of established image, the American self, like the God of the ancient Hebrew, began with a word void of imagery, a conceptual hole. Unlike the hole of Hebrew that emerged due to an inability to paint pictures in words, the American hole was the result of the lack of a unified image. There were too many languages spoken by the new American immigrants ... the gallery of competing portraits was overcrowded.[54]

America had the unique notion that it could understand global matters without traveling anywhere. This was the first imperial boy who had never developed a fascination about other cultures, because he believed that he had the whole of mankind within his own boundary. He confused his ethnical diversity with cultural diversity because his notion of cultural difference was only skin deep.

American cultural identity had been imprisoned in the limited and shaded language of black and white. There was no color on the American palette. This presentation and argument persisted from the time of Mark Twin until the beginning of the twenty-first century. American vision of self and the outside world remained shallow and resisted the temptation to penetrate the skin.[55]

Among many of his contemporary golden boys, the American was the only one who had yet to outgrow his isolating self-worship. He had not yet been rejected, defeated, and therefore, enlightened. He was still living in a fantasy world of his own. His self-centered vision was limited to the illumination provided by his own light. He could not see the darkness beyond his light and he could not see the galaxies beyond his limited vision.

American soldiers had been around the world, but not their writers, especially those of the second half of the twentieth century. The generation of

Ernest Hemingway had died. Since then, American literature had imprisoned itself within its border and sang the same song of self-worship. The only thing foreign in America were the wives and concubines of American solders and the children they fathered while away. Americans did not need to fall in love; love just fell in their laps because of their association with money and power. American globalization was a financial transaction that was negotiated in American English. The world was forced to listen to the American songs of bravado.

While England produced many generations of scholars who devoted their entire lives to the study and understanding of the people of the world, America recruited foreign scholars to produce images of outsiders and present them to the American eyes and minds. One had to agree to be a spice in the American stew before they could enter the American soil. One had to surrender his soul first. From Victorian times, English scholars began to learn Sanskrit, Chinese, Hebrew, Arabic, and Persian. They produced and accumulated volumes and volumes of scholarly work to research the literature, arts, language, customs, and laws of other people. Americans produced one loud voice, called the "science" of humanity and imposed a "universal" structure to organize an empire of information about the world.

In this empire of information, computerized or not, there was only one vision in one language. Every form of scholarship had to choose between the two eyes of America, the left or the right. Within the domain of American vision, there was no need for distinct perspectives. American freedom was compelled to speak American English, which ended at the edge of the melting pot.

American blindness and bias were not based on racism. Compared with other European cultures, America developed a most tolerable attitude toward ethnical distinction and minority rights, thanks to the long tradition of the civil rights movement led by African Americans.

American limitation lies within a formal conformity of its cultural expression and a lack of perspectives or intolerance to non–American perspectives. The triumphs of visual art forms — film and TV — although they inspired imagination, overshadowed verbal and written expression. Visual images, which are supported by commercial and political interests, hold language hostage, and, to a great extent, American culture remains illiterate. In this illiterate democracy, people turned to television for all types of information. They allowed the TV Gods and Goddesses to decide for them what to wear, what to eat, what to read (or not read), and what to think.

American culture, which used to be the most innovative and creative culture of the world, has become a culture of sequels, with its repetition of idea, plot, and sometimes even faces. It is a culture with enormous images that carry shallow meanings. Images that used to inspire poetry and songs, now repress words and smother literacy.

10. Confidence and Tolerance

Confidence and tolerance do not come as moral or political decisions, as sociologists believe. They begin to evolve in a culture as it outgrows its rigid boundary of self and expands its horizon. Confidence emerges from knowledge — knowledge about the world and about oneself, which calms the fear of the unknown. One must know what is outside one's defensive barriers to be comfortable enough to let them down. One needs to come out from behind his defensive wall and has to demystify the imagined enemy. To come out of the shell and feel secure, one has to know oneself and his neighbors well enough to feel unthreatened and simply be one of them, rather than overseeing them. Tolerance comes from seeing and living with diversities which cultivate empathy and flexibility.

Like any culture, imperialist boys were not born with the qualities of confidence and tolerance. They had to learn through accumulation of cultural idioms in which self-images were painted, cultural boundaries were constructed, and distinction bridged.

A sure sign of maturity is the ability to know and accept one's own limitations. With this awareness, it is much easier to accept the way that other people live. And it makes it much easier to talk to other people. The most mature civilizations have learned to speak other languages; they have learned to exchange ideas. With this exchange, connections became tolerance, and tolerance became understanding.

Some of our boys are now men. Some are fathers, and others are grandfathers. Each has the wisdom to know his place in the world ... a place that no one can take from him. Each has learned from his past actions that we all come from many different places, and that we are all at different points on the road that is humanity.... And we are all one.

The pioneer of the new vision was lyrical poetics, which challenged and deviated from the established and rigid ideologies. The poetics here were a literary form, rather than the romantic scheme that is often attached to poetry. It was not a genre, clearly cut and isolated from other literary forms. Although every imperialist boy's rigid vision began to be fragmented by its lyrical poetics, when and how this poetry emerged was often determined by the totality of their literary tapestry.

During the past two centuries, Greek poetics have been largely read and understood as if they spoke Latin or German.[1] Western literature had not yet developed a capacity to present and comprehend multi-dimensional visions from various perspectives, and did not begin to cultivate them until it had accumulated variations in its own languages.

Greek began to penetrate the interior of the human soul through its ancient tragedies as its philosophical tradition evolved to explore the exterior of human life. For more than ten centuries, Greek literature, and later Western literatures attempting to reproduce classical tradition, had followed a theological, philosophical, and rhetoric discourse that dealt with the same metaphysical issues and filled up the experimental gaps between the ideological categories. Romantic writers represented the first generation that was unable to live as easily as their great predecessors within the same ideological comforts which had been fashioned and maintained by their literature. It was a struggle against one's own language and upbringing. It brought deeply troubled feelings and self-doubt to the point where one questioned if he was actually as mad as society presumed. In this particular sense, literary rebellion served as a vanguard of ideological transformation that lagged along for a few centuries. The internalization of vision transformed humanity from an object to a subject which was self-projecting and realizing. The sense of self began with a personal voice rather than a literary genre.[2]

The first epigrams, as fully literary forms, emerged from Greece at the beginning of the Hellenistic age. In fact, they became a favorite form used by those on the cutting edge of literary development.[3] Initiating from oral composition or performance, epigrams presented an unusual presence of erotic, sympotic, and satiric feelings, rather than dedicatory and sepulchral themes. Compared to archaic elegy, these new epigrams had a shorter and yet more focused flow. The continuity and individuality of poetic narrative transformed from the subject, such as Theognis' Cyrnus or Mimnermus' Nanno, to the poet. As his love objects were continually varied by name and nature, as well as by sex, the condition depicted in each epigram was specific to the individual lover in a given time and place. Although the poet could adapt the imagery and motifs of earlier lyric, the speaker of an erotic epigram was a lover whose speech act was dramatized as a monologue (speech directed to himself) or as a dialogue (speech directed to another or divided between two speakers).

It was a different kind of communication, a briefer, more fragmentary, yet more intense and refined style, which evoked particular and momentary emotional states, such as delight, despair, or delusion. While the love poetry of earlier periods evoked feelings by sharing all the customary and common experience of love relations, Hellenistic epigrams stirred readers' emotions by remedial inference of the same feelings in various relations and situations.[4] Hellenistic poets reworked imageries and motifs which conveyed general truth typical to elegy and changed them into a language of specific experience and highly personal feelings.[5]

Hellenistic poetics transformed the general and abstract concepts familiar to archaic elegies into unique and concrete allusion. For example, Asclepiades describes love making (one cloak covering two lovers) as sweeter than an icy drink in summer or sailing to a land of peace after a storm. Asclepiades' preamble on sweetness came from a tradition of generalizing preambles illustrated by a Delian epigram that justice is good, health is the best, but best of all is to gain what one desires.[6] Here he collected and focused on a single allusion of one of the three concepts. He stretched pleasure and desire by adding sensual feelings. Asclepiades bolstered his attempt to remodel erotic desire as a higher pleasure by extending the archaic goal of sexual conquest, as expressed in the Delian epigram, with a different goal of mutual affection — one cloak but a dual honoring of the Cyprian.[7]

This transformation was not only about the attitude towards sexuality or women's roles, but also about the way in which love affairs were described and narrated. Compared with the dialogue-framed narrative of Idyll 14, Asclepiades' epigrams reduced each love affair into a single, brief speech act whose dramatic setting may or may not be discernible. As the archaic reader stood beside the poet to see the suffering of the lover, Aschlepiades' erotic personal speech distilled and intensified the lover's emotion to the point where the reader had to feel his feelings.[8]

Similar complication through poetic form also occurred in poetic irony. As emotional variations were portrayed by the diverse speech acts of erotic poetry, distinct and contrary ideas were expressed in varied tones. One is a life of extreme happiness without knowledge or seafaring; another is a life that flows on waves. Two people were used to project an expressive contrast and an emotional utterance. The reality of the man's existence was evoked with vigorous yet haunting poetry. By reapplying the language of knowledge which Callimachus had used, the author delicately highlighted the contrast of tone. The pedantry of the dramatic character added another ingredient to a rich mixture.[9]

Poetry became more and more suggestive rather than straight forward, and expressed a shifting rather than a controlling perspective.[10] The violence of Homer, the exchange of insults among the herdsmen, was replaced by an exchange of heart felt speech in highly emotional drama.[11] With centuries of poetic accumulation, poetic imagery evolved various allusions and layers of meanings. Hellenistic poets needed a much higher awareness of past poetic texts ... "souls worked out in books." It involved not only familiarity with details of earlier writing, but also embarked on a search for novelty in narrative and technique through an active response to and manipulation of the texts of the past.[12]

Poets had to begin with a web of imageries and allusions that connected them with the past. Their individual voice and vision emerged from a collective thematic continuity, from which they immediately distanced themselves.[13] Initially, it was a combination and mixture of imprecision and specificity, as well as precision and blurring.[14]

Hellenistic poets often picked and reworked Homeric imageries and motifs, which were characterized by short, vivid descriptive passages. They exploited and expanded these imageries by adding new forms and voices. For example, the grander and violent scenes in *Odyssey* were diffused into finer and more focused pastoral images. The third person narration was replaced by the multi first person narratives, which created a much wider space for the reader's interpretations. As there was no authoritative narrator (like Homer) to strip the disguise and analyze the exchange of words between characters, stories gave the impression of observing a strangely playful encounter, where the reader could never quite grasp the rules of game.[15]

As a result, Hellenistic Greek poetry turned epic tradition, which was sung by a soloist, into a polyphony in which there were many voices and visions from various perspectives.[16] In this new network of images and voices, there were songs within a song, stories within a story, a vague authority orchestrated by many voices.[17]

Hellenistic poets announced their withdrawal from public persona. "I loathe everything to do with the people," wrote Callimachus.[18]

Hellenistic masks symbolized the beginning of personal imagination distinct from the collective. Roman masks did not have the opportunity to be personalized enough to be free from the tyranny of words. It had less to do with the basic concepts of mask and performance than with the choices available to Latin writers. Unlike Greek masks, which served as barriers between various layers of personality, Latin persona and masks represented an unbridgeable gap. The Latin word *persona* was a fairly exact translation of the Greek *prosopon*. However, there was no precise Greek equivalent to the Latin synonym *larva*. Larva derived etymologically from *lar*, which meant a household god; *larva* meant a ghost or dead person.[19] Unlike Hellenistic Greek, which had penetrated its rigid opposition, Latin was still obsessed with god/man and death/life opposition — an obsession which centralized all of its cultural activities and institutions. Latin saw total darkness beyond the light and nothing beyond words except their absolute opposites. Gladiators fought to the death. To win was to live and to lose was to die. Greeks often left a mask in a tomb, assuming it would provide a form to create a life beyond death. Latin masks represented a gap rather than a bridge between the opposites. The most revealing example of this fundamental difference was the life cult of Dionysus and the death cults of Rome.

Like any Latin conceptual opposition, there was a deep gap between mask and face, as that between man and God, life and death, and real and unreal. This rigidity was evident from the materials and construction of masks. Dionysus' mask was made of linen rags and glue, while the mask worn for the worship of the Roman Bacchus was made of wood.[20]

Latin inherited the Greek stock of masks and transformed it by polarization and separation of the mask from what was beyond.[21] There were two kinds of masks for different cultural functions. Imago was a mold of a dead person, a man of noble family. A person who had the same physique as the deceased and had been trained in life to imitate him (sometimes a professional actor) would participate in the funeral as the living incarnation of the dead man. Mask, in this context, represented immortality and social nobility.[22] In Latin, positive masks were associated with god or extraordinary humans.

However, Latin comedy masks portrayed a negative image. Unlike Hellenistic masks, which evolved in variations and distortions constructed upon a normative base, such as male or female beauty, Roman masks were the inversion of a noble imago and were necessarily an emblem of ignobility. The animal references in Curculio were more than coincidental and included a lioness, a wolf, a weasel. While the mulier looked like an owl, the leno, with his stomach and green eyes, resembled a frog. With the name of the miles, Therapontigonus suggested a "beast born from the sea." Plautus' characters did not act with the noble qualities of men but with the instincts of beasts. The masks of Plautus preserved the structured outline of the Greek system, but their meaning was completely changed.[23]

The purpose of the early Roman mask was to conceal rather than reveal. It was designed to mask the identity of the face behind it. For example, during the Imperial period, behind masks, actors could express forbidden political views, or pursue an acting career (which was considered improper if one came from a good family). The ritual of masks was used to protect and legitimatize behaviors that were not approved by God or man (society).

Roman masks were much less conventional than Greek masks. Roman masks carried no connotation of past or future. As slaves, for instance, detached from their homeland, with no hope for freedom, they lived only for the present. Young men, likewise, were interested in sex rather than relationships. Prostitutes were welcome, as they offered immediate gratification.[24]

Without the fixed convention that Greek theater had evolved during its long history, the early Roman masks were a play of contrary, unexpected identities, and non (or reversed) identities. There was no such norm or ideal implicit in Plautine theater, where a theatrical mask was the inversion of a noble imago, and was necessarily an emblem of ignobility. Lacking the necessary visual and verbal variations to bridge this gap, Latin commedia created the half-mask. While the Greek mask consumed the actor's personality, the commedia mask left part of the face visible and established the sense that a particular actor had a unique physical presence. While Greek actors slipped from one mask to another, the Latin commedia actors developed a close relationship with their masks, which they wore throughout their careers. The formal distinction between mask and face, a source for novel imagery in Greek theater, vanished in Latin. As the Latin mask was presented with the face of the actor, the character became a real person, and the gap created by the formal distinction, which had made it possible for Greek drama to constantly produce novel imagery and expression, finally began to close.[25] The space between actor and his mask, which constituted the foundation of theatrical creativity, was not recognized by Latin writers. Plautus' masks were created and functioned under the assumption that the audience was aware of the actor's physical presence. Plautus had offered the audience the same apprehension as the role of the player behind the mask. The half mask made actors more visible. An even more revealing mask, which emphasized the mouth and eyes (of the New Comedy mask) allowed the features of the actor to be discerned. The most striking example was a figurine from Asia Minor of the third century. Here the trumpet mouth of the slave became a kind of picture frame, allowing the audience to observe the movement of the actor's mouth. Such a mask would well suit the role of the slave as a "poet" in a drama within a drama.[26]

The comedy of Terence moved closer to the Greek comedy of Menander, where supremacy of the writer dominated. His plays invited the audience to be aware of the aesthetic control which he, the writer, maintained over the performance. Terence consciously reduced the use of masks and visual gesture. Words regained control of theatrical gesture and produced a monopolizing effect. Actions became the means to serve moral argument. In *The Brothers*, present actions were seen as having consequences in future life. The freedom of masks and gestures in Roman theater was short lived. Terence returned narrative back to a clear opposition between those who surrendered to pleasure and those who rejected emotion in preference for duty.

Terence was not in a position to reproduce the nuances of Menander's system of masks. Terence's Roman audience did not possess the same cultural references as the Greek audience. Without Menander's familiarity, Terence was unable to pursue the finer points of Menander's theater and returned to generalization. When theater became nothing more than a mouthpiece of ideology, it simply died.

Like ancient Greek, Arabic, until the time of modern politics, had the least ethnic and territorial consciousness. There is no word that signified the place, Arabia, as in other linguistic tradition. It is most commonly known as "the country of the Arabs." The land was attributed to the people, not the people to the land. In addition, the word for "Arabs," a collective noun, not a plural, derived from a root which most commonly denotes articulateness or expressiveness. Arabs were, originally, those who could make themselves understood. For example, a woman who wore her heart on her sleeve was said to be *arub*. Ancient Arabs had the same attitudes towards alien people as the Greeks. They recognized and defined the human distinction less in terms of geography and ethnic features than language. They used to call foreigners, for example, Persians, *ajam*, which was derived from a root that primarily meant "crunching with the teeth," a metaphor that often connoted indistinctness in speech.[27]

Unlike Western Europeans, whose sense of self was associated with geographic and ethnic origins, Arabs had never created these barriers. The center of Islamic culture had shifted among various places and languages, since the first century of Islam. Although engaged with endless debate and rhetoric with one another, the Medieval Arabs could find compromise and did not resort to war in solving their differences. Meanwhile, medieval Europe was constantly seeking a military solution for its disputes.

Arabic nationalism, unlike Western Europe, whose national identity was a combination of geography, language, ethnical origin, and culture, was nothing but an ideological and political being. The Muslim identity, which focused on pride rather than fear or insecurity, emerged from a civilization that was old enough to grow into conservatism and cynicism. In order to revive a culture, mining the past glory was the only effective tool. This type of nationalism emerged from the civilizations of older languages, during the second half of the twentieth century in China, Iran, Syria, Iraq, and Egypt, just to mention a few. Unlike the imperial boys of the West, who had difficulty when they found themselves in a larger world, the speakers of Old languages knew who they were, and where they wanted to be. Their challenge was to evolve and agree upon a single voice and pin down what they wanted and how to get it. Millions of voices, words, images, portraits, and dreams screamed at the same time competing with one another.

Islamic hegemony was cultural and partially linguistic, because like

Christianity, Islam did not insist that Muslims speak Arabic in everyday life. Even the most radical branches of Islam insisted on political and religious distinction, rather than race.

Performable literature was a middle stage between literacy and illiteracy, and occurred in the history of many cultures. Performable images inspired verbal expression and imagination as language emerged from its infancy, because they were needed to convey meanings that words could yet specifically define. This was the case in the English of the Renaissance theater, as words had not yet developed a density of their own. The function of gesture, at the time, was to build connections toward meaning. With the help of music, scenery, and gesture, theatrical performance carried words on and built a dwelling place for them. By the twentieth century, English had matured and was able to imagine and depict like a camera. Words now had places in the verbal universe. Performance now stretched the words and constructed an extension to the established meaning as they lost their "redundance, a fullness to excess."[28]

In order to make room for visual expression, the words of a formative language chose to retreat from their advanced level of efficiency and expressiveness, which had been achieved through centuries of writing, reading, and discussion. They became hollow (or incomplete) and thin (poor).[29] As writers of drama and screenplay chose to mute their thoughts back to other communicators (actors, musicians, special effects engineers) as an opportunity to portray meaning, they either reluctantly betrayed their own media, or happily covered their lack of verbal talent. After centuries of refining visual images through theater and film, it became harder and harder to find a new story or script. Verbal expression became poorer while visual imagery got richer.[30] American culture became a culture of actors, a culture of poor text, and a culture of illiteracy.

This illiterate tendency could also be observed in political rhetoric. As Aristotle pointed out twenty-five hundred years ago, "When compared, the works of 'writers' appear thin in public debates, while those of orators, when held in the hand and read carefully, appear amateurish — the reason being that they suit debate. So when performance is removed, speeches made to be performed do not fulfil their proper function but appear banal — for instance asyndeton and frequent repetition, properly disallowed in writing, are part of the debating style of orators, for they are performable."[31]

After visual images flourished in films and musical theater, the text behind them began to degenerate. As images advanced and became highly technical, they became hollow. Cultural images became highly repetitive and constantly recycled without adding any new meanings. Verbal language began to die and ideas began to stagnate.

To write about others was more then just speaking for them. It also created a distinct perspective about oneself. It challenged established self-image. If the self-contained lyric represented a claimed clear idea about self-consciousness, the dialogue with self became mocking, jaded, and self-critical. This change of communicative form paved the way to a much larger repertoire of idioms. From a desolate landscape, or some ruined paradise, as in Tennyson's "Mariana" or "Oenone," to a vast mindscape where every mood of the mind had its own outward world, or rather filled the world, it became cluttered with objects that the mind could inhabit.[32]

English civilization, like that of the Romans, began with language of law as well as poetry. Growing up in a formative yet written language, the early English community was much more structured and organized than that of Greek.[33]

English internal enlightenment began well before the colonial period. Global expansion did not initiate the cultural and spiritual cultivation of English. It simply provided it with wider perspective and a richer repertoire of idioms to accelerate the pursuit that had begun since the later medieval.[34]

English of the thirteenth and fourteenth century was not lyrical in any sense of the word, although it had developed relatively rich and diverse prose writing. Italian and French described passionate, dramatic, and exuberant "love" for God, while the English connection with God was a divine touch or mystic marriage, a union with God. The personal encounter with the Divine (which was depicted in autobiographical writing using the word "I,") was intended to be used in the reader's prayers.[35] At this stage of linguistic development, English was capable only of describing men and God as collective categories rather than individuals.

The written language still needed a visual aid. Rolle's text was presented with its full illustrations. It showed Christ on the cross with the instrument of passion. The illustration also indicated that Christ was addressing to mankind, "O mankynde," when he was being crucified with his heart wounded and bleeding. The poem "Ihesu my luf my ioy my reste" was placed underneath his picture, and included a note on the number of the drops of blood that Christ had shed (the nowmer of our lords droppes alle). With such infantile poetic, English did not create a single mystical poet as great as those of the Italian, French, or Spanish.[36]

English faced a much larger challenge to imitate and reproduce Latin visions, compared to the Romantic vernaculars. As the English were writers of contemplative saints, they had to struggle with their formative language. They evolved their own style.[37] These writings pushed English expressive capacity to a new level of intensity and complexity.

Like Biblical Hebrew, English of the fourteenth and fifteenth centuries was a simple and concrete language which had no vocabularies for abstract speculation. This is probably why the Latin language was not widely learned by English speakers. It simply did not appeal to them. Englishmen chose to establish a different kind relation with the Divine. They chose to cultivate devotion and spiritual connection with God using concrete human metaphors. This is why English mystics used the same language as the common prayers. As they communicated emotions as vague as "sweetness" and "love," without Latin specification, English mystics could only fall back on the language of human relationships and of sensual perception. Yet, to do so, they knew that they were risking falsification and confusion.[38]

Unlike Hebrew, which used an external negation to describe the non-definable Divine, English juxtaposed the describable in a positive way to illustrate the abstract. They conveyed mystical love by association with the urgency of desire and courtship in everyday life. To portray oneself as the lover and friend of God, they described the feelings for God in concrete and familiar imageries, such as a comparison of the symptoms of lovesickness, and a shrewd analysis of the gradations between spiritual and physical love. In the opening of *Ego Dormio*, Rolle cast himself as a proxy to woo the recipient, not for himself, but for his lord to bring her to Christ's bed. Margery Kempe heard God spelling out to her the conjugal intimacies that would follow her mystical marriage to the Godhead.

English imagination, as that of many other European vernaculars, took the form of prophecies during the late medieval period. Visual and verbal infinity was pursued under the name of God, or an association with God in various degrees.[39] The descriptive capacity of the English language outgrew the dream visions of religious ecstasy and produced more and more real and sensual visions. The English mind learned to imagine a mixture of visual and mental visions, and so did its language.

Once language could express complex images, it eventually disposed of religion as the source of inspiration as well as the basic framework of the mind. Poetic voice replaced the voice of God. As Blake declared: "I saw no God, nor heard any, in a finite organical perception; but my senses discovered the infinite in everything, and as I was then persuaded, and remain confirmed, that the voice of honest indignation is the voice of God, I cared not for the consequences but wrote."[40]

However, it took English literature many centuries to completely outgrow its Christian framework and replace the vision of God with that of the poets. It was not the simple and linear evolution of science and rationality replacing religion that post–Enlightenment scholars have portrayed. It was a process of revelation, through which Englishmen gradually found themselves with their own words. Both the rise and the fall of English Christianity were deeply rooted in the formal evolution of its literary language. It began from the fifteenth century, when Christianity, which had been articulated in Latin for centuries, was re-imagined and reproduced by a formative English, whose imagery was merely used as allegorical illustration of an established divine vision. Constant writing and rewriting of the same inherited ideas repeatedly sharpened the English poetic vision, as concrete and fresh images were invented and accumulated. When English began to mature, homegrown concrete images began to replace religious allegory. The idea of God had been compared with many familiar and detailed images. It ceased to be a well-structured pyramid and became an extended network of metaphors. As its language expanded, the familiar habit of the English mind was forgotten. Ideas no longer had to carry potentially religious meanings.

This liberation gave poetry and poetic imagination permission to fly beyond established Christian ideology. In this sense, the visions of the Romantic writers marked the end of God's language and the beginning of poetic prophecy. The former was a vision that was perceived as divine because of its direct association with God, while the latter was a vision that contained divine images without him. Traditional monasticism increasingly came under attack from the newer and more evangelical orders in the twelfth century. Unlike the medieval prophetic poets, who uttered original imageries in the name of God, William Blake, prophetic writer in the canon of English literature, challenged the divine origin of any word ever spoken in the English language.[41]

English self-image was one of the fastest developing in history because English writers were prolific, serious, and would go to the ends of the world to write. Perched on the edge of the British Empire, they produced the most original and amazing narratives, which served as a multitude of mirrors to reflect on the image of the English. The non–English image of humanity gradually moved closer and closer, from the periphery to the center. It shocked the English eyes as well as their minds. It took them centuries to recognize and understand what it meant, and what it could do with their own consciousness.[42] The richer repertoire provided opportunities for writers to have more than one life. They had a great variety of selves to call upon, far more than they could find room for.[43]

Fantasizing about others was, more than anything else, about self-reflection and expanding. The images of other people had more to say about oneself than about anyone else.[44] What has been called romanticism after the enlightenment was a natural evolution of cultural expression. English went through a period of clarification and classification which established boundaries of basic concepts of nationhood, as well as legal and social rhetoric. It began to grow away from the rigid shadow of Latin literature. With the accumulation of expressions in various literary and dramatic forms, for the first time, Englishmen experienced a different cultural perspective. It was a different way of seeing, hearing, and understanding. As Hazlitt put it: "It is seeing with the eyes of others, hearing with their ears, and pinning our faith on their understandings."[45]

"Taken over by other" registered a sense of internal dislocation of metropolitan culture that offered itself as a site of resistance for the subjugated. "Troubled or uneasy in mind about some uncertain event, being in painful or disturbing suspense, fraught with trouble or solicitude, distressing, worrying." Confusing self and other, "I was the idol; I was the priest; I was worshiped; I was sacrificed." This passage illustrates Byron's worst dreams ... the squandering of civic and personal identity in the imperialist project.[46]

Racism was a self-defense, an attempt to build walls to protect and to deal with pre-assumed self degeneration by other's diseases.[47] The romantic exotic image was not simply an object appearing out of context, a distant object surviving incongruously in present space; rather, its function was to envelope or absorb the present or familiar within the distant or unfamiliar.[48] The romantic exotic image, like the souvenir, "solicits a grounding narrative." It brings a context with it, "assimilat[ing] its objects to a generalized homogeneity, a wealth of inscrutable detail that is the perquisite of the knowing European to articulate."[49]

In this respect, it differs markedly from the exotic curiosity of an earlier period which, in departing from the aesthetic norm, really served to consolidate neoclassical notions of a standard of taste. In the Romantic eyes, other cultures, which were represented and understood in a new mode of expression, formulated a distinct part of the same world, called oriental.[50] Other cultures that had formerly been regarded in terms of sheer and even immutable difference, were now seen from a properly all-embracing perspective by the late nineteenth century.

The self-image of Imperialist Great Britain gradually changed with its poetry. During the early nineteenth century, Southey's *Life of Horatio, Lord Nelson* (1813) was the most influential book. Published in thirteen editions over forty years, it became the textbook to be in "the chest of every seaman, from the admiral to the cabin boy," and to be carried by sailors "till he has treasured up the example in his memory and his heart."[51] The biography was designed to define British imperialism by embodying it in a paternalist, dutiful manner, through Southey's interpretation and presentation of a Protestant hero.[52] In life, colonies remained "other" but became a safe and manageable uncanny combination of similarity and difference.

Colonization brought Britain into the same realm as other cultures. The interaction with the conquered and subjugated, no matter how unwilling at first, left a great mark on English culture. People from different places were simply perceived as walking mirrors of the English self. Disease, fear of infection and degeneration were the first reactions.

Fear was not only a physical thing. It was moral and psychological too. There was apprehension, of not only pagan beliefs, but also any non–Protestant interpretations of the same Christian God. "Religious madness is infectious," Southey wrote. The revival of monasteries allowed the Catholic clergy to "communicate the contagion." Such contagion would be made political as well as religious by emancipation, and would "introduce a church, which Buonaparte has ostentatiously restored."[53] In the rhetoric of fear, all different cultures could be received as reversible subjects of moral fear of infection. Irish Catholicism was compared with the notorious savage kings of Africa. Religious idolatry and superstition became associated with Jacobinism, Hinduism, and Catholicism. Anyone who resisted British rule was savage and should be kept at distance.[54] The East, sitting apart from other cultures, presented a different kind of fear. In India, Englishmen felt that they were swallowed by climate, landscape, intrigue, madness and death.[55]

There was also guilt. Englishmen had a high opinion of themselves. They saw themselves as highly civilized and just. They were the champions of liberty, independence, and freedom. In its adventure literature, English outgrew and stepped away from the boundary that had been created, meditated, and maintained by Renaissance and classical writings. A new perspective about self-image evolved. Kipling's writing, with its new vision from a different perspective, created a new revision. His work combined the presentation of the texts of the European masters and his more immediate sensual impressions. In his fictions, Kipling recognized and depicted the unstable opposite sides of the English soul, which was constantly in conflict with itself. With a superficial review, all that one could see was a narrative of the distinct worlds of England/empire and India/jungle. Underlying this, however, was the division, contradiction and confusion of the English self-image. His principle character was motivated by an unacknowledged desire and a longing to explore beyond the boundary, and he was restrained by fear. The fear of every boy, whose security depended on a well-defined boundary, was to be seduced by the embrace of Indian life and Indian women. If he transgressed these racial and mental boundaries, he would lose his Englishness.[56]

Kipling portrayed levels of self in a constant conflict between desire and dread. He used metaphor and metonymy to blur the distinctive levels. He achieved this by balancing forward movements of discovery with regressive movements, controlled by fear and dreams that threatened his being. He risked the assertion of similarity between the self and other, between narrative voice and the blind face that silently cries and could not wipe its eyes (*la nuit blanche*). He compared Englishmen whose insomnia drove "the night into my head," and Indians in the cities of "dreadful night." [57]

However, writing about darkness was, in itself, a process to enlighten the dark experience. Writing about this fear was therapeutic. As the English writers slayed their dragons of fear and destruction, the English language became enlightened again. Gradually, English was able to see beyond darkness and isolation, and it became an internal light that carried past the visual boundaries. Writers were constantly traveling, examining the outside from shifting perspectives, and describing the hidden and the forbidden. The vision of the English universe kept expanding until it enveloped the world.

Like Latin, the English of the nineteenth century was a language that created a self-image based on visual imitation. Self-portrait was extremely important to the English mind. Disorder and contradiction were shielded by this inflated and armored image. This external origin of self-image required a large army to protect its interests. Until the twentieth century, it was essential for the English soul to see and touch its boundary. This made them feel secure and confident. The fear described in Kipling's stories was real and internal. The mind of the culture of a young language was much like a boy who was afraid to close his eyes, hoping that by keeping his eyes open, "ill dreams and power of darkness" would not drive him into an early grave.[58]

This internalization of images and transformation from "other worldly" curiosity to absorptive expression was supported by the development of English culture itself. English imagination needed a brand new world to feed it. Other cultures became a safe place to explore new and fresh images. After the mass production of highly abstract ideas during the classic period, language and imagination became quite rigid and dry. This left a deep gap between ideas and reality, between empty notions and concrete images. The stock of novel presentation and exotic "verisimilitude" served the purpose well in the "return of the visible."[59] The exploration and presentation of other cultures became a literary tool to destabilize and reverse the established ideology of the previous era.

English poets had long careers as priests; their words lifted man's heart to the holy.[60] Their preaching language remained the same although they kept changing the god. They became the priests of nature during the Romantic period. They eventually became God themselves. Wordsworth, Coleridge, and John Keats might have been terrified if they knew that they would be worshiped as gods of letters. During their times, God was much more sacred. They did not know that the modern men would use their words, but not pursue the same God to whom they originally had written. Now, their words were used to paint new idolatry. They worshiped their words, not as a means to search for God, but to give them freedom to create and collect their own gods.

They worshiped poets because they refused to bow down their minds to take orders.[61] Poets were worshiped because their words were the only ones that could stretch ideas enough to accommodate a community of independent, imaginative minds. They provided the weapon to fight against oneself, wings to fly from the prison of a doctrine to a higher creed.[62] Poets were the only men who had the ability to be their own god.

While the British Empire collapsed as a military and political institution, English literature expanded and flourished in territories that the English monarchy had never dreamed of occupying. English became the language in which the best and most original writers chose to write. Although English was not yet the most expressive language of the world, its worldwide following was hungry for words and books.

While it matured, English became more sensitive and more expressive. Many talented writers whose first language was something else chose to write in English while they could freely express themselves. The nuances of English allowed a harmonious transition between words and feelings. Besides, English readers were very serious about their words. English could activate more intense emotions and stir deeper feelings than any of the older, worn out, and highly ritualized languages. English readers were hungry for good stories, expression, and they read with a sense of tragedy and urgency. They could debate ideas and exchange insults, but they never slipped away using the excuses of abstraction, intellect, or mystery. Their minds were thirsty for inspiration rather than numbed by slippery dancing words. They engaged the expression of feelings and new ideas. As a young language, English was more instinctive and less politicized (compared to German) and ritualized (compared to Italian), therefore less contained and controlled by tyranny.[63]

By loaning itself to non–English speakers, English substantially expanded its cultural horizon and ability to comprehend the world. Non-English speakers wrote in English during the second half of the twentieth century both by choice and necessity. To escape political repression and pursue freedom, they came from languages with much older and richer traditions, and their words were more precisely sensitive and emotionally provocative. Reading English of the late twentieth century was like living many lives in many places. One could live in India by reading Nepal, Pakistan by reading Rushdie, Sir Lanka by reading Michael Angelo, and China by reading Gu. Most importantly, English reading and understanding was continuing to deepen. It was alive, not only in its characters (as a subject), but also in the minds of the readers ... a most engaging experience of novel forms of expression. The literature of non–English speakers, especially those from older civilizations, transplanted new seeds of imagination into English. The soil of the English flower was fertilized, and the blooms flourished!

Writers whose first languages were richer in narrative and poetics than English substantially expanded English's capacity to clearly envisage. English words began to project thought as clearly, precisely, and as engagingly as motion pictures. For example, in Salman Rushdie's *Midnight's Children*, Saleem witnesses his mother having an affair in a café, then mocks her indirect kiss, and finally censors the scene by tearing himself from the window.[64]

The first reason why it took America much longer to mature was historical circumstance rather than choice. America, emerging after World War II, hardly had any real interaction with other cultures. American intervention in world affairs had been mainly through diplomacy, and with very little human contact. Although American military involvement spread around globe, Americans had never presented themselves an opportunity to live side by side with other people in different lands. Yes, American soldiers brought Asian wives home, but they became American citizens, a piece of the American stew. However, taking immigrants from various parts of the world gave them an opportunity to observe alien cultures in a secure setting. As the most racially diversified country on earth, America felt that its land represented the whole world. There was no need to search out the unknown. America confused immigration policy and foreign policy. The former was to embrace anyone who surrendered his own language and was willing to jump into the American pot ... to be colored and flavored by American culture. The latter was to learn to speak other people's languages and to meet them halfway.

Most Americans could not tell the difference due to their lack of knowledge about world history and other cultures. They were always wondering why anyone would not want to be an American. They thought that America was the best and most powerful country in the world. If every country in the world behaved as Americans, the whole world would live happily ever after. Not everyone believed this childish dream. For many, America was a god who had bullied his way to a position of authority. He had the ability to repress anyone who did not agree with him. Being an American, decorated with glittering images of money and power, was a heady experience. It was not only gratifying, it was satisfying to be able to do whatever one wished to the people of other countries.

The British and French invested centuries in learning the national languages of their colonies. They always looked for a way to cultivate relationships with them. The scholarship of Orientalism, with all its prejudice and bias, initiated a dialogue with other cultures. It had established that there was difference in language and mindset which was beyond translation. Americans did not even have a desire to do that. They had better solutions. They compelled the entire world to speak English, their English. With endless funding for research, they simply paid foreign scholars, with dollars or green cards, to produce literature about other cultures in American English.

This was a brilliant strategy. It replaced cultural diversity with politics and global perspective with ethnic mixture. America understood global culture and history only as deep as the color of skin. It allowed resident non–American scholars a very narrow spectrum of choice ... the inch and a half between the eyes ... from the American right to its left.

America did not intend to limit anyone's vision. It had proclaimed itself the land of opportunity and freedom. However, vision could not be free if one could not change vantage points. Global understanding was impossible if one spoke only a fragment of a single language in a world community that spoke hundreds of tongues.

As a young culture, American views were contra, polarized, highly classified, and segregated. Popular culture was governed by highly controlled images that produced simplified stories and ideas. Brilliant visual variations accumulated and repeated the same values. God was renamed and yet imitated and worshiped with the same passion. When money and sex became the new God, he demanded a new sacrifice — the celebrities. They shared God's light and glory but not his wisdom. What did wisdom have to do with God anyway, if one could be successful without knowing the ways of the world? There was another god, worshiped by a different crowd — the people of "high culture." American intellectuals had built their own temple to worship their own God — science — the totality of knowledge applicable to universal affairs. One needed highly specified training to be a part of these chosen few. It was a different kind of association with God, and was centered in a special language. With highly abstract jargon, American intellectuals built their Babel with words — words that no one could understand except themselves. But, mysticism was always a sign of power, and even of the divine.

American popular culture was highly visualized and illiterate. The habit of watching and hearing rather than reading and writing suppressed cultural idioms and promoted a low level of literacy. Americans do not yet know the cost of this shortcoming in global matters, as they depend on their rhetoric of war to mold world opinions. And, it does. However, boys usually fight until their nose and legs are broken, because they always refuse to listen to anyone except themselves.

Russian Enlightenment was never as abstract and rational as that in the West. Russian Romanticism was based on a combination rather than an opposition to nationalism. Russian mysticism actually was immersed in the spirit of eighteenth-century rationalism and showed influence of the Romantic Movement. It was a conscious and eclectic choice. Russian thinkers did not believe that they were incompatible with the rest of the world.

Romanticism was the first abstract thought that Russian had ever produced. Looking at the world from the heights of the absolute, Russian writers, first of all, turned away from political interest. With this burden removed, they were encouraged to despise earthbound "empiricism" and to shut their eyes to the burning social and political issues of the day.[65]

Lermontov, in the late years of his life, experienced the same anguish about unity as did the English writers and poets. Unlike the writing inspired by Georgia, late Lermontov's portrayal of the Muslim tribes conveyed a suspicion that their conquest was a spiritually losing proposition for Russia. His self-mocking reference to Napoleon's claim: "les grands noms se font a l'Orient," and his taste for the "addictive form of gambling" of military aggression, suggested that he was troubled by Russia's imperial commitment. However, like most English poets, he was too loyal to the existing collective cultural image to associate Russia with the brutal Romans. He created the high-minded German hero (Franz) to guard his sanity. Franz hid a heroine (Ambra) in his tent, moralistically declined her sexual invitation, and tried to marry her after the military authority had forced her to go home to her father, a powerful sheik. After describing the Bedouin woman as an erotic slave of love, Lermontov let her die a brutal death.[66]

Lermontov's blurring depiction of distinct identities was much more vivid and penetrating than any of the English novelists of the nineteenth century. As a profound poet who would never describe directly his political or theoretic intent (such as the genteel coat of civilization to cover the savage within), Lermontov visualized a pattern of degeneration into the primitive. Over a seven year period, a chivalrous Christian soldier gradually submitted to savage standards. Now a daunting intriguer, he teased the proud young princess into falling in love with him, ruined her reputation, provoked a duel with her rejected admirer, and slayed him.

In Lermontov's eyes, Asia was, after all, not as alien, remote, or contrary as portrayed in English literature. Asia needed not to have a single ethnic origin or a cultural inferiority. "Asia" was within the sight of every Russian. By readily adhering to savage standards, Pechorin regressed to release the "Asia" within him, that realm of depravity, which Belinsky's essay on Polezhaev would proclaim as a monstrous part of everybody. In this specific sense, Lermonov dismantled the therapeutic fiction of oriental alterity. This had not been done in Western Europe until the latter nineteenth century.

The reason why Russian, the youngest literary language in Europe, could penetrate quicker and deeper in the description of the human mind was, until the twentieth century, Russian, as a literature, had very little interruption from abstract ideas. While the literatures of Western Europe were struggling with their rigid ideological boundaries of civility/primitive, self/other, masculine/feminine, and correct/incorrect, Russian had already muted these boundaries through literary and poetic meditation. This process did not begin in Western literature until a century later. The expansion of Russian expression traveled the road of storytelling, instead of philosophy or psychology.

Like English literature (until the twentieth century), otherness (or cross boundary), Caucasus in Russian literature was the birthplace of poetry.[67] Unlike the English Romanticism that initiated an individual vision of the world, Russian Romanticism associated with nationalism, a collective individuality. Although the wisdom-lovers emphasized the spiritual part of national culture, as distinct from the Decembrists' "body politic" of legislation and an "aggregation of citizens," they conceived the nation as a whole, transcending its individual parts. By the latter half of the 1820s, the Russians made a clean break from the English romanticism of nature and focused on the philosophy of history. They transformed the conceptual ground of philosophical debate from rational and irrational, as normally conceived in the Western Enlightenment, into an opposition between native culture of Russia and that of the West.

By the late nineteenth century, Russian evolved into a language capable of abstract thinking. The time and sequence of the Russian reception of abstract thought were extremely important to the way in which it chose and assimilated German philosophy. Unlike English, whose verbal world was literally created under the influence of the established philosophy Russian only occasionally flirted with philosophy, until its literary and political language became mature enough to branch out an abstract level of expression. On this much more elaborate and diversified literary base, Russian chose the philosophy of Hegel, which was most compatible to its own worldview.

With German philosophy, Belinsky finally established a system that rationalized all the opposite tendencies that had evolved in Russian history and made them a whole. However, unlike the Germans, whose philosophy was based on an abstract notion of reason, the Russian whole came from a concrete image: Russia. When Hegelian negation was applied to Russian history, variations and opposite tendencies became interpreted as a linear growth from Russia as a people to Russia as a nation.

Belinsky's vision of pre–Petrine Russia was surprisingly similar to that presented by the Slavophiles, although he came to a different conclusion. Before Peter the Great, the Russian people (the nation in the age of immediacy) had been a close-knit community held together by faith and custom. These very qualities allowed no room for the emergence of rational thought or individuality, and thus prevented dynamic social change. To break up a stagnant society, Russia had to develop a gap between the cultivated elite and the common people. (This gap would disappear in time, with the progress of civilization.) The Petrine reforms, which initiated social gap, were the first step toward modern Russia. Before Peter the Great, Russia was merely a people of a geography. She became a nation (*natsiia*) thanks to the reform.

The Petrine reform thus represented the radical negation of the natural immediacy of ancient Russia. In accordance with the dialectical process, however, this antithesis had to be followed by a synthesis, a dialectical return to "immediacy" on a higher plane. The reform of the Enlightenment negated ancient Russian immediacy in the name of the universal human values represented by European civilization. These universal values had, in turn, to assume national form so that the negation of immediate instinctive nationality could lead to the positive emergence of a new conscious national awareness.[68]

According to this national awareness, the individual voice within the society was completely negated by the Russian speaking German Hegelian logic. As Belinsky put it: "Nationalities are the individualities of mankind. Without nations mankind would be a lifeless abstraction, a word without content, a meaningless sound. In this respect I would rather join the Slavophiles than stay with the humanist cosmopolitans because even if the former make mistakes they err like living human beings, whereas the latter make even the truth sound like the embodiment of some abstract logic.... Therefore, as long as a man had a nationality he did not need an individuality. Since great men were always children of their country, sons of their nation, for they are great just because they are representatives of their nation."[69]

The Russian cult of Hegelian totality eventually uprooted philosophy from German soil and transplanted it in Russian, a language that had just started to build the notions of abstract meanings.

———

Arabic poetics was a language of freedom. It was a formal freedom that had not yet been seen in English until the twentieth century. It went far beyond ideological rebellion and superficial word play. It was free because, after long history of poetic elaboration, its imagery became extremely refined, vivid, and highly fluid. Unlike an English poet who had to dissect images into pieces and reassemble them, Arabic poets could just pick up the images, which were already in pieces, and make them flow. These images not only transcended all the boundaries between light and darkness, between life and death, and between man and God, they also created a panoramic view that changes every minute according to human emotion. For example, while English described nature as an abstract image (such as the beauty walks with Wordsworth), nature in Arabic flows as water in various forms, shapes and colors as carried by the mood of the poet. One poet asked his lover to take him as he was rather than to capture or contain him like a cloud, a rainbow, a dam, a waterfall or a lake. He warned her that his waters would pour into her and yet rush on. Like a river that hated containment, he would slip over the rocks of her waterfall. He advised her to be wide and deep to accept him so he could pour into her.[70]

With these loosely connected images, Arabic poetic created a universe of words that penetrated and flowed seamlessly with emotion. Instead of the pretty irrigation system dug by formative languages, Arabic words flowed as naturally as water and as effortlessly as air. As water, it rained, poured, arrested, clouded, contained, froze, distilled, and overflowed dams, lakes, and oceans. As air it burned, exploded, and evaporated. Charged with this dynamic energy, Arabic created many lives and worlds, each of which looked and felt different. Khalil Hawi's sharp and biting ideas were expressed in his very simple dramatic imagery and diction: midnight, Christmas Eve, no breath, an empty street, unholy corridor, caves of the city and night of the tombs. A god of the lost was hidden from the land of civilization and ideas were born among the borrowed faces and minds in the caves of the underworld. Under the red lantern, a door named earthly paradise where roses had no thorns and the naked were innocent.[71]

Arab poets were also uncompromising and penetrating about matters concerning their God. They asked direct questions: "What does a disc of light do to my country?" "What does the moon do to us, so that we lose our pride and live to beseech the heavens?" With precision of imagery, Arabic poetic could depict passion as well as cynicism. "The wall fell between God and myself," "when I cut my pocket into swaddling clothes, and my sleeve into a blanket," "when I warmed the bones of the children with my flesh," and when I undressed my wound to bandage the gash of others. As the poet being crucified, he sees "the eyes of guns block my path." "They plot my death with their iron and fire" while the "remembrance and love are the eyes of my people."[72]

Like English imagination that germinated in religious languages, Arabic poetry was both the seeds and fruit of Islamic mysticism, especially Sufism. An ascetic and mystical element that was implicitly present in Islam since its very inception became explicit during the first Islamic centuries (the seventh and eighth centuries A.D.). This period witnessed the appearance of the first Muslim devotees and "moral athletes" who formed primitive ascetic communities in the central and eastern lands of Islam, primarily in Mesopotamia, Syria and Eastern Iran. By the thirteenth century, such early communities had spread all over the Islamic world. Together, they formed a new social institution, the *tariqas* (brotherhoods), which had their distinct devotional practices, lifestyle, moral and ethical system, educational philosophy, and a semi-independent economy. In the later Middle Ages (the twelfth to sixteenth century) Sufism became a dominant feature of the Muslim social order. Its common textbooks and authorities, its networks of *tariqas* institutions and its distinctive lifestyles became the spiritual and intellectual glue that held together the culturally and ethnically diverse societies huddled up under the Islamic umbrella. Unlike Christian mysticism, which was overshadowed and marginalized by the secularizing and rationalistic tendencies in Western European societies that culminated in the Enlightenment, its Muslim counterpart, Sufism, retained its pervasive influence on the spiritual and intellectual life of Muslims until the beginning of the twenty-first century.[73]

Early Sufis paid close attention to the underlying motives of their actions and sought to impregnate them with a deeper spiritual meaning. This goal was achieved through a meticulous contemplation on the Qur'anic revelation through imitation of the Prophet's piety, introspection, as well as voluntary poverty, and self-motification. Strenuous efforts aimed at self-purification and self-improvement (*jihad, mujahada*) were sometimes accompanied by voluntary military service in which many renowned early ascetics settled in search of a pure life and livelihood, or as the case may be, martyrdom in the path of God. The acts of penitence and self-renunciation were justified by their practitioners through references to certain Qur'anic verses and the Prophet's utterances.

They believed that the truly God-fearing person should try to save himself by withdrawing from the overbearing world and its sinful and unjust ways. As an outward sign of this pietistic withdrawal, some of them adopted a distinct dress code, which often featured a rough woolen robe. This robe set them apart from people wearing more expensive silk or cotton. Willing or not, the early Muslim religiosi came to resemble Christian monks and ascetics, who also donned coarse woolen clothes as a symbol of penitence and contempt for worldly luxuries.[74]

While most early Muslim ascetics emphasized personal purity, moral uprightness, fear of God, and strict compliance with the letter of the divine law, there were those who carried their search of God's favor a bit further. The latter group, who could be viewed as the forerunners of the Sufi movement, strove to achieve a psychological and experiential proximity with God through self-imposed deprivations (such as abstinence from food and sex). They insisted on self-effacing humility, supererogatory religious practices, long vigils, pious meditation on the meaning of the Qur'anic text, and a single-minded concentration on the divine object. In their ardent search for intimacy with God, they sought inspiration in the following Qur'anic verses: "If My servants ask thee concerning Me, I am indeed close: I listen to the prayer of every suplicant, when he calleth on me" (2: 185/186); "We are nearer to him [man] than his jugular vein" (50:15/16), and "Withersoever ye turn, there is the Face of God" (2:144–5).

Likewise, the primitive Muslim mystics pondered on those Islamic traditions (hadith) which pointed to God's imminent presence in this world. Thus, in one tradition, God said: "I am present when My servant thinks of Me.... And whosoever seeks to approach me by a span, I approach him by a cubit;

and he who seeks to approach me by one cubit, I will seek to approach him by two fathoms; and whoever walks towards me, I will run towards him."[75]

In another popular hadith, the Prophet encouraged believers to serve God as if they could see him, to count themselves among the dead, to know that the little quantity that sufficed them was better than the abundance that distracted them (from the worship of their Lord) and to realize that a pious deed persists forever, while a transgression is never forgotten (by God). In meditating on these and similar scriptural passages and on the precepts attributed to the Prophet's pious followers, the representatives of the nascent Sufi movement developed a strict code of behavior which encouraged repentance, abstinence from worldly delights, frugality and voluntary poverty.

Qur'anic verse (5:54/57): "He [God] loves them, and they love Him." Inspired by this and similar verse and traditions, the early mystics began to celebrate their longing for the beloved Divine in poems and utterances of exceptional beauty and verve. It was this exalted love and longing which, in their eyes, justified the austerities to which they subjected themselves in order to demonstrate their faithfulness to the heavenly beloved. In the teachings and statements of the early mystics, their feeling of intimacy with God was often mixed with an intense fear of divine retribution for the slightest slippage in or through action exhibited by God's servant, or even for his momentary neglectfulness of divine grace (*ghafla*). Also prominent in early mystical speculations was the idea of an eternal covenant between God and the human race, prior to their creation as individual human beings endowed with sinful and restive bodies. Basing themselves on the Qur'an (7:172), Sufi theorists described the emergence from "the reins of the sons of Adam" as human souls in the form of particles of light. The particles bore testimony to the sovereignty of their Lord in pre-eternity and promised him their faithfulness and devotion. However, once the human souls had acquired their bodies and found themselves in the corrupt world of false idols and appearances, they forgot their promise and succumbed to temptations.

The mystic's goal, therefore, consisted of "recapturing the rapture" of the day of covenant in an effort to reinforce the state of primordial purity and faithfulness that characterized the soul-particles before their actual creation.[76] In an attempt to achieve this goal the mystic had to contend not only with the corruptive trappings of the world, but also with his own base emotions, which Sufis saw as the self-serving evil lusts and passions that impeded their progress towards God. It was therefore his task to look into himself and exercise self-restraint, with the aim of doing away with the self and all the impulses emanating from it. For as long as self was enduring, true Islam, true surrender to God's will, was not possible.[77]

Rabi'a often described two types of love: one that seeks its own satisfaction, and one that is directed toward God alone. But the love that is worthy of him, she implied, was the love of his beauty "which He revealed to her." The latter was far superior to the former. Anticipating the theosophical speculations of later Muslim mystics, Rabi'a described her arduous attempts to achieve union with the Divine (*wasl*). According to one of her verses, "My hope is for union with Thee, for that is the goal of my desire!" Elsewhere, she said, "I have ceased to exist and annihilated my own self. I have thus become one with God and am now altogether His." In later accounts of her life and teaching, Rabi'a presented herself as a true mystic inspired by an ardent love of God and conscious of having entered into unitive life with him. Her emphasis on love of God distinguished her from contemporary ascetics and quietists who were preoccupied with abstention from earthly delights, maintaining ritual purity, voluntary poverty, fear of God, and meticulous observance of religious duties. In the later Sufi tradition, Rabi'a is portrayed as the first exponent and the very embodiment of pure, disinterested love of God for his own sake alone. In a similar vein, she is depicted as the first to combine the preaching of divine love with the doctrine of unveiling (*tajalli*; *kashf*) of God before as his lover.[78]

In the ninth century, Basra and to lesser extent Kufa remained the main centers of ascetic and mystical life in Islam. In Syria, Abu Sulayman al-Darani (d. 830) placed special emphasis on trust in God. He also preached a total, unconditional acceptance of the divine will (*rida*). He seems to have viewed these concepts as the pinnacle of ascetic piety (*zuhd*). He said: "There is nothing in either this world or the next ... of sufficient importance to keep men back from God: everything that distracts man from God, whether family or child, is to be regarded as misfortune." The true knowledge of God was to be obtained by strict obedience. This single-minded commitment helped to explain Abut Sulayman's preference for celibacy. According to him, "The sweetness of adoration and undisturbed surrender of the heart, which the single man can feel, the married man can never experience." Seen from this perspective, women were the major distraction from God. In his words, "There is nothing on earth more pleasant than women." Paradoxically, his thinking did not prevent him from having a wife and a son. In contrast to Shaqiq, he was not a fighter for religion. He regarded the struggle against the passions and drives of one's self as a much more noble, albeit also more difficult task. One should constantly watch over one's heart to keep him from engaging in sinful actions.[79]

With a mature poetic, Islamic writer al-Muhasibi developed a mystical psychology during the later Middle Ages, centuries before the Christian West. The term al-Muhasibi derived from the phrase *muhasaba al-nafs* (taking account of oneself or examining one's conscience).[80] His principle work, *Kitab al-n'aya li-huquq Allah* (*Book of Observance of What Is Due to God*), was the first to give a detailed account of the science of scrupulous introspection to be practiced by anyone who aspired to a godly life and sincere worship of God. This work revealed profound knowledge of human nature and its weaknesses and suggested means to combat these weaknesses to attain to the single-hearted service of God.

Al-Muhasibi's analysis of the most secret motions of the soul and heart allowed him to go beyond the simple ascetic piety of his predecessors which manifested itself in spectacular feats of self-abnegation, voluntary poverty and mortification of the flesh. Wary of this superficial asceticism, al-Muhasibi encouraged his followers to avoid an ostentatious display of righteousness. He warned that it often results in *riya'*, a concept that in his discourse connotes simultaneously such vices as "hypocrisy," "vainglory," and "complacency." Abu Yazid al-Bistami (d.848) describes:

> I saw that my spirit was borne to the heavens. It looked at nothing and gave no heed, though Paradise and Hell were displayed to it, for it was freed of [apparent] phenomena and veils. Then I became a bird, whose body was of Oneness and whose wings were of Everlastingness, and I continued to fly in the air of the Absolute, until I passed into the sphere of Purification, and gazed upon the field of Eternity and beheld there the tree of Oneness. When I looked, I myself was all those. I cried: "O Lord, with my I-ness I cannot attain to Thee, and I cannot escape from my selfhood. What am I to do?" God spake: "O Abu Yazid, thou must win release from thy thou-ness by following my Beloved [Muhammad]. Smear thine eyes with the dust of his feet and follow him continually."

In describing one of his most intense encounters with the Divine Reality: "I gazed upon Him with the eye of truth, and said to Him: 'Who is this?' He said: 'This is neither I nor other than I. There is no God but I.' Then he changed me out of my identity into His selfhood.... Then I ... communed with Him with the tongue of His Grace, saying: 'How fares it with me with Three?' He said: 'I am Thine through thee: there is no God but Thou.'"[81]

Here the boundary between man and divine became blurred and eventually vanished; God and worshiper reversed the role; they became an undifferentiated one.[82] Al-Hallaj described the union with God in a more vivid manner, as if his spirit and that of God mingled as amber mixed with fragrant musk, and as if they reside (*halalna*) in a single body. This line of thinking reaches its culmination in the poetic lines that became emblematic of al-Hallaj's entire teaching: God's humanity manifested in the form of one who eats and drinks.[83]

During the middle of the tenth to the middle of the eleventh century, Sufi tradition was codified into systems.[84] Sufi science reached its maturity at the hands of al-Ghazali. His *The Revival of the Religious Science* (*Ihya' 'ulum al-din*) was a detailed synthesis of theological and mystical sciences accumulated by the Muslim community over the centuries.[85]

The seemingly diverse poetic expression and mystical experience of Sufism were rooted in and bound by the same common use of poetic Arabic, which was capable of expressing subtle connotation and multi-dimensional association. The Arabic self was multi-dimensional because it was expressed in an open-ended poetic. At times it could be self-expressive and even self-assertive, as well as self-annihilative. At times it could verbalize personal sentiment or be a silent contemplation of God. The accumulation of subtle variations of emotional and formal expression increased the elasticity of the language and extended the chain of association.

Different cultural maturity defines various degrees in which the mind's eyes can see and the ear can hear. The best Islamic poetry made one see the moon appearing in the morning sky. Everything emerged and fell in and out of a divine ocean of forms and flakes.... Arabic eyes could see various manifestations in every tree, rock, and animal and hear the inner voice of meaning.[86]

Arabic cultivated thousands of highly personal and overlapping images of God and his Muslim community. Islam became a huge umbrella or wide spectrum of ideologies, with highly extreme and modest variations. The words of Allah could be interpreted to justify any human activities from the most noble to the cruelest.

Russian had an interpretation of Greek classical culture similar to that of Germany. Russian ideals were just as abstract as that of German.[87] Alexander Herzen grew up in a world dominated by French and German historical romanticism. It did not take Russians long to find and reach the limitation of French romanticism and to replace words for things. Russians chose to be the "cold" head of Romantics. Herzen thought that both French romanticism and German idealism were too hollow to have anything to do with real life. Although growing up with an ideal of personal freedom, Herzen, as a Russian who had a particular distinct sense of form, knew that fanaticism, enforced virtues, and official and rhetorical moralities could not substitute for life. He had the good sense to know that "the masses are indifferent to individual freedom, liberty of speech; the masses love authority. They are still blinded by the arrogant glitter of power, they are offended by those who stand alone. By equality they understand equality of oppression ... they want a social government to rule for their benefit, and not, like the present one, against it. But to govern themselves doesn't enter their heads."[88]

In Russian mind, words, especially seemingly magical words, were seen as untrue, and essentially a representation distinct from reality. Western Europe did not reach this conclusion until the latter part of the twentieth century. Russia saw abstract ideas such as liberty, social justice, and equality as cruel altars upon which many innocent people had sacrificed their lives because they were excited, fascinated, and inflamed by the empty words.[89] In this particular sense, Russian had not truly believed in either Romanticism or classicism. It flew beyond both because it did not have a Latin phase in its history. It did not take the detour that Western Europe did.

The Russian mind, after critically absorbing French Romanticism and German idealism, possessed a large and wide horizon that was much more fluid than that of Western Europe. Both Russian thinkers and writers could easily move back and forth in between polarized Western concepts such as realism and idealism, civility and cruelty, complex diversity and primitive harmony. This repeated fluid conversion altered all rigid moral, religious, and political convictions ... religious/secular, spontaneity/obligation, right/wrong, civilization/brutality and education/manipulation. Russian philosophers and writers did not find answers for all of these contradictions and they did not attempt to reconcile them. However, their search and struggle with these ideas as well as the questions that they raised made Russian writing and meaning universal.[90]

Russian "nihilists" of the nineteenth century were different from those of Germany. They were first class literary writers. They did not challenge Romanticism to pursue mystical illumination or integration. They were not interested in the protocol of chasing a god. But through their sharp eyes, they could perceive distinctions overlooked by philosophers. They found the incoherence in philosophical logic. They were scrupulously empirical, rational, tough-minded and realistic. The rebellion of words could only show what was not. They simply wiped the paint off the face of the Godhead and made it empty again. They told habitual worshipers, who had rushed to new sacrifice for the new god, that the Romantic prophet was not the new god. God existed, but he was somewhere else. Verbal reality could not be cheated and explained away with philosophy.[91]

The reason Russian literature and philosophy accelerated to modern form much more quickly than that of Western Europe was its language. Instead of being twice reoriented, Russian was rooted in its original oral poetic and codified by Greek Orthodox. Its original fluidity made philosophical adaptation much easier than for the European vernaculars, especially those of Germanic origin. It was very much like the Islamic Arabic, which had difficulty classifying meanings and stabilizing conceptual boundaries during the classical time, and then, internalizing and juxtaposing contraries into a conceptual whole well before the modern period. Russian, which was less fluid and refined than Arabic, due to its comparatively short time in oral form, had no trouble expanding its conceptual horizon to consider the abstract and quickly returning to meditate in between. (Spanish was another example of this much swifter transformation from classical/romantic opposition to modern fluidity because of its much later and smoother transition from Latin to Castilian, as well as its assimilation of mature Arabic.[92])

Russians worshiped writers because they were the ones who could see, make one see unseen visions, and provoke awareness. Unlike American and English writers, who created characters, often conflicting characters who reflected one particular social or racial group, Russian writers created gods for the Russian worshipers whose lives had no meaning except to devote and sacrifice. The gallery of cultural images in American English was a collection of diverse mirrors competing for the attention of admirers. As a competition, the goal of the game was to create a dominant hero or anti-hero. Lacking of this single-minded purpose, the Russian gallery of literary images was not a competition to be divine. It was a world of worshipers who saw the divine in various lights and understood him from various perspectives. Each image, the god, the worshiper, the good, and the evil had its own unique voice, consciousness, perspective, and soul.

In this specific sense, the author became an invisible God who impassively viewed his handiwork and presented his drama with pretended indifference, "silently paring his fingernails."[93] The Russian writer's disappearance in their fiction was highly skillful and magical. Its symphony of voices had a more powerful moral and rhetorical impact than that of English fictions. Within the span of a century, Russian literature, which was only a regional concern of Eastern Europe, evolved into a literary giant. It demonstrated a level of fluidity and refinement that took English and other Western vernaculars many more decades to attain.

Russian writers were also the first ones to create non-moral gods. And they began writing criticism against everyone's moral gods. Turgenev was the first such writer in Europe.[94]

Unlike other imperialist boys, America was a nation built by a single and mature literary language. With its rich and diverse sub-verbal expression, American English substantially stretched and reinvented the British English in a new cultural environment. American culture evolved through constant interaction between its transplanted words and native sub-verbal images and between written English and the spoken and performed American language. American literature meditated, assimilated, and transformed the images and ideas that had accumulated in Europe.

However, compared to the pre–Renaissance English, the Latin of republic period, pre–Islamic Arabic, and Medieval Russian, the language of American English enjoyed a much higher degree of stability and consistency. Because of this literary maturity and verbal consistency, new cultural activities in

North America did not alter the structure of the English language or radically change its worldview, which had established its basic conceptions before the seventeenth century. American cultural innovation expanded and reinterpreted English language. It opened new frontiers of imagination and widened its horizon, but it did not shift its viewpoint. During the latter part of the seventeenth century, when English was transplanted to North America, it was already a language mature enough to function as a legal, political, and later, scientific language. With English, America inherited established and sophisticated philosophical, religious, and political ideas. However, American English, at the time, was a transplanted language that left its entire childhood and youth in England. American English was a language of the Bible cut off from its medieval literary canon of Christianity, which had embraced classical literature and philosophy of both platonic and mystic traditions. American English was the language of Shakespeare without its theatrical repertoire, which had envisaged and cultivated English eyes and minds.

Initially, the transplanted English was a language uprooted from its oral language articulated in speech and performance, and a language without voice.[95] However, it was a strong and vibrant seed which took deep roots in the North American soil. To survive in a cultural vacancy, American English had to create its voice by composing its own speech and performance. The form of American speech and performance would determine not only the nature of American English, but also the nature of American cultural identity.

Growing in a wild and vacant land, void of cultural expression during the first few centuries, American cultural activities were mainly formulated and controlled by the written words which they brought from Europe. In a way similar to the Russian experience, although for different reasons, the initial speech and performance of American English was devoted to explanation and understanding of the word of God in the English Bible. This reinterpretation attempted to build a relationship with God in a new world that was much more formless and restless than the old.

As the Christian God began to speak American English, He did so with a collection of literature as thin and poor as the orthodox Christian that Russian inherited from Byzantine Greek. The English Bible and books of prayers, compiled by Puritan and Calvinist churches, were the place where American literature began its new journey. However, compared to the emerging written Russian, English was a much richer and more mature language whose inner strength survived. As soon as the American English created it own speech and performance, its literature quickly flourished and triumphed.

By leaving its multi-lingual childhood behind, American English did not inherit a verbal and ideological gap between abstract and concrete, public and private, and between legal and religious expression. By the seventeenth century, this gap in English had been substantially narrowed by the accumulation of dramatic and poetic literature since the English Renaissance. The English idea of the unwritten nature law, which constantly interacted and supervised human law, did not take root in America. This historic reservation on human words and their rhetorical function would never be a part of the American culture and political philosophy.

Like many young cultures, America was built on a transparent language and an abstract idea. The debate about its specific name, image, and form was the engine that drove and inspired its nation's creativity. It was the same idea that the English language had coined yet did not have the opportunity to reach its completion. Freedom and equality could not be practiced to its ultimate form in a land filled with social ladders and formal rituals. On the barren land of America of the seventeenth and eighteenth centuries, physically as well as literally (without the formal hierarchy that was established in England), each American faced God individually and equally, and contributed to the society indiscriminately. Each gave two shillings a year to the public library, regardless if he was a major in the militia, the Baptist deacon, or the member of Congress. Money equalized every single citizen, the Baptists, the Methodists, the saved and the damned, the learned and the vulgar, the authorized, and the unauthorized. This created a freemasonry of tolerance and self-improvement.

Unlike early Latin, Middle English, or pre–Classical Russian, which grew through a codifying voice with letters, American English accumulated its vocabulary and expression by repeating, reinventing, and imitating previously written words. American English was a written rhetoric rather than an oral eloquence. In written rhetoric, words always dominate and control the performance of language. Unlike a shared assumption or abstract principles, whose meaning could be enacted through writing, the American constitution was a document whose meaning expanded and multiplied through reinterpretation. American English was a dialogue that was recorded as soon as it was spoken. American ideas were formulated by building a network of written words through interpretation.

Until the twentieth century, American English was primarily an ongoing dialogue and a verbal contest. Various perspectives made themselves heard through a grand symphony where each sound, rhythm, and word counterbalanced one another. None of these voices alone could make the music. In a young and transparent language, like the ancient Greek during the Athenian democracy, each individual voice had the same volume although various distinct characteristics were apparent. It was a contest of oral rhetoric, whose dominance and influence began, ended, and was determined with each speech and each performance.

During the nineteenth century, as America gradually created its own canon of literature, written language and rhetoric played an increasingly important role in cultural development. Like many emerging empires, whose language of prose clarified and redefined national image, the language of distinction in America was abstract and hollow. Without established cultural idioms and social hierarchy, the balance of the verbal contest in America was determined by number — the number of votes required to ratify proposals of idea and social value. From the very beginning, Americans realized that it was impossible to formulate a country like England, an ideal commonwealth with one king, one godhead (church), and one tongue. Americans had to build a union from the believers of dozens of religions factors, who lived in various regional sections, each with a unique set of values and characteristics. Added to this already complex mix was the constant flow of new Americans who were seduced by the new ideas of freedom and individual pursuit. A national rivalry emerged as the number of nationalized citizens grew.[96] The only imaginable language capable of carrying negotiation among these diverse groups and interests was the language of numbers, which defined and limited each by representation. This interlocking control system was later verbalized and legalized as a form of federalism that fragmented and limited political power of state institutions. This secured individual rights and kept democracy at its grassroots.

As the language of democracy accumulated layers of meanings and connotations through centuries of political rhetoric, ideas became diversified and less transparent. As the level of diversity expanded, a more absolute collective value was required to secure the rift in ideology and culture. During the first two centuries of American history, this linguistic glue was the Christian God. Unlike in England, religion was perceived as opposite to science and material life. American English, in a highly personal tone, always associated God with commercial success and social mobility. Personal prosperity was often read as a sign of divine approval. God's will was believed to be revealed within the human lifetime rather than fixing exclusively on future rewards and punishment. By the end of the eighteenth century, most Protestant leaders in America had accepted the fundamental premise of a free market and the morality of individuals making private decisions about their resources, including the free use of their time and talents.

In America, God became the witness and supporter of the human contest for material gain. The Second Great Awakening reshaped American Christianity, pulling ordinary people, black and white, into the dense circuitry of meetings and services of the proselytizing denominations. This reinvigorated men's and women's religious affections through vernacular preaching about the anguish of individual sinners. America's free churches, like its free men, appeared to thrive on expanded choices, personal autonomy, and ardent striving. Having reached new converts by preaching a very personal message about sin and redemption, evangelical ministers found it easy to look to individual success as a sign of divine approval.[97]

The focal point of the American ideological redefinition did not concern itself with the specific image of God or nature, as it had in the philosophical debate of eighteenth century England. American English did not produce poetry, painting a natural world filled with vivid images. American God or nature was a much grander notion, which had a much more personal relationship with them. It was not about the otherness of the world, but rather about how I, as an individual, related to God and made him work for me.

In America, unlike in England, where man had to choose between man and God (or nature), this world and the other, God became a blessing for human utility, justification, and manipulation. Instead of converting to God, Americans converted God and made him their ally and servant through reinterpretation and ritualization of the words of God. In both cases, what was written had become assumed, but no longer spoken. The gap between man and God (or nature) in British English did not exist in fluid American English. Any American, individual or institution, with God-given right regardless of education or moral conduct, could speak for him.

The divine right to speak for someone else, even someone like God or the founding fathers of the nation, became an assumption, no longer spoken, yet taken for granted.[98] This assumption confused original imagination with reinterpretation or revision, and literary authorship with political (or instrumental) rhetoric. With centuries of political discourse about the same ideas, American dialogue became louder and noisier, yet had less and less substance. The high level of conformity and repetition silenced the real voices which once made America original. As Americans repeated God's words and began to feel and sound like Him, they forgot their human limitations. When they began to enjoy their own voice more than a symphony of various sounds, they lost their ears and eyes. They could no longer hear anyone else in the world.

Chapter Notes

Chapter 1

1. Edward, 1979, *Kadmos the Phoenician: A Study in Greek Legends and the Mycenaean Age*, Amsterdam: Adolf M. Hakkert, 15, 45–65; M. C. Astour, 1967, *Hellenosemitica: An Ethnical and Cultural Study in West Semitic Impact on Mycenaean Greece*, Leiden: Brill, 1–112; Braun, 2006a, "The Greeks in Near East" *The Cambridge Ancient History Pt. 3. The Expansion of the Greek World, Eighth to Sixth Centuries B.C.*, Cambridge: Cambridge University Press, 1–31; Braun, "The Greeks in Egypt," *Ibid.*, 32–56; A. I. Baumgarten, 1981, *The Phoenician History of Philo of Byblos: A Commentary*, Leiden: Brill, 8–139; A. Bernstein, 1993, *The Formation of Hell: Death and Retribution in the Ancient and Early Christian Worlds*, Ithaca, NY: Cornell University Press, 1–130; J. Boardman, 1999, *The Greeks Overseas: Their Early Colonies and Trade*, New York: Thames and Hudson, 39–69; R. Brown, 1977, *Semitic Influence in Hellenic Mythology*, New York: Arno Press, 4–22, 41–76; J. Chadwick, 1976, *The Mycenaean World*, New York: Cambridge University Press, 1–34, 61–101; Hagg, 1983, *The Greek Renaissance of the Eight Century B.C.: Tradition and Innovation*, Stockholm: Svenska institutet, 8–51; D. G. Hogarth, 1909, *Ionia and the East*, Oxford: Clarendon Press, 7–98; H. R. Immerwahr, 1990, *Attic Scrip: A Survey*, Oxford: Clarendon Press, 7–23; Jastrow, 1905–12, *Die Religion Babyloniens und Assyriens*, Giessen, A. Topelmann, vol. 2, 11–13, 484–455; Mondi, 1970, *Greek and Near Eastern Mythology: Approaches to Greek Myth*, Baltimore, MD: Johns Hopkins University Press, 141–198; R. Parker, 1996, *Athenian Religion: A History*, Oxford: Clarendon, 1–121; B. B. Powell, 1991, *Homer and the Origin of the Greek Alphabet*, Cambridge: Cambridge University Press, 114–226; T. B. L. Webster, 1958, *From Mycenae to Homer*, London: Methuen, 1–90; Dunbabin and Boardman, 1957, *The Greeks and Their Eastern Neighbours: Studies in the Relations Between Greece and the Countries of the Near East in the 8th and 7th Centuries B.C.*, London: Soc. for the Promotion of Hellenic Studies, 21–58; L. R. Farnell, 1911, *Greece and Babylon: A Comparative Sketch of Mesopotamian Anatolian and Hellenic Religions*, Edinburgh: T. Clark, 5–39.

2. Bernal, 1987, *Black Athena: The Afroasiatic Roots of Classical Civilization*, New Brunswick, NJ: Rutgers University Press, 121–188; Bernal, 1996, *Black Athena 2. The Archaeological and Documentary Evidence*, New Brunswick, NJ: Rutgers University Press, 63–153; Bernal, 2001, *Black Athena Writes Back: Martin Bernal Responds to His Critics*, Durham: Duke University Press, 165–248.

3. Guthrie, 1962–1981, *A History of Greek Philosophy*, 6 vols. Cambridge: Cambridge University Press, I: 33–5; Aristotle, 1976, *Aristotle's Metaphysics*, Oxford: Clarendon Press, 981 b 23; R. Turcan, 1996, *The Cults of the Roman Empire*, New York: Blackwell, 75–129.

4. C. Freeman, 2004. *Egypt, Greece, and Rome: Civilizations of the Ancient Mediterranean*, Oxford: Oxford University Press, 136–7.

5. Freeman, 2004, 137–8.

6. T. Rasmussen and N. Spivey, 1991, *Looking at Greek Vases*, Cambridge: Cambridge University Press, 37–102; Boardman, 1974, *Athenian Black Figure Vases*, New York: Oxford University Press, 31–51; Boardman, 1975, *Athenian Red Figure Vases*, New York: Oxford University Press, 89–178.

7. R. Neer, 1995, *The Lion's Eye: Imitation and Understanding in Attic Red-figure Representations* 51: 118–53; Steiner, 2001, *Images in Mind, Statues in Archaic and Classical Greek Literature and Thought*, Princeton, NJ: Princeton University Press, 19–52.

8. Boardman, 1999, 4–38; H. V. Herrmann, 1975, "Hellas," *Reallexikon der Assyriologie und vorderasiatischen Archaeologie* (Berlin) 4: 303–311; Akurgal, 1968, *The Birth of Greek Art: The*

Mediterranean and the Near East, London: Methuen, 10–39; Dunbabin and Boardman, 1957, 24–34.

9. Haskell, 1993, *History and Its Images: Art and the Interpretation of the Past*, New Haven, CT: Yale University Press, 159–200; Buxton, 1994, *Imaginary Greece*, Cambridge: Cambridge University Press, ii–xiv.

10. Guthrie, 1962–1981, I: 28.

11. Sampson, 1985, *Writing Systems: A Linguistic Introduction*, Stanford: Stanford University Press, 44–119; Foster and Foster, 2009, *Civilizations of Ancient Iraq*, Princeton, NJ: Princeton University Press, 51–66; Cross, 1991, "The Invention and Development of the Alphabet," *The Origin of Writing*, Lincoln: University of Nebraska Press, 77–90; Daniels and Bright, 1996, *The World's Writing Systems*, New York: Oxford University Press, 19–87; Senner, 1991, *The Origins of Writing*, Lincoln: University of Nebraska Press, 43–90; Houston, 2004, *The First Writing: Script Invention as History and Process*, Cambridge: Cambridge University Press, 71–99, 274–312; Kuhrt, 1995, *The Ancient Near East c. 3000–330 B.C.*, London: Routledge, 4–6; Nissen, 1988, *The Early History of the Ancient Near East, 9000–2000 B.C.*, Chicago: University of Chicago Press, 136–137, 150–152, 179–180; Woods, 2010, *Visible Language: Inventions of Writing in the Ancient Middle East and Beyond*, Chicago: Oriental Institute of the University of Chicago, 1–62.

12. Driver, 1976, *Semitic Writing from Picture to Alphabet*, Oxford: Oxford University Press, 137–8.

13. Immerwahr, 1989, "Historiography," *The Cambridge History of Classical Literature*, Cambridge: Cambridge University Press, 14–24, 65–66; Kennedy, 1989, "Language and Meaning in Archaic and Classic Greece," *The Cambridge History of Literary Criticism*, Cambridge: Cambridge University Press, 1: 87–88.

14. W. Harris, 1989, *Ancient Literacy*, Cambridge, MA: Harvard University Press, 147–174.

15. A. M. Anderson, 1994, *Music and Musicians in Ancient Greece*, Ithaca, NY: Cornell University Press, 27–57; Barker, 1984, *Greek Musical Writings, Vol. I: The Musician and His Art*, Cambridge: Cambridge University Press, 195–210; Sach, 1943, *The Rise of Music in the Ancient World, East and West*, New York: W. W. Norton, 30–47; Hagel, 2010, *Ancient Greek Music: A New Technical History*, Cambridge: Cambridge University Press, 53–96; Landels, 1999, *Music in Ancient Greece and Rome*, London: Routledge, 163–205; Mathiesen, 1999, *Apollo's Lyre, Greek Music and Music Theory in Antiquity and Middle Age*, Lincoln: University of Nebraska Press, 23–158; M. West, 1994a, *Ancient Greek Music*, Oxford: Clarendon Press, 129–217; West and Pohlmann, 2001, *Documents of Ancient Greek Music:* *The Extant Melodies and Fragments*, Oxford: Clarendon Press, 5–21.

16. Nunn, 1996, *Ancient Egyptian Medicine*, Norman: University of Oklahoma Press, 163–90; Cassar, 1974, "Surgical Instruments on a Tomb Slab in Roman Malta," *Medical History* 18: 89–92.

17. K. Kerenyi, 1980, *The Gods of the Greeks*, New York: Thames and Hudson, 74–111; M. P. O. Morford and L. J. Lenardon, 2006, *Classical Mythology*. Oxford University Press, 503–542; Woodard, 2007, *The Cambridge Companion to Greek Mythology*, Cambridge: Cambridge University Press, 503–541.

18. Guthrie, 1962–1981, especially vols. 1 and 2.

19. Carr, 2010, *An Introduction to the Bible: Sacred Texts and Imperial Contexts*. Malden, MA: Wiley-Blackwell, 221–268; Carr, 2011, *The Formation of the Hebrew Bible: A New Reconstruction*, New York: Oxford University Press, 153–179.

20. J. H. Taylor, 2001, *Death and the Afterlife in Ancient Egypt*. Chicago: University of Chicago Press, 2–135; Nunn, 1996, 42–63.

21. Pinch, 2004, *Egyptian Mythology: A Guide to the Gods, Goddesses, and Traditions of Ancient Egypt*, Oxford: Oxford University Press, 149–151; Wilkinson, 2003, *The Complete Gods and Goddesses of Ancient Egypt*, New York: Thames and Hudson, 257–259; Armour, 1986, *Gods and Myths of Ancient Egypt*, Cairo: American University in Cairo Press, 54–59.

22. Parkinson, 1991, *Voices from Ancient Egypt: An Anthology of Middle Kingdom Writings*, London: British Museum, 145–51; Hare, 1999, *Remembering Osiris: Number, Gender, and the Word in Ancient Egyptian Representational Systems*, Stanford: Stanford University Press, 137–147.

23. Cockburn, 1975, "Autopsy of an Egyptian Mummy," *Science* 187: 1155–60; Cockburn, 1998, *Mummies, Disease and Ancient Cultures*, Cambridge: Cambridge University Press, 15–37; Dollery, 1994, "Medicine and the Pharmacological Revolution," *Journal of the Royal College of Physicians* 28: 59–69; Estes, 2004, *The Medical Skills of Ancient Egypt*, Sagamore Beach, MA: Science History Publications, 43–45; Majno, 1975, *The Healing Hand: Man and Wound in the Ancient World*, Cambridge, MA: Harvard University Press, 29–140; Nunn, 1996, 163–90; Cassar, 1974, 89–92.

24. Dodson, 2003, *The Hieroglyphs of Ancient Egypt*, London: Sterling, 6–8; Wilson, 2003, *Sacred Signs: Hieroglyphs in Ancient Egypt*, Oxford: Oxford University Press, 17–37.

25. The only graphic language to survive over five thousands years unmarried to another language was ancient Chinese, because Chinese was a far better developed written language. By 12th century B.C., it already had more than 3,000

words, while Akkadian, inherited and developed from Sumerian, only had 600 words and syllable signs.

26. Driver, 1976, 78–127.

27. Westenholz, 1997, *Legends of the Kings of Akkade: The Texts*, Winona Lake, IN: Eisenbrauns, 24–29; Linvingstone, 1989, *Court Poetry and Literary Miscellanea*, Helsinki: Helsinki University Press, 4–10; Denning-Bolle, 1982, *Wisdom in Akkadian Literature: Expression, Instruction, Dialogue*, Leiden: Ex Oriente Lux, 13–35; Grayson, 1975, *Babylonian Historical-literary Texts*, Toronto: University of Toronto Press, 3–15; Lambert, Millard and Civl, 1999, *Atra-hasis: The Babylonian Story of the Flood*, Winona Lake, IN: Eisenbrauns, 1–24; Guinan, 2006, *If a Man Builds a Joyful House: Assyriological Studies in Honor of Erle Verdun Leichty*, Leiden: Brill, 209–222; Melville and Slotsky, 2010, *Opening the Tablet Box: Near Eastern Studies in Honor of Benjamin R. Foster*, Leiden: Brill, 3–35.

28. Westenholz, 1997, 52–56.

29. Freeman, 2004, 60.

30. Driver, 1976, 78–127.

31. Harrison, 1991, 257–321; Bremmer, 1994, *Greek Religion*, Oxford: Oxford University Press, 69–83; Hadley, 2000, *The Cult of Asherah in Ancient Israel and Judah: Evidence for a Hebrew Goddess*, New York: Cambridge University Press, 188–205; Hurwit, 1999, *The Athenian Acropolis: History, Mythology, and Archaeology from the Neolithic Era to the Present*, Cambridge: Cambridge University Press, 235–245; Patai, 1990, *The Hebrew Goddess*, Detroit, MI: Wayne State University Press, 23–33.

32. Faulkner, 2011, *The Homeric Hymns Interpretative Essays*, Oxford: Oxford University Press, 10–14; Hine, 2005, *Works of Hesiod and the Homeric Hymns*, Chicago: University of Chicago Press, 53–94; Lloyd-Jones, 1971, *The Justice of Zeus*, Berkeley: University of California Press, 2–32; J. Griffin, 1983, *Homer on Life and Death*, Oxford: Oxford University Press, 144–204; Griffin, 1980, *Homer*, New York: Hill and Wang, 16–76.

33. Alden, 2000, *Homer Beside Himself: Paranarratives in the Iliad*, Oxford: Oxford University Press, 153–178; Calame, 1999, *The Poetics of Eros in Ancient Greece*, Princeton, NJ: Princeton University Press, 13–38; Friedrich, 1978, *The Meaning of Aphrodite*, Chicago: University of Chicago Press, 7–25; Diggle, 1970, *Euripides: Phaeton*, Cambridge: Cambridge University Press, 4–7.

34. S. N. Kramer, 1956, *Twenty-five Firsts in Man's Recorded History: From the Tablets of Sumer*, Indian Hills, CO: Falcon's Wing Press, 143–144, 170–171; Kramer, 1989, *Myth of Enki, the Crafty God*, Oxford: Oxford University Press, 1–5, 38–40; Kramer, 1997, *Sumerian Mythology: A Study of Spiritual and Literary*

Achievement in the Third Millennium B.C., Philadelphia: University of Pennsylvania Press, 44–110; Dalley, 2009, *Myths from Mesopotamia: Creation, the Flood, Gilgamesh, and Others*, Oxford: Oxford University Press, 39–153.

35. Harrison, 1991, 263–321.

36. C. Kerenyi, 1975, *Zeus and Hera: Archetypal Image of Father, Husband, and Wife*, London: Routledge & Kegan, 3–28.

37. Patai, 1990, 62–3; Cross, 1997, *Canaanite Myth and Hebrew Epic: Essays in the History of the Religion of Israel*, Cambridge, MA: Harvard University Press, 4–6.

38. M. L. West, 1988, *Hesiod's "Theogony" and "Works and Days,"* Oxford: Oxford University Press; R. Lamberton, 1986, *Homer the Theologian: Neoplatonist Allegorical Reading and the Growth of the Epic Tradition*, Berkeley: University of California Press, 1–10.

39. Long, 1999, *The Cambridge Companion to Early Greek Philosophy*, Cambridge: Cambridge University Press, 1–4.

40. Romm, 1998, *Herodotus*, New Haven, CT: Yale University Press, 13–16.

41. West, 1988, 4–11; West, 1985, *The Hesiodic Catalogue of Women: Its Nature, Structure, and Origins*, Oxford: Clarendon Press, 31–54; Lefkowitz, 2003, *Greek Gods, Human Lives: What We Can Learn From Myths*, New Haven, CT: Yale University Press, 209–33.

42. Burkert, 1985, *Greek Religion*, Cambridge, MA: Harvard University Press, 182.

43. Plato, *Republic*, 2, 365; Nilsson, 1948, *Greek Piety*, Oxford: Clarendon Press, 84–91; Heisserer, 1980, *Alexander the Great and the Greeks: The Epigraphic Evidence*, Norman: University of Oklahoma Press, 1–23; Hammond, Griffith, and Walbank, 1979, *A History of Macedonia*, Oxford: Clarendon Press, 152–8; Fishwick, 1991, *The Imperial Cult in the Latin West: Studies in the Ruler Cult of the Western Provinces of the Roman Empire*, Leiden: Brill, 6–12.

44. Ps. 6: 8–9, 18: 6, 20: 5–6, 22, 27: 6, 34, 40: 1–2, 56: 13; Exod. 5: 22–6: 1, 32: 11–14, Judg. 6: 22–3, 10: 10–6, 13: 8–9; 1 Kgs. 3: 6–14, 17: 17–24; 2 Kgs. 6: 17–20, 19: 14–20; Miller, 1994, *They Cried to the Lord: The Form and Theology of Biblical Prayer*, Minneapolis: Fortress Press, 136–77.

45. Brinkman, 1984, *Prelude to Empire: Babylonian Society and Politics, 747–626 B.C.*, Philadelphia: University Museum, 2–34; Kramer, 1989, 99–126; Kramer, 1981, 60–4; Oppenheim, 1964, *Ancient Mesopotamia*, Chicago: University of Chicago Press, 180–1, 295–6; Jacobsen, 1976, *The Treasure of Darkness*, New Haven, CT: Yale University Press, 21, 110–6; S. Langdon, 1919, *Sumerian Liturgies and Psalms*. Philadelphia: University of Pennsylvania Museum, 36; Wilson, 1965, "An Introduction to Babylonian Psychiatry," *Assyriological Studies* 16: 289–98;

Hooke, 1963, *Babylonian and Assyrian Religion*, Norman: University of Oklahoma Press, 29–40; Buren, 1938, *The Flowing Vase and the God with Streams*, Berlin: H. Schoetz., 115–43.

46. Harrison, 1991, 3.

47. Guthrie, 1962–1981, I: 30.

48. Bowersock, 1990a, *Hellenism in Latin Antiquity*, Cambridge: Cambridge University Press, 41–44; Hopkinson, 1994, "Homeric Episodes in Nonnus," *Studies in the Dionysiaca of Nonnus*, 9–42; Hollis, 1994, "Nonnus and Hellenistic Poetry," *Studies in the Dionysiaca of Nonnus*, Cambridge: Cambridge University Press, 43–62; Chulvin, 1991, *Mythologies et geographie dionysiaque: Recherches sur l'oeuvre de Nonnos de Panopolis*, Clermont-Ferrand: Adosa, 11–21; Whitby, 1985, "The Occasion of Paul in the Silentiary's Ekphrasis of S. Sophia," *Cambridge Quarterly* 36: 215–28.

49. Momigliano, 1987, *On Pagans, Jews, and Christians*, Middletown: Wesleyan University Press, 79–99; B. Croke, 1990, *The Early Development of Byzantine Chronicles: Studies in John Malalas*, Sydney: Australian Association for Byzantine Studies, 27–54.

50. R. Markus, 1990, *The End of Ancient Christianity*, Cambridge: Cambridge University Press, 223–48.

51. MacCoull, 1988, *Dioscorus of Aphrodito: His Work and His World*, Berkeley: University of California Press, 134–46; Liebeschuetz, 1979, *Continuity and Change in Roman Religion*, Oxford: Clarendon Press, 228–30; Liebeschuetz, 1989, *Barbarians and Bishops: Army, Church, and State in the Age of Arcadius and Chrysostom*, Oxford: Clarendon Press, 3–24; Liebeschuetz, 2006, *Decline and Change in Late Antiquity: Religion, Barbarians and their Historiography*, Burlington, VT: Ashgate, 2–5; Zayadine, 1989, "Peintures et mosaiques mythologiques en Jordanie," *Iconographic Classique et Identities Regionales*, Paris: Flammarion, 406–32.

52. Wiseman, 1995, *Remus: A Roman Myth*, Cambridge: Cambridge University Press, 129–32; Sandbach, 1977, *The Comic Theater of Greece and Rome*, New York: Norton, 103–5; Cornell, 1991b, "The Tyranny of the Evidence: A Discussion of the Possible Uses of Literacy in Etruria and Latium in the Archaic Age," *Literacy in the Roman World*, Ann Arbor, MI: Journal of Roman Archaeology, 1–24.

53. Salmon, 1982, *The Making of Roman Italy*, Ithaca, NY: Cornell University Press, 1–3.

54. Sandbach, 1977, 108–17.

55. Mawer, 1960, *The Art of Mime: Its History and Technique in Education and Theater*, London: Methuen, 89–91, 125–126; Lust, 2000, *From the Greek Mimes to Marcel Marceau and Beyond: Mimes, Actors, Pierrots, and Clowns: A Chronicle of the Many Visages of Mime in the Theatre*, Lanham, MD: Scarecrow Press, 19–35;

Laberius, 2010, *Decimus Laberius: the Fragments*, Cambridge: Cambridge University Press, 1–15; 57–66.

56. Sandbach, 1977, 113–6.

57. Conte, 1994b, *Latin Literature: A History*, Baltimore: Johns Hopkins University Press, 29–38; Duckworth, 1952, *The Nature of Roman Comedy: A Study in Popular Entertainment*, Princeton, NJ: Princeton University Press, 39–72; Lowe, 2007, *Comedy*, Cambridge: Cambridge University Press, 81–114; Sandbach, 1977, 111–117; Wright, 1974, Dancing in Chains: The Stylistic Unity of the Comoedia Palliata, Rome: American Academy, 63–87; Segal, 1968, *Poetry and Myth in Ancient Pastoral: Essays on Theocritus and Virgil*, Princeton, NJ: Princeton University Press, 3–25; Hunter, 1985, *The New Comedy of Greece and Rome*, Cambridge: Cambridge University Press, 1–58. Arnott, 1968, *Menander, Plautus, Terence*, Oxford: Oxford University Press, 55–60.

58. Sandbach, 1977, 14–5; Wilson, 2000, *The Athenian Institution of Khoregia: The Chorus, the City and the Stage*, Cambridge: Cambridge University Press, 11–25; Arnott, 1989, *Public Performance in the Greek Theatre*, London: Routledge, 44–104; Dale, 1969, "The Chorus in the Action of Greek Tragedy," *Collected Papers*, 210–220, Cambridge: Cambridge University Press, 210–220; W. Mullen, 1982, *Choreia: Pindar and Dance*, Princeton, NJ: Princeton University Press, 3–12; Csapo and Miller, 2007, *The Origins of Theater in Ancient Greece and Beyond: From Ritual*, Cambridge: Cambridge University Press, 77–95; Lawler, 1964, *The Dance of Ancient Greek Theatre*. Iowa City: University of Iowa Press, 22–62; Ley, 2007, *The Theatricality of Greek Tragedy: Playing Space and Chorus*, Chicago: University of Chicago Press, 9–23.

59. Llyne, 1989, Words and the Poet: Characteristic Techniques of Style in Vergil's Aeneid, Oxford: Oxford University Press, 135–68; Heinze, 2000, Vergil's Epic Technique. Bristol: Classical Press, 4–26; Hinds, 1997, Allusion and Intertext, Dynamics of Appropriation in Roman Poetry, Cambridge: Cambridge University Press, 1–16; Wills, 1996, Repetition in Latin Poetry: Figures of Allusion, Oxford: Oxford University Press, 17–51; O'Hara, 1996, *True Names. Vergil and the Alexandrian Tradition of Etymological Wordplay*, Ann Arbor: University of Micigan Press, i–x; 1–5..

60. Edwards, 2002, *Sound, Sense, and Rhythm*, Princeton, NJ: Princeton University Press, 99–124; Davis, 1991, *Polyhymia: The Rhetorica of Horatian Lyric Discourse*, Berkeley: University of California Press, 11–22.

61. Leishman, 1956, *Translating Horace: Thirty Odes Translated into the Original Metres with the Latin Text and an Introductiory and Critical Essay*, Oxford: Oxford University Press,

80–2; D. West, 1966, *Reading Horace,* Edinburgh: University of Edinburgh Press, 88; Stack, 1985, *Pope and Horace,* Cambridge: Cambridge University Press, 100–2.

62. Anderson, 1994, 124–35; Bakker and Kahane, 1997, *Written Voice, Spoken Signs: Tradition, Performance, and the Epic Text,* Cambridge, MA: Harvard University Press, 7–26; R. W. B. Burton, 1985, *The Chorus in Sophocles' Tragedies,* Oxford: Clarendon Press, 52–62 Landels, 1999, 1–23; Mackay, 1999, *The Oral Tradition and Its Influence in the Greek and Roman World,* Leiden: Brill, 65–78, 155–142; Pohlsander, 1964, *Metrical Studies in the Lyrics of Sophocles,* Leiden: Brill, 147–159, 172–174; W. C. Scott, 1984, *Musical Design in Aeschylean Theater,* Hanover, NH: Dartmouth College, 7–26; W. C. Scott, 1996, *Musical Design in Sophoclean Theater,* Hanover, NH: Dartmouth College, 34–56; Taplin, 1992, *Homeric Soundings: The Shaping of the Iliad,* Oxford: Clarendon Press, 1–7.

63. Wiles, 1991, *The Masks of Menander Sign and Meaning in Greek and Roman Performance,* Cambridge: Cambridge University Press, 6–8, 34–5; Cairns, 1972, *Generic Composition in Greek and Roman Poetry,* Edinburgh: Edinburgh University Press, 36–43.

64. Conte, 1994b, 60.

65. Sedley, 1998, *Lucretius and the Transformation of Greek Wisdom,* Cambridge: Cambridge University Press, xv, 35–61.

66. Ovid, 1998, *Metamorphoses, Book II,* Oxford: Oxford University Press, I: 1–4; Myers, 1994, *Ovid's Causes Cosmogony and Aetiology in the Metamorphoses,* Ann Arbor: University of Michigan Press, 1–2; Fantham, 2004, *Ovid's Metamorphoses,* Oxford: Oxford University Press, 3–20, 89–104.

67. Myer, 1994, 27–61, 133–166; Hutchinson, 1988, *Hellenistic Poetry,* Oxford: Oxford University Press, 340–2; Krostenko, 2001, *Cicero, Catullus, and Language of Social Performance,* Chicago: University of Chicago Press, 21–31.

68. Quoted in Feldherr, 1998, *Spectacle and Society in Livy's History,* Berkeley: University of California Press, 1.

69. Krostenko, 2001, 24, 86–8.

70. B. A. Krosteniko, ibid., 1–3.

71. Habinek, 1998, *The Politics of Latin Literature, Writing, Identity, and Empire in Ancient Rome,* Princeton, NJ: Princeton University Press, 39–40, 54–55; Krostenko, 2001, 32–4.

72. Briscoe, 1993, *A Commentary on Livy's Books XXXI–XXXIII,* Oxford: Oxford University Press, 13, 146–51; Kraus, 1988, "Verba Tene: Form and Style in Livy," Dissertation, Harvard University, 1–20.

73. Oakley, 1997, *A Commentary on Livy Book vi–x,* Oxford: Oxford University Press, 7–10; Fower, 1995, *Theoppompus of Chios: History and Rhetoric in the Fourth Century B.C.,* Oxford: Ox-

ford University Press, 42, 62; Woodman, 1988, *Rhetoric in Classical Historiography,* London: Croom Helm, 70–116.

74. Briscoe, 1993, 150–1.

75. Veyne, 1962, "Les honneurs posthumes de Flavia Domitilla et les dédicaces grecques et latines," *Latomus* 21: 49–98; 1988, *Roman Erotic Elegy Love Poetry and the West,* Chicago: University of Chicago Press, 19–61.

76. Wyke, 2002, *The Roman Mistress,* Oxford: Oxford University Press, 18; Braund and Gill, 1997, *The Passions in Roman Thought and Literature,* Cambridge: Cambridge University Press, 89–127.

77. Lupoi, 2000, *The Origins of the European Legal Order,* Cambridge: Cambridge University Press, 5–46; Bellomo, 1995, *The Common Legal Past of Europe: 1000–1800,* Washington, DC: Catholic University of America Press, 34–54.

78. C. H. W. Johns, 2000, *The Oldest Code of Laws in the World: The Code of Laws Promulgated by Hammurabi, King of Babylon, B.C. 2285–2242,* Union, NJ: Lawbook Exchange, 1–25; A. R. W. Harrison, 1968–71, *The Law of Athens,* Oxford: Oxford University Press, 1–2, 122–124; MacDowell, 1978, *The Law in Classical Athens,* Ithaca, NY: Cornell University Press. 41–52; Arnaoutoglou, 1998, *Ancient Greek Laws: A Sourcebook,* London: Routledge, 1–6.

79. Jolowicz, 1972, *Historical Introduction to the Studies of Roman Law,* Cambridge: Cambridge Unviersity Press, 8–57; Buckland, 1963, *Textbook of Roman Law from Augustine to Justinian,* Cambridge: Cambridge University Press, 1–55, 604–718; Kelling, 1992, *A Short History of Western Legal History,* Oxford: Oxford University Press, 39–78.

80. Zimmermann, 1990, *The Law of Obligations: Roman Foundation of the Civilian Tradition,* Capetown: Juta, 177–90; Markensinis, 1990, *The German Law of Torts,* Oxford: Oxford University Press, 10–12, 50–2; Kretzmer, 1984, "Transformation of Tort Liability in the Nineteenth Century: The Visible Hand," *Oxford Journal of Legal Studies* 4: 46.

81. Daube, 1969, *The Forms of Roman Legislation,* Oxford: Clarendon Press, 11–2.

82. P. Stein, 1966, *Regulae Iuris From Juristic Rules to Legal Maxims,* Edinburgh: Edinburgh University Press, 5.

83. Kern, 2006, *Kingship and Law in Middle Ages,* New York: The Lawbook Exchange, 151.

84. Schulz, 1936, *Principles of Roman Law,* Oxford: Clarendon Press, 40.

85. Gu, 2006, *The Boundaries of Meaning and the Formation of Law,* Montreal: McGill-Queen's University Press, 5–39, 109–134.

86. A. Watson, 1991, *Legal Origins and Legal Change,* London: Rio Grande, 3–108; P. Stein, 1966, 5–7; Jolowicz, 1972, 85–6.

87. Jolowicz, 1972, 85–6; A. Watson, 1974,

Law Making in the Later Roman Republic, Oxford: Clarendon Press, 19–39; Schulz, 1936, 7–11.
88. Schulz, 1936, 11–13.
89. Jolowicz, 1972, 99, 106–112.
90. P. Stein, 1988, 151–66.
91. Fishwick, 2005, *The Imperial Cult in the Latin West Studies in the Ruler Cult of the Western Provinces of the Roman Empire*, Leiden: Brill, 195–239; Halsborghe, 1972, *The Cult of Sol Invictus*, Leiden: Brill, 26–44; Rogers, 1991, *The Sacred Identity of Ephesos*, London: Routledge, 136–148.
92. Bossbach, 1999, Gnostic Wars: The Cold War in the Context of a History of Western Spirituality, Edinburgh: Edinburgh University Press, 72–102; Filoramo, 1990, *A History of Gnoticism*, Cambridge, MA: Blackwell, 3–26.
93. Frend, 1974, "The Two Worlds of Paulinus of Nola," *Latin Literature of the Fourth Century*, London: Routledge and K. Paul, 58–99; Isbell, 1974, "Decimus Malgnis Ausonius: The Poet and His World," *Latin Literature of the Fourth Century*, London: Routledge & K. Paul, 22–57.
94. G. B. Matthers, 1999, *The Augustinian Tradition*, Berkeley: University of California Press, 27–38; L. Holsher, 1986, *The Reality of Mind: St. Augustine's Arguments for Human Soul as a Spiritual Substance*, London: Routledge, 11–42; Matthew, 1992, *Thought's Ego in Augustine and Descartes*. Ithaca, NY: Cornell University Press, 1–51; Rist, 1994, *Augustine: Ancient Thought Baptized*, Cambridge: Cambridge University Press, 23–40; Stock, 1996, *The Reader: Meditation, Self-Knowledge, and the Ethics of Interpretation*, Cambridge, MA: Harvard University Press, 243–272; Wetzel, 1992, *Augustine and the Limits of Virtue*, Cambridge: Cambridge University Press, 1–16.
95. 10. 26. 37, Matthew, 1999, 32–4.
96. Matthew, 1999, 34.
97. Fishwick, 1991, I: 46; Bowersock, 1965, 113.
98. Fishwick, 1991, 1: 6–12.
99. Fishwick, 1991, 1: 62–72; S. Weinstock, 1971, *Divus Julius*, Oxford, Clarendon, Press, 270–2, 364–7, 401; Beaujeu, 1978, "Le paganisme romain sous le Haut Empire," *Aufstieg und Niedergang der römischen Welt* 2, 16, 1: 3–26.
100. A. Wallace-Hadrill, 1981, "The Emperor and His Virtues," *Historia*, 30: 298–323; J. R. Fears, 1981, "The Cult of Virtues and Roman Imperial Ideology," *Aufstieg und Niedergang der römische Welt*, 2: 827–948.
101. Fishwick, 1990a, "Dio and Maecenas: The Emperor and the Ruler Cult," *Phoenix* 44: 267–275; Fishwick, 1990b, "Prudentius and the Cult of Divus Augustus," *Historia* 39: 475–486; Fishwick, 1990c, "Votive Offerings to the Emperor?" *Zeitschrift für Papyrologie und Epigraphik* 80: 121–130; 2005, 195–239; Friesen, 1993, *Twice*

Neokoros: Ephesus, Asia, and the Cult of the Flavian Imperial Family, Leiden: Brill, 1–28; Friesen, 2001, *Imperial Cults and the Apocalypse of John: Reading Revelation in the Ruins*, New York: Oxford University Press, 25–38.

Chapter 2

1. Ando, 2008, *The Matter of the Gods: Religion and the Roman Empire*, Berkeley: University of California Press, 1–20; Bowden, 2010, *Mystery Cults of the Ancient World*. Princeton, NJ: Princeton University Press; Court, 1990, *The New Testament World*. Cambridge: Cambridge University Press, 18–28; Heyman, 2007, *The Power of Sacrifice: Roman and Christian Discourses in Conflict*, Washington, DC: Catholic University of America Press, 95–160; Schurer, 1991, 63–89; Vermes, 1983, *Jesus the Jew: A Historian's Reading of the Gospels*, London: SCM Press, 83–222; 1984, *Jesus and the World of Judaism*. Philadelphia: Fortress, 44–65; Frend, 1984, *The Rise of Christianity*. Philadelphia: Fortress Press, 53–84; Fox, 1987, *Pagans and Christians*, New York: Knopf, 282–284; Rives, 2007, *Religion in the Roman Empire*, Malden, MA: Blackwell, 89–104; Turcan, 1996, *The Cults of the Roman Empire*, New York: Blackwell, 1–27; Warrier, 2006, *Roman Religion*, Cambridge: Cambridge University Press, 1–26.
2. Knohl, 2000, *The Messiah Before Jesus: The Suffering Servant of the Dead Sea Scrolls*, Berkeley: University of California Press, 1–26.
3. The non–Christian community who accepted Jesus as the new Jewish messiah. Freeman, 2004, 486.
4. Carrington, 1957, *The Early Christian Church*, Cambridge: Cambridge University Press, i: 16–23.
5. C. Stead, 1994, *Philosophy in Christian Antiquity*, Cambridge, Cambridge University Press, 95–108; W. Eichrodt, 1967, *Theology of the Old Testament*, Philadelphia, Westminster Press, 103–5, 210–11.
6. Stanton, 1989, *The Gospels and Jesus*, Oxford: Oxford University Press, 7–8.
7. Stanton, 1989, 10–11.
8. Plato, 2000, *The Republic*, Cambridge: Cambridge University Press, 7. 533.
9. Carrington, 1957, 146.
10. Freeman, 2004, 488–90.
11. McMullen, 1981, *Paganism in Roman Empire*, New Haven, CT: Yale University Press, 18–34, 105–54; Turcan, 2000, 51–104, 99–154; Rives, 1995, 199.
12. Turcan, 1996, 12–4, 98–101.
13. R. Bloch, 1976, "Interpretatio," *Recherches sur les religon de 'ltalie antique*. Geneva, 32–5.
14. Turcan, 1996, 23; Rives, 1995, 250–310; McMullen, 1981, 24–5, 42–8.

15. Bowersock, 1995, 1–2; D. Boyarin, 1999, *Dying for God Martyrdom and the Making of Christian and Judaism*, Stanford: Stanford University Press, 1–21.

16. Barnes, 1971, *Tertullian*, Oxford: Oxford University Press, 132–42; Bowersock, 1995, 2–3; Gibbons, 1954, *Gibbons' Decline and Fall of the Roman Empire in Six Volumes*, New York: E. P. Dutton, 4: 121; Cartledge, Millett and Todd, 1990, *Nomas: Essays in Athenian Law Politics and Society*, Cambridge: Cambridge University Press, 5.

17. Gibbons, 1954, ii: 110; Bowersock, 1995, 3–4.

18. Augustine, "On the Predestination of the Saints," 5, *Patrologiaa Latina*, 44: 962–63.

19. Freeman, 2004, 491–2.

20. Ovid, *Amores, Metamorphoses, Book 11.* A.D. Oxford: Oxford University Press, Book 2: 2: 25–6.

21. *Epigrams*, Book 11, 47: 3–4; Higob, 1975, *The Cult of Isis Among Women in the Graeco-Roman World*, Leiden: Brill, 118–9.

22. Mark, 3, 31–5; VI. 3; Matthew 7, 4, 12, 46–50; Luke, 8, 21; 12, 28; John 2, 1–11.

23. Carroll, 1986, *The Cult of the Virgin Mary*, Princeton, NJ: Princeton University Press, 4–5; Laurentin, 1965, *The Question of Mary*, New York: Holt, Rinehart and Winston, 41; Hirn, 1957, *The Sacred Shrine: A Study of the Poetry and Art of the Catholic Church*, Boston: Beacon Press, 188–9; Graef, 1963, *Mary: A History of Doctrine and Devotion*. London: Sheed and Ward, 60–78; Elm, 1994, '*Virgins of God:' The Making of Asceticism in Late Antiquity*. Oxford: Oxford University Press, 1–24, 106–136.; Cooper, 1996, *The Virgin and Bride: Idealized Womanhood in the Late Antiquity*, Cambridge, MA: Harvard University Press, 1–19.

24. Graef, 1963, 46; Carroll, 1986, 5–8.

25. Freeman, 2004, 58–75; Hodgson, 1974, *The Venture of Islam*. Chicago: University of Chicago Press, i:103.

26. Cross, 1997, *Canaanite Myth and Hebrew Epic: Essays in the History of the Religion of Israel*, Cambridge, MA: Harvard University Press, 77–144.

27. Lambert, 1960, *Babylonian Wisdom Literature*, Oxford: Clarendon Press, 1:73–77, 104–6, 2: 139–40; E. R. Daalglish, 1962, *Psalm Fifty-one in the Light of Ancient Near Eastern Patternism*, Leiden: Brill, 73–102; Roberts, 1972, *The Earliest Semitic Pantheon: A Study of the Semitic Deities Attested in Mesopotamia Before Ur III*, Baltimore: Johns Hopkins University Press, 12–35; Keel, 1978, *The Symbolism of the Biblical World: Ancient Near Eastern Iconography and the Book of Psalms*, New York: Seabury Press, 308–24; Cross, 1997, 1–76; Miller, 1994, 1–31; Albright, 1925, "The Evolution of the West-Semitic Divinity 'An-'Anat-'Atta," *American Journal of Semitic Languages and Literatures* 41: 73–101.

28. Exodus 6: 2–3, 3: 13–15; F. M. Cross, 1997, 5.

29. Albright, 1968, *Yahweh and the Gods of Canaan*, New York: Doubleday, 226–32; R. A. Wilson, 1966, 1–100; Van der Toorn, 2007, *Scribal Culture and the Making of the Hebrew Bible*, Cambridge, MA: Harvard University Press, 109–172.

30. M. Smith, 2002, *The Early History of God: Yahweh and Other Deities in Ancient Israel*, Grand Rapids, Mich. xxxv–xl; 46–50.

31. Most Syrian Christians were monophysites. For earlier urban life of Syria, see A. H. M. Jones, 1971, *The Cities of the Eastern Roman Provinces*, Oxford: Clarendon Press, 226–94.

32. Donner, 1981, *The Early Islamic Conquests*, Princeton, NJ: Princeton University Press, 94–5; L. E. Goodman, 1983, "The Syrian Impact on Arabic Literature," *Arabic Literature to the End of the Umayyad Period*, Cambridge: Cambridge University Press, 497–501.

33. Hodgson, 1974, I: 237.

34. Abdulla El Tayin, 1983, Pre-Islamic Poetry: Arabic Literature to the End of the Umayyad Period, Cambridge: Cambridge University Press, 27–113; Stetkevych, S. P. 1993, *The Mute Immortals Speak: Pre-Islamic Poetry and Poetics of Ritual (Myth and Poetics)*. Ithaca, NY: Cornell University Press, 3–54, 2002, 2009, 55–78, 2010, 1–27; Beeston, 1983, *Arabic Literature to the End of the Umayyad Period*, Cambridge: Cambridge University Press, 22–23.

35. They were called "queens of Arabia," *Twrm* (Bull) was a well-known name of the Moon-god. Winnett and Reed, 1970, *Ancient Records from North Arabia*, Toronto: University of Toronto Press, 69; Beeston, 1983, 22–4. Pritchard, 1955, *The Ancient Near East in Pictures Relating to the Old Testament, Ancient Near Eastern Texts*, Princeton, NJ: Princeton University Press, 299–305, 346; Bowen and Albright, 1958, *Archaeological Discoveries in South Arabia*, Baltimore: Johns Hopkins University Press, 150–53; Reed, 1949, *The Asherah in the Old Testament*, Fort Worth, TX: Christian University Press, 69–96, 167–71; Cook, 1930, *The Religion of Ancient Palestine in the Light of Archaeology*, Oxford: Oxford University Press, 126–7.

36. Donner, 1981, 14, 169–171.

37. Hodgson, 1974, i: 9.

38. Bravemann, 1972, *The Spiritual Background of Early Islam: Studies on Ancient Arab Concepts*, Leiden: Brill, 1–122.

39. Hodgson, 1974, i: 162; Wiggins, 2007, *A Reassessment of Asherah: With Further Considerations of the Goddess*, Piscataway, NJ: Gorgias Press, 151–188.

40. Beeston, 1983, 13; Court, 1990, 8–35; Fox, 1991, 10–29; Hodgson, 1974, i: 184–5.

41. Qur'an, xxxiii, 72; ii, 28–34; xxxviii, 71–85; xvii; xvii, 61–7; xcii, 5–13; vii, 171–2.

42. Beeston, 1983, 7.
43. Liebeschuetz, 2001, 318; Riche, 1976, *Education and Culture in the Barbarian West*, Columbia: University of South Carolina Press, 3–24.

Chapter 3

1. R. Allen, 2005, *The Arabic Literary Heritage: The Development of its Genres and Criticism*, Cambridge: Cambridge University Press, 103–202; Gibb, 1974, *Introduction to Arabic Literature*, Oxford: Oxford University Press, 4; Coulson, 1964, *A History of Islamic Law*, Edinburgh: Edinburgh University Press, 19–20; Wenger, 1982, "Islamic and Talmudic Jurisprudence: The Four Roots of Islamic Law and Their Talmudic Counterparts," *The American Journal of Legal History* 26: 25–71; 'Abdullah el Tayib, 1983, 27–113; Beeston, 1969, *Arabic Historical Phraseology*, Cambridge: Cambridge University Press, 1–3; Beeston, 1983, 1–113; Beeston, 1984, *Sabaic Grammar*. Manchester: Manchester University Press; Haidar, 2008, *The Prose Poem and the Journal Shi'r: A Comparative Study of Literature, Literary Theory and Journalism*, Reading, UK: Ithaca Press, 1–38; Stetkevych, 1983, "Structualist Interpretations of pre–Islamic Poetry," *Journal of Near Eastern Studies* 42 (2): 85–107; Stetkevych, 1993, *The Mute Immortals Speak: Pre-Islamic Poetry and Poetics of Ritual (Myth and Poetics)*, Ithaca, NY: Cornell University Press, 3–160; Stetkevych, 2002, *The Poetics of Islamic Legitimacy: Myth, Gender, and Ceremony in the Classical Arabic Odes*, Bloomington: Indiana University Press, 48–79; Stetkevych, 2009, *Early Islamic Poetry and Poetics*, Burlington, VT: Ashgate, 1–54; Stetkevych, 2010, *The Mantle Odes: Arabic Praise Poems to the Prophet Muhammad*, Bloomington: Indiana University Press, 1–29.
2. Arberry, 1957, *The Seven Odes: The First Chapter in Arabic Literature*, New York: Macmillan, 13–24; Tayib, 1983, 29; Mornroe, 1972, "Oral Composition in Pre-Islamic Poetry," *Journal of Arabic Literature* 3: 1–53; M. V. McDonald, 1978, "Orally Transmitted Poetry in Pre-Islamic Arabia and Other Pre-Literate Societies," *Journal of Arabic Literature* 9: 14–31.
3. Mutallammins, *Kitab al-Aghain*, xxi: 187–8. trans. Tuetey, 21, 98.
4. Lichtenstadter, 1974, *Introduction to Classical Arabic Literature: with Selections from Representative Works in English Translation*, New York: Twayne Publishers, 10–11, 149–90; Lichtenstadter, 1939, *Muhammad Ibn Habib and his Kitāb al-Muhabbar*, London: Royal Asiatic Society.
5. *Hamasa*, Nicholson, 1969, *A Literary History of the Arabs*, London: Cambridge University Press, 83.
6. Henninger, 1981, "Pre-Islamic Bedouin

Religion," *Studies on Islam*, Oxford: Oxford University Press, 3–22; Ibn al-Kalbi, 1924, *Kitab al-Asnam*, Cairo, Matba'at dar al-kutub almisriyah, trans. by N. A. Faris as *The Book of Idols*, Princeton, NJ: Princeton University Press, 1952.
7. Al-Mutalammis was addressing 'Amr b Hind the king of Hirah. *Kitab al-Aghani*, xxi: 313.
8. These goddesses were mentioned in Quran I iii/19–20; M.Ibn Ishāq and Quillaume, 1955, *The Life of Muhammad*, Karachi: Oxford University Press, 38–9; Henninger, 1959, "La religion bedouine preislamique," *L'antica societa beduina*, Rome: Centro di studi Semitici, Instituto di studi Orientali-Universita, 115–140.
9. Ibn al-Kalbi, 1924, 14.
10. Ibid., 19–25, 39–42, 110.
11. Beeston, 1983, 4–5.
12. Abbott, 1972, *Studies in Arabic Literary Papyri: III. Language and Literature*, Chicago: University of Chicago Press, 3, 33–4.
13. Sa'id al-Dani, 1960, *al-Muhkam fi naqt al-masahif*, Damascus: Arab Academy.
14. Âh?mad ibn 'Abd al-Wahhab al-Nuwayri, 1929–1935, *Nihayat al-arab fi funun al-adab*, 18 vols., Cairo: Dar al-kutub al-Mistriyyah, ix: 214–8.
15. Abbott, 1972, 3: 27–9.
16. Bravemann, 1972, 8–12.
17. Bravemann, 1972, 12.
18. Bravemann, 1972, 13.
19. Ibn Hisam, quoted in Bravemann, 1972, 13.
20. Watt, 1973, *The Formative Period of Islamic Thought*, Edinburgh: Edinburgh University Press, 90–3.
21. Qur'an, xvi/80–90, xiv/37–9, xxix/61–8. Translation is modified from Arberry, 1976, *The Koran interpreted*, New York: Macmillan, ii: 295–6.
22. Ahmad ibn Muhammad ibn Hanbal, 1949, *al-Musnad*, 6 vols., Cairo, Dar al-Ma'rif, iv: 91–102, 244–55; Muhammad ibn Isma'il al-Bukhari, 1908, *al-Jaami' al-Sahih*, Leiden, Brill, iv: 256, 423; 'Ali Hasan Abd al-Qadir, 1965, *Nazrah 'Ammah fi tarikh al-fiqh al-Islami*, Cairo, Dar al-Kutub al-H?adithah, 24–49, 78–108.
23. Muhammad Yusuf Gurayn, 1982, *Judicial System Under the Holy Prophet and the First Two Pious Caliphs*, Lahore, Himayat al-Islam, 60–8; Abd al-Qadir, 1965, 9–27; Jawad 'Ali, 1950–1959. *al-Mufassal fi tarikh al-'Arab qabl al-Islam*, 8 vols., Baghdad, n.p. iv: 24–5, 48–50, v: 186–234, 349–56.
24. Watt, 1956, *Muhammad in Medina*, Oxford: Oxford University Press, 289–93, 331–406.
25. Muslim, 1955–1956, *Sahih*, Cairo, Dar Ihya' al Kutub al-'Arabiyya, viii: 229–30.
26. Muhammad ibn Sa'd, 1904–1940, *Kitab at -Tabaqat al — Kabir*, Leiden: Brill, iii: 207–8; Isma'l Bukhari, 1908, *Kitab al-Jami' al-Sahih*,

Leiden: Brill, 232–4, 309–15; Ibn Khaldun, 1958, *The Muqaddimah; An Introduction to History*, New York: Pantheon Books, I: 192–3, 223, iii: 88–9; Abbott, 1972, 7–10, 56–7.

27. Mahmassani, 1961, *Falsafat al-tashri fi al-Islam, The Philosophy of Jurisprudence in Islam*, Leiden: Brill, 72.

28. Al-Kindi, 1908, The Governors and Judges of Egypt, New York: Columbia University Press, 3–37; Juynboll, 2008, *Muslim Tradition: Studies in Chronology, Provenance and Authorship of Early Hadith*, Cambridge: Cambridge University Press, 79–95.

29. Juynboll, 1969, The Authenticity of the Tradition Literature: Discussions in Modern Egypt. Leiden: Brill; Juynboll, 1996, Studies on the Origins and Uses of Islamic Ha?dith. Brookfield, VT: Variorum; M. A. Rauf, 1983, "Hadith Literature I," *Arabic Literature to the End of the Umayyad Period*, Cambridge, Cambridge University Press, 271–88; Abbott, "Hadith Literature II," *Arabic Literature to the End of the Umayyad Period*, Cambridge, Cambridge University Press, 289–98.

30. Crone and Hinds, 2003, *God's Caliph: Religious Authority in the First Centuries of Islam*. Cambridge: Cambridge University Press, 43–57.

31. Abbott, 1972, ii: 22–3.

32. Azami, 1967. *Studies in Early H?adith Literature*, Riyad: Riyad University Press, 3–25; Juynboll, 2008, 9–76.

33. Fu'ad 'Abd al-Baqi, 1949, *al-Lu' lu' wa almarjan fi al-ma'tafaq 'alaybi al-shaykhan*, Cairo, Dar Ah?yah al-Kutub al-'Arabiyah, 10–49; Sahair el-Caalamawy, 1983, "Narrrrative Elements in Hadith Literature," *Arabic Literature to the End of the Umayyad Period*, Cambridge, Cambridge University Press, 308–16.

34. B. A. Malik, *Muwatta*, 1951. Cairo, Dal Ahyah al-Kutub al-A'rabiyah, 50, 89, 314, 487, 513, 567; Muhammad b. al-Hasan Shaybani, 1965, *al-Hujjaa 'ala aahl al-Madina*, Hyderabad, Lajnat Ihya' al-Ma'rifah, i: 186, 287, 315, 342; Azami, 1967, 30–4.

35. Shaybani, 1965, i: 342, ii: 399.

36. Malik, 1951, 487; Azami, 1967, 33.

37. Shaybani, 1965, i: 186; Azami, 1986, 33.

38. Malik, 1951, 487, Azami, 1967, 34.

39. A.Rahim, 1963, *The Principles of Muhammadan Jurisprudence*, Lahore: All Pakistan Legal Decisions, 54.

40. Juynboll, 2008, 77–95; Guraya, 215–300.

41. Qur'an xxxviii/25; Arberry, 1976, ii: 160.

42. Abu al-Faraj 'Ali b. al-Husayn al-Isfahani, 1927–74 *Kitab of al-Aaghani*, Cairo, Dar al-fikr al-Arabi, xxii: 124; Crone and Hinds, 2003, 44–5.

43. Schacht, 1964, *An Introduction to Islamic Law*, Oxford, Clarendon Press, 15–8; Schacht,

1950, The Origins of Muhammadan Jurisprudence, Oxford, Clarendon Press, 190–213.

44. Crone and Hinds, 2003, 12–23.

45. Al-San'ani, 2000, *Musannaf*, Beirut, Dar Kutub al-'Imiyah, vi: 10866, vii: 12325, viii: 15664.

46. Abbott, 1972, ii: 24–32.

47. Ibn al-Salah, 1936, *Ikhtis?ar 'ulum al-hadith*, Cairo, s.n., 5–34; Jamal al-Din al-Qasimi, 1979, *Qawa'id al-tahdith min funun mustalab al-hadith*, Bayruit: Dar Ih?yah al-Sunnah al-Nabawiyah, 52–62.

48. Al-Shafi'i, 1997, *Tartib Musnad al-Shafi'i*, Beirut, Dar al-Fikr; Ahmad ibn Hanbal, 1949, *al-Musnad*, Cairo, Dar al-Ma'rif.

49. Muhhib Allah ibn 'Abd al-Shakur al-Bahari, 1950–1951, *Muslim al-thubut*, Cairo, Matba't Muhammad 'Ali Subayah, ii: 79–92; Saayf al-Din al-'Amidi, 1968, *al-Ihkaam fi usul al-Ahkam*, Cairo, Matba't Muhammad 'Ali Subayha, i: 161–4; Ibn Hazm, 1968, *Ihkaam*, Cairo: Maktaba't al-'A'zimah, i:108–118.

50. Abbott, 1972, ii: 73–4.

51. Abbott, 1972, ii: 77–8; Siddiqi, 1961, *Hadith Literature: Its Origin, Development, Special Features and Criticism*, Calcutta: Calcutta University Press, 164–204.

52. Siddiqi, 1961, 88–125.

53. al-Bukhari, 1908, *Kitab al-Jami' al-Sahih*, 4 vols. Leiden, Brill, 1908; Muslim, 1955–1956, *Sahih*, 5vols. Cairo, 'Isa Babi al-Halabi; Tirmidhi, 1931–4, *Sahih*, 13vol. Cairo, Mustafa al-Bali al-Habali.

54. Hanafi, quoted in Mahassani, 1961, *Falsafat al-tashri fi al-Islam, The Philosophy of Jurisprudence in Islam*, Leiden: Brill, 19–20.

55. 'Abdullah ibn Mas'ud, quoted in Mahassani, 1961, 77.

56. Coulson, 1969, 20–31.

57. Iibn Hazim, 1968, i: 130, iv: 147; Saayf al-Din al-'Amidi, 1968, 253–346.

58. Shafi'i, 1961, *Kitab al-umm*, Cairo: Maktabat al-Kulliyyat al-Azhariyya, ii: 277–336; Coulson, 1969, 53–4; Schacht, 1950, 315.

59. Shafi'i, 1961, ii: 151–77, 338–40.

60. Coulson, 1964, 56–7.

61. Al-Shafi'i, 1961, i: 3, 35, 366–8.

62. Al-Shafi'i, ibid., i:177–8.

63. Al-Shafi'i, ibid., i: 217–330.

64. Al-Shafi'i, ibid., i: 123–38.

65. Al-Shafi'i, ibid., i: 40–1; Schacht, p. 14.

66. Al-Shafi'i, ibid., i: 5; al-Shafi'i, 1969, *Risalah*, Cairo: Mustafa Babi al-Halabi, 33.

67. Al-Shafi'i, 1969, 9–11, 17–31; al-Shafi'i, 1985, Ikhtilaf al-Hadith, Bayruit: Mu'assasat al-Kutub al-Thaqafiyah, 41–8.

68. Coulson, 1961, 60–1.

69. S. Gu, 2006, 5–39, 109–134.

70. In my opinion, Britishness lies less in law or God than in the way in which two counterparts interacted and complemented one another.

I agree and disagree partially with each side of the discourse. P. Christianson, 1978, *The Reformers and Babylon: English Apocalyptic Vision*, Toronto: Toronto University Press; Claydon and McBride, 1998, *Protestantism and National Identity: Britain and Ireland, 1650–1850*, Cambridge: Cambridge University Press; K. R. Firth, 1979, *The Apocalypic Tradition in Reformation Britiain*, Oxford: Oxford University Press; R.Bouckham, 1978, *Tudoor Apocalypose*, Oxford: Oxford University Press; L. Colleey, 1992, "Britishness and Otherness: An Argument," *Journal of British Studies* 31: 309–29.

71. Lehman, 1985, "The First English Law," *The Journal of Legal History* 6 (19): 9; Baube, 1956, *Roman Law, Linguistic, Social and Philosophical Aspects*, Edinburgh: Edinburgh University Press, 6–8.

72. Robertson, 1925, "The Law of Ethelbert," *The Laws of the Kings of England from Edmund to Henry I*, Cambridge: Cambridge University Press, 16–17; Thorpe, 2002, *Ancient Laws and Institutes of England*, Union, NJ: Law Book Exchange, i: 2–25.

73. Simpson, 1987, *Legal Theory and Legal History: Essays on the Common Law*, Ronceverte, WV: Hambledon Press, 3–4.

74. Baube, 1956, 7–8.

75. "The Law of Hlothhere and Eadric, Kings of Kent," "The Law of Wihtred, King of Kent," Thorpe, 2002, i: 26–43.

76. "The Laws of Ine," Thorpe, 2002. i: 101–51.

77. "The Laws of Alfred," Thorpe, 2002, i: 44–101.

78. "The Code of Edgar" 2, 3, 4, Thorpe, 2002, i: 262–5, 270–9; Robertson, 1925, 20–39.

79. "The Code of Ethelred" 3, 5, and 7, Thorpe, 2002, i: 292–9, 304–13, 336–9, 343–51; Robertson, 1925, 154–219, 108–29.

80. "The Laws of Cnut Kings," Thorpe, i: 358–425; Robertson, 1925, 154–219.

81. Simpson, 1987, 5–13.

82. Richardson and Sayles, 1974, *The Governance of Mediaeval England from the Conquest to Magna Carta*, Edinburgh: Edinburgh University Press, 5–6.

83. Lehman, 1985, 13.

84. Pollock and Maitland, 1968, *The History of English Law Before the Time of Edward I*, Cambridge: Cambridge University Press, i: xxvii.

85. Jolliffe, 1967, *The Constitutional History of Medieval England*, London: Adam and Charles Black, 2–3; Pollock and Maitland, 1968, 32–3.

86. "II Aethelstan," in Jolliffe, 1967, 6.

87. Pollock and Maitland, 1968, 31–2.

88. Lehman, 1985, 4–9; Richardson and Sayles, 1974, 5–6.

89. Richardson and Sayles, 1941, *Selected Cases of Procedure Without Writ Under Henry III*, London: B.Quaritch, Ix: xxv–xxvi.

90. Maitland, 1989, *The Forms of Action at Common Law*, Cambridge: Cambridge University Press, 299.

91. Maitland, 1999, *The Collected Papers of Frederic William Maitland*, Holmes Beach, FL: Gaunt, ii: 476.

92. Plucknett, 2001, A Concise History of the Common Law, Union, NJ: Lawbook Exchange, 48; Van Caegenem, 1959, *Royal Writs in England from the Conquest to Glanvill, Studies in the Early History of the Common Law*, London: Selden Society, 47.

93. Maitland, 1999, ii: 20–52; Van Caegenem, 1959, 49.

94. Maitland, 1999, ii: 466; Plucknett, 1922, *Statutes and their Interpretation in the First Half of the Fourteenth Century*, Cambridge: University Press, xxi–xxiii.

95. Bracton, in Maitland, 1989, 6.

96. "The Laws of Ethelbert and Laws of Alfred," Liebermann, 1902–1916, *Die Gesetze der Angelsachsen*, Halle: S. Max Niemeyer, i: 3–8, 46–87.

97. Thorpe, 2002, i: 47.

98. Stubbs, 1979, *The Constitutional History of England*, Chicago: University of Chicago Press, 24.

99. "The Code of Ethelred" viii, 42, *English Historical Documents*, 413–4.

100. "The Laws of Cnut," ibid., p. 419; Thorpe, 2002, i: 358; Liebermann, 1902–1916, 273–9.

101. Chibnall, 1986, *Anglo-Norman England, 1066–1166*, Oxford: Oxford University Press, 161–2.

102. Maitland, 1987, 80–1. L. J. Downer, 1972, *Leges Henrici primi*, Oxford: Clarendon Press, 78.

103. Richardson and Sayles, 1974, 42–4; Downer, 1972, 12–30; Chibnall, 1986, 170–1.

104. Downer, 1972, 84–5.

105. Ibid., 128–9.

106. Ibid., 92–101, 112–5, 152–5, 228–9.

107. Ibid., 90–1.

108. Maitland, 1987, 81.

109. Downer, 1972, 122–9.

110. Maitland, 1987, 82.

111. Downer, 1972, 123–7.

112. Ibid., 108–9.

113. Ibid., 94–5; T. A. Green, 1972, "Societal Concepts of Criminal Liability for Homicide in Medieval England," *Speculum* 47: 669–94; J. M. Kaye, 1965, "The Early History of Murder and Manslaughter," *Law Quarterly Review* 83 (July and October): 95, 569–601.

114. Downer, 1972, 96–7; F. J. West, 2005, *The Justiciarship in England, 1066–1232*, Cambridge: Cambridge University Press, 10–22, 31–53.

115. J. A. Green, 1986, *The Government of England Under Henry I*, Cambridge, Cambridge

University Press, 95–132; D. Crouch, Geoffrey de Clinton, 1982, "Roger Earl of Warwick: New Men and Magnates in the Reign of Henry I," *Bulletin of the Institute of Historical Research* 55: 113–24; J. A. Green, 1981, "Last Century of Danegeld," *English Historical Review* 96: 241–58; C. W. Hollister, 1978, "The Rise of Administrative Kingship: Henry I and Philip Augustus," *American Historical Review* 83: 867–905.

116. The Latin word *iusticiis*, at the time, had no connotation of English word "right," In legal writs, the translated English word "right" had a Latin origin of *rectum* and *recti*. The word *iustitiae* meant only English justice rather than right. Van Caenegem, 1959, 414–41, 448, 461–3, 469–474.

117. F. J. West, 2005, 3, 10–12; Van Caenegem, 1959, 473–83.

118. F. J. West, 2005, 1.

119. Richardson and Sayles, 1964, 157–72; F. J. West, 2005, 13–23.

120. P. R. Hyams 1974, "The Proof of Villein Status in the Common Law," *English Historical Review* 89: 721–49; D. W. Sutherland, 1973, *The Assize of Novel Disseisin*, Oxford, 216–71; Palmer, 1982, *County Courts of Medieval England*, Princeton, NJ: Princeton University Press, 174–219.

121. Palmer, 1982, 175–9.

122. Palmer, 1982, 181–7; H. Bracton, 1968, *Delegibus et constuetudinibus Angliae*, Cambridge, Cambridge, University Press; H. Cam, *The Hundred and the Hundred Rolls*, 117–8; Glanvill, 1968. *The Treatise on the Laws and Customs of the Realm of England, Commonly Called Glanvill*, Cambridge, MA: Harvard University Press, 68–9, 112–4, 137–41; E. de Haas and G. D. G. Hall, 1970, *Early Registers of Writs*, London: Quaritch, 8–14.

123. Rotuli de Litterarum Causarum, I, 19b, Palmer, 1982, 188.

124. Palmer, 1982, 176.

125. Plucknett, 1949, 8–12.

126. Maitland, 1999, ii: 465–75.

127. Plucknett, 1952, "State Trials under Richard II," *Transactions of the Royal Historical Society* 5th Ser.: 159–71.

128. Maitland, 1999, ii: 476–80.

129. Plucknett, 1922, *Statutes and their Interpretation in the First Half of the Fourteenth Century*. Cambridge: Cambridge University Press, 21, 86–88.

130. D. Bethurum, 1932, "Stylistic Features of the Old English Laws," *Modern Language Review* 27: 270–1; W. A. Chaney, 1970, *The Cult of Kingship in Anglo-Saxon England*, Manchester, Manchester University Press, 7–42, 174–220.

131. E. Levy, 1942, "Reflections on the First Reception of Roman Law in Germanic States," *American Historical Review* 48: 23–4; Chanchy, 1970, 177.

132. Glanvill, in Plucknett, 1922, xi; Chanchy, 13, 129, 165; Maitland, 1999, I: 166.

133. Bracton, in Maitland, 1999, ii: 19–22.

134. Holdworth, 1938, *Some Makers of English Law*, Cambridge, Cambridge University Press, 15–24.

135. Van Caenegem, 1987, 4–16.

136. H. Cam, 1963, *Law-Finders and Law-Makers in Medieval England*, New York: Barnes & Noble, 132–58.

137. Maitland, 1987, 9.

138. Van Caenegem, 1973, 32–4; Milsom, 1976, 2–3.

139. Palmer, 1982, 179–80, 206–7.

140. Maitland, 1989, 20–52.

141. J. F. Baldwin, 1969, *The King's Council in England During the Middle Ages*, Oxford: Oxford University Press, 7–68.

142. A. Pagden, 1987, *The King's Council in England During the Middle Ages*, Oxford: Oxford University Press, 1–16.

143. Kenyon, 1986, *The Stuart Constitution 1603–1688*, Cambridge: Cambridge University Press, 74–110.

144. Fortescue, 1980, "De Natura Legis Naturae," New York: Garland Pub, I, xxx, 200–1; Chrimes, 1978, *English Constitutional Ideas in the Fifteenth Century*, Cambridge: Cambridge University Press, 199.

145. E. F. Jacob, 1934, "Sir John Fortescue and the Law of Nature," *Bull. J. R. L.* 18: 37–48.

146. Fortescue, 1980, 200.

147. Fortescue, 1980, 193–6, 207–8; Fortescue, 1942, *De Laudibus Legum Anglie*. Cambridge: Cambridge University Press, xciv, 43–9; 1926, 109–16.

148. Fortescue, 1926, *The Governance of England: Otherwise Called the Difference Between an Absolute and a Limited Monarchy*, Oxford: Oxford University Press, 109–10; Gilbert, 93–5.

149. Fortescue, 1942, 26–7; Fortescue, 1980, 192–3.

150. Fortescue, 1980, 208–9.

151. Baumgold, 1988, *Hobbes' Political Theory*, Cambridge: Cambridge University Press; Hood, 1987, *The Divine Politics: Literalism in the Philosophies of Hobbes, Locke, and Rousseau*, Ithaca, NY: Cornell University Press, 12–5, 25–112, 168–76.

152. Hobbes, 1971, *A Dialogue Between a Philosopher and a Student*, Chicago: University of Chicago Press, 50–77; Hobbes, 1983, *De Cive*, Oxford: Oxford University Press, 41–85; 1969, 28–31, 70–81; Sacksteder, 1984, "Hobbes: Philosophical and Rhetorical Artifice," *Philosophy and Rhetoric* 17: 30–46; Johnston, 1984, *The Rhetoric of Leviathan*. Princeton, NJ: Princeton University Press, 3–65; Rapaczynski, 1987, *Nature and Politics: Liberalism in the Philosophies of Hobbes, Locke, and Rousseau*, Ithaca, NY: Cor-

nell University Press, 74–82; Whenlan, 1985, "Language and its Abuses in Hobbes's Political Philosophy," *American Polticial Science Review* 75: 59–75.

Chapter 4

1. Pattison, 1970, *Music and Poetry of English Renaissance*, London: Methuen, 21.
2. *Beowulf,* I 2197 in Pattison, 1970, 22–4, 39–40.
3. G. Petrie, 2002, *The Petrie Collection of the Ancient Music of Ireland*, Cork: Cork University Press, 27–40; S. Williams, 2010, *Focus: Irish Traditional Music*, New York: Routledge, 25–102; W. Nash, 2006, *A Departed Music: Readings in Old English Poetry*, Hockwold-cum-Wilton: Anglo-Saxon Books, 8–29.
4. The influence of music could be heard in the metrical structure of Old English poetry. Minkova, 2003, *Alliteration and Sound Change in Early English*. Cambridge: Cambridge University Press, 22–70; Russom, 1998, *Beowulf and old Germanic Metre*, Cambridge: Cambridge University Press, 60–96.
5. D. Hiley, 1993, *Western Plain Chant*, Oxford: Oxford University Press, 1–45; K. Kevy, 1998, *Gregorian Chant and the Carrolingians*, Princeton, NJ: Princeton University Press, 19–30, 82–108; J. Roche, 1990, *The Madrigal*, New York: Oxford University Press, 6–24; T. Karp, 1998, *Aspects of Orality and Formularity in Grogerian Chant*, Evanton, North Western University Press, 1–58; R. L. Crocker, 2000, *An Introduction to Gregorian Chant*, New Haven, Yale University Press, 22–63; Crocker, 1977, *Early Medieval Sequence*, Berkeley: University of California Press; J. McKinnon, 2000, *The Advent Project*, Berkeley: University of California Press, 101–153; J. Cumming, 1999, *The Motet in the Age of Du Fay*, Cambridge, Cambridge University Press, 1–4; Pattison, 1970, 29.
6. N. Temperley, 1979, *The Music of English Parish Church*, Cambridge; E. Wellesz, Early Christian Music, *Early Medieval Music, New Oxford History of Music* 2: 3–5.
7. T. Georgiades, 1982, *Music and Language: The Rise of Western Music as Exemplified in Settings of the Mass*, Cambridge, Cambridge University Press, 35–36.
8. T. Georgiades, 1982, 24, 42.
9. S. Prickett, 1975, *Wordsworth and Coleridge: The Lyrical Ballads*, London: Edward Arnold, 16–19, 60–61; S. M. Parrish., 1973, *The Art of the Lyrical Ballads*, Cambridge, MA: Harvard University Press, 34–79; L. Kramer, 1984, *Music and Poetry: The Nineteenth Century and After*, Berkeley: University of California Press, 25–124.
10. Fowler, 1991, *A History of English Litera-*ture. Cambridge, MA: Harvard University Press, 66–69.
11. Fowler, 1991, 69–70.
12. Shakespeare, 1926, *Comedy of Error.* ed. R. D. French, New Haven, CT: Yale University Press.
13. J. L. Styan, 1967, *Shakespeare's Stagecraft,* Cambridge, Cambridge University Press, 71, 195–8.
14. T. Middleton, 1975, *Women Beware Women*, London: Methuen, Act II.
15. Shakespeare, *Macbeth*; B. Evans, 1979, *Shakespeare's Tragic Practice*, Oxford, 181.
16. For mannerism in English literature, see H. Gardner, 1957, *Metaphysical Poets*, Oxford University, xix–liv; C.Sullivan, 2008, *The Rhetoric of the Conscience in Donne, Herbert, and Vaughan*, Oxford: Oxford University Press, 1–38.
17. G. Parfitt, 1992, *English Poetry of the Seventeenth Century*, Berkeley: University of California Press, 1–29; B. Vickers, 1968, *Francis Bacon and Renaissance Prose*, Cambridge, Cambridge University Press, 141–173.
18. Johnson, "The Sad Shepherd," "Inviting a Friend to Supper"; Edmund Waller, "At Penshurst," "On St. James's Park"; Cotton, "The Wonders of the Peak"; John Denham, "Cooper's Hill"; Lord Lansdowne, "To Flavia"; Charles Hopkins, "White-hall"; Marvell's "The Garden"; and Pope, "Summer," Quoted in Fowler, 1991, 102–6.
19. Thomas Browne, 1958, *Urne Buriall: And the Garden of Cyrus*, Cambridge, Cambridge University Press, 7–114; H. Gardner, 1967, *The Metaphysical Poets*, London: Oxford University Press, xix–xxxiv; A. M. Witherspoon and F. J. Warnke, 1963, *Seventeenth Century Prose and Poetry*, New York: Harcourt, Brace & World; R. S. Peterson, 1981, *Imitation and Praise in the Poems of Ben Johnson*, New Haven, Yale University Press, 1–34.
20. I. Walton, 1825, *The Lives of Dr. John Donne, Sir Henry Wotton, Mr. Richard Hooker, Mr. George Herbert, and Dr. Robert Sanderson*, London: John Major.
21. Lucy Hutchinson, 1973, *Memoirs of the life of Colonel Hutchinson*, New York: Oxford University Press; T. Sprat, 1958, *History of the Royal Society*, St. Louis, Washington University.
22. W. Ralegh, 1972, *History of the World*, Phila.: Temple University Press; The Earl of Clarendon, 1888, *The History of the Rebellion and Civil Wars in England Begun in the Year 1641*, Oxford, Clarendon Press.
23. Thomas Hobbes, 1839–1845, *The English Works of Thomas Hobbes of Malmesbury*, London: J. Bohn; Thomas Hobbes, 1994, The Elements of Law, Natural and Politic, Oxford: Oxford University Press; F. Bacon, 1861–1879, *The Works of Francis Bacon*, London: Longman;

B. Vickers, 1996, *Francis Bacon*, Oxford: Oxford University Press, xv–xliv; G. Williamson, 1951, *The Senecan Amble: A Study in Prose from Bacon to Collier*, Chicago: University of Chicago Press, 11–120; F. P. Wilson, 1960, *Seventeenth Century Prose: Five Lectures*, Cambridge, Cambridge University Press, 1–25; D. Johnston, 1986, *The Rhetoric of Leviathan: Thomas Hobbes and Politics of Cultural Transformation*, Princeton, NJ: Princeton University Press, xv–65.

24. Lenhart, 1956, *Musical Influence on American Poetry*, Athens: University of Georgia Press, 1–28.

25. Lenhart, 1956, 1.

26. Renaissance England was a land of song, where popular ballads were sung on the streets and metrical psalmody swept the court. G. Reese, 1959, *Music in the Renaissance*, New York: W. W. Norton, 763–815; F. W. Sternfeld, 1973, *Music from the Middle Ages to the Renaissance*, London: Weidenfeld and Nicolson, 255–323.

27. Lenhart, 1956, 4–5.

28. A. A. Parker, M. A. Leach, and W. Lichtenwanger, *Church music and musical life in Pennsylvania in the eighteenth century: prepared by the Committee on Historical Research*, Philadelphia, The National Society of Colonial Dames of America in the Commonwealth of Pennsylvania, 1927, 163; Lenhart, 1956, 9.

29. Lenhart, 1956, 20–21; E. H. Krehbiel, 1892, *The Philharmonic Society of New York*, New York: Novello, Ewer & Co., 23–4; J. T. Howard, *Our American Music*, 1946, New York: T. Y. Crowell, 33–4.

30. R. Wuthnow, 2003, *All in Sync: How Music and Art are Revitalizing American Religion*, Berkeley: University of California Press, 21–55, 79–182.

31. Lenhart, 1956, 29.

32. K. Heiler, 2003, *Confronting Identities in German Art: Myths, Reactions, and Reflections*, Chicago: University of Chicago Press, Chapters 1–3; P. M. Daley, 2000, *Images of Germany: Perceptions and Conceptions*, New York: Peter Lang, 51–84; J. Henretta and J. Heideking, 2000, *Republicanism and Liberalism in America and the German States, 1750–1850*, Cambridge, Cambridge University Press, 1–34; M. B. Levinger, 2000, *Enlightened Nationalism: The Transformation of Prussian Political Culture, 1806–1848*, Oxford: Oxford University Press, 19–40, 97–126.

33. Quoted by Daiches, *God and the Poets*, Oxford: Oxford University Press, 162.

34. E. Peters, 1993, *Lyrics of the Afro-American Spiritual*, Westport, CO: Greenwood Press, 1–110, 341–380; Rosenthal, 1992, *Hard Bop: Jazz and Black Music, 1955–1965*, Oxford: Oxford University Press, 3–60.

35. M. Williams, 1983, *The Jazz Tradition New and Revised Edition*. Oxford: Oxford University Press, 7–8.

36. M. Williams, 1983, 10–12, 52–64.

37. H. Reich, 2003, *Jelly's Blues: The Life, Music, and Redemption of Jelly Roll Morton*, Cambridge, MA: Da Capo, 1–52.

38. R. M. Radano, 2003, *Lying Up A Nation: Race and Black Music*, Chicago: University of Chicago Press, 164–187.

39. E. Redmond, 1976, *Drumvoices: The Mission of Afro-American Poetry: A Critical History*, Garden City: Anchor Press, 27–42.

40. Daiches, 1984, 98–99.

Chapter 5

1. Wachtel, 1994, *An Obsession with History: Russian Writers Confront the Past*, Stanford: Stanford University Press, 1–2, 219–226.

2. Kelly and Lovell, 2000, *Russian Literature, Modernism and the Visual Arts*. Cambridge: Cambridge University Press, 1–146; Moser, 1992, *The Cambridge History of Russian Literature*, Cambridge: Cambridge University Press, 92–188; Terras, 1991, *A History of Russian Literature*, New Haven, CT: Yale University Press, 115–378.

3. Wachtel, 1998, xi.

4. Platt, 1997, *History in a Grotesque Key: Russian Literature and the Idea of Revolution*, Stanford: Stanford University Press, 1–65; Ram, 2003, *The Imperial Sublime: A Russian Poetics of Empire*, Madison: University of Wisconsin Press, 3–27, 63–120.

5. Groys, 1992, *The Total Arts of Stalinism*. Princeton, NJ: Princeton University Press, 48–9; Wachtel, 1994, 3.

6. A. Weiner, 1998, *By Authors Possessed: The Demonic Novel in Russia*, Evanston, IL, North Western University Press, 1–56; V. Boss, 1991, *Milton and the Rise of Russian Satanism*, Toronto, University of Toronto Press, 1–58; D. B. Johnson, 1985, *Worlds in Regression: Some Novels of Vladimir Nabokov*, Ann Arbor: Adis, 47–78; Pattison and Thompson, 2001, *Dostoevsky and the Christian Tradition*. Cambridge: Cambridge University Press, 1–27; D. O. Thompson, 1991, *The Brothers Karamazov and Poetics of Memory*, Cambridge, Cambridge University Press, 273–318; Coates, 1998, *Christianity in Bakhtin: God and the Exiled Author*. Cambridge: Cambridge University Press, 126–176; Cornwell, 1999, *The Gothic-Fantastic in Nineteenth-Century Russian Literature*, Amsterdam: Rodopi, 3–22.

7. Vinokur, 1971, 1–9; Auty, 1977; N. K. Chedwick, 1964, 1–158.

8. Chedwick, 1964, *Russian Heroic Poetry*, New York: Russell and Russell, 10–11; Terra, 1991, 1–14; W. R. S. Ralston, 2005, *Songs of the Russian People*, Whitefish, MT: Kessinger, 36–54.

9. Chadwick, 1964, xi–xii, 15–19.

10. Chadwick, 1964, 3–42.

11. Moser, 1996, 1–44; Auty, 1977, "The Russian Language," *An Introduction to Russian Language and Literature*, Cambridge: Cambridge University Press, 35–37; J. Fennel and Antony Stoke, 1974, *Early Russian Literature*, Berkeley: University of California Press, 11–79.

12. Moser, 1996, 3–4.

13. Moser, 1996, 4; Vinokur, 1971, *The Russian Language: A Brief History*. Cambridge: Cambridge University Press, 1–67.

14. J. Bortnes, 1996, "The Literature of Old Russia, 988–1730," *The Cambridge History of Russian Literature*, Cambridge: Cambridge University Press, 1–44; Terras, 1991, 15–84; Obolensky, 1971, *Byzantine and Slaves: Collected Studies*, London: Variorum, 3–27; Fedotov, 1988, *The Russian Religious Mind*. 2 vols. Belmont, MA: Notable and Academic Books, 63–93.

15. Sherbowitz-Wetzor and Cross, 1973, *The Russian Primary Chronicle: Laurentian Text*, Cambridge, MA: Mediaeval Academy of America, 21–2, 62–3, 101–37; Meyendorff, 1981, *Byzntium and the Rise of Russia*, Cambridge: Cambridge University Press, 17–23.

16. Fedotov, 1988, vol. 1.

17. Vinokur, 1971, 24.

18. Fedotov, 1988, 344–362; M. Gimbutas, 1974, *Gods and Goddesses of Old Europe, 7000–3500 B.C: Myths, Legends, and Cult Images*, Berkeley: University of California Press, 112–95.

19. Hubbs, 1988, *Mother Russia: The Feminine Myth in Russian Culture*, Bloomington: Indiana University Press, 145–55.

20. Pattison and Thompson, 2001, *Dostoevsky and the Christian Tradition*, Cambridge: Cambridge University Press, 1–30; Coates, 1998, *Christianity in Bakhtin: God and the Exiled Author*, Cambridge: Cambridge University Press, 1–24, 126–151; Bethea, 1989, *The Shape of Apocalypse in Modern Russian Fiction*, Princeton, NJ: Princeton University Press, 1–26.

21. Hubbs, 1988, 87–9.

22. P. I. Barta, 2001, *Gender and Sexuality in Russian Civilization*, New York: Routledge, 1–88.

23. Prof. Wachtel called it "intergeneric dialogue," I changed the word because I want to suggest a much wider range of cultural expression, including verbal and sub-verbal. Wachtel, 1994, 219–28.

24. Mosor, 1996, 45–91, 136–188; Ram, 2003, 28–62, 160–211.

25. Marina Ritzarev, 2006, *Eighteenth-Century Russian Music*, Aldershot: Ashgate; Marina Ritzarev, "*Russian Music before Glinka: A Look from the Beginning of the Third Millennium*" on Israel Studies in Musicology Online, up dated 2002; A. Nelson, 2004, *Music for the Revolution: Musicians and Power in Early Soviet Russia*, University Park, PA: Penn State University Press, 1–40; R. B. Anderson and P. Debreczeny, 1994, *Russian Narrative & Visual Art: Varieties of Seeing*, Gainesville: University Press of Florida, 11–40, 63–77.

26. Auty and Obolensky, 1977, *An Introduction to Russian Language and Literature*, Cambridge, Cambridge University Press, 133–147; Debreczeny, *The Other Pushkin: A Study of Alexander Pushkin's Prose Fiction*, Stanford, Stanford University Press; B.Gasparov, "Poetry of the Silver Age," *The Cambridge Companion to Twentieth-Century Russian Literature*, Cambridge, Cambridge University Press, 1–20.

27. Bristol, 1991, *A History of Russian Poetry*, Oxford: Oxford University Press, 104–111.

28. Wachtel, 2004, *The Cambridge Introduction to Russian Poetry*, Cambridge, Cambridge University Press, 146–155; A.Smith, 2006, *Montaging Pushkin: Pushkin and Visions of Modernity in Russian Twentieth-century Poetry*, New York: Rodopi, 11–102.

29. O. G. T. Sonneck, 1972, *Report on the Star-Spangled Banner, Hail Columbia, America, Yankee Doodle*, New York: Dover Publications, 79–156; J. A. Lomax, 1994, American Ballads and Folk Songs, New York: Dover, 521.

Chapter 6

1. Gurhrie, 1962–1981, 2: 361–83; E. Hussey, 1972, *The Presocratics*, London: Duckworth, 1–10, 107–126; Kirk, Raven and Schofield, 1983, The Presocratic Philosophers, *Cambridge: Cambridge University Press*, 7–75; A. Lesky, 1966, *A History of Greek Literature*, London: Hackket, 190–3; A. P. D. Mourelatos, ed., 1974, *The Presocratics*, New York: Anchor Press, Parts 1–4.

2. G. S. Kirk, 1962, *Heraclitus: The Cosmic Fragments*, Cambridge: Cambridge University Press, 13–30; C. H. Kahn, 1979, *The Art and Thought of Heraclitus*, Cambridge: Cambridge University Press, 3–24.

3. H. Diels and W. Kranz, 1951–2, *Die Fragmente der Vorsokratiker I–ii*, Berlin; K. Freeman, 1956, *Ancilla to the Pre-Socratic Philosophers*, London: Blackwell; J. Barnes, 1979, *The Presocratic Philosophers*, London: 3–56.

4. G. S. Kirk, 1962, 13–26; C. H. Kahn, 1960, *Anaximander and the Origins of Greek Cosmology*, New York: Hackket, 11–24, 75–118; Kahn, 1973, *The Verb "Be" in Ancient Greek; The Art and Thought of Heraclitus*, Cambridge: Cambridge University Press.

5. Kirk, *Heraclitus*, quoted in Long, 1999, "Early Greek Philosophy," 7–8.

6. G. Kennedy, 1989, "Sophists and Physicians of the Greek Enlightenment," *The Cambridge History of Classical Literature*, vol. 1, part 3, 63–4; L. Y. Kim, 2010, Homer between History and Fiction in Imperial Greek Literature, Cambridge: Cambridge University Press, 175–

216.

7. This verbal path for philosophy is not completely unique in Greek. One can see the same pattern in ancient Chinese, and Sanskrit, that distilled abstract words rather than borrowed them through translation.

8. Sandbach, 1989, "Plato and Socratic Work of Xenophon," in *Cambridge History of Classical Literature*, I (3): 70–83; Plato, 1963, *The Collected Dialogues of Plato*: Including the Letters, eds. E.Hamilton; and H.Cairns, Princeton, NJ: Princeton University Press; R. Robinson, 1947, *Plato's Earlier Dialectic*, Oxford: Clarendon, 93–96; R. K. Sprague, 1962, *Plato's Use of Fallacy*, New York: Barnes and Nobles; H. Thesleff, 1967, *Studies in the Style of Plato*, Helsinki, 1–60, 107–128.

9. Plato, *Laws*; Sandbach, 1989, 71–2.

10. Plato, *Republic, Phaedrus, Symposium*, in *The Collected Dialogues of Plato*, E. Hamilton and H. Cairn, 1961, Princeton, NJ: Princeton University Press; G. Watson, 1988, *Phantasia in Classical Thought*, Galway: Galway University Press, 80–93.

11. G. Kennedy, 1963, *The Art of Persuasion in Greece*, Princeton, NJ: Princeton University Press, 26–70; J. Walker, 2000, *Rhetoric and Poetics in Antiquity*, Oxford: Oxford University Press, 139–276.

12. Walker, 2000, 108–9.

13. Shepard, 1994, "Plato and the Neoplatonists," *Platonism and the English Imagination*, Cambridge: Cambridge University Press, 6.

14. Aristotle, 1937, *Parts of Animals*, Cambridge: Cambridge University Press; Aristotle, 1943, *Generation of Animals*, Cambridge, Cambridge University Press; Aristotle, 1965–70, *Historia Animalium, Books 1–6*, Cambridge, Cambridge University Press; P. Pellegrin, 1986, *Classification of Animals*, trans. Berkeley: University of California Press; R. B. B. Wardy, 1990, *The Chain of Change: A Study of Aristotle's Physics VII*, Cambridge: Cambrige University Press, 71–120; G. E. R. Lloyd, 1966, *Polarity and Analogy; Two Types of Argumentation in Early Greek Thought*, Cambridge, Cambridge University Press, 15–171; Lloyd, 1996, *Aristotelian Exploration*, Cambridge: Cambridge University Press, 7–37; S. Broadie, 1993, "Aristotle's Perceptual Realism," *Southern Journal of Philosophy* 31: 137–59; G. Freudenthal, 1995, *Aristotle's Theory of Material Substance: Heat and Pneuma, Form and Soul*, Oxford: Clarendon Press, 1–35; A. Gotthelf and J. G. Lexnnox, 1987, *Philosophical Issues in Aristotle's Biology*, Cambridge: Cambridge University Press, 5–64.

15. A. A. Long, 1985, "Aristotle," *Cambridge History of Classical Literature*, vol. 1, part 3, 118–20.

16. Long, 1985, 120–2; G. M. A. Grube, 1965, *The Greek and Roman Critics*, London:

Methuen, 93–4.

17. Aristotle, 1952, *Meteorologica*, Cambridge, MA: Harvard University Press, 185–202; Aristotle, 1975, *Posterior Analytics* 71b 17–22, 78a 30–36, J. Barnes, ed., Oxford: Clarendon; Lloyd, 1996, 7–37; Guthrie, 1939, *Aristotle, On the Heavens*, Cambridge, MA: Harvard University Press; R. Boton, 1987, "Definition and Scientific Method in Aristotle's *Posterior Analytics* and *Generation of Animals*," Gotthelf and Lennox, eds., 120–66; E. Berti, ed., 1981, *Aristotle on Science: The Posterior Analytics*, Padua; C. Rossitto, 1984, "La dimostraziooone diaaalettica in Aristotele," *La Nottola* 3: 5–40; S. Waterlow, 1982, *Nature, Change and Agency in Aristotle's Physics*, Oxford: Oxford University Press.

18. H. Chadwick, 1967, "Philo," *The Cambridge History of Later Greek and Early Medieval Philosophy*, Cambridge, Cambridge University Press, 137–57; C. Bigg, 1913, *The Christian Platonists of Alexandria*, Oxford, 31–50; D. J. Riunia, 1986, *Philo of Alexandria and the Timaeus of Plato*, Leiden.

19. D. Feeney, 1998, *Literature and Religion at Rome Culture, Contexts, and Beliefs*, Cambridge, Cambridge University Press, 1–2; G. B. Conte, 1994b, *Latin Literature: A History*, Baltimore, Johns Hopkins University Press, 4–5, 23, 108–10; E. J. Kennedy, 1993, *The Arts of Love*, Cambridge, Cambridge University Press, 7–8.

20. Lamberton, 1986, *Homer the Theologian: Neoplatonist Allegorical Reading and the Growth of the Epic Tradition*, Berkeley: University of California Press, 11–12; L. H. Pratt, 1993, *Lying and Poetry from Homer to Pindar: Falsehood and Deception in Archaic Greek Poetics*, Ann Arbor: University of Michigan Press, 36–7; R. Parker, 1983, *Miasma: Pollution and Purification in Early Greek Religion*, Oxford: Oxford University Press, 16–7.

21. Conte, 1994b, 29–109; A. S. Gratwick, 1982, "Drama," *Cambridge History of Classical Literature* 2: 77–137; R. C. Beacham, 1991, *The Roman Theatre and Its Audience*, Cambridge, MA: Harvard University Press, 86–116; H. D. Jocelyn, 1967, *The Tragedies of Ennius*, Cambridge, Cambridge University Press, 3–43; G. E. Duckworth, 1994, *The Nature of Roman Comedy: A Study in Popular Entertainment*, London: Bristol Classical Press, 39–73; F. H. Sandhabch, 1977, *The Comic Theatre of Greece and Rome*, New York: Norton, 15–36; W. S. Anderson, 1993, *Barbarian Play: Plautius Roman Comedy*, Toronto: University of Toronto Press, 1–59; J. Wright, 1974, *Dancing in Chains: The Stylistic Unity of the Comoedia Palliata*, Rome: American Academy, 1–30; E. Segal, *Roman Laughter*, New York: Oxford University Press, 1–14; 1987; R. L. Hunter, 1985, *The New Comedy of Greece and Rome*, Cambridge: Cambridge University Press, 1–23, 83–94, 147–151;. G. Manuwald, 2011,

Roman Republican Theatre Cambridge: Cambridge University Press, 26–48.

22. Conte, 1994b, 57–41. Like the Greeks centuries ago, Latin character building had to begin with masks whose stereotyped features were more efficient than primitive words for depiction and allowed instinct identification of characters and their intended traits. A. Pickard, 1988, *Dramatic Festivals of Athens*, Oxford: Oxford University Press, 218–20; S. O'Bryhim, 2001, *Greek and Roman Comedy*, Austin: University of Texas Press, 153–4.

23. Pickard, 1988, 218–20; S. O'Bryhim, 2001, 153–4.

24. F. H. Sandbach, 1977, *The Comic Theatre of Greece and Rome*, London; E. Frankel, 1960, *Elementi plautini in Plauto*, Florence; W. G. Arnott, 1968, *Menander, Plautus, Terence*, Oxford; D. Konstan, 1983, *Roman Comedy*, Ithaca; N. W. Slater, 1985, *Plautus in Performance*, Princeton, NJ: Princeton University Press, 97–138; H. W. Prescott, 1932, "Criteria of Originality in Plautus," *Transactions and Proceedings of the American Philological Association* 63: 103–24; D. Bain, 1979, "Plautus vortit barbare: Plautus Bacchides 526–61 and Menannder Dis Exapaton 102–12," in *Creative Imitation in Latin Literature*, D. West and A. J. Woodman, eds., Cambridge: Cambridge University Press, 17–34; N. Zagagi, 1980, *Tradition and Originality in Plautus*, Gottingen: Vandenhoeck und Ruprecht, 15–34.

25. Plautus, 1986, *Bacchiedes*, trans. J. Barsby, Wiltshire: Aris & Phillips.

26. D. Wiles, 2000, *Greek Theatre Performance*, Cambridge: Cambridge University Press, 176–8; A. Pickard, 1988, 218–220.

27. Conte, 1994b, 60–61.

28. Conte, 1994b, p. 82; O. Ribbeck, 1962, *Scaenicae Rmanorum Poesis Fragmenta*, Hildesheim, iii 1897–8; English translation, E. H. Warmington, 1979, *Remains of Old Latin*, London: W. Heinemann; W. Beare, 1984, *The Roman Stage*, London: Metheun, 86–90; J. Wright, 1974, *Dancing in Chains: The Stylistic Unity of the Comoedia Palliata*, Rome: American Academy, 87–126; L. H. Stevens, 1988, *Aulus Gellius*, Chapel Hill: University of North Carolina Press, 145–8.

29. J. Vahlen, 1963, *Ennianae Poesis Reliquiae*, Amsterdam; Conte, 1994b, 81–2.

30. Terence, 1960, *Andria*, ed. G. P. Shipp, Melbourne; Terence, 1988, *Heautontimorumenos*, ed. A. J. Brothers, Warminster: Aris & Phillips; Terence, 1959, *Phormio*, ed. R. M. Martin, London: Methuen; Terence, 1963, *Hecyra*, ed. T. F. Carney, Pretoria: Classical Association of Rhodesia and Nyasaland; W. G. Forehand, 1985, *Terence*, Boston; G. Norwood, 1923, *The Art of Terence*, Oxford: Clarendon Press, 2–14; S. M. Goldberg, 1986, *Understand-*

ing Terence, Princeton, NJ: Princeton University Press; E. Karakasis, 2005, Terence nd the Language of Roman Comedy, Cambridge: Cambridge University Press, 2005. 1–43, 118–125.

31. Conte, 1994a, *Genres and Readers: Lucretius, Love Elegy, Pliny's Encyclopedia*, Baltimore: Johns Hopkins University Press, 1–34; J. K. Newman, 1967, *The Concept of Vates in Augustan Poetry*, Bruxelles, Latomus, revue d'e´tudes latines, 7–24.

32. P. Conte, 1994b, 12; G. S. Irk, J. E. Raven, and M. Schofield, 1983, *The Presocratic Philosophers*, Cambridge, Cambridge University Press, 360–1.

33. Cicero, 1999, *On the Commonwealth and, On the Laws*, ed. J. E. G. Zetel Cambridge: Cambrdige University Press, 1–102.

34. Cicero, *De Legibus*; Conte, 1994b, 190–1.

35. Conte, 1994b, 83–4, 134–5.

36. J. W. Crawford, 1984, *M. Tullius Cicero: The Lost and Unpublished Orations*, Gottingen: Vandenhoeck & Ruprecht, 1–32; M. Fox, 1996, *Roman Historical Myth: The Regal Period in Augustan Literature*, Oxford: Oxford Univeristy Press, 5–28; A. Vasaly, 1993, *Representations: Images of the World in Ciceronian Oratory*, Berkeley: University of California Press, 1–14, 40–87; E. Rawson, 1985, *Intellectual Life in Late Roman Republic*, Baltimore: Johns Hopkins University Press, 3–19, 38–56; P. Mackendrick, 1989, *The Philosophical Books of Cicero*, London.

37. Conte, 1994b, 169–99.

38. Sallust, 1991, *Works*, ed. L. D. Reynolds, Oxford; R. Syme, 1964, *Sallust*, California; D. C. Earl, 1961, *The Political Thought of Sallust*, Cambridge; U. Paananen, 1972, *Sallust's Political-Social Terminology*, Helsinki; T. F. Scanlon, 1980, *The Influence of Thucydides on Sallust*, Heidelberg; E. Rawson, 1991, "Sallust in the 80s," *Roman Culture and Society*, Oxford; Conte, 1994b, 235–242.

39. R. Parker, 1983, *Miasma: Pollution and Purification in Early Greek Religion*, Oxford: Clarendon Press, 1–31; W. Burkert, 1985, *Greek Religion*, Cambridge, MA: Harvard University Press, 10–118, 119–89; A. W. Bulloch, E. S. Gruen, A. A. Ong, and A. Steward, eds., 1993, *Images and Ideologies: Self-Definition in the Hellenistic World*, Berkeley: University of California Press, 245–298; Buxton, 1994, *Imaginary Greece: The Contexts of Mythology*, Cambridge: Cambridge University Press, 9–17; P. F. Dorcey, 1992, *The Cult of Silvanus: A Study in Roman Folk Religion*, Leiden: Brill, 84–144; D. C. Feeney, 1991, *The Gods in Epic: Poets and Critics of the Classical Tradition*, Oxford: Oxford Universit Press, 5–56; G. Nagy, 1979, *The Best of the Achaeans: Concepts of Hero in Archaic Greek Poetry*, Baltimore: Johns Hopkins University Press, 211–242; D. Potter, 1994, *Prophets and Emperors: Human and Divine Authority from Augustus to Theodo-*

sius, Cambridge, MA: Harvard University Press, 10–34; L. H. Pratt, 1993, *Lying and Poetry from Homer to Pindar: Falsehood and Deception in Archaic Greek Poetics*, Ann Arbor: Michigan University Press, 1–10; H. S. Versnel, 1990, *Inconsistencies in Greek and Roman Religion*, Leiden: Brill, 231–253; J. Scheid, 1990, *Romulus et ses Freres: Le college des freres arvaales, modele du culte public dans la Rome des empereurs*, Rome, Ecole francaise de Rome, 475–675; S. R. F. Price, 1984, *Rituals and Power: The Roman Imperial Cult in Asia Minor*, Cambridge: Cambridge University Press, 170–206; D. C. Feeney, 1998, 80–1.

40. R. Gordon, 1979, "The Real and the Imaginary: Production and Religion in the Greco-Roman World," *Art History*, 2: 5–34.

41. Plautus, 1986, 120.

42. Prudentius, *Hamartigenia*, 79–82, quoted in D. Fowler, 2000, *Roman Constructions*, New York: Oxford University Press, 218–9, 225–31.

43. Feeney, 1998, 22, 76; T. J. Cornell, 1995, *The Beginnings of Rome: Italy and Rome from the Bronze Age to the Punic Wars*, London: Routledge, 161–2.

44. A. H. Armstrong, 1967, *St. Augustine and Christian Platonism*, Villanova, Villanova University Press, 3–37; W. Jaeger, 1961, *Early Christianity and Greek Paideia*, Oxford.

45. Philo, 1923–53, *Philo with an English Translation*, trans. F. H. Colson and G. H. Whitaker, 12 vols., Cambridge, MA; Harvard University Press; Proclus, 1963, *Elements of Theology*, ed. E. R. Dodds, Oxford: Oxford University Press; S. Rappe, 2000, Reading neoplatonism: non-discursive thinking in the texts of Plotinus, Proclus, and Damascius, Cambridge: Cambridge University Press, 1–44.

46. Sheppard, 1994, "Plato and the Neoplatonists," *Platonism and the English Imagination*, A. Baldwin and S. Hutton, eds., Cambridge: Cambridge University Press, 6–7.

47. Louth, 1989, "Apathetic Love in Clement of Alexandria," *Studia Patristica*, 18: 413–19; Chadwick, 1967, "'Clement of Alexandria' and 'Origen,'" *Cambridge History of Later Greek and Early Medieval Philosophy*, Cambridge: Cambridge University Press, 168–92.

48. J. Marenbon, 1983, *Early Medieval Philosophy 480–1150, An Introduction*, London: Routledge & K. Paul, 18–20; C. S. Lewis, 1964, *The Discarded Image*, Cambridge: Cambridge University Press, 70–4.

49. Augustine of Hippo, 1972, *The City of God*, trans. H. Bettenson, Harmondsworth; Augustine of Hippo, 1991, *Confessions*, trans. H. Chadwick, Oxford: Oxford University Press.

50. H. J. Blumenthal and R. A. Markus, 1981, *Neoplatonism and Early Christian Thought*, London: Variorum, 204–211; Markus, *End of Ancient Christianity*, Cambridge: Cambridge University Press, 48–56; Marcus, 1970, *Saeculum, History and Society in the Theology of St. Augustine*, Cambridge: Cambridge University Press, 87–92; J. Coleman, 1994, "The Christian Platonism of St. Augustine," in *Platonism and the English Imagination*, A. Baldwin and S. Hutton. Cambridge: Cambridge University Press, 27–36.

51. Baldwin, 1994, "Introduction," Chapter 2, in *Platonism and the English Imagination*, A. Baldwin and S. Hutton, eds., Cambridge: Cambridge University Press, 21.

52. O. Leaman, 1985, *An Introduction to Medieval Islamic Philosophy*, Cambridge, Cambridge University Press, 1–9; F. E. Peters, 1996, "Greek and Syriac Background," *History of Islamic Philosophy*, ed. S. H. Nasr, London: Routledge, I: 40–51; F. Rosenthal, 1992, *The Classical Heritage in Islam*, Berkeley: University of California Press, 17–27; F. Peters, 1968, *Aristotle and the Arabs: The Aristotalian Tradition in Islam*, Albany: State University of New York Press, 3–35; C. Jambet, 2006, The Act of Being: the Philosophy of Revelation. in Mullā Sadraā, Cambridge, MA: MIT Press, 19–44; H. A. Davidson, 1992, Alfarabi, Avicenna, and Averroës on Intellect: Their Cosmologies, Theories of the Active Intellect, and Theories of Human Intellect, Oxford University Press, 7–43; D. Gutas, 1975, *Greek Wisdom Literature in Arabic Translation*, New Haven, CT: American Oriental Society, 1975, 1–8; T. Greene, 1992, *City of the Moon God*, Leiden: Brill, 74–93.

53. Hodgson, 1974, *The Venture of Islam*. Chicago: University of Chicago Press, i: 412–4.

54. Hodgson, 1974, i: 422–5.

55. Hodgson, 1974, i: 423–4.

56. Hodgson, 1974, ii:170–175:

57. M. S. Mahdi, 2001, *Affarabi and Foundation of Islamic Political Philosophy*, Chicago: University of Chicago Press.

58. Mahdi, 2001, 58–62; Hodgson, i: 433–7.

59. Mahdi, 2001, 69–70.

60. J. A. Aertsen, 1999, *Averroës and the Aristiotlian Tradition Sources, Constitution and Reception of the Philosophy of Ibn Rushd (1126–1198)*, Leiden: Brill, 246–271; W. B. Hallag, 1993, *Ibn Taaymiyya Against the Greek Logicians*, Oxford: Clarendon, 3–24; Hallag, *The Origins and Evolution of Islamic Law*, Cambridge: Cambridge University Press, 22–25.

61. "Early Kalam," in *History of Islamic Philosophy*, ed. S. H. Nasr, London: Routledge, i: 71–88.

62. Y. H. Farghal, 1972, *Nash't al-ara wa'l-madhahib wal-fraqal-Kalamiyyah*, Cairo, I: 25, 36; M.'Abdd-al-Raziq, 1966, *Tambidli larikh al-falsafah-al-islamiyah*, Cairo, p. 266, quoted by Abdel Heleem.

63. D. Margoliouuth, trans., 1905, "The Dis-

cussion Between Abu Bishr Matta and Abu Sai'd al-Sirafi on the Merits of Logic and Grammar," *Journal of Royal Asiatic Society* 37: 79–129; Leaman, 1985, 9–10; Ibn Khaldun, 1955, *Al Muqaddma: An Introduction to History*, trans. F. Rosenthal, New York: Pantheon, III: 34, 155.

64. A. G. Chejne, 1984, "Ibn Hazmof Cordova on Logic," *Journal of American Oriental Society* 104 (1): 57–72; I. Hadoot, 1990, "The Life and Work of Simplicius in Greek and Arabic Sources," *Aristotle Transformed*, ed. R. Sorabji, Ithaca, Cornell University Press, 275–303; F. Zimmermann, 1987, "Philoponus' Impetus Theory in Arabic Tradition," in *Philoponus and the Rejection of Aristotlian Science*, Ithaca, Cornell University Press, 121–9; J. Pavlin, 1996, "Sunni Kalam and Theological Controversies," in , *History of Islamic Philosophy*, ed. S. H. Nasr, London: Routledge, 105–7.

65. G. Hourani, 1971, *Islamic Rationalism: The Ethics of 'Abd -Ajabbar*, Oxford; Hourani, 1985, *Reason and Tradition in Islamic Ethics*, Cambridge; Leaman, 1985, 3–8.

66. Reinhart, 1995, *Before Evolution: The Boundaries of Muslim Moral Thought*, Albany: State University of New York Press, 1–26; N. Robinson, 1991, *Christ in Islam and Christianity*, Albany: State Univeristy of New York Press, 1–7; A. Avry, 1976, "Aal-Kindi and the Mu'tazila: A Philosophical and Political Reevaluation," *Oriens*, 25–6, 69–85; B. Gimaret, 1980, *Theories de l'acte humain en theologie muslmane*, Paris; I. Goldziher, 1931 *Introduction to Islamic Theology and Law*, Princeton; E. G. T. Beeth, 1983, *Aristotlian Aporetic Ontology in Islam and Christian Thinkers*, Cambridge: Cambridge University Press, 95–150.

67. G. Endress and J. A. Aertsen, 1999, *Averroës and the Aristotlian Tradition Source, Constitution and Reception of the Philosophy of Ibn Rushd, 1126–1198*, Leiden: Brill, 36–43; Leam, 2009, Islamic Philosophy: An Introduction, Malden, MA: Polity, 2009. 3–12.

68. W. J. Sedgefield, ed., 1899, *King Alfred's Old English Version of Boethius De Consolatione Philosophiae*, Oxford: Clarendon Press; T. A. Carnicelli, ed. , 1969, *King Alfred's Version of St. Augustine's Soliloquies*, Cambridge, MA: Harvard University Press.

69. J. Bately, 1994, "Boethius and King Alfred," *Platonism and the English Imagination*, eds. A. Baldwin and S. Hutton, Cambridge, Cambridge University Press, 38–41.

70. K. Poole, 2000, *Radical Religion from Shakespeare to Milton: Figures of Nonconformity in Early Modern England*, Cambridge, Cambridge University Press, 2.

71. Poole, 2000, 1–15.

72. Nietzsche, 1974, *The Gay Science*, New York:Johnson Reprint, 137–8.

73. R. Lyne, 2001, *Ovid's Changing Worlds:*

English Metamorphoses, 1567–1632, Oxford: Oxford University Press, 3.

74. R. Helgerson, 1988, "Barbarous Tongues: The Ideology of Poetic Form in Renaissance England," *The Historical Renaissance: New Essays on Tudor and Stuart Literature and Culture*, eds. H. Dubrow and R. Strier, Chicago: University of Chicago Press, 273; Helgerson, 1992, *Forms of Nationhood: The Elizabethan Writing of England*, Chicago: University of Chicago Press, 25–59.

75. Quoted from "A Defense of Rhyme," in Samuel Daniel, 1965, *Poems and a Defense of Rhyme*, ed. A. C. Sprague, Chicago: University of Chicago Press, 158.

76. T. Howell, 1560, *The Fable of Ovid Treting of Narcissus*, London; F. S. Boas, 1950, "Ovid and the Elizabethans," in *Queen Elizabeth in Drama and Related Studies*, London: Allen & Unwin, 101–21.

77. T. Howell, 1560, 29–35; R. Lyne, 2001, 35–6.

78. Golding, 1965, *Ovid's Metamorphoses: The Arthur Golding Translation*, ed. J. F. Nims, New York.

79. G. Kennedy, 1989, "Sophists and Physicians of he Greek Enlightenment," in *Cambridge History of Classical Literature*, vol. 1, part 3, 64–5.

80. Plotinus, 1966–8, *Plotinus with an English Translation*, ed., trans. A. H. Armstrong, 6 vols., London; E. N. Tigerstedt, 1974, *The Decline and Fall of the Neoplatonic Interpretation of Plato*, Helsinki; J. M. Rist, 1967, *Plotinus: The Road to Reality*, Cambridge.

81. Hippocratic works *On the Sacred Disease*. Aristotle, *Metaphysics*; for modern writers, see Guthrie, 1962, 26–38; G. Lloyd, 1979, *Magic, Reason, and Experience: Studies in the Origin and Development of Greek Science*, Cambridge, chapter 1–3; Lloyd, 1987, *The Revolutions of Wisdom: Studies in the Claims and Practice of Ancient Greek Science*, Berkeley: University of California Press, 50–70; Ostwald, 1992, 338–69; Hornblower, 1987, *Thucydides*, Baltimore: Johns Hopkins University Press, 110–35; J. R. Hankinson, 1992, "Doing Without Hypotheses: The Nature of Ancient Medicine," in J. A. Lopez Ferez, ed., *Tratados Hippocraticos*, Madrid; J. Longrigg, 1993, *Greek Rational Medicine: Philosophy and Medicine from Alcmaeon to the Alexandrians*, London.

82. W. Burkert, 1995, *The Orientalizing Revolution: Near Eastern Influence of Greek Culture in the Early Archaic Age*, Cambridge, MA: Harvard University Press, 1.

83. E. Hall, 1989, 16–7, 59–60.

84. J. Bately, 1994, "Boethius and King Alfred," in *Platonism and the English Imagination*, eds. A. Baldwin and S. Hutton, Cambridge: Cambridge University Press, 38–9; Bately, 1985 "Anglo-Saxons on the Mind," in *Learning and*

Literature in Anglo-Saxon England, eds. M. Lapidge and H. Gneuss, Cambridge: Cambridge Universit Press, 296–9; M. Gibson, 1981, *Boethius, his Life, Thought, and Influence*, Oxford: Blackwell, chapter 1; J.Marebon, 2003, *Boethius*, Oxford: Oxford University Press, 17–42.

85. G. B. Evans, 1974, *The Riverside Shakespeare*, Boston; R. L. Colie, 1974, *Shakespeare's Living Art*, Princeton; W. H. Clemen, 1951, *The Development of Shakespeare's Imagery*, London; A. C. Bradley, 1904, *Shakespeare's Tragedy*, London; A. Barton, 1984, *Ben Jonson, Dramatist*, Cambridge; G. Braden, 1985, *Renaissance Tragedy and the Senecan Tradition*, New Haven; E. L. Jones, 1971, *Scenic Form in Shakespeare*, Oxford; A. H. Gomme, 1969, *Jacobean Tragedies*, London.

86. Augustine, *Confessions*, III 6.11.

87. Louth, 1994, "Platonism in the Middle English Mystics," *Platonism*

88. *and the English Imagination*, eds. A. Baldwin and S. Hutton, Cambridge:

89. Cambridge University, 55–6.

90. H. More, 1878, *Utopia, Written in Latin*, trans. R. Robyson, Boston: Constable; More, 2002, *Utopia*, eds. G. M. Logan and R. M. Adams, Cambridge: Cambridge University Press; A. R. Hall, 1996, *Henry More and Scientific Revolution*, Cambridge: Cambridge University Press, 82–106; D. C. Fouke, 1997, *The Enthusiastical Concerns of Dr. Henry More: Religious Meaning and the Psychology of Delusion*, Leiden: Brill, 18–34.

91. J. Knapp, 1992, *An Empire Nowhere: England, America, and Literature from Utopia to the Tempest*, Berkeley: University of California Press, 18; C. McEachern, 1996, *The Poetics of English Nationhood, 1590–1612*, Cambridge: Cambridge University Press, 5.

92. J. Knapp, 1992, 63–9.

93. J. S. Scarisbrick, 1984, *The Reformation and the English People*, Oxford; C. Haigh, ed., 1987, *The Reformation Revised*, Cambridge: Cambridge University Press, 34–57; E. Carlson, ed., 1998, *Religion and English People, 1500–1640: New Voices/New Perspective*, Kirksville, MO: Thomas Jefferson University Press, 23–48; C. Marsh, 1998, *Popular Religion in Sixteenth-Century England: Holding Their Peace*, New York: McMillam, 27–95; M. C. McClendon, 1999, *The Quiet Reformation: Magistrates and the Emergence of Protestantism in Tudor Norwich*, Stanford: Stanford University Press, 88–151; P. Lake, 1982, *Moderate Puritans and the Elizabethan Church*, Cambridge: Cambridge University Press, 55–92; P. Marshal and A. Ryrie, eds., 2002, *The Beginnings of English Protestantism*, Cambridge; P. Marshall, 1997, "Introduction," in *The Impact of the English Reformation 1500–1640*, New York: Arnold, 4–19; N. Jones, 2002, *The English Reformation Religion and Cultural*

Adaptation, Oxford: Oxford University Press, 7–28; E. Duffy, 1992, *The Stripping of the Altars: Traditional Religion in England 1400–1580*, New Haven, CT: Yale University Press, 89–130.

94. D. Norton, 2000, *A History of the English Bible as Literature*, Cambridge: Cambridge University Press, 1–2; C; Cross, 1978, "Great Reasoners in Scripture: The Activities of Women Lollards, 1380–1530," *Medieval Women*, Oxford: Oxford University Press, 359–80.

95. Hudson ed., 1978, *Selections from English Wycliffite Writings*, Cambridge: Cambridge University Press, 67–72, 174–6; Norton, 2000, 7–9.

96. Norton, 2000, 1–2, 7.

97. R. Hooker, 1593, *The Laws of Ecclesiastical Polity*, ed. A. S. McGrade, 1989, Cambridge: Cambridge University Press, 87; J. Milton, 1957, "Tenure of Kings and Magistrates," *Complete Poems and Major Prose*, ed. M. Y. Hughes, New York.

98. Norton, 2000, 8, 15–6.

99. Davies, 2002, *A Religion of the Word The Defense of the Reformation in the Reign of Edward VI*, Manchester: Manchester University Press, lx–x.

100. F. Yates, 1975, *The Imperial Theme in the Sixteenth Century*, London: Routledge, 12–23; W. Oram, 1984, "Elizabethan Fact and Spenserian Fiction," *Spenser Studies* 4: 33–47; S. Orgel, 1975, *The Illusion of Power*, Berkeley: University of California Press, 37–87; R. Strong, 1977, *The Cult of Elizabeth: Elizabethan Portraiture and Pageantry*, London: Thames & Hudson, 114–128.

101. E. Spenser, 1932–1957, *Works: A Variorum Edition*, ed. E. Greenlaw, et al., Baltimore: John Hopkins Press, Book 4, The Faerie Qveene; P. Alpers, 1977, "The Narration of *Faerie Queene*" *English Literary History* 44(1): 19–39; J. H. Anderson, 1982, "'In Living Colors and Right Hew:' The Queen of Spenser's Central Books," in *Poetic Tradition of English Renaissance*, eds. M. M. Mack and G. D. Llord, New Haven, CT: Yale University Press, 47–66.

102. McEachern, 1996, *The Poetics of English Nationhood, 1590–1612*, Cambridge: Cambridge University Press, 1–33.

103. The ambivalent effects of Shakespeare's Henry V became a focus of critical reading. See Rabkin, 1977, "Rabbits, Ducks, and Henry V," *Shakespeare Quarterl*, 28: 281–96; W. Cohn, 1985, *Drama of a Nation: Public Theater in Renaissance England and Spain*, Ithaca, NY: Cornell University Press, 20–39; C. Belsey, 1985, *The Subject of Tragedy: Identity and Difference in Renaissance Drama*, London: Methuem, 8–15.

104. T. Eliot, 1531, *The Boke Named the Governour*, ed. H. H. S. Croft, 1883, 2 vols., London, vol. 239; C. McEachern, 1996, *The Poetics of English Nationhood*, Cambridge: Cambridge

University Press, 86–7.

105. Hill, 1986, "The Protestant Nation," *Collected Essays II: Religion and Politics in Seventeenth Century England*, Brighton: Harvester Press, 28–9.

106. E. H. Kantorowicz, 1957, *The King's Two Bodies*, Princeton, NJ: Princeton University Press, 86.

107. C. Jordan, 1993, "The Household and the State: Transformation in the Representation of an Analogy from Aristotle to James I," *Modern Language Quarterly*, 54 (3): 307–26.

108. McEachern, 1996, 126.

109. M. Yazawa, 1985, *From Colonies to Commonwealth: Familial Ideology and the Beginnings of the American Republic*, Baltimore: Johns Hopkins University Press, 111.

110. C. C. Eldridge, 1996, *The Imperial Experience: From Carlyle to Forester*, New York: St. Martin's Press, 2.

111. H. W. Wyatt, 1897, "The Ethics of Empire," *Nineteenth Century* (April), 526; Eldridge, 1996, 104.

112. J. E. Cwelldon, 1910, "The Early Training of Boy into Citizenship," *Essays on Duty and Discipline*, 12–3; Eldridge, 1996, 103.

113. Lord Rosebery, 1900, "Inaugural Address as Rector of the University of Glasgow, 16 Nov. 1900," *Question of Empire*, 37; R. Kipling, 1893, "A Song of the English"; R. William, 1991, *Defending the Empire: The Conservative Party and British Defense Policy, 1899–1915*, New Haven; W. M. R. Louis, 1992, "*In the Name of God, Go!*" New York; Eldridge, 1996, 105–6.

114. John Davidson, 1902, "The Testament of an Empire Builder," p. 81, Eldridge, 1996, 7–8.

115. N. Forester, 1962, *Image of America: Our Literature from Puritanism to the Space Age*, Nortre Dame: University of Notre Dame Press, 1–2.

116. Greene, 1969, "Political Mimesis: A Consideration of the Historical and Cultural Roots of Legislative Behavior in the British Colonies in the Eighteenth Century," *American Historical Review* 75: 343–6; F. Syme, 1958, *Colonial Elites: Rome, Spain, and the Americas*, London; G. C. Bolton, 1968, "The Idea of a Colonial Gentry," *Historical Studies* 13: 307–28; Greene, 1969, *Imperative*, 159–61.

117. B. Kuklick, 2001, *A History of Philosophy in America*, Oxford: Oxford University Press, 1–3.

118. R. Middlekauff, 1971, *The Mothers: Three Generations of Puritan Intellectuals, 1596–1728*, Berkeley: Universit of California Press, 113–161.

119. O. Ritschl, 1926, *Dogmengeschichte des Protestantismus*, Gottingen, 412–58; R. L. Greaves, 1968, "The Origins and Early Development of English Covenant Thought," *The Historian*, 31: 21–35; E. B. Holifield, 1974, *The Covenant Sealed: The Development of Puritan*

Sacramental Theology in Old and New England, 1570–1720, New Haven, CT: Yale University Press, 169–196; R. T. Kandall, 1979, *Calvin and English Calvinism to 1649*, Oxford: Oxford University Press, 1–28; J. New, 1964, *Anglican and Puritan: The Basis of Their Opposition*, London.

120. Kuklick, 2001, 5–6.

121. Forest, 1962, 3–8.

122. Forest, 1962, 8.

123. J. P. Greene, 1992, *Imperatives, Behaviors, and Identities: Essays in Early American Cultural History*, Charlottesville: University Press of Virginia, 113–142; *The Intellectual Construction of America: Exceptionalism and Identity from 1492–1800*, Chapel Hill: University of North Carolina Press, 8–33.

124. Kuklick, 2001, 35–42.

125. Jennings, 2000, *The Creation of America through Evolution to Empire*, Cambridge: Cambridge University Press, 111–6, 171.

126. C. H. Lincoln, 1901, "The Revolutionary Movement in Pennsylvania, 1760–1776," Ph.D. dissertation, Philadelphia, 284; R. L. Brunbouse, 1942, *The Counter-revolution in Pennsylvania, 1776–1790*, Harrisburg, p. 19; Jennings, 2000, 184.

127. About how "undemocratic" America was at the time, see Jennings, 2000, 180–92, 195–7.

128. H. Adams, 1961, *The Education of Henry Adams: An Autobiography*, Boston, 105–1.

129. C. G. Calloway, 1995, *The American Revolution in Indian Country*, Cambridge, p. xv.

130. R. Carwardine, 2002, "Charles Sellers's 'Antinomians' and 'Arminians': Methodists and the Market Revolution," in *God and Mammon, Protestants, Money, and the Market, 1790–1860*, ed. M. A. Noll, Oxford, 76.

131. Van Alstyne, 1965, *The Rising American Empire*, reprint, Chicago: University of Chicago Press, 6–7; Jennings, 2000, p. 199.

132. Burstein, 1999, *Sentimental Democracy: The Evolution of America's Romantic Self-image*, New York: Hill and Wang, 325–6.

133. Burstein, 1999, p. 334.

134. Perry Miller, 1967, "Declension in a Bible Commonwealth," in *Nature's Name*, Cambridge: Cambridge University Press, 14–49; Miller, 1953, *The New England Mind*, Cambridge.

135. Heimert, 1966, *Religion and the American Mind from the Great Awakening to the Revolution*, Cambridge, MA, 27–9; Greene, 1992, 145–6.

136. F. B. Tolles, 1948, *Meeting House and Counting House: The Quaker Merchants of Colonial Philadelphia*, Chapel Hill, 123–5, 234–6; Greene, 1992, 146–7.

137. Scottow, 1715, *Old Men's Tears for their Own Declensions*, reprint, Boston, p. 19; J. Webb, 1734, *The Duty of a Degenerated People to Pray for the Reviving of God's Work*, Boston, 3: 25–6; Miller, 1953, *The New England Mind: From Col-*

ony to Province, Cambridge, ix–x; Greene, 1992, 147.

138. R. L. Bushman, 1967, *From Puritan to Yankee: Character and the Social Order in Connecticut, 1690–1765*, Cambridge, MA: Harvard University Press, 147–235; W. Williams, 1719, *A Plea for God, and an Appeal to the Consciousness of a People Declining in Religion*, Boston, 23–5; Greene, *Imperative*, 148, 153–6.

139. J. P. Diggins, 2000, *On Hallowed Ground: Abraham Lincoln and the Foundations of American History*, New Haven, p. 2.

140. R. Wiebe, 1995, *Self-Rule: A Cultural History of American Democracy*, Chicago: University of Chicago Press 14–15.

141. John Adams, 1991, quoted in I. Kramnick, *Republicanism and Bourgeois Radicalism*, Ithaca, p. 138, and R. H. Lee, 1911–4, in *The Letters of Richard Henry Lee*, ed. J. C. Ballagh, 2 vols., New York:MacMillan, quoted in *Self-Ruled*, p. 34.

142. J. Meyendorff, 1981, *Byzantium and the Rise of Russia: A Study of Byzantino-Russia Relations in the Fourteenth Century*, Cambridge: Cambridge University Press, 2–3; H. Ram, 2003, *The Imperial Sublime: A Russian Poetics of Empire*, Madison: University of Wisconsin Press; B. Holmgren, 2003, *The Russian Memoir: History and Literature*, Evanston, IL: Northwestern University Press.

143. S. H. Cross and O. P. Sherbowitz-Wetzor, trans., 1953, *The Russian Primary Chronicle*, Cambridge, MA: Harvard, University Press, p. 111.

144. Meyendorff, 1981, 17–18; Cross and Sherbowitz-Wetzor, 1953, 38–44, 59–85.

145. Cross and Sherbowitz-Wetzor, 1953, 62–4, 137–8; Meyendorff, 1981, 19–23.

146. Obolensky, 1971, *Commonwealth*, 151–3; G. P. Fedotov, 1946–66, *The Russian Religious Mind*, Cambridge, MA: Harvard University Press, 39–40.

147. Florovsky, 1937, *Ways of Russian Theology*, Paris; Meyendorff, 1981, 21–8; Meyendorff, 1975, *Byzantine Theology: Christ in Eastern Christian Thought*, 2nd ed., Crestwood, NY: St. Valdimir's Seminary Press; G. Pattison and D. O. Thompson, 1991, *Dostoevsky and the Christian Tradition*, Cambridge: Cambridge University Press; R. Coates, 1998, *Christianity in Bakhtin: God and the Exiled Author*, Cambridge: Cambridge University Press, 1–24.

148. M. Cherniavsky, 1969, *Studies in Russian Myth*, New York: Random House, 114–20; J. H. Billington, 1966, *The Icon and the Axe: An Interpretative History of Russian Culture*, New York: Knopf, 48–52, 93–4; G. Hosking, 1997, *Russia: People and Empire 1552–1917*, London: Harper Collins; N. V. Riasanovsky, 1993, *A History of Russia*, Oxford: Oxford University Press; Ram, *The Imperial Sublime*, Madison: University of

Wisconsin Press; C. D. Ely, 2002, *This Meager Nature: Landscape and Natural Identity in Imperial Russia*, DeKalb: Northern Illinois University Press.

149. deMarderiaga, 1982, "Autocracy and Sovereignty," *Canadian-American Slavic Studies* 16 (Fall-Winter): 369–87.

150. C. H. Whittaker, 1970, 37–50.

151. Walicki, 1979, *A History of Russian Thought from the Enlightenment to Marxism*, Stanford, CA: Stanford University Press, 2–8.

152. L. Livak, 2003, How it Was Done in Paris, Russian Émigré Literature and French Modernism, Madison; R. Hellebust, 2003, Flesh to Metal: Soviet Literature and the Alchemy of Revolution, Ithaca, NY: Cornell University Press; C. Kelley, 2001, Russian Literature: A Very Short Introduction, Oxford: Oxford University Press; P. M. Waszink, 2003, Don't Weep a Gold Chain: Observations on Primary and Secondary Systems in Russian Classical and Romantic Art and Literature, Munchen: Verlag Otto Sagner; C. Kelley, 2001, Refining Russia: Advice Literature, Political Culture, and Gender from Catherine to Yeltsin, Oxford: Oxford University Press; M. Sendich, 1999, English Counter Russian: Essays on Criticism of Literary Translation in America, New York: Peter Lang; M. D. Steinburg, 2002, Proletarian Imagination: Self, Modernity, and the Sacred in Russia, 1910–1925, Ithaca, NY: Cornell University Press.

153. Walicki, trans. H. Andrews-Rusiecka, 1979, A History of Russian Thought From the Enlightenment to Marxism, Stanford, CA: Stanford University Press, ix; C. H. Whittaker, 1998, "The Idea of Autocracy Among Eighteenth-Century Russian Historians," in Imperial Russia: New Histories for the Empire, eds. J. Burbank and D. L. Ransel, Bloomington: Indiana University Press, 32–59; J. Hartley, 1990, in Bartlett and Hartley, 1990, 167–202.

154. R. Wortman, 1998, "The Russian Imperial Family as Symbol," in Imperial Russia: New Histories for the Empire, Bloomington: Indiana University Press, 60–86; Wortman, 1995, Scenarios of Power, Myth and Ceremony in Russian Monarchy, Vol. 1, From Peter the Great to the Death of Nicholas I, Princeton, NJ: Princeton University Press; W. B. Lincoln, 1978 Nicholas I: Empire and Autocrat of All the Russia, Bloomington: Indiana University Press, 22–7.

155. Baehr, 1991, The Paradise Myth in Eighteenth Century Russia, Stanford: Stanford University Press, 14–40.

156. R. Wortman, 1995, Scenarios of Power, Myth and Ceremony in Russian Monarchy, Vol. 1, From Peter the Great to the Death of Nicholas I, Princeton, NJ: Princeton University Press, 169–70.

157. Wortman, 1995, p. 169; L. Colley, 1992,

Britons: Forging the Nation, 1707–1837, New Haven, CT: Yale University Press, 21–8; M. Ozouf, 1988, *Festivals and the French Revolution*, Cambridge, MA: Harvard University Press, 262–81.
158. Wortman, 1995, 171–92; R. McGrew, 1992, *Paul I of Russia*, Oxford: Oxford University Press, 209–228.
159. Wortman, 1995, 171–92, 200–1, 232–47.
160. Wortman, 1995, p. 381.
161. Rogger, 1960, *National Consciousness in Eighteenth Century Russia*, Cambridge, MA: Harvard University Press; I. Serman, 1990, "Russian National Consciousness and its Development in the Eighteenth Century," *Russia in the Age of the Enlightenment*, New York: St. Martin's Press, 40–56; M. Raeff, 1975, "The Well-Ordered Police State and the Development of Modernity in Seventeenth- and Eighteenth Century Europe," *American Historical Review* 80, 1230–45; D. C. Gillespie, 1992, *Iurii Trifonov: Unity Through Time*, Cambridge: Cambridge University Press; E. A. Dobrenko, 2001, *The Making of the State Writer: Social and Aesthetic Origins of Soviet Literary Culture*, Stanford, CA: Stanford University Press.
162. Dostoevsky, *Diary of a Writer*, in *Complete Works of Dostoevsky*, vol. 23, p. 47; A. B. Wachtel, 1994, p. 4.
163. J. Billington, 1970, 58.

Chapter 7

1. Cartledge, 1993, 11–13; B. M. W. Knox, 1990, *Essays Ancient and Modern*, Baltimore: Johns Hopkins University Press, 55.
2. *Iliad*, 2.804, 4.437–8; R. Janko, 1982, *Homer, Hesiod and the Hymns: Diachronic Development in Epic Diction*, Cambridge: Cambridge University Press, 180; Nagy, 1978, 7–8, 115–20.
3. Cartledge, 1993, 11–14.
4. B. Watson, 1962, *Records of the Grand Historian in China*, New York: Columbia University Press, 155–92; H. Bielenstein, 1980, *The Bureaucracy of Han Times*, Cambridge: Cambridge University Press, 48, 100–123; Di Cosmo, 2004, 93–126; S. N. Kramer, 1963, *Sumerians: Their History, Culture, and Character*, Chicago: University of Chicago Press, 282–6; A. L. Oppenheim, 1977, *Ancient Mesopotamia*, Chicago: University of Chicago Press, 261; S. Diamond, 1974, *In Search of Primitive: A Critique of Civilization*, New Brunswick, NJ:Transaction Books; 120–122, 207–212.
5. Cartledge, 1993, 11–3.
6. E. Hall, 1989, 5.
7. H. Limet, 1972, "L'etranger dans la societe sumerienne," in D. O. Edzard, ed., *Gesellschaftsklassen im alten Zweistromland und in den*

angrenzenden Gebienten; W. Bauer, 1980, *China und die Fremden*, Munich. The ancient Egyptians called foreign land a part of "chaos," but the term wasn't specific enough to specify people from non–Egyptian land. W. Helck, 1964, "Sie Agypter und die Fremden," *Speculum* 15:104–9.
8. E. Hall, 1989, 9–10.
9. I. Weiler, 1968, "The Greek and non–Greek World in the Archaic Period," *Greek, Roman, Byzantine Studies* 9: 21–9.
10. Quoted in Freeman, 2004, 166–7. S. Perlman, 1968, "Athenian Imperial Expansion in the Fourth Century," *Classical Philology* 63: 257–67; Perlman, 1976, "Panhellenism, the Polis and Imperialism," *Historia* 25: 1–30; Meiggs, 1972; M. I. Finley, 1978, "The Fifth-century Athenian Empire: A Balance-sheet," *Imperialism in the Ancient World*, eds. P. D. A. Garnsey and C. R. Whittaker, Cambridge: Cambridge University Press, 103–126.
11. H. Dorrie, 1972, "Die Wertung der Barbaren in Urteil der Griechen," in *Antik und Universalgeschichte*, R. Stiehl and G. Lehmann, eds. Munster, 146–75; H. Bengston, 1954, "Hellenen und Barbaren: Gedanken zum Problem des griechischen Nationalbewusstseins," in *Unser Geschichtsbild*, K. Rudinger, ed., Munich, 25–40; G. S. Kirk, 1985, *The Iliad: A Commentary* I, Cambridge: Cambridge University Press, 262; E. Hall, 1989, 9–10.
12. *Odyssey*, I 3. 272, I 4. 288–97, I 5. 415–81, I 5. 279–80, 6.10, 9.130–135; Snodgrass, 1971, 3–4; J. K. Davies, 1984, *The Trojan War: Its Historicity and Context*, eds. L. Foxhall and J. K. Davies, Bristol: Classical Press, 95–96; Burkert, 1982, 24; J. H. Finley, 1979, *The World of Odysseus*, Harmondsworth, 61; Vidal-Naquet, 1986, 21–6; E. Hall, 1989, 15–6.
13. G. Walser, 1984, *Hellas und Iran: Studien zu den griechisch-persischen Beziehungen vor Alexander*, Darmstadt: Wissenschaftliche Buchgesellschaft.
14. G. Nagy, 1979, *The Best of Achaeans: Concepts of the Hero in Archaic Greek Poetry*, Baltimore: Johns Hopkins University Press, 7–8, 115–7, 119–20; E. Hall, 1989, 17, 21.
15. Bowra, 1930, *Tradition and Design*, Oxford: Clarendon Press, 209–10, 241; F. Dornseiff, 1935, "Homerphilologie," *Hermes* 70: 241–4; M. H. A. L. H. van der Valk, 1966, "The Formulaic Character of Homeric Poetry and the Relation Between the *Iliad* and the *Odyssey*," *L'Antiquite Classique* 35: 5–70; M. Willcock, 1976, *Companion to the Iliad*, Chicago: University of Chicato Press, 80, 151; J. Pinsent, 1984, "Trojans in the Iliad," *Trojan War: Its Historicity and Context*, L. Foxhall and J. K. Davies, eds., Bristol, 137–62; Kirk, 1985, 261; S. Weil, 1986 *Simone Weil: An Anthology*, S. Miles, ed., London: 182–215.
16. Schwable, 1962, p. 23; H. Oliver, 1960, *Demodratia, the Gods, and the Free World*, Bal-

timore, 142–5; A. Momigliano, 1979, "Persian Empire and Greek Freedom," in *The Idea of Freedom: Essays in Honour of Isaiah Berlin*, A. Ryan, ed., Oxford: Oxford University Press, 139–51; E. Hall, 1989, 16.

17. E. Hall, 1989, 56–100.

18. Said, 1978, 56–7.

19. Plato, *Republic*, 4.427e 10–11; O. Kunsemuller, 1979, *Die Herkunft der platonischen Kardinaltugenden*, New York: Arno Press, 8–10, 35–45.

20. H. North, 1966, *Sophrosyne: Self-knowledge and Self-restraint in Greek Literature*, Ithaca, NY: Cornell University Press, 32–85.

21. Euripides, 1984, *It and Helen*, i, ii, iii, J. Diggle; G. Murray, 1913.

22. Bosworth, 1988, 278.

23. Pindar, *Pyth*, v. 93–4.

24. Pindar, *OL*, 1.113–5, 111.43–5.

25. Aristotle, *Pol*, 1284a10–1; 1332b16–23; NE, 1154a18–27.

26. Isocr. lx.72; Rhet. 1361a34–6.

27. Bosworth, 1988, 280.

28. Bosworth, 1988, 281.

29. Bosworth, 1988, 290.

30. D. C. Earl, 1961, *The Political Thought of Sallust*, Cambridge: Cambridge University Press, 420–46.

31. Brunt, 1990b, 161–2.

32. Brunt, 1971, 1990a, 1990b.

33. C. Edwards and G. Woolf, eds., 2003, *Rome the Cosmopolis*, Cambridge: Cambridge University Press, 23; M. Beard, 1998, "The Triumph of the Absurd: Roman State and Army," 21–43; W. V. Harris, 1992, 25–6; J. R. Patterson, 2000, *Political Life in the City of Rome*, London: Bristol Classical, 31–3; J. J. Pollitt, 1983, *The Art of Rome C. 753 B.C.–A.D. 337*, Cambridge: Cambridge Universit Press, 24–5, 42–8.

34. K. Hopkins, 1978, *Conquerors and Slaves: Sociological Studies in Roman History*, Cambridge: Cambridge University Press, i: 27; J. Scheid, 1993, "The Priest," in A. Giardina, ed., *The Romans*, Chicago: University of Chicago Press, 213–30; L. B. Warren, 1970, "Roman Triumphs and Etruscan Kings: The Changing Face of the Triumph," *Journal of Roman Studies* 60: 49–66; S. Weinstock, 1971, *Divus Julius*, Oxford: Clarendon Press, 66–8; R. Brilliant, 1999, "'Let the Trumpets Roar!' The Roman Triumph," *The Art of Ancient Spectacle*, New Heaven: Yale University Press, 221–9.

35. Livy, 7.6.3.

36. Brunt, 1990b, 170.

37. Cicero, *de offic.* 1.34–40 and 80; *de rep*, 2.31, 3.34–6; F. W. Walbank, 1965, "Political Morality and the Friends of Scipio," *Journal of Roman Studies* 55: 1–16.

38. Cicero, *de offic.* 1.20–4.

39. P. Brown, 1992, 7; J. Matthews, 1989, 252–6.

40. Smith, 2001, 61–3.

41. Smith, 2001, 49.

42. A. R. W. Green, 2003; Penchansky, 2005; Smith, 2001.

43. T. Husayn, al-Ayyam, Cairo, 1972; F. Malti-Douglas, 1988, *Blindness and Auto Biography: Al-Ayyam of Taha Husayn*, Princeton, NJ: Princeton University Press.

44. I *Sam.*, xxvi, 19; *Jer.*, ii, 11; *Ruth.*, I, 14.

45. *Deut.*, iv, 19; 1 *Sam.*, iv 7; xxx, 26.

46. Smith, 2001, 28–83, 213–243, 312–53.

47. D. T. Rice, 1971, *Islamic Painting: A Survey*, Edinburgh.

48. Rosenthal, 2000, 9.

49. R. Atwan, G. Dardess and P. Rosenthal, eds., 1988, *Divine Inspiration: The Life of Jesus in World Poetry*, Oxford; C. Eagan, ed., 1962, *Poems of Prudentius*, Washington, DC.

50. Rosenthal, 2000, p. 13.

51. Rosenthal, 2000, p. 14; Bennett, 1982; P. Dronke, 1970, *Poetic Individuality in the Middle Ages*, Oxford: Clarendon Press.

52. J. Kraye, 2002, "The Transformation of Platonic Love in the Italian Renaissance," *Platonism*, 76–85; J. Hankins, 1990, *Plato in Italian Renaissance*, 2 vols., Leiden; B. K. Lewalski, 1979, *Protestant Poetics and the Seventeenth-century Religious Lyric*, Princeton, NJ: Princeton University Press; K. Kavanaugh and O. Rodriguez, trans., 1991, *The Collected Works of Saint John of the Cross*, Washington, DC.; L. L. Marz, 1962, *The Poetry of Meditation*, New Haven; J. Summers, 1954, *George Herbert: His Religion and Art*, London.

53. K. Hopkins, 1983, *Death and Renewal Sociological Studies in Roman History*, II, Cambridge.

54. Noy, 2000, 17–8.

54. C. Edwards and G. Woolf, eds., 2003, *Rome the Cosmopolis*, Cambridge: Cambridge University Press, p. 1.

56. Ovid, *Fasti*, 2.684; C. Nicolet, 1991, *Space, Geography and Politics in the Early Roman Empire*, Ann Arbor, 98–114; M. Griffin, 1991, "Urbs Roma, plebs und princeps," in L. Alexander, ed., *Images of Empire*, Sheffield, 19–46. E. Guwer, 1995, "From Capitol to Cloace: The Anatomy of Rome," *Journal of Roman Studies* 85: 23–32; C. Edwards, 1996, *Textual Approaches to the City*, Cambridge: Cambridge University Press, 99–100.

Chapter 8

1. Dodds, 1951, *The Greeks and Irrational*, Berkeley: University of California Press, Chapter 2; Douglas, 1984, *Purity and Danger: An Analysis of Concepts of Pollution and Taboo*, London: Taylor and Francis, 11–3; R. Parker, 1983, *Miasma*, Oxford: Clarendon Press,

1–31.

2. Plato, *Soph*, 226d; Parker, 1983, 18.

3. Loyd-Jones, 1971, 74–6; Dodd, 1951, 36.

4. Homer, *Iliad*, 1. 449, 6.266–8; 16. 228–30; *Odyssey*, 1.146, 4.750–2; Moulinier, 1975, 26–7, 71–4; Parker, 1983, 20–5.

5. Parker, 1983, 3.

6. Homer, *Iliad*, 23.571, 6.209; Solon, fr.32, 3; Pind. Pyth. 4. 100; Nem. 3.16; Eur. Hel. 1000.

7. Ar. Eq. 304. Pax. 182–4, Ran. 465–8; Xen. Hell. 7.3.6; Dem. 8.68, 19.17, 278, 309, 21. 69, 98, 123, 143, 25.27, 35.26, 47.81; Parker, 1983, 4–7.

8. Thuc. 1.126–36, 3.104.1–2, 157, 4.97.2–99, 5.32.1; Parker, 1983, 1–3.

9. Childs, 2001, *Modernism and Eugenics*, Cambridge: Cambridge University Press, 1–2.

Chapter 9

1. Barton, 2001, *Roman Honor the Fire in the Bone*. Berkeley: University of California Press, 56–61.

2. Cicero, *De finibus*, 5.22.61; Barton, 2001, 11.

3. Melville, 1967, *Moby Dick*. New York: W. W. Norton; Layton, 2005, 17–24.

4. Rihll, 1999, *Greek Science*. New York: Oxford University Press, 89–90.

5. J. Evans, 1991, *Herodotus, Explorer of the Past: Three Essays*. Princeton, NJ: Princeton University Press, 168; Freeman, 2004, 167.

6. Cartledge, 1993, *The Greeks: A Portrait of Self and Others*. Oxford: Oxford University Press, 38–9; J. Boardman, 1999, 115–6; Cohen, 2006.

7. Raeck, 1981, Zum Barbarenbild in der Kunst Athens im 6. und 5. Jahrhundert. Bonn: R. Habelt, 152.

8. E. Hall, 1989, *Inventing the Barbarian*. Oxford: Oxford University Press, 80–81.

9. E. Hall, 1989, 80–81.

10. M. Willcock, 1976, *A Companion to the Iliad*. University of Chicago Press, 151–2, 205–7; G. S. Kirk, 1985, *The Iliad: A Commentary*, Cambridge: Cambridge Universit Press, 261–2; Hall, 1989, 19–20, 2002, 83.

11. Herodotus, 1.6.1, 1.203.1, 4.5, 17, 4.99, 108, 4.171–172, 4. 183–197, 5. 77. 4, 7.161.3, 8.73.1–2, quoted by Hall, 1997, *Ethnic Identity in Greek Antiquity*, Cambridge: Cambridge University Press, 34.

12. Homer, *Iliad*, 2.87–91; 2.459–469; 3.32; 7.115; 11.724; *Odyssey*, 10.526; W. Donlan, 1985, "The Social Groups of Dark Age Greece," *Classic Philology* 80: 295; E. Tonkin, M. McDonald, and M. Chapman, 1989, "Introduction," *History and Ethnicity*, eds. Tonkin, et al., London: Routledge, 12–3. Herodotus, 1.56.2–3; 1.145–148; 5.88; 6.106; 7.99.3; 7.206; 8.31–43; 8.73.2;

Hall, 1997, 39–46.

13. J. Hall, 1997, 47–8; C. M. Antonaccio, 2001, "Ethnicity and Colonization," in *Ancient Perceptions of Greek Ethnicity*, ed. I. Malkin, Cambridge, MA: Harvard University Press, 113–50.

14. J. J. Price, 2001, 127–189.

15. J. J. Price, 2001, 4, 22–28, 373.

16. Price, 2001, 39.

17. Price, 2001, 49

18. Price, 2001, 83.

19. Price, 2001, 88–90.

20. Aristotle, *Politics*, 1327b, 29–32; A. Bulloch, 1993, "Introduction," *Image and Ideologies Self-definition in the Hellenistic World*, Berkeley: University of California Press, 12.

21. P. R. Hardie, 1986, *Virgil's* Aeneid: *Cosmos and Imperium*, Oxford: Oxford University Press, 293–331; E. W. Leach, 1988, *The Rhetoric of Space*, Princeton, NJ: Princeton University Press, 27–72; E. Oliensis, 1998, *Horace and the Rhetoric of Authority*, Cambridge: Cambridge University Press, 1–5; R. C. M. Lyn, 1995, *Horace: Behind the Public Poetry*, New Haven, CT: Yale University Press, 75–89.

22. Conte, 1996, 27–8.

23. Conte, 1994b, 32–33; N. Horsfall, 1991–1992, "'Generic Composition' and Petronius' Satyricon," *Scripta Classica Israelica* II: 129–138.

24. Price, 2001, 90; 38; F. Bonner, 1977, *Education in Ancient Rome*, Berkeley: University of California Press, 213–4; Conte, 1994b, 47–51.

25. S. Bartsch, 1994, *Actors in the Audience: Theatricality and Doublespeak from Nero to Hadrian*, Cambridge, MA: Harvard University Press, 10–12; Conte, 1994b, 70–2.

26. E. Oliensis, 1998, *Horace and the Rhetoric of Authority*, Cambridge: Cambrdige University Press, 6–7; A. Barchiesi, 1993, "Insegnare ad Augusto: Orazio Epistolez 1 e Ovidio, Fristia," *MD* 31: 149–84; C. O. Brink, 1971, *Horace on Poetry*, 2: *The "Ars Poetica*," Cambridge: Cambridge University Press, 85–6; Frischer, 1991, 74–85; N. Rudd, 1989, *Horace: Epistles II and "Arts Poetica*," Cambridge: Cambridge University Press, 150.

27. Plato, *PHdr*, 267–73; R. Brinkmann, 1966, *Wirklichkeit und Illusion*, Stuttgart.

28. G. Williams, 1985, *Figures of Thought in Roman Poetry*, New Haven, CT: Yale University Press, 1–19, 21–3; R. G. M. Nisbet and M. Hubbard, 1970, *A Commentary on Horace: Odes Book I*, Oxford: Clarendon, 26–27; 156–8; 326–30; F. Ahl, 1985, *Metaformations: Soundplay and Wordplay in Ovid and Other Classical Poets*, Ithaca, NY: Cornell University Press, 201–235.

29. J. Fabian, 1983, *Time and the Other: How Anthropology Makes its Object*, New York: Columbia University Press, 2–6; M. L. Pratt, 1992, 15–6; D. Porter, 1991, *Haunted Journeys: Desire and Transgression in European Travel Writing*,

Princeton, NJ: Princeton University Press, 10–11; J. V. Gunn, 1982, *Autobiography: Toward a Poetics of Experience*, Philadelphia, PA: University of Pennsylvania Press, 59–60.

30. Bartram, 1988, 312–3.

31. J. Campbell, 1968, *The Hero with a Thousand Faces*, Princeton, NJ: Princeton University Press, 3–25; M. Campbell, 1988, 15–20, 209–10.

32. H. Weber, 1812, *The Tales of the East*, London, quoted in P. L. Caracciolo, "Introduction," *The Arabian Nights*, 1; Moussa-Mahmoud, 1988, "English Travellers and the Arabian Nights," *The Arabian Nights in English Literature*, New York: McMillam, 95–110.

33. Layton, 2005, 38–41.

34. Pushkin, quoted in Layton, 200, 97–99; R. Reid and J. Andrew, 2003–2004, Two Hundred Years of Pushkin, Amsterdam: Rodopi, 1–36.

35. Translation, Layton, 2005, 61–2.

36. Shishkov, *Ketevana*, p. 426, quoted in Layton, 2005, p. 203.

37. D. N. Lang, 1957, *The Last Year of the Georgian Monarch, 1658–1832*, New York: Columbia University Press, 52–53, 253–85; R. G. Suny, 1989, *The Making of the Georgian Nation*, Bloomington, IN: Indiana University Press, 20–30, 46–55, 83–4; Layton, 2005, 205–7.

38. Pushkin, "The Fountain of Bakhchisarai" *Works by Aleksandr Pushkin* at Project Gutenberg; J. Andrew, 1996, *Women in Russian Literature, 1780–1863*, Oxford: Clarendon Press, 54–60.

39. Layton, 2005, 205.

40. R. P. Geraci, 2001, *Window on the East National and Imperial Identity in Late Tsarist Russia*, Ithaca, NY: Cornell University Press, 1–3.

41. S. Zenkovsky, 1953, "A Century of Tatar Revival," *American Slavic and East European Review*, 12 (October): 303–19; P. W. Werth, 1996, "Subjects for Empire: Orthodox Mission and Imperial Governance in the Volga-Kama Region, 1825–1881," Ph.D. dissertation, University of Michigan; P. W. Werth, *At the Margins of Orthodoxy: Mission, Governance, and Confessional Politics in Russia's Volga-Kama Region, 1827–1905*, Ithaca, NY: Cornell University Press, 44–95, 177–199; L. Tillett, 1969, *The Great Friendship: Soviet Historians on the Non-Russian Nationalities*, Chapel Hill, University of North Carolina Press, 3–34; J. W. Slocum, 1993, "The Boundaries of National Identity: Religion, Language, and National Politics in Late Imperial Russia," Ph.D. dissertation, University of Chicago; D. B. Saunders, 1982, *Slavonic and East European Review* 60 (January): 44–62; V. A. Shnirelman, 1996, *Who Gets the Past? Competition for Ancestors Among Non-Russian Intellectuals in Russia*, Washington: Woodrow Wilson Center Press, 13–35; M. Kemper, A. von Kugelgen and

D. Yermakov, 1996, *Muslim Culture in Russia and Central Asia from the 18th to the Early 20th Centuries*, Berlin: Schwarz, 1–35; R. P. Geraci, 2001, *Of Religion and Empire: Missions, Conversion, and Tolerance in Tsarist Russia*, Ithaca, NY: Cornell University Press, 1–37; S. Becker, 1986, "The Muslim East in Nineteenth-century Russian Popular Historiography," *Central Asian Survey* 5: 25–27; Becker, 1991, "Russia Between East and West: The Intelligensia, Russian National Identity and the Asian Borderlands," *Central Asian Survey* 10: 47–64.

42. Geraci, 2001, 15–194.

43. B. G.Smith, 2000, 24–28, 34–54, 93–110; Harland-Jacobs, 2007, 130–281.

44. L. Greenfield, 1992, *Nationalism: Five Roads to Modernity*, Cambridge, MA: Harvard University Press, 50–76; G. Hammond, 1996, "How They Brought the Good News to Halifax: Tyndale's Bible and the Emergence of the English Nation State," *Reformation* 1: 11–28; K. Kumar, 2003, *The Making of English National Identity*, Cambridge: Cambridge University Press, 103–5; J. C. D. Clark, 2000, "Protestantism, Nationalism, and National Identity, 1600–1832," *The Historical Journal* 43.1: 272–76.

45. J. W. McKenna, 1982, "How God Became an Englishman," in Guth and McKenna, eds., *Tudor Rule and Revolution*, Cambridge: Cambridge University Press, 25–43; Hastings, 1977, *The Construction of Nationhood: Ethnicity, Religion, and Nationalism*, Cambridge: Cambridge University Press, 59–60; Collinson, 1977, "Biblical Rhetoric: The English Nation and National Sentiment in the Prophetic Mode," E. McEachern and D. Shuger, *Religion and Culture in Renaissance England*, Cambridge: Cambridge University Press, 15–45; J. C. D. Clark, 2000, "Protestantism, Nationalism and National Identity, 1660–1832," *The Historical Journal*, 43.1: 249–76.

46. Coleridge, 1912, "Eolian Harp," *The Complete Poetical Works of Samuel Taylor Coleridge*, ed. E. H. Coleridge, 2 vols., Oxford: Clarendon Press, I: 102; J. Mileur, 1982, *Vision and Revision: Coleridge's Art of Immanence*, Berkeley: University of California Press, 37; Paley, 1996, 37–61; G. Whalley, 1964, "'Late Autumn's Amaranth': Coleridge's Late Poems," *Transactions of the Royal Society of Canada*, 4th ser.

47. Paley, 1996, 39; M. Schulz, 1963, *The Poetic of Coleridge*; J. L. Mahoney, 1990, "Coleridge, Keats and the Imagination: Romanticism and Adam's Dream," *Essays in Honor of Walter Jackson Bate*, ed. R. Barth, S. J. J. and J. L. Mahoney, Columbia: University of Missouri Press, 121–2.

48. J. Mileur, 1982, *Vision and Revision: Coleridge's Art of Immanence*. Berkeley: University of California Press, 125–6.

49. Coleridge, 1912, "Dejection: An Ode,"

Coleridge, *The Complete Poetical Works Samuel Taylor Coleridge*, Oxford: Clarendeon Press, 2: 821; E. Kessler, 1979, *Coleridge's Metaphors of Being*, Princeton, NJ: Princeton University Press, 105; Paley, 1996, 19–20.

50. Coleridge, 1912, "Ne Plus Ultra," 2: 670–3.

51. R. Parker, 1975, *Coleridge's Meditative Art*, Ithaca, NY: Cornell University Press, 242; J. Boulger, 1961, *Coleridge as Religious Thinker*, New Haven, CT: Yale University Press, 110; E. Kessler, 1979, 101–2; F. Burwick, 1985, "Coleridge 'Limbo' and 'Ne Plus Ultra': The Multeity of Intertexuality," *Romanticism Past and Present* 9: 73–95; S. Prickett, 1970, *Coleridge and Wordsworth: The Poetry of Growth*, Cambridge: Cambridge University Press, 202–3; E. L. Griggs, 1956–72, *Collected Letters of Samuel Taylor Coleridge*, 6 vols., Oxford: Clarendon Press, 2: 810; Ryan, 1997, 129–30, 73. J. J. McGann, 1986, *Byron, the Complete Poetic Works*, vol. 5, "Don Juan," Oxford; J. McGann, 1968, *Fiery Dust: Byron's Poetic Development*, Chicago: University of Chicago Press, 36–40; E. Bostetter, 1963, *The Romantic Ventriloquists: Wordsworth, Coleridge, Keats, Shelley, Byron*, Seattle: University of Washington Press, 282–3.

52. Ryan, 1997, 138.

53. S. E. Fish, 1967, *Surprised by Sin: The Reader in Paradise Lost*, New York: St. Martin's Press, 43–44.

54. S. Samuels, 2000, "Miscegenated America: The Civil War," in Reynolds and Hutner, 2000, *National Imaginaries, American Identities*, Princeton, NJ: Princeton University Press, 141–3.

55. H. K. Bhabha, 1994, *The Location of Culture*, London; G. Brown, 1990, *Domestic Individualism: Imagining Self in Nineteenth Century America*, Berkeley; J. Fliegelman, 1993, *Independence: Jefferson's National Language and the Culture of Performance*, Stanford; N. Hudson, 1996, "From 'Nation' to 'Race': The Origin of Racial Classification in Eighteenth Century Thought," *Eighteenth Century Studies* 29: 247–64; M. Jehlen, 1990, "The Ties That Bind: Race and Sex in Pudd'nhead Wilson," *American Literary History* 2: 39–55; R. Wiegman, 1995, *American Anatomies: Theorizing Race and Gender*, Durham; E. Lott, 2000, "The Whiteness of Film Noir," *National Imaginaries*, Princeton, NJ: Princeton University Press, 159–181; W. Boelhower, 1984, *Through a Glass Darkly: Ethnic Semiosis in American Literature*, Oxford: Oxford University Press, 9–40; T. Gripps, 1997, *Slow Fade to Black: The Negro in American Film*, 1900–1942, New York: Oxford University Press, 90–149.

Chapter 10

1. Hutchinson, 1988, *Hellenistic Poetry*, Oxford: Oxford University Press, 1–2.

2. Paige, 2001, *Being Interior: Autobiography and the Contradictions of Modernity in Seventeenth-century France*, Philadelphia: University of Pennsylvania Press, 180–1; M. Mascush, 1998, *Origins of Individual Self-autobiography and Self-identity in England, 1591–1791*, Stanford, Stanford University Press, 1–24; J. Olney, 1980, *Autobiography: Essays Theoretical and Critical*, Princeton, NJ: Princeton University Press, 3–25.

3. Page and Gow, 1965, *The Greek Anthology: Hellenistic Epigrams*, Cambridge: Cambridge University press, i: viii–xxvii; Page and Gow, 1981, *The Greek Anthology, Further Greek Epigrams: Epigrams before A.D. 50 from the Greek Anthology and other Sources*, Cambridge: Cambridge University press, 3–16; S. L. Taran, 1979, *The Art of Variation in the Hellenistic Epigram*, Leiden: Brill, 1–6, 162–167; Bulloch, 1985, "Hellenistic Poetry," *Cambridge History of Classical Literature*, Cambridge University Press, i: 616–8; K. J. Gutzwiller, 1998, *Poetic Garlands: Hellenistic Epigrams in Context*, Berkeley: University of California Press, 3–6, 15–46.

4. K. J. Gutzwiller, 1998, 118–20; R. Meiggs, 1988, *A Selection of Greek Historical Inscriptions to the End of the Fifth Century B.C.*, Oxford: Clarendon Press, 288–9; Page and Gow, 1965, 525–8; M. L. West, 1974, *Studies in Greek Elegy and Iambus*, Berlin: de Gruyter, 10–3, 40–59; Bowra, 2000, *Greek Lyric Poetry*. Oxford: Clarendon Press, 373–97; M. van der Valk, 1974, "On the Composition of the Attic Skolia," *Hermes* 102: 1–20; E. L. Bowie, 1986, "Early Greek Elegy, Symposium and Public Festival," *Journal of Hellenic Studies* 106: 13–35; G. Nagy, 1985, "Theognis and Megara: A Poet's Vision of his City," *Theognis of Megara: Poetry and the Polis*, Baltimore, Johns Hopkins University Press, 48–50.

5. Gow and Page, 1965, ii: 114–5, 148; A. Cameron, 1990, "Two Mistresses of Ptolemy Philadelphus," *Greek, Roman, and Byzantine Studies* 31: 291–4; Cameron, 1981 "Asclepiades' Girl Friends," *Reflections of Women in Antiquity*, New York: Gordon and Breach Science Publishers, 295; G. Giangrande, 1968, "Sympotic Literature and Epigram," *L'epigramme grecque, Entretiens sur l'antiquite classique*, 14 (Geneva): 119–72, 122–25; L. Defreyne, 1993, "Erotes and Eros in the Epigrams of Asclepiades," *Aaevum Antiquum* 6: 199–236.

6. Aristotle, *Ethics*, 1099a 25–8; West, 1974, 45, 58–9; M. Gronewald, 1975, "Theognis 255 and Pap. Oxy. 2380," *Zeitschrift für Papyrologie und Epigraphik* 19: 178–9.

7. Gutzwiller, 1998, 130.

8. Gutzwiller, 1998, 135.

9. Hutchinson, 1988, 28.

10. Goldhill, 1991, *The Poet's Voice: Essays on Poetics and Greek Literature*. Cambridge: Cam-

bridge University Press, 228–9; A. Gow, 1950, *Theocritus*, Cambridge, Cambridge University Press, 127–35; C. Segal, 1981, *Poetry and Myth in Ancient Pastoral: Essays on Theocritus and Virgil*, Princeton, NJ: Princeton University Press, 119–29; F. Williams, 1971, "A Theophany in Theocritus," *Classical Quarterly* 21: 137–45; E. Brown, 1981, "The Lycidas of Theocritus, Idyll 7," *Harvard Studies in Classical Philology* 86: 59–100.

11. Halperin, 1983, *Before Pastoral: Theocritus and the Ancient Tradition of Bucolic Poetry*. New Haven, CT: Yale University Press, 227–8; J. Van Sickle, 1976, "Theocritus and the Development of the Conception of Bucolic Genre," *Ramus* 5: 18–44.

12. Goldhill, 1991, 224.

13. Theocritus, Idyll 7; Halperin, 1983, 224–7; Hatzikosta, 1982, *A Stylistic Commentary on Theocritus' Idyll VII*, Amsterdam: A. M. Hakkert, 35–6; N. Krevans, 1983, "Geography and Literary Tradition in Theocritus," *Transactions and Proceedings of the American Philological Association*, 113: 201–220; K. Dover, 1971, *Theocritus: Selected Poems*, London: Macmillan, 150–151; G. Arnott, 1979, "The Mound of Brasilas and Theocritus' Seventh Idyll," *Quaderni Urbinati di Cultura Classica*, 32: 99–105; Goldhill, 1991, 226.

14. E. Segal, 1981, 163.

15. Halperin, 1983, 245; Segal, 1981, 125; Goldhill, 1991, 229–30.

16. Goldhill, 1986, "Framing and Polyphony: Readings in Hellenistic Poetry," *Proceedings of the Cambridge Philological Society* 32: 25–52; Segal, 1981, 135–48.

17. Goldhill, 1986, 135–48; Goldhill, 1991, 223–283.

18. S. Goldhill, 1991, 223.

19. Wiles, 1991, p. 129.

20. Virgil, *Georgics*, 2: 385; Wiles, 1991, *The Masks of Menander: Sign and Meaning in Greek and Roman Performance*, Cambridge: Cambridge University Press.

21. A. C. Gratwick, 1982, in *Cambridge History of Classical Literature*, vol. 2, *Latin Literature*, ed. E. J. Kenney, Cambridge, Cambridge University Press, 83–104; Dupont, 1985, *L'Acteur roi: ou le theátre dans la Rome antique*, Paris: Les Belles Lettres, 1985. 147–55; Segal, 1987, *Roman Laughter*, New York: Oxford University Press, 31–4.

22. Polybius, 6: 53, Ovid, *Fasti*, I: 591; Juvenal, 8: 19–21.

23. Wiles, 133–7; J. Wright, 1974, 104–5.

24. Segal, 1981, 141–8; Wiles, 1989, "Marriage and Prostitution in Classical New Comedy," *Themes in Drama: Women and Theater*, ed. J. Redmond, Cambridge, Cambridge University Press, 31–48.

25. Chiarini and Tessari, 1983, *Teatro del corpo, teatro della parola*, Paris, 109–14.

26. Wiles, 1991, 141–2.

27. Cachia, 2002, *Arabic Literature: An Overview*. London: RoutledgeCurzon, 31.

28. Dupont, 1985, 252; R. Barthes, 1983, "Writing Degree Zero," *Selected Writings*, London: Fontana/Collins, 54–8; Wiles, 1991, 211.

29. Wiles, 1991, 209.

30. E. Decroux, 1985, *Words on Mime*, trans. M. Piper, Claremont, CA: Pomona College Theatre Dept., 33–6.

31. Aristotle, *Rhetoric*, III. i.4.1403b; Wiles, 1991, 210.

32. D. Shaw, 1999, *Origins of the Monologue: The Hidden God*, Toronto, University of Toronto, 190–1.

33. Van Caenegem, 1973, *The Birth of the English Common Law*, Cambridge: Cambridge University Press, 9; P. Wormald, 1999, *The Making of English Law*, Oxford, Blackwell, i: 104–6; H. R. Loyn, 1984, *The Governance of Anglo-Saxon England, 500–1087*, Stanford: Stanford University Press, 107–22; R. Colls, 2002, *Identity of England*, Oxford: Oxford University Press, 13–33.

34. P. Keen, 1999, *The Crisis of Literature in the 1790s: Print Culture and the Public Sphere*, Cambridge, Cambridge University Press, 206–35; C. A. Bayly, 1989, *Imperial Meridian: The British Empire and the World, 1780–1830*, London: Longman, 1–15; Leask, 1992, *British Romantic Writers and the East: Anxieties of Empire*, Cambridge: Cambridge University Press, 12–5.

35. Gray, 1975, *A Selection of Religious Lyrics*. Oxford: Oxford University Press, 203.

36. Gray, 1975, 210; R. Woolf, 1968, *The English Religious Lyric in the Middle Ages*, Oxford: Oxford University Press, 159–79; P. Dronke, 1968, *The Medieval Lyric*, London: Hutchinson, 59–63, 81–2; H. E. Allen, ed., 1931, *English Writings of Richard Rolle*, Oxford: Oxford University Press. 43–7, 107; V. Gillespie, 1982, "Mystics Foot: Rolle and Affectivity," *The Medieval Mystical Tradition in England* II, Exeter: University of Exeter Press, 99–230.

37. Windeatt, 1994, *English Mystics of the Middle Ages*. Cambridge: Cambridge University Press, 1–5; Roger Dahood, 1984, "Ancrene Wisse, the Katherine Group, and the Wohunge Group" *Middle English Prose: A Critical Guide to Major Authors and Genres*, New Brunswick, NJ: Rutgers University Press, 3–26; Szarmach, 1984, *An Introduction to the Medieval Mystics of Europe*, Albany: State University of New York Press; Riehle, 1981, *The Middle English Mystics*, London: Routledge and Kegan Paul; M. Glasscoe, 1980–2, *The Medieval mystical tradition in England*, Exeter: University of Exeter Press; M.Glasscoe, 1993 *English Medieval Mystics: Games of Faith*, London: Longman; A. I. Boyle,

1964, "A Text Attributed to Ruusbrec Circulating in England" *Dr. L. Reypens Album*, Antwerp: Ruusbroec-Genootschap, 153–71; M. G. Sargent, 1983, "Ruusbroec in England: The Chastising of God's Children and Related Works," *Historia et Spiritualititas Cartusienses: Colloquii Quarti Internationalis Acta*, Destelbergen: J. De Grauwe, 303–12.

38. D. Gray, 1997, "Medieval English Mystical Lyrics," in *Mysticism and Spirituality in Medieval England*, Rochester, NY: D. S. Brewer, 203–18; P. S. Diehl, 1985, *The Medieval European Religious Lyric*, Berkeley: University of California Press, 69–70; W. Hilton, 1991, *The Scale of Perfection*, New York: Paulist Press, 24–7, 44; M. G. Sargent, 1992, *Nicholas Love's "Mirror of the Blessed Life of Jesus Christ*," New York: Garland, 10–11; Windeatt, 1994, 7–8.

39. Kerby-Fulton, 1990, *Reformist Apocalypticism and Piers Plowman*. Cambridge: Cambridge University Press; D. Aers, 1980, *Chaucer, Langland and the Creative Imagination*, London: Routledge & Kegan Paul, 1–37; Lerner, 1983, *The Power of Prophecy: The Cedar of Lebanon Vision from the Mongol Onslaught to the Dawn of the Enlightenment*. Berkeley: University of California Press, 25–36; Leyser, 1984; Patrides and Wittreich, 1984, *The Apocalypse in English Renaissance Thought and Literature*. Ithaca, NY: Cornell University Press, 2–73; Tambling, 2010, *Allegory*, New York: Routledge, 36–61; Pendergast, 2006, *Religion, Allegory, and Literacy in Early Modern England, 1560–1640: The Control of the Word*, Burlington, VT: Ashgate, 1–36.

40. W. Blake, 1972, "The Marriage of Heaven and Hell," *Blake: Complete Writings*, ed. G. Keynes, Oxford: Oxford University Press, 153.

41. K. Kerby-Fulton, 1990, 201–3.

42. S. Rushdie, 1988, *Satanic Verses*, New York: Viking, 343; G. Viswanathan, 1989, *Masks of Conquest: Literary Study and British Rule in India*, New York: Columbia University Press, 45–117; H. Trivadi, 1993, *Colonial Transactions: English Literature and India*, Manchester: Manchester University Press, 82–175.

43. V. Woolf, 1992, *Orlando*, Oxford: Oxford University Press, 294–5.

44. English images and ideas about the East have only been interpreted in terms of international politics, which I believe is essentially a sidebar. Said, 1985, *Orientalism*, London: Homi Bhabha, 1985, "Signs Taken for Wonders," in *Europe and its Others*, Colchester: Exeter University Press, i: 89–106; Leask, 1992, 68–169.

45. Hazlitt, 1967, "On the Ignorance of the Learned," *The Complete Works of William Hazlitt*, ed. P. P. Howe, 21 vols., New York: AMS, viii:73.

46. Leask, 1992, 4–5.

47. D. Pick, 1989, *Faces of Degeneration: A European Disorder c. 1848–c. 1918*, Cambridge;

Barrell, 1991.

48. S. Stewart, 1986, *On Longing: Narratives of the Miniature, the Gigantic, the Souvenir, the Collection*, Baltimore: Johns Hopkins University Press, 150–2; N. Leask, 1989, "'Wandering through Eblis," *Absorption and Containment in Romantic Exoticism*, Cambridge, Cambridge University Press, 165–188.

49. H. Guest, 1992, "Curiously Marked: Tattooing, Masculinity, and Nationality in 18th Century British Perceptions of the South Pacific," *Painting and the Politics of Culture: New Essays on British Art 1700–1850*, Oxford: Oxford University Press, 102; Leask, 1992, 170.

50. Makdisi, 1998, *Romantic Imperialism*, Cambridge: Cambridge University Press, 13.

51. D. Eastwood, 1991, "Patriotism Personified: Robert Southey's 'Life of Nelson' Reconsidered," *The Mariner's Mirror* 77: 143–49; Tim Fulford, 1998, "Romanticism and Colonialism: Races, Places, Peoples," Fulford and Kitson, 1998, Cambridge: Cambridge University Press, 37.

52. Fulford and Kitson, 1998, 37.

53. R. Southey, 1832, *Essays Moral and Political*, London: John Murry, ii: 280; Fulford and Kitson, 1998, 38.

54. D. V. Erdman, ed., 1978, *Essays on His Times: Collected Works of Samuel Taylor Coleridge*, 3 vols., London: Routledge and K. Paul, ii, 384–409.

55. Sullivan, 1993, *Narratives of Empire: The Fictions of Rudyard Kipling*, Cambridge: Cambridge University Press, 25.

56. Sullivan, 1993, 1–2, 9–13.

57. Sullivan, 1993, 13.

58. Kipling, 1987, *Life's Handicap*, ed. A. O. J. Cockshut, Oxford: Oxford University Press, 46–150.

59. Galperin, 1993, *The Return of the Visible in British Romanticism*. Baltimore: Johns Hopkins University Press, 19–35.

60. J. Keble, 1912, *Lectures on Poetry, 1832–1841*, trans. E. K. Francis, 2 vols., Oxford: Clarendon Press, 8–26; Ryan, 1997, *The Romantic Reformation, Religious Politics in English Literature, 1789–1824*, Cambridge: Cambridge University Press, 80.

61. W. Wordsworth, 1967, *The Letters of William and Dorothy Wordsworth: The Early Years, 1787–1805*, Oxford: Clarendon Press, 76.

62. Wordsworth, 1979, *The Prelude: 1799, 1805, 1850*, eds. J. Wordsworth, M. H. Abrahams, and S. Gill, New York: Norton, 10, 278–280.

63. V. S. Naipaul, 2002, *The Writer and the World*, New York: A. A. Knopf, 512–3.

64. R. Y. Clarke, 2001, *Stranger Gods: Salman Rushdie's Other Worlds*, Montreal: McGill-Queen's University Press, 11.

65. Walicki, 1979, 71–5.

66. Layton, 2005, 133–155.
67. Layton, 2005, 230.
68. Walicki, 1979, 77–8, 137–8.
69. Walicki, 1979, 143–4.
70. Ghada al-Samman, in Asfour, 1988, *When the Words Burn: An Anthology of Modern Arabic Poetry, 1945–1987*, Dunvegan, Ontario: Cormorant Books, 133–4.
71. Khalil Hawi, in Asfour, 1988, 153–4.
72. Badr Shakir al-Sayyab, in Asfour, 1988, 140–2.
73. Knysh, 2000, *Islamic Mysticism: A Short History*, Leiden: Brill, 1–2.
74. A. Voobus, 1960, *Syrian and Arabic Documents Regarding Legislation Relevant to Syrian Asceticism*, Stockholm, Etse, 20, 58–61, 101–3; Van Ess, 1992, *Theologie und Gesellschaft im 2 und 3 Jahrhundert Hidschra*, Berlin: de Gruyter, ii: 88–9, 94–5; Knysh, 2000, 6–7.
75. Smith, 1995, 145.
76. G. Bowering, 1980, *The Mystical Vision of Existence in Classical Islam*, Berlin: de Gruyter, 145–65.
77. Knysh, 2000, 9–10.
78. G. J. H. van Gelder, 1990, "Rabi'a's Poem on the Two Kinds of Love: A Mystification?" in *Verse and the Fair Sex*, a collection of papers presented at the 15th Congress of the UEAI; Knysh, 2000, 30–31.
79. Knysh, 2000, 36–7.
80. Van Ess, 1992, *Theologies*, vol. 4, p. 197; Knysh, 2000, 44.
81. Arberry, 1990, *Sufism*, New York: Unwin Paperbacks, 54–55; Arberry, 1957, *Revelation Reason in Islam*, London: Allen & Unwin, 100–101; Ernst, 1985, *Words of Ecstasy in Sufism*, Albany: State University of New York Press, 44–45.
82. Hodgson, 1974, i: 405; L. Massignon, 1997, *Essay on the Origins of the Technical Language of Islamic Mysticism*, Notre Dame: University of Notre Dame Press, 185–90.
83. Baldick, 1989, 53.
84. Knysh, 2000, 116–149; Bowering, 1980, 21–35; Arberry, 1990, 65–7.
85. Knysh, 2000, 140–8; Moosa, 2005, *Ghazali and the Poetics of Imagination*, Chapel Hill: University of North Carolina Press, 1–32, 169–180.
86. Banani, 1994, *Poetry and Mysticism in Islam: The Heritage of Rumi*, Cambridge: Cambridge University Press, 12–3.
87. Russian influenced by German idealism, see I. Berlin, et al., 1978, 82–113.
88. Herzen, 1847–1848, "My Past and Thought," "From the Other Shore," vi. 123–6, and "Letters from France and Italy," tenth letters: v. 175–6; E.Acton, 1979, *Alexander Herzen and the Role of the Intellectual Revolutionary*, 1–24; Berlin, 1978, 88–89.
89. Herzen, 1956, *From the Other Shore, and the Russian People and Socialism, an Open Letter to Jules Michelet*, New York: G. Braziller, 31–5.
90. Berlin, 1978, 238–60.
91. Berlin, 1978, 77.
92. Burke, 1998, *Desire Against the Law: The Juxtaposition of Contraries in Early Medieval Spanish Literature*, Stanford: Stanford University Press, 1–26, 231–246.
93. W. C. Booth, 1984, "Introduction," Bakhtin, *Problems of Dostoevsky's Poetics*, Minneapolis: University of Minnesota Press, 23.
94. Berlin, 1978, 70–2.
95. K. Wallace, 1954, *A History of Speech Education in America*. New York: Appleton-Century-Crofts, 80–115; Wolfe, 1988, *The Book Culture of a Colonial American City: Philadelphia Books, Bookmen, and Booksellers*, New York: Oxford University Press, 1–77; W. L. Hedges, 1987, "Telling Off the King: Jefferson's Summary View as American Fantasy," *Early American Literature* 22 (2): 166–75; Karamer, 1992; H. L. Mencken, 2000, *The American Language*, New York: Alfred A. Knopf, 3–89; E. J. Monaghan, 1983, *A Common Heritage: Noah Webster's Blue-Back Speller*, Hamden: Hamden, CO: Archon Books, 11–38; M. Warner, 1990, *The Letters of the Republic: Republication and the Public Sphere in Eighteenth Century America*. Cambridge, MA: Harvard University Press, 1–31; Ziff, 1997, *Writing in the New Nation: Prose, Print, and Politics in the Early United States*, New Haven, CT: Yale University Press, 7–32.
96. E. Foner, 1970, *Free Soil, Free Labor, Free Men: The Ideology of the Republican Party Before the Civil War*, New York: Oxford University Press, 40–72, 261–300; Hatch, 1989, *The Democratization of American Christianity*, New Haven, CT: Yale University Press, 17–48; Keller, 2007, 7–66; Appleby, 2000, *Inheriting the Revolution: The First Generation of Americans*, Cambridge, MA: Harvard University Press, 239–41.
97. Wigger, 1998, *Taking Heaven by Storm: Methodism and the Rise of Popular Christianity in America*, Oxford: Oxford University Press, 3–20, 104–124; Andrews, 2000, The Methodists and Revolutionary America, 1760–1800: The Shaping of an Evangelical Culture. Princeton, NJ: Princeton University Press, 3–10.
98. Fliegelman, 1993, *Declaring Independence: Jefferson, Natural Language and the Culture of Performance*, Stanford: Stanford University Press, 3–4.

Bibliography

Abbott, N. 1972. *Studies in Arabic Literary Papyri: III. Language and Literature.* Chicago: University of Chicago Press.

Ahl, F. 1984. "The Art of Safe Criticism in Greece and Rome." *American Journal of Philology* 105: 174–208.

Akurgal, E. 1968. *The Birth of Greek Art: The Mediterranean and the Near East.* London: Methuen.

Albright, W. F. 1925. "The Evolution of the West-Semitic Divinity 'An-'Anat-'Atta.'" *American Journal of Semitic Languages and Literatures* 41: 73–101.

_____. 1968. *Yahweh and the Gods of Canaan.* New York: Doubleday.

Alcock, S. E. 1993. *Graecia Capta: The Landscapes of Roman Greece.* Cambridge: Cambridge University Press.

_____. 1997. *The Early Roman Empire in the East.* Oxford: Oxbow.

Alden, M. J. 2000. *Homer Beside Himself: Paranarratives in the* Iliad. Oxford: Oxford University Press.

Alexander, L., ed. 1991. *Images of Empire.* Sheffield, UK: Sheffield Academic Press.

Alexander, P. S. 1991. "The Family of Caesar and the Family of God: The Image of the Emperor in the Heikhalot Literature." *Images of Empire,* 276–297. L. Alexander, ed. Sheffield, UK: Sheffield Academic Press.

Allen, R. M. A. 2005. *The Arabic Literary Heritage: The Development of its Genres and Criticism.* Cambridge: Cambridge University Press.

_____, and D. S. Richards, eds. 2006. *Arabic Literature in the Post-classical Period.* Cambridge: Cambridge University Press.

Alster, B. 1975. *Studies in Sumerian Proverbs.* Copenhagen: Akademisk Forlag.

Amory, P. 1997. *People and Identity in Ostrogothic Italy, 489–554.* Cambridge: Cambridge University Press.

Anderson, A. M. 1994. *Music and Musicians in Ancient Greece.* Ithaca, NY: Cornell University Press.

Anderson, B. 1983. *Imagined Communities: Reflections on the Origin and Spread of Nationalism.* New York: Verso.

Anderson, J. G. C. 1913. "Festivals of Mên Askaênos in the Roman Colonia at Antioch of Pisidia." *Journal of Roman Studies* 3: 267–300.

Ando, C. 1993. "Review of H. W. Bird, *Eutropius.*" *Bryn Mawr Classical Review* 4: 420–422.

_____. 1996. "Pagan Apologetics and Christian Intolerance in the Ages of Themistius and Augustine." *Journal of Early Christian Studies* 4: 171–207.

_____. 1997. "Tacitus, *Annales* VI: Beginning and End." *American Journal of Philology* 118: 285–303.

_____. 2000. *Imperial Ideology and Provincial Loyalty in the Roman Empire.* Berkeley: University of California Press.

_____. 2008. *The Matter of the Gods: Religion and the Roman Empire.* Berkeley: University of California Press.

Andrews, D. E. 2000. *The Methodists and Revolutionary America, 1760–1800: The Shaping of an Evangelical Culture.* Princeton, NJ: Princeton University Press.

Appleby, J. 2000. *Inheriting the Revolution. The First Generation of Americans.* Cambridge, MA: Harvard University Press.

Arberry, A. J. 1957. *The Seven Odes: The First Chapter in Arabic Literature.* New York: Macmillan.

Aristotle, 1976. *Aristotle's Metaphysics: Books [mu] and [nu].* J. Annas, trans. Oxford: Clarendon Press.

_____. 1999. *Metaphysics. Book [beta] and Book [kappa] 1–2.* A. Madigan, trans. Oxford: Clarendon Press.

Armour, R. A. 1986. *Gods and Myths of Ancient Egypt.* Cairo: American University in Cairo Press.

Arnaoutoglou, L. 1998. *Ancient Greek Laws: A Sourcebook.* London: Routledge.

Arnaud-Lindet, M.-P. *L. Ampelius: Aide-mémoire (Liber memorialis).* Paris: Les Belles Lettres.

Arnott, P. D. 1989. *Public Performance in the Greek Theatre.* London: Routledge.

Arnott, W. G. 1968. *Menander, Plautus, Terence.* Oxford: Oxford University Press.

Asfour, J. M. 1988. *When the Words Burn: An Anthology of Modern Arabic Poetry, 1945–1987.* Dunvegan, Ontario: Cormorant Books.

Astour, M. C. 1967. *Hellenosemitica: An Ethnic and Cultural Study in West Semitic Impact on Mycenaean Greece.* Leiden: Brill.

Aubineau, M. 1983. *Un traité inédit de christologie de Sévérien de Gabala* In Centurionem et Contra Manichaeos et Apollinaristas. Geneva: P. Cramer.

Augustine. On the Predestination of the Saints, 5. *Patrologia Latina,* 44: 962–63.

Aune, D. E. 1983. "The Influence of Roman Imperial Court Ceremonial on the Apocalypse of John." *Biblical Research* 28: 5–26.

Austin, N. J. E. 1972. "A Usurper's Claim to Legitimacy." *Rivista Storica dell' Antichità* 2: 77–83.

Auty, R. 1977. "The Russian Language." *An Introduction to Russian Language and Literature,* 35–37. R. Auty and D. Obolensky, eds. Cambridge: Cambridge University Press.

Avenarius, G. 1956. *Lukians Schrift zur Geschichtsschreibung.* Meisenheim am Glan: Anton Hain.

Avery, W. T. 1940. "The *Adoratio Purpurae* and the Importance of the Imperial Purple in the Fourth Century of the Christian Era." *Memoirs of the American Academy in Rome* 17: 66–80.

Axtell, H. L. 1907. *The Deification of Abstract Ideas in Roman Literature and Inscriptions.* Chicago: University of Chicago Press.

Azami, M. M. 1967. *Studies in Early Hadith Literature.* Riyad: Riyad University Press.

_____. 1986. *On Schacht's Origins.* New York: Wiley.

Badian, E. 1989. "The *Scribae* of the Roman Republic." *Klio* 71: 582–603.

_____. 1993. *From Plataea to Potiaea.* Baltimore: Johns Hopkins University Press.

Bagnall, R. 1991. "The Beginnings of the Roman Census in Egypt." *Greek, Roman, and Byzantine Studies* 32: 255–265.

_____. 1992. "Landholding in Late Roman Egypt: The Distribution of Wealth. " *Journal of Roman Studies* 82: 128–149.

_____, A. Cameron, S. R. Schwartz, and K. A. Worp. 1987. *Consuls of the Later Roman Empire.* Atlanta: Scholars Press.

_____, and B. W. Frier. 1994. *The Demography of Roman Egypt.* Cambridge: Cambridge University Press.

Baharal, D. 1996. *Victory of Propaganda: The Dynastic Aspect of the Imperial Propaganda of the Severi—The Literary and Archaeological Evidence, A.D. 193–225.* Oxford: Tempus Reparatum.

Bakhtin, M. 1984. *Problems of Dostoevsky's Poetics.* Minneapolis: University of Minnesota Press.

Bakker, E. J., and A. Kahane, eds. 1997. *Written Voice, Spoken Signs: Tradition, Performance, and the Epic Text.* Cambridge, MA: Harvard University Press.

Baldick, J. 1989. *Mystical Islam: An Introduction to Sufism.* New York: New York University Press.

Baldwin, B. 1974. "The Victories of Augustus. " *Journal of Roman Studies* 64: 21–26.

_____. 1978. *The Sources of the* Historia Augusta (Collection Latomus, 155). Brussels: Revue d'Études Latines.

Baldwin, B. 1979. "The *Acta Diurna.* " *Chiron* 9: 189–203.

_____. 1981. "Acclamations in the *Historia Augusta.*" *Athenaeum* 69: 138–149.

_____. 1981. *Constantine and Eusebius.* Cambridge, MA: Harvard University Press.

_____. 1982. *The New Empire of Diocletian and Constantine.* Cambridge, MA: Harvard University Press.

_____. 1985. "Constantine and the Christians of Persia." *Journal of Roman Studies* 75: 126–136.

_____. 1989. "Panegyric, History and Hagiography in Eusebius' *Life of Constantine.*" In *The Making of Orthodoxy,* 94–123. R. Williams, ed. Cambridge: Cambridge University Press.

_____. 1993. *Athanasius and Constantius: Theology and Politics in the Constantinian Empire.* Cambridge, MA: Harvard University Press.

_____. 1997. "Christentum und dynastische Politik (300–325)." *Paschoud and Szidat,* 99–109.

Baldwin, J. F. 1969. *The King's Council in England During the Middle Ages.* Oxford: Oxford University Press.

Banani, A., R. Hovannisian and G. Sabach. 1994. *Poetry and Mysticism in Islam: The Heritage of Rumi.* Cambridge: Cambridge University Press.

Barker, A. 1984. *Greek Musical Writings, Vol. I: The Musician and His Art.* Cambridge: Cambridge University Press.

Barnes, T. D. 1971. *Tertullian.* Oxford: Oxford University Press.

_____. 1973. "Lactantius and Constantine." *Journal of Roman Studies* 63: 29–46.

Barrell, J. 1991. *The Infection of Thomas De Quincey: A Psychopathology of Imperialism.* New Haven: Yale University Press.

Barrett, M. 1991. *The Politics of Truth from Marx to Foucault.* Stanford: Stanford University Press.

Barron, J. P. 1964. "Religious Propaganda of the Delian League." *Journal of Hellenic Studies* 84: 35–48.

Bartlett, R., and J. Hartley. 1990. *Russian in the Age of the Enlightenment.* New York: St. Martin's Press.

Barton, C. A. 2001. *Roman Honor the Fire in the Bone.* Berkeley: University of California Press.

Bartram, W. 1988 [reprint]. *Travels Through North & Southern Carolina, Georgia, East & West Florida, the Cherokee Country.* New York: Penguin.

Batiffol, P. 1913a. "La conversion de Constantin et la tendance au monothéisme dans la religion romaine." *Bulletin d'Ancienne Littérature et d'Archéologie Chrétiennes* 3: 132–141.

_____. 1913b. "Le règlement des premiers conciles africains et le règlement du sénat romain." *Bulletin d'Ancienne Littérature et d'Archéologie Chrétiennes* 3: 3–19.

_____. 1920. "L'église et les survivances du culte impérial." *Les survivances du culte impérial romain* 5–34. Paris: Picard.

Bats, M. 1994. "Les débuts de l'information politique officielle à Rome au premier siècle avant J.-C." *La mémoire perdue. À la recherché des archives oubliées, publique et privées de la Rome antique.* Paris: Publications de la Sorbonne, 19–43.

Baube, D. 1956. *The Forms of Roman Legislation.* Oxford: Clarendon Press.

Bauman, R. 1974. *Impietas in Principem: A Study of Treason Against the Roman Emperor with Special Reference to the First Century A.D.* Münchener Beiträge zur Papyrusforschung und Antiken Rechtsgeschichte, 67. Munich: Beck.

Baumgarten, A. I. 1981. *The Phoenician History of Philo of Byblos: A Commentary.* Leiden: Brill.

Baumgold, D. 1988. *Hobbes' Political Theory.* Cambridge: Cambridge University Press.

Bay, A. 1972. "The Letters *SC* on Augustan *aes* Coinage." *Journal of Roman Studies* 62: 111–122.

Baynes, N. H. 1931. *Constantine the Great and the Christian Church.* Reprinted as a monograph, Oxford: Clarendon Press, 1972.

_____. 1933. "Eusebius and the Christian Empire." *Mélanges Bidez, Annuaire de l'Institut de Philologie et d'Histoire Orientales* No. 2, 13–18. Brussels: Secrétariat de l'Institut.

_____. 1935. "Review of J. Vogt and E. Kornemann, *Römische Geschichte* (Leipzig: Teubner, 1933)." *Journal of Roman Studies* 25: 81–87.

_____. 1946a. "Review of McGeachy, 'Quintus Aurelius Symmachus and the Senatorial Aristocracy of the West' (dissertation, University of Chicago, 1942)." *Journal of Roman Studies* 36: 173–177.

_____. 1946b. "Review of Setton, 1941." *Journal of Roman Studies* 36: 135–140.

Beard, M., J. North, and S. Price. 1998. *Religions of Rome, Vol. 1: A History.* Cambridge: Cambridge University Press.

Beaujeu, J. 1955. *La religion romaine à l'apogée de l'empire: La politique religieuse des Antonins (96–192).* Paris: Les Belles Lettres.

_____. 1978. "Le paganisme romain sous le Haut Empire." *Aufstieg und Niedergang der römischen Welt* 2, 16, 1: 3–26.

Bebster, T. B. L. 1958. *From Mycenae to Homer.* London: Methuen.

Beck, H.-G. 1980. "Constantinople: The Rise of a New Capital in the East." *Age of Spirituality*, 29–37. K. Weitzmann, ed. New York: Metropolitan Museum of Art.

Beeston, A. F. 1969. *Arabic Historical Phraseology.* Cambridge: Cambridge University Press.

_____. 1984. *Sabaic Grammar.* Manchester: Manchester University Press.

_____, et al., eds. 1983. *Arabic Literature to the End of the Umayyad Period.* Cambridge: Cambridge University Press.

Behr, C. A. 1981. *P. Aelius Aristides: The Complete Works.* Vol. 2, *Orations*, 17–53. Leiden: Brill.

Bellinger, A. R., and M. A. Berlincourt. 1962. *Victory as a Coin Type.* New York: American Numismatic Society.

Bellomo, M. 1995. *The Common Legal Past of Europe: 1000–1800.* L.G. Cochrance, trans. Washington, DC: Catholic University of America Press.

Bendix, R. 1960. *Max Weber.* New York: Doubleday.

Benjamin, A., and A. E. Raubitschek. 1959. "Arae Augusti." *Hesperia* 28: 65–85.

Benner, M. 1975. *The Emperor Says: Studies in the Rhetorical Style in Edicts of the Early Empire.* Göteborg: Acta Universitatis Gothoburgensis.

Bennett, J. A. W. 1982. *Poetry of the Passion: Studies in Twelve Centuries of English Verse.* Oxford: Clarendon Press.

Béranger, J. 1953. *Recherches sur l'aspect idéologique du principat.* Schweizerische Beiträge zur Altertumswissenschaft, 6. Basel: Reinhardt.

_____. 1975. *Principatus.* Publications de la Faculté des Lettres de l'Université de Lausanne, 20. Geneva: Droz.

Berlin, I., et al. 1978. *Russian Thinkers.* New York: Viking Press.

Bernal, M. 1987. *Black Athena: The Afroasiatic Roots of Classical Civilization.* New Brunswick, NJ: Rutgers University Press.

_____. 1996. *Black Athena 2: The Archaeological and Documentary Evidence.* New Brunswick, NJ: Rutgers University Press.

_____. 2001. *Black Athena Writes Back: Martin Bernal Responds to His Critics.* Durham: Duke University Press.

Bernstein, A. 1993. *The Formation of Hell: Death and Retribution in the Ancient and Early Chris-*

tian Worlds. Ithaca, NY: Cornell University Press.

Beskow, P. 1962. *Res Gloriae: The Kingship of Christ in the Early Church.* Stockholm: Almqvist and Wiksell.

Bethea, D. M. 1989. *The Shape of Apocalypse in Modern Russian Fiction.* Princeton, NJ: Princeton University Press.

Birley, A. R. 1988. *The African Emperor Septimius Severus.* London: Batsford.

_____. 1997. *Hadrian: The Restless Emperor.* London: Routledge.

Bisbee, G.A. 1988. *Pre-Decian Acts of Martyrs and Commentarii.* Series *Harvard Dissertations in Religion*, 22. Philadelphia: Fortress Press.

Bishop, M. C., and J. C. N. Coulston. 1993. *Roman Military Equipment: From the Punic Wars to the Fall of Rome.* London: Batsford.

Blagg, T., and M. Millett, eds. 1990. *The Early Roman Empire in the West.* Oxford: Oxbow.

Bloch, R. 1976. "Interpretatio." *Recherches sur les religon de 'ltalie antique.* Geneva.

Blockley, R. C. 1975. *Ammianus Marcellinus: A Study of His Historiography and Political Thought.* Collection Latomus, 141. Brussels: Revue d'Études Latines.

_____. 1980. "Was the First Book of Zosimus' New History Based on More Than Two Sources?" *Byzantion* 50: 393–402.

_____. 1981. *The Fragmentary Classicising Historians of the Later Roman Empire.* Vol. 1. Liverpool: Francis Cairns.

_____. 1983. *The Fragmentary Classicising Historians of the Later Roman Empire.* Vol. 2. Liverpool: Francis Cairns.

Boardman, J. 1974. *Athenian Black Figure Vases.* New York: Oxford University Press.

_____. 1975. *Athenian Red Figure Vases.* New York: Oxford University Press.

_____. 1993. *The Oxford History of Classical Art.* Oxford: Oxford University Press.

_____. 1999. *The Greeks Overseas: Their Early Colonies and Trade.* New York: Thames and Hudson.

Boatwright, M. T. 1987. *Hadrian and the City of Rome.* Princeton, NJ: Princeton University Press.

Borch, M. F. 2004. *Conciliation, Compulsion, Conversion: British Attitudes Towards Indigenous Peoples, 1763–1814.* New York: Rodopi.

Bortnes, J. "The Literature of Old Russia, 988–1730." *The Cambridge History of Russian Literature*, 1–44. Charles Moser, ed. Cambridge: Cambridge University Press.

Boschung, D. 1993. *Die Bildnisse des Augustus.* Das Römische Herrscherbild 1.2. Berlin: Gebr. Mann.

Bossbach, S. 1999. *Gnostic Wars: The Cold War in the Context of a History of Western Spirituality.* Edinburgh: Edinburgh University Press.

Bosworth, A. B. 1988. *Conquest and Empire: The Reign of Alexander the Great.* Cambridge: Cambridge University Press.

Bottero, J., and A. Finet, et al. 2001. *Everyday Life in Ancient Mesopotamia.* Edinburgh: Edinburgh University Press.

Bouckham, R. 1978. *Tudoor Apocalypose.* Oxford: Oxford University Press.

Bowden, H. 2010. *Mystery Cults of the Ancient World.* Princeton, NJ: Princeton University Press.

Bowen, R. L. B., and F. P. Albright. 1958. *Archaeological Discoveries in South Arabia.* Baltimore: John Hopkins University Press.

Bowersock, G. W. 1965. *Augustus and the Greek World.* Oxford: Clarendon Press.

_____. 1973. "Syria under Vespasian." *Journal of Roman Studies* 63: 133–140.

_____. 1978. *Julian the Apostate.* Cambridge, MA: Harvard University Press.

_____. 1982. "The Imperial Cult: Perceptions and Persistence." *Jewish and Christian Self-definition*, 171–182. B. F. Meyer and E. P. Sanders, eds. London: SCM Press.

_____. 1986. "From Emperor to Bishop: The Self-conscious Transformation of Political Power in the Fourth Century A.D." *Classical Philology* 81: 298–307.

_____. 1990a. *Hellenism in Latin Antiquity.* Cambridge: Cambridge University Press.

_____. 1990b. "The Pontificate of Augustus." *Between Republic and Empire: Interpretations of Augustus and His Principate*, 380–394. Raaflaub and Toher, eds. Berkeley: University of California Press.

_____. 1991. "The Babatha Papyri, Masada, and Rome." *Journal of Roman Archaeology* 4: 336–344.

_____. 1995. *Martyrdom and Rome.* Cambridge: Cambridge University Press.

Bowie, E. L. 1970. "Review of Levick 1967." *Journal of Roman Studies* 60: 202–207.

Bowman, A. K., 1967. "The Crown-tax in Roman Egypt." *The Bulletin of the American Society of Papyrologists* 4: 59–74.

_____. 1971. *The Town Councils of Roman Egypt.* Series *American Studies in Papyrology* 11. Toronto: Hakkert.

_____. 1985. "Landholding in the Hermopolite Nome in the Fourth Century A.D." *Journal of Roman Studies* 75: 137–163.

_____, and D. Rathbone. 1992. "Cities and Administration in Roman Egypt." *Journal of Roman Studies* 82: 107–127.

Bowra, C. M. 2000. *Greek Lyric Poetry.* Oxford: Clarendon Press.

Box, H., trans. 1939. *Philonis Alexandrini in Flaccum.* London: Oxford University Press.

Boyarin, D. 1999. *Dying for God Martyrdom and the Making of Christian and Judaism.* Stanford: Stanford University Press.

Braun, T. F. R. G. 2006a. "The Greeks in Near

East." *The Cambridge Ancient History*, Part 3: *The Expansion of the Greek World, Eighth to Sixth Centuries B.C.*, 1–31. Boardman, ed. Cambridge: Cambridge University Press.

_____. 2006b. "The Greeks in Egypt." *The Cambridge Ancient History*, Part 3: *The Expansion of the Greek World, Eighth to Sixth Centuries B.C.*, 32–56. Boardman, ed. Cambridge UK: Cambridge University Press.

Braund, S. M., and G. Christopher. 1997. *The Passions in Roman Thought and Literature*. Cambridge: Cambridge University Press.

Bravmann, M. M. 1972. *The Spiritual Background of Early Islam: Studies on Ancient Arab Concepts*. Leiden: Brill.

Bréhier, L. 1949. *Les institutions de l'empire byzantin*. Paris: Albin Michel.

Bremmer, J. N. 1994. *Greek Religion*. Oxford: Oxford University Press.

Bridges, E., E. Hall, and P. J. Rhodes. 2007. *Cultural Responses to the Persian Wars: Antiquity to the Third Millennium*. New York: Oxford University Press.

Brilliant, R. 1963. *Gesture and Rank in Roman Art*. Memoirs of the Connecticut Academy of Arts and Sciences, 14. New Haven: The Academy.

Brinkman, J. A. 1984. *Prelude to Empire: Babylonian Society and Politics, 747–626 B.C.* Philadelphia: University Museum.

Briscoe, J. 1993. *A Commentary on Livy's Books XXXI–XXXIII*. Oxford: Oxford University Press.

Brock, S. 1982. "Clothing Metaphors as a Means of Theological Expression in Syriac Tradition." *Typus, Symbol, Allegorie bei den östlichen Vätern und ihren Parallelen im Mittelalter*, 11–38. M. Schmidt, ed. Regensburg: Pustet.

Brown, P. 1992. *Power and Persuasion in Late Antiquity Towards Christian Empire*. Madison: University of Wisconsin Press.

Brown, R. 1977. *Semitic Influence in Hellenic Mythology*. New York: Arno Press.

Browne, G. M. 1975. "A Panegyrist from Panopolis." *Proceedings of the 14th International Congress of Papyrologists* 61: 39–33. E.E.S. Graeco-Roman Memoirs. London: Egypt Exploration Society.

Browning, R. 1952. "The Riot of A.D. 387 in Antioch: The Role of the Theatrical Claques in the Later Empire." *Journal of Roman Studies* 42: 13–20.

Brundage, A., and R. A. Cosgrove. 2007. *The Great Tradition: Constitutional History and National Identity in Britain and the United States, 1870–1960*. Stanford: Stanford University Press.

Brunt, P. A. 1971. *Italian Manpower 225 B.C.–A.D. 14*. Oxford: Clarendon Press.

_____. 1982. "The Legal Issue in Cicero, *Pro Balbo*." *Classical Quarterly* 32: 136–147.

_____. 1984. "The Role of the Senate in the Augustan Regime." *Classical Quarterly* 34: 423–444.

_____. 1988. *The Fall of the Roman Republic and Related Essays*. Oxford: Clarendon Press.

_____. 1990a. *Roman Imperial Themes*. Oxford: Clarendon Press.

_____. 1990b. Laus Imperii. *Imperialism in the Ancient World*, 159–192. P. D. Garnsey, ed. Cambridge: Cambridge University Press.

_____, and J. M. Moore. 1967. *Res gestae Divi Augusti*. Oxford: Oxford University Press.

Bruun, P. 1976. "Notes on the Transmission of Imperial Images in Late Antiquity." *Studia Romana in Honorem Petri Krarup Septuagenarii*, 122–131. K. Ascani, et al., eds. Odense: Odense University Press.

Buckland, W. W. 1963. *Textbook of Roman Law from Augustine to Justinian*. Cambridge: Cambridge University Press.

Buckler, W. H. 1935. "Auguste, Zeus Patroos." *Revue de Philologie* 3d series, 9: 177–188.

Bulloch, A. W. 1985. "Hellenistic Poetry." *Cambridge History of Classical Literature I*: 616–8. Cambridge: Cambridge University Press.

Buren, E. D. Van. 1938. *The Flowing Vase and the God with Streams*. Berlin: H. Schoetz.

Bureth, P. 1964. *Les titulatures impériales dans les papyrus, les ostraca, et les inscriptions d'Égypte (30 a. C.–284 p. C.)*. Papyrologica Bruxellensia, 2. Brussels: Fondation Égyptologique Reine Élisabeth.

Burke, J. F. 1998. *Desire Against the Law: The Juxtaposition of Contraries in Early Medieval Spanish Literature*. Stanford: Stanford University Press.

Burkert, W. 1982. *Structure and History in Greek Mythology and Ritual*. Berkeley: University of California Press.

_____. 1985. *Greek Religion*. Cambridge, MA: Harvard University Press.

_____. 1995. *The Orientalizing Revolution: Near Eastern Influence of Greek Culture in the Early Archaic Age*. Cambridge, MA: Harvard University Press.

Burnett, A., and S. Walker. 1981. *The Image of Augustus*. London: The British Museum.

Burton, A. 1998. *At the Heart of the Empire: Indians and the Colonial Encounter in Late-Victorian Britain*. Berkely: University of California Press.

Burton, G. P. 1976. "The Issuing of Mandata to Proconsuls and a New Inscription from Cos." *Zeitschrift für Papyrologie und Epigraphik* 21: 63–68.

_____. 1993. "Provincial Procurators and the Public Provinces." *Chiron* 23: 13–28.

Burton, R. W. B. 1985. *The Chorus in Sophocles' Tragedies*. Oxford: Oxford University Press.

Buxton, G. 1994. *Imaginary Greece*. Cambridge: Cambridge University Press.

Cachia, P. 2002. *Arabic Literature: An Overview.* London.

Cairns, F. 1972. *Generic Composition in Greek and Roman Poetry.* Edinburgh: Edinburgh University Press.

Calame, C. 1999. *The Poetics of Eros in Ancient Greece.* Princeton, NJ: Princeton University Press.

The Cambridge Ancient History 3. The Expansion of the Greek World, Eighth to Sixth Centuries B.C. J. Boardman, ed. Cambridge: Cambridge University Press.

The Cambridge Ancient History, 4, Persia, Greece and the Western Mediterranean C. 525 to 479 B.C. 2008. J. Boardman, A. K. Bowman, J. B. Bury, and A. Cameron, eds. Cambridge: Cambridge University Press.

The Cambridge Ancient History, 5, Fifth Century B.C. 2008. D. M Lewis, et al., eds. Cambridge: Cambridge University Press.

The Cambridge Ancient History, 6, The Fourth Century B.C. 2006. A. K. Bowman, J. B. Bury, A. Cameron, eds. Cambridge: Cambridge University Press.

Cameron, A. 1931. "Latin Words in the Greek Inscriptions of Asia Minor." *American Journal of Philology* 52: 232–262.

Cameron, A. D. E. 1965a. "Palladas and Christian Polemic." *Journal of Roman Studies* 55: 17–30.

_____. 1965b. "Wandering Poets: A Literary Movement in Byzantine Egypt." *Historia* 14: 470–509.

_____. 1967. "Rutilius Namatianus, St. Augustine, and the Date of the *De Reditu.*" *Journal of Roman Studies* 57: 31–39.

_____. 1970. *Claudian: Poetry and Propaganda in the Court of Honorius.* Oxford: Clarendon Press.

_____. 1973. *Porphyrius the Charioteer.* Oxford: Clarendon Press.

_____. 1976. *Circus Factions.* Oxford: Clarendon Press.

_____, J. Long, and L. Sherry. 1993. *Barbarians and Politics at the Court of Arcadius.* Berkeley: University of California Press.

Cameron, Av. 1983. "Eusebius of Caesarea and the Rethinking of History." *Tria corda: Scritti in onore di Arnaldo Momigliano,* 71–88. E. Gabba, ed. Como: Edizioni. New Press.

Campbell, J. B. 1984. *The Emperor and the Roman Army, 31 B.C.–A.D. 235.* Oxford: Clarendon Press.

Campbell, M. 1988. *The Witness and the Other World: Exotic European Travel Writing, 400–1600.* Ithaca, NY: Cornell University Press.

Canterbury, D. C. 2010. *European Bloc Imperialism.* Leiden: Brill.

Carr, D. M. 2010. *An Introduction to the Bible: Sacred Texts and Imperial Contexts.* Malden, MA: Wiley-Blackwell.

_____. 2011. *The Formation of the Hebrew Bible: A New Reconstruction.* New York: Oxford University Press.

Carrington, P. 1957. *The Early Christian Church.* Cambridge: Cambridge University Press.

Carroll, M. 1986. *The Cult of the Virgin Mary.* Princeton, NJ: Princeton University Press.

Cartledge, P. M. 1993. *The Greeks: A Portrait of Self and Others.* Oxford: Oxford University Press.

_____, and S. Todd, eds. 1990. *Nomas: Essays in Athenian Law Politics and Society.* Cambridge: Cambridge University Press.

Cassar, P. 1974. "Surgical Instruments on a Tomb Slab in Roman Malta." *Medical History* 18: 89–92.

Cawkwell, G. 1997. "Thucydides and the Empire." *Thucydides and the Peloponnesian War,* 92–106. London: Routledge.

Chadwick, H. 1986. *Augustine.* Oxford: Oxford University Press.

Chadwick, J. 1976. *The Mycenaean World.* New York: Cambridge University Press.

Cerfaux, L., and J. Tondriau. 1956. *Un concurrent du christianisme: Le culte des souverains dans la civilisation gréco-romaine.* Tournai: Desclée and Cie.

Charanis, F. 1940. "Coronation and its Constitutional Significance in the Later Roman Empire." *Byzantion* 15: 49–66.

Chedwick, N. K. 1964. *Russian Heroic Poetry.* New York: Russell and Russell.

Chestnut, G. F. 1986. *The First Christian Histories.* 2d ed. Macon: Mercer University Press.

Chibnall, M. 1986. *Anglo-Norman England, 1066–1166.* Oxford: Oxford University Press

Childs, D. J. 2001. *Modernism and Eugenics.* Cambridge: Cambridge University Press.

Chilver, G. E. F. 1979. *A Historical Commentary on Tacitus' Histories I and II.* Oxford: Clarendon Press.

Chilver, G. E. F., and G. B. Townend. 1985. *A Historical Commentary on Tacitus' Histories IV and V.* Oxford: Clarendon Press.

Chrimes, S. B. 1978. *English Constitutional Ideas in the Fifteenth Century.* Cambridge: Cambridge University Press.

Christ, F. 1938. *Die römische Weltherrschaft in der antiken Dichtung.* Tübinger Beiträge zur Altertumswissenschaft, 31. Stuttgart: Kohlhammer.

Christianson, P. 1978. *The Reformers and Babylon: English Apocalyptic Vision.* Toronto: Toronto University Press.

Christol, M. 1994. "Pline l'Ancien et la *formula* de la province narbonnaise." *La mémoire perdue: À la recherché des archives oubliées, publiques et privées, de la Rome antique,* 45–63. Ségolène Demougin. Paris: Publications de la Sorbonne.

Chuvin, P. 1991. *Mythologies et geographie*

dionysiaque: Recherches sur l'oeuvre de Nonnos de Panopolis. Clermont-Ferrand: Adosa.

Claydon, T., and I. McBride, eds. 1998. *Protestantism and National Identity: Britain and Ireland, 1650–1850.* Cambridge: Cambridge University Press.

Coates, R. 1998. *Christianity in Bakhtin: God and the Exiled Author.* Cambridge: Cambridge University Press.

Cockburn, A. 1975. "Autopsy of an Egyptian Mummy." *Science* 187: 1155–60.

_____, E. Cockburn, and T. A. Reyman. 1998. *Mummies, Disease and Ancient Cultures.* Cambridge: Cambridge University Press.

Cockle, W. E. H. 1984. "State Archives in Graeco-Roman Egypt from 30 B.C. to the Reign of Septimius Severus." *Journal of Egyptian Archaeology* 70: 106–122.

Cohen, G. M. 2006. *The Hellenistic Settlements in Syria, the Red Sea Basin, and North Africa.* Berkeley: University of California Press.

Cohen, T. V., and E. S. Cohen. 1993. *Words and Deeds in Renaissance Rome: Trial Before the Papal Magistrate.* Toronto: University of Toronto Press.

Coles, R. 1966. *Reports of Proceedings in Papyri.* Papyrologica Bruxellensia, 4. Brussels: Fondation Égyptologique Reine Élisabeth.

Colleey, L. 1992. "Britishness and Otherness: An Argument." *Journal of British Studies* 31: 309–29.

Collini, S. 1991. *Public Moralists.* Oxford: Oxford University Press.

Colley, L. 2002. *Captives: Britain, Empire and the World, 1600–1850.* London: J. Cape.

Constantakopoulou, C. 2007. *The Dance of the Islands: Insularity, Networks, the Athenian Empire, and the Aegean World.* Oxford: Oxford University Press.

Conte, G. B. 1994a. *Genres and Readers: Lucretius, Love Elegy, Pliny's Encyclopedia.* Baltimore: Johns Hopkins University Press.

_____. 1994b. *Latin Literature: A History.* Baltimore: John Hopkins University Press.

_____. 1996. *The Hidden Author.* Berkeley: University of California Press.

Cook, S. A. 1930. *The Religion of Ancient Palestine in the Light of Archaeology.* Oxford: Oxford University Press.

Cooper, K. 1996. *The Virgin and Bride: Idealized Womanhood in the Late Antiquity.* Cambridge, MA: Harvard University Press.

Corcoran, S. 1996. *The Empire of the Tetrarchs.* Oxford: Clarendon Press.

Cornell, T. J. 1991a. "Rome: The History of an Anachronism." *City States in Classical Antiquity and Medieval Italy,* 53–69. Molho, Raaflaub, and Emlen, eds. Stuttgart: F. Steiner.

_____. 1991b. "The Tyranny of the Evidence: A Discussion of the Possible Uses of Literacy in Etruria and Latium in the Archaic Age." *Literacy in the Roman World.* Ann Arbor, MI: Journal of Roman Archaeology.

Cornwell, N. 1999. *The Gothic-Fantastic in Nineteenth-Century Russian Literature.* Amsterdam: Rodopi.

Cotton, H. 1993. "The Guardianship of Jesus Son of Babatha: Roman and Local Law in the Province of Arabia." *Journal of Roman Studies* 83: 94–108.

_____. 1994. "A Cancelled Marriage Contract From the Judaean Desert?" *Journal of Roman Studies* 84: 64–86.

_____, et al. 2009. *From Hellenism to Islam: Cultural and Linguistic Change in the Roman Near East.* Cambridge: Cambridge University Press.

Coudry, M. 1994. "Sénatus-consultes et *acta senatus:* Rédaction, conservation et archivage des documents émanant du sénat, de l'époque de César à celle des Sévères." *La mémoire perdue: À la recherché des archives oubliées, publiques et privées, de la Rome antique,* 65–102. Ségolène Demougin. Paris: Publications de la Sorbonne.

Coulson, N. J. 1964. *A History of Islamic Law.* Edinburgh: Edinburgh University Press.

_____. 1969. *Conflicts and Tensions in Islamic Jurisprudence.* Chicago: University of Chicago Press.

Court, J., and K. Court. 1990. *The New Testament World.* Cambridge: Cambridge University Press.

Craddock, P. B. *Edward Gibbon, Luminous Historian, 1772–1794.* Baltimore: Johns Hopkins University Press.

Crawford, M. 1970. "Money and Exchange in the Roman World." *Journal of Roman Studies* 60: 40–48.

_____. 1988. "The Laws of the Romans: Knowledge and Diffusion." *Estudios sobre la Tabula Siarensis,* 127–139. González and Arce, eds. Madrid: Centro de Estudios históricos.

Croke, B. 1990. *The Early Development of Byzantine Chronicles: Studies in John Malalas, 27–54.* Sydney: Australian Association for Byzantine Studies.

Crone, P., and M. Hinds. 2003. *God's Caliph: Religious Authority in the First Centuries of Islam.* Cambridge: Cambridge University Press.

Cross, F. M. 1997. *Canaanite Myth and Hebrew Epic: Essays in the History of the Religion of Israel.* Cambridge, MA: Harvard University Press.

_____. 1991. "The Invention and Development of the Alphabet." *The Origin of Writing,* 77–90. W.M. Senner, ed. Lincoln: University of Nebraska Press.

Csapo, E., and M. C. Miler. 2007. *The Origins of Theater in Ancient Greece and Beyond: From*

Ritual. Cambridge: Cambridge University Press.

Curty, O. 1995. *Les parentés légendaires entre les cités grècques*. Hautes Études du Monde Greco-Romain, 20. Geneva: Droz.

Dagron, G. 1968. "L'empire romain d'orient au IVᵉ siècle et les traditions politiques de l'hellénisme: Le témoignage de Thémistios." *Travaux et Mémoires* 3: 1–242.

_____. 1984. *Naissance d'une capitale: Constantinople et ses institutions de 330 à 451*. 2d ed. Bibliothèque Byzantine, Études, 7. Paris: Presses Universitaires de France.

_____. 1987. 'Ceux d'en face': Les peuples étrangers dans les traités militaires byzantins." *Travaux et Mémoires* 10: 207–228.

_____. 1996. *Empereur et prêtre: Étude sur le 'césaropapisme' byzantin*. Paris: Gallimard.

Daiches, D. 1984. *God and the Poets*. Oxford: Oxford University Press.

Dale, A. M. 1969. "The Chorus in the Action of Greek Tragedy." *Collected Papers*, 210–220. Cambridge: Cambridge University Press.

Dalglish, E. R. 1962. *Psalm Fifty-One: In the Light of Ancient Near Eastern Patternism*. Leiden: Brill.

Dalley, S., trans. 2009. *Myths from Mesopotamia: Creation, the Flood, Gilgamesh, and Others*. Oxford: Oxford University Press.

Daniels, P. T., and W. Bright, eds. 1996. *The World's Writing Systems*. New York: Oxford University Press.

D'Arms, J. H. 1981. *Commerce and Social Standing in Ancient Rome*. Cambridge, MA: Harvard University Press.

Daube, D. 1969. *Roman Law, Linguistic, Social and Philosophical Aspects*. Edinburgh: Edinburgh University Press.

Daunton, M., and R. Halpern. 1999. *Empire and Others: British Encounters with Indigenous Peoples, 1600–1850*. Philadelphia: University of Pennsylvania Press.

David, J.-M. 1997. *The Roman Conquest of Italy*. A. Nevill, trans. Oxford: Blackwell.

Davies, P. S. 1989. "The Origin and Purpose of the Persecution of A.D. 303." *Journal of Theological Studies* 40: 66–94.

Davies, W. V., and R. Walker. 1993. *Biological Anthropology and the Study of Ancient Egypt*. London: British Museum Press.

Davis, G. 1991. *Polyhymia: The Rhetorica of Horatian Lyric Discourse*. Berkeley: University of California Press.

Dawson, W. R. 1932–1934. *Studies in the Egyptian Medical Texts* 1–3. London: Egypt Exploration Society.

Demougin, S., ed. 1994. *La mémoire perdue: À la recherche des archives oubliées, publiques et privées, de la Rome antique*. CNRS, Série Histoire Ancienne et Médiévale, 30. Paris: Publications de la Sorbonne.

den Boeft, J., D. den Hengst, and H. C. Teitler. 1987. *Philological and Historical Commentary on Ammianus Marcellinus 20*. Groningen: Egbert Forsten.

den Boer, W. 1975. "Trajan's Deification. *Proceedings of the 14th International Congress of Papyrologists* (Oxford, 1974), E.E.S. Graeco-Roman Memoirs, No. 61, 85–90. London: Egypt Exploration Society.

Denning-Bolle, S. 1992. *Wisdom in Akkadian Literature: Expression, Instruction, Dialogue*. Leiden: Ex Oriente Lux.

De Polignac, F. 1995. *Cults, Territory, and the Origins of the Greek City-state*. Chicago: University of Chicago Press.

de Romilly, J. 1963. *Thucydides and Athenian Imperialism*. New York: Barnes and Noble.

Dick, M. B. 1999. *Born in Heaven, Made on Earth: The Making of the Cult Image in the Ancient Near East*. Winona Lake, IN: Eisenbrauns.

Di Cosmo, Nicola. *Ancient China and its Enemies: The Rise of Nomadic Power in East Asian History*. Cambridge: Cambridge University Press.

Diggle, J. 1970. *Euripides: Phaeton*. Cambridge: Cambridge: University Press.

Dilke, O. A. W. 1971. *The Roman Land Surveyors: An Introduction to the* Agrimensores. New York: Barnes and Noble.

DiMaio III, M., J. Zeuge, and N. Zotov. 1988. "*Ambiguitas Constantiniana*: The *caeleste signum Dei* of Constantine the Great." *Byzantion* 58: 333–360.

Dodds, E. R. 1951. *The Greeks and Irrational*. Berkeley: University of California Press.

Dodge, H. 1990. "The Architectural Impact of Rome in the East." *Architecture and Architectural Sculpture in the Roman Empire*, 108–120. M. Henig, ed. Oxford University Committee for Archaeology Monographs, No. 29. Oxford: Institute of Archaeology.

Douglas, M. 1984. *Purity and Danger: An Analysis of Concepts of Pollution and Taboo*. London: Ark.

Dodson, A. 2003. *The Hieroglyphs of Ancient Egypt*. London: New Holland.

Dollery, C. 1994. "Medicine and the Pharmacological Revolution." *Journal of the Royal College of Physicians* 28: 59–69.

Donner, F. M. 1981. *The Early Islamic Conquests*. Princeton, NJ: Princeton University Press.

Dover, K. 1971. *Theocritus: Selected Poems*. London.

Downey, G. 1940. "The Pilgrim's Progress of the Byzantine Emperor." *Church History* 9: 207–217.

Downey, G. 1941. "Ethical Themes in the Antioch Mosaics." *Church History* 10: 367–376.

Drake, H. A. 1976. *In Praise of Constantine: A Historical Study and New Translation of Euse-*

bius' Tricennial Orations. Berkeley: University of California Press.

Drinkwater, J.F. 1987. *The Gallic Empire.* Historia Einzelschriften, 52. Stuttgart: Steiner.

Driver, G. R. 1976. *Semitic Writing from Picture to Alphabet.* Oxford: Oxford University Press.

Duckworth, G. E. 1952. *The Nature of Roman Comedy: A Study in Popular Entertainment.* Princeton, NJ: Princeton University Press.

Dufraigne, P. 1994. *Adventus Augusti, adventus Christi: Recherche sur l'exploitation idéologique et littéraire d'un cérémonial dans l'antiquité tardive.* Collection des Études Augustiniennes, Série Antiquité, 141. Paris.

Dunbabin, T. J., and J. Boardman. 1957. *The Greeks and Their Eastern Neighbours: Studies in the Relations Between Greece and the Countries of the Near East in the 8th and 7th Centuries B.C.* London: Society for the Promotion of Hellenic Studies.

Dvornik, F. 1934. "The Authority of the State in the Oecumenical Councils." *The Christian East* 14: 95–108.

_____. 1966. *Early Christian and Byzantine Political Philosophy.* Washington, DC: Dumbarton Oaks.

Dyck, A. R. 1996. *A Commentary on Cicero. De Officiis.* Ann Arbor: University of Michigan Press.

Dyson, S. 1971. "Native Revolts in the Roman Empire." *Historia* 20: 239–274.

Eck, W. 1979. *Die staatliche Organisation Italiens in der hohen Kaiserzeit.* Vestigia, 28. Munich: Beck.

Eck, W., A. Caballos, and F. Fernández. 1996. *Das senatus consultum de Cn. Pisone patre.* Vestigia, 48. Munich: Beck.

Eder, W. 1990. "Augustus and the Power of Tradition: The Augustan Principate as Binding Link Between Republic and Empire." *Between Republic and Empire: Interpretations of Augustus and His Principate,* 71–122. Raaflaub and Tohe, eds. Berkeley: University of California Press.

Edmondson, J. C. 1990. "Romanization and Urban Development in Lusitania." *The Early Roman Empire in the West,* 151–178. Blagg and Millett, eds. Oxford: Oxbow.

_____. 1992/93. "Creating a Provincial Landscape: Roman Imperialism and Rural Change in Lusitania." *Historia Antigua* 10/11: 13–30.

_____. 1996. "Roman Power and the Emergence of Provincial Administration in Lusitania During the Republic." *Pouvoir et imperium,* 163–211. E. Hermon, ed. Naples: Jovene.

Edward, R. P. 1979. *Kadmos the Phoenician: A Study in Greek Legends and the Mycenaean Age.* Amsterdam: Adolf M. Hakkert.

Edwards, M. W. 2002. *Sound, Sense, and Rhythm.* Princeton, NJ: Princeton University Press.

Ehrhardt, C. T. H. R. 1984. "Roman Coin Types and the Roman Public." *Jahbuck für Nimismatik un Geldgeschichte* 34: 41–54.

Ehrmn, B. D. 2003. *Lost Christianities: The Battles for Scripture and the Faiths We Never Knew.* New York: Oxford University Press.

Elm, S. 1994. *'Virgins of God:' The Making of Asceticism in Late Antiquity.* Oxford: Oxford University Press.

Erim, K. T. 1982. "A New Relief Showing Claudius and Britannia from Aphrodisias." *Britannia* 13: 277–281.

Erskine, A. 1988. "Rhodes and Augustus." *Zeitschrift für Papyrologie und Epigraphik* 88: 271–275.

_____. 1990. *The Hellenistic Stoa: Political Thought and Action.* Ithaca, NY: Cornell University Press.

_____. 1997. "Greekness and Uniqueness: The Cult of the Senate in the Greek East." *Phoenix* 51: 25–37.

_____. 2001. *Troy Between Greece and Rome: Local Tradition and Imperial Power.* Oxford: Oxford University Press.

_____. 2010a. *Roman Imperialism.* Edinburgh: Edinburgh University Press.

_____, and D. H. Berry. 2010b. *Form and Function in Roman Oratory.* Cambridge: Cambridge University Press.

Estes, J. W. 2004. *The Medical Skills of Ancient Egypt.* Sagamore Beach, MA: Science History Publications.

Evans, J. A. 1991. *Herodotus, Explorer of the Past: Three Essays.* Princeton, NJ: Princeton University Press.

Fantham, E. 2004. *Ovid's Metamorphoses.* Oxford: Oxford University Press.

Farnell, L. R. 1911. *Greece and Babylon: A Comparative Sketch of Mesopotamian Anatolian and Hellenic Religions.* Edinburgh: T. Clark.

Faulkner, A. 2011. *The Homeric Hymns Interpretative Essays.* Oxford: Oxford University Press.

Fears, J. R. 1977. *Princeps a diis electus: The Divine Election of the Emperor as a Political Concept at Rome.* Papers and Monographs of the American Academy at Rome, 26.

Fedotov, G. P. 1988. *The Russian Religious Mind.* 2 vols. Belmont, MA: Notable and Academic Books.

Feenly, D. C. 1991. *The Gods in Epic: Poets and Critics of the Classical Tradition.* Oxford: Oxford University Press.

Feldherr, A. 1988. *Spectacle and Society in Livy's History.* Berkeley: University of California Press.

Feldman, L. H. 1993. *Jew and Gentile in the Ancient World.* Princeton, NJ: Princeton University Press.

Ferguson, J. 1970. *The Religions of the Roman Empire.* Ithaca, NY: Cornell University Press.

Filoramo, G. 1990. *A History of Gnoticism.* Cambridge, MA: Blackwell.

Fink, R. O., A. S. Hoey, and W. F. Snyder. 1940. "The Feriale Duranum." *Yale Classical Studies* 7: 1–222.

Firth, K. R. 1979. *The Apocalyptic Tradition in Reformation Britiain*. Oxford: Oxford University Press.

Fishwick, D. 1970. "Flamen Augustorum." *Harvard Studies in Classical Philology* 74: 299–312.

_____. 1978. "The Federal Cult of the Three Gauls." *Les Martyrs de Lyon (177)*, 33–45. J. Rougé and R. Turcan, eds. Colloques Internationaux du CNRS, 575. Paris: Éditions du CNRS.

_____. 1990a. "Dio and Maecenas: The Emperor and the Ruler Cult." *Phoenix* 44: 267–275.

_____. 1990b. "Prudentius and the Cult of Divus Augustus." *Historia* 39: 475–486.

_____. 1990c. "Votive Offerings to the Emperor?" *Zeitschrift für Papyrologie und Epigraphik* 80: 121–130.

_____. 1991. *The Imperial Cult in the Latin West*. 2 vols. Leiden: Brill.

_____. 2005. *The Imperial Cult in the Latin West Studies in the Ruler Cult of the Western Provinces of the Roman Empire*. Leiden: Brill.

Fontaine, J. 1971. "Vienne, carrefour du paganisme et du christianisme dans la Gaule du IVe siècle." *Bulletin de la Société des Amis de Vienne* 67: 17–36.

_____. 1996. *Ammien Marcellin, Histoire. Tome III, Livres XX–XXII*. Paris: Les Belles Lettres.

Ferguson, W. S. 2001. *Greek Imperialism*. Kitchener, ON: Batoche.

Fliegelman, J. 1993. *Declaring Independence: Jefferson, Natural Language and the Culture of Performance*. Stanford: Stanford University Press.

Fornara, C. 1983. *The Nature of History in Ancient Greece and Rome*. Berkeley: University of California Press.

_____. 1989. "Eunapius' Epidemia in Athens." *Classical Quarterly* 39: 517–523.

Fortescue, Sir J. 1926. *The Governance of England: Otherwise Called the Difference Between an Absolute and a Limited Monarchy*. C. Plummer, ed. Oxford: Oxford University Press.

_____. 1942. *De Laudibus Legum Anglie*. S. B. Chrimes, ed. Cambridge: Cambridge University Press.

_____. 1980. "De Natura Legis Naturae." New York: Garland Pub.

_____. 1997. *On the Laws and Governance of England*. S. Lockwood, ed. Cambridge: Cambridge University Press.

Foster, B. R., and K. P. Foster. 2009. *Civilizations of Ancient Iraq*. Princeton, NJ: Princeton University Press.

Fowden, G. 1994. "The Last Days of Constantine: Oppositional Versions and Their Influence." *Journal of Roman Studies* 84: 146–170.

Fower, M. A. 1995. *Theoppompus of Chios: History and Rhetoric in the Fourth Century B.C.* Oxford: Oxford University Press.

Fowler, A. 1991. *A History of English Literature*. Cambridge, MA: Harvard University Press.

Fox, R. L. 1987. *Pagans and Christians*. New York: Knopf.

_____. 1991. *The Unauthorised Version: Truth and Fiction in the Bible*. London: Vintage.

Frederiksen, M. W. 1965. "The Republican Municipal Laws: Errors and Drafts." *Journal of Roman Studies* 55: 183–198.

Freeman, C. 2004. *Egypt, Greece, and Rome: Civilizations of the Ancient Mediterranean*. Oxford: Oxford University Press.

Freeman, P. W. M. 1993. "'Romanisation' and Roman Material Culture." *Journal of Roman Archaeology* 6: 438–445.

Friedrich, P. 1978. *The Meaning of Aphrodite*. Chicago: University of Chicago Press.

French, D. 1981. *Roman Roads and Milestones of Asia Minor*. Fasc. 1, *The Pilgrim's Road*. BAR International Series, 105. Oxford: Tempus Reparatum.

_____. 1988. *Roman Roads and Milestones of Asia Minor*. Fasc. 2, *An Interim Catalogue of Milestones*. 2 parts. BAR International Series, 392. Oxford: Tempus Reparatum.

Frend, W. H. C. 1956. "A Third-century Inscription Relating to *Angareia* in Phrygia." *Journal of Roman Studies* 46: 46–56.

_____. 1965. *Martyrdom and Persecution in the Early Church*. Oxford: Blackwell.

_____. 1974. "The Two Worlds of Paulinus of Nola." *Latin Literature of the Fourth Century*, 58–99. J. W. Binns, ed. London: Routledge and K. Paul.

_____. 1984. *The Rise of Christianity*. Philadelphia: Fortress Press.

Friedlaender, L. 1922. *Darstellung aus der Sittengeschichte Roms in der Zeit von Augustus bis zum Ausgang der Antonine*. G. Wissowa, ed. Leipzig: S. Hirzel.

Frier, B. W. 1979. *Libri annales pontificum maximorum: The Origins of the Annalistic Tradition*. Papers and Monographs of the American Academy in Rome.

_____. 1985. *The Rise of the Roman Jurists*. Princeton, NJ: Princeton University Press.

Friesen, S. J. 1993. *Twice Neokoros: Ephesus, Asia, and the Cult of the Flavian Imperial Family*. Leiden: Brill.

_____. 2001. *Imperial Cults and the Apocalypse of John: Reading Revelation in the Ruins*. New York: Oxford University Press.

Frischer, B. 1991. *Shifting Paradigms: New Approaches to Horace's Ars Poetica*. Atlanta: Scholars Press.

Fulford, T., and P. J. Kitson, eds. 1998. *Roman-*

ticism and Colonialism: Writing and Empire, 1780–1830. Cambridge: Cambridge University Press.

Furtwängler, A. 1900. *Die antiken Gemmen: Geschichte der Steinschneidekunst im klassischen Altertum.* Leipzig: Giesecke.

Gabba, E. 1982. "Political and Cultural Aspects of the Classicistic Revival in the Augustan Age." *Classical Antiquity* 1: 43–65.

_____. 1984. "The Historians and Augustus." *Caesar Augustus: Seven Aspects*, 61–88. Millar and Segal, eds. Oxford: Clarendon Press.

_____. 1991. *Dionysius and the History of Archaic Rome.* Berkeley: University of California Press.

Galinsky, K. 1996. *Augustan Culture: An Interpretive Introduction.* Princeton, NJ: Princeton University Press.

Galperin, W. H. 1993. *The Return of the Visible in British Romanticism.* Baltimore: John Hopkins University Press.

Geertz, C. 1973. *The Interpretation of Cultures: Selected Essays.* New York: Basic Books.

_____. 1983. *Local Knowledge: Further Essays in Interpretive Anthropology.* New York: Basic Books.

Georgacas, J. G. 1947. "The Names of Constantinople." *Transactions and Proceedings of the American Philological Association* 78: 347–367.

Geraci, R. 2001. *Window on the East: National and Imperial Identities in Late Tsarist Russia.* Ithaca, NY: Cornell University Press.

Gibb, H. A. R. 1974. *Introduction to Arabic Literature.* Oxford: Oxford University Press.

Gibbon, E. 1972. *The English Essays of Edward Gibbon.* P. B. Craddock, ed. Oxford: Clarendon Press.

Gibbons, E. 1954. *Gibbons' Decline and Fall of the Roman Empire in Six Volumes.* New York: E. P. Dutton.

Gichon, M. 1972. "The Plan of a Roman Camp Depicted upon a Lamp from Samaria." *Palestine Exploration Quarterly* 104: 38–58.

Giddens, A. 1983. "Four Theses on Ideology." *Canadian Journal of Political and Social Theory* 7: 18–21.

Giddens, A. 1984. *The Constitution of Society.* Berkeley: University of California Press.

Gilliam, J. F. 1969. "On *Divi* Under the Severi." *Hommages à Marcel Renard*, 102, 2: 284–289. ed. J. Bibauw, Brussels: Latomus, Revue d'etudes latines.

_____. 1975. "Notes on Latin Texts from Egypt." *Le monde grec: Hommages à Claire Préaux*, 766–774. J. Bingen, G. Cambier, and G. Nachtergael, eds. Brussels: Éditions de l'Université de Bruxelles.

_____. 1978. "Some Roman Elements in Roman Egypt." *Illinois Classical Studies* 3: 115–131.

Goldhill, S. 1986. "Framing and Polyphony: Readings in Hellenistic Poetry." *Proceedings of the Cambridge Philological Society* 32: 25–52.

_____. 1991. *The Poet's Voice: Essays on Poetics and Greek Literature.* Cambridge: Cambridge University Press.

_____. 2001. *Being Greek Under Rome: Cultural Identity, the Second Sophistic and the Development of Empire.* Cambridge: Cambridge University Press.

Goodman, L. E. 1983. "The Syrian Impact on Arabic Literature." *Arabic Literature to the End of the Umayyad Period, 497–501.* A. F. L. Beeston, et al., eds. Cambridge: Cambridge University Press.

Goodman, M. 1991a. "Babatha's Story. Review of Y. Yadin, *The Documents from the Bar Kokhba Period: Greek Papyri* (Jerusalem: Israel Exploration Society, 1989)." *Journal of Roman Studies* 81: 169–175.

_____. 1991b. "Opponents of Rome: Jews and Others." *Images of Empire*, 222–238. Sheffield, UK: Sheffield Academic Press.

Goodman, M. 1994. *Mission and Conversion: Proselytizing in the Religious History of the Roman Empire.* Oxford: Clarendon Press.

Gordon, R. L. 1979. "Production and Religion in the Graeco-Roman World." *Art History* 2: 5–34.

Grabar, A. 1968. *Christian Iconography: A Study of its Origins.* Princeton, NJ: Princeton University Press.

Graef, H. 1963. *Mary: A History of Doctrine and Devotion.* London: Sheed and Ward.

Grant, M. 1946. *From* Imperium *to* Auctoritas: *A Historical Study of* aes *Coinage in the Roman Empire 49 B.C.–A.D. 14.* Cambridge: Cambridge University Press.

_____. 1950. *Roman Anniversary Issues: An Exploratory Study of the Numismatic and Medallic Commemoration of Anniversary Years, 49 B.C.–A.D. 375.* Cambridge: Cambridge University Press.

Gray, D., ed. 1975. *A Selection of Religious Lyrics.* Oxford: Oxford University Press.

Grayson, A. K. 1975. *Babylonian Historical-literary Texts.* Toronto: University of Toronto Press.

Green, A. R. W. 2003. *The Storm-god in the Ancient Near East.* Winona Lake, IN: Eisenbrauns.

Green, R.L. 1977. *The Early English Carols.* Oxford: Oxford University Press.

Greene, J. P. 2011. *The Constitutional Origins of the American Revolution.* New York: Cambridge University Press.

Griffel, F. 2009. *Al-Ghazali's Philosophical Theology.* Oxford: Oxford University Press.

Griffin, J. 1980. *Homer.* New York: Hill and Wang.

_____. 1983. *Homer on Life and Death.* Oxford: Oxford University Press.

Griffin, M. 1991. "Urbs Roma, Plebs, and Princeps." *Images of Empire*, 19–46. Alexander, ed. Sheffield, UK: Sheffield Academic Press.

Griffith, S. H. 1987. "Ephraem the Syrian's Hymns 'Against Julian': Meditations on History and Imperial Power." *Vigiliae Christianae* 41: 238–266.

van Groningen, B. A. 1956. "Preparatives to Hadrian's Visit to Egypt." *Studi in onore di Aristide Calderini e Roberto Paribeni*, vol. 2, *Studi di papirologia e antichità orientali*, 253–256. Milan: Ceschina.

Groys, B. 1992. *The Total Arts of Stalinism*. Princeton, NJ: Princeton University Press.

Gruen, E. S. 1992. *Culture and National Identity in Republican Rome*. Ithaca, NY: Cornell University Press.

Grünewald, T. 1990. *Constantinus Maximus Augustus: Herrschaftspropaganda in der zeitgenössischen Überlieferung*. Historia Einzelschriften, 64. Stuttgart: Steiner.

Gu, S. 2006. *The Boundaries of Meaning and the Formation of Law*. Montreal: McGill-Queen's University Press.

Guinan, A. K. 2006. *If a Man Builds a Joyful House: Assyriological Studies in Honor of Erle Verdun Leichty*. Leiden: Brill.

Guraya, M. Y. 1982. *Judicial System Under the Holy Prophet and the First Two Dious Caliphs*. Lahore: Himayat al-Islam.

Gurval, R. A. 1995. *Actium and Augustus: The Politics and Emotions of Civil War*. Ann Arbor: University of Michigan Press.

Guthrie, W. K. C. 1962–1981. *A History of Greek Philosophy*. 6 vols. Cambridge: Cambridge University Press.

Gutzwiller, H. 1942. *Die Neujahrsrede des Konsuls Claudius Mamertinus vor dem Kaiser Julian*. Freiburg: Paulus.

Gutzwiller, K. J. 1991. *Theocritus' Pastoral Analogies: The Formation of a Genre*. Madison: University of Wisconsin Press.

_____. 1998. *Poetic Garlands: Hellenistic Epigrams in Context*. Berkeley: University of California Press.

Habinek, T. 1998. *The Politics of Latin Literature, Writing, Identity, and Empire in Ancient Rome*. Princeton, NJ: Princeton University Press.

Hadley, J. M. 2000. *The Cult of Asherah in Ancient Israel and Judah: Evidence for a Hebrew Goddess*. New York: Cambridge University Press.

Hagel, S. 2010. *Ancient Greek Music: A New Technical History*. Cambridge: Cambridge University Press.

Hagg, R. 1983. *The Greek Renaissance of the Eighth Century B.C.: Tradition and Innovation*. Stockhom: Svenska institutet.

Haidar, O. 2008. *The Prose Poem and the Journal Shi'r: A Comparative Study of Literature, Literary Theory and Journalism*. Reading, UK: Ithaca Press.

Halfmann, H. 1979. *Die Senatoren aus dem östlichen Teil des Imperium Romanum bis zum Ende des 2. Jahrhunderts n. Chr.* Hypomnemata, 58. Göttingen: Vandenhoeck and Ruprecht.

_____. 1986. *Itinera principum: Geschichte und Typologie der Kaiserreisen im römischen Reich*. Heidelberger Althistorische Beiträge und Epigraphische Studien, 2. Stuttgart: Steiner.

Hall, C. 2000. *Cultures of Empire: A Reader*. Manchester: Manchester University Press.

Hall, E. 1989. *Inventing the Barbarian*. Oxford: Oxford University Press.

Hall, J. M. 1997. *Ethnic Identity in Greek Antiquity*. Cambridge: Cambridge University Press.

_____. 2002. *Hellenicity: Between Ethnicity and Culture*. Chicago: University of Chicago Press.

Halperin, D. 1983. *Before Pastoral: Theocritus and the Ancient Tradition of Bucolic Poetry*. New Haven: Yale University Press.

Halsborghe, G. H. 1972. *The Cult of Sol Invictus*. Leiden: Brill. Hammer, R., trans.

_____. 1986. *Sifre: A Tannaitic Commentary on the Book of Deuteronomy*. New Haven: Yale University Press.

Hammond, M. 1948. "Ancient Imperialism: Contemporary Justifications." *Harvard Studies in Classical Philology* 58–59: 105–161.

_____. 1951. "Germana patria." *Harvard Studies in Classical Philology* 60: 147–174.

_____. 1957. "Composition of the Senate, A.D. 68–235." *Journal of Roman Studies* 47: 74–81.

Hammond, N. G. L., G. T. Griffith, and F. W. Walbank. 1979. *A History of Macedonia*. Oxford: Clarendon Press.

Hannestad, N. 1988. *Roman Art and Imperial Policy*. Aarhus: Aarhus University Press.

Hanson, A. E. 1997. "Isodorus of Psophthis, Augustan Cultivator: An Update." *Akten der 21. internationalen Papyrologenkongresses (Berlin, 13.–19.8.1995)*, 1: 413–429. B. Kramer, et al., eds. Leipzig: Teubner.

Hare, T. 1999. *Remembering Osiris: Number, Gender, and the Word in Ancient Egyptian Representational Systems*. Stanford: Stanford University Press.

Hariman, R. 1995. *Political Style: The Artistry of Power*. Chicago: University of Chicago Press.

Harl, K. 1987. *Civic Coins and Civic Politics in the Roman East, A.D. 180–275*. Berkeley: University of California Press.

Harland-Jacobs, J. 2007. *Builders of Empire: Freemasons and British Imperialism, 1717–1927*. Chapel Hill: University of North Carolina Press.

Harris, W. V. 1989. *Ancient Literacy*. Cambridge, MA: Harvard University Press.

_____. 1992. *War and Imperialism in Republican*

Rome, 327–70 BC. Oxford: Oxford University Press.

Harrison, A. R. 1968–1971. *The Law of Athens*. Oxford: Oxford University Press.

Harrison, J. E. 1991. *Prolegomena to the Study of Greek Religion*. Princeton, NJ: Princeton University Press.

Harrison, T. 2002. *Greeks and Barbarians*. New York: Routledge.

Haskell, F. 1993. *History and Its Images: Art and the Interpretation of the Past*. New Haven: Yale University Press.

Hassall, M., M. Crawford, and J. Reynolds. 1974. "Rome and the Eastern Provinces at the End of the Second Century B.C.: The So-called 'Piracy Law' and a New Inscription from Cnidos." *Journal of Roman Studies* 64: 195–220.

Hatch, N. O. 1989. *The Democratization of American Christianity*. New Haven: Yale University Press.

Hatzikosta, S. 1982. *A Stylistic Commentary on Theocritus' Idyll VII*. Amsterdam: A.M. Hakkert.

Heather, P. 1991. *Goths and Romans 332–489*. Oxford: Clarendon Press.

Heinze, R. 2000. *Vergil's Epic Technique*. Bristol: Classical Press.

Heisserer, A. J. 1980. *Alexander the Great and the Greeks: The Epigraphic Evidence*. Norman: University of Oklahoma Press.

Henninger, J. 1959. "La religion bedouine preislamique." *L'antica societa beduina*, 115–40, F. Gabreli, ed. Rome: Centro di studi Semitici, Instituto di studi Orientali-Universita.

———. 1981. "Pre-Islamic Bedouin Religion." *Studies on Islam*, 3–22. M. L. Swartz, ed. Oxford: Oxford University Press.

Henry III, P. 1967. "A Mirror for Justinian: The *Ekthesis* of Agapetus Diaconus." *Greek, Roman, and Byzantine Studies* 8: 281–308.

Herington, J. 1985. *Poetry into Drama: Early Tragedy and the Greek Poetic Tradition*. Berkeley: University of California Press.

Herrmann, H. V. 1975. "Hellas." *Reallexikon der Assyriologie und vorderasiatischen Archaologie* (Berlin) 4: 303–311.

Heyman, G. 2007. *The Power of Sacrifice: Roman and Christian Discourses in Conflict*. Washington, DC: Catholic University of America Press.

Hidber, T. 1996. *Das klassizistische Manifest des Dionys von Halikarnass: Die Praefatio zu De oratoribus veteribus*. Stuttgart: Steiner.

Higob, S. K. 1975. *The Cult of Isis Among Women in the Graeco-Roman World*. Leiden: Brill.

Hill, P. V. 1989. *The Monuments of Ancient Rome as Coin Types*. London. B. A. Seaby.

Hinds, S. 1997. *Allusion and Intertext, Dynamics of Appropriation in Roman Poetry*. Cambridge: Cambridge University Press.

Hine, D. 2005. *Works of Hesiod and the Homeric Hymns*. Chicago: University of Chicago Press.

Hirn, Y. 1957. *The Sacred Shrine: A Study of the Poetry and Art of the Catholic Church*. Boston: Beacon Press.

Hobbes, T. 1969. *The Elements of Law*. M.M. Goldsmith, ed. London: Cass.

———. 1971. *A Dialogue Between a Philosopher and a Student*. J. Cropsey, ed. Chicago: University of Chicago Press.

———. 1983. *De Cive*. H. Warrender, ed. Oxford: Oxford University Press.

Hobson, D. W. 1993. "The Impact of Law on Village Life in Roman Egypt." *Law, Politics and Society in the Ancient Mediterranean World*, 193–219. B. Halpern and D. W. Hobson, eds. Sheffield, UK: Sheffield Academic Press.

Hodgson, M. G. S. 1974. *The Venture of Islam*. Chicago: University of Chicago Press.

Hoff, M. C., and S. I. Rotroff, eds. 1997. *The Romanization of Athens*. Oxford: Oxbow.

Hogarth, D. G. 1909. *Ionia and the East*. Oxford: Clarendon Press.

Hollis, A. "Nonnus and Hellenistic Poetry." *Studies in the Dionysiaca of Nonnus*, 43–62. N. Hopkinson, ed. Cambridge: Cambridge University Press.

Hölscher, T. 1967. *Victoria Romana*. Mainz: von Zabern.

Hölscher, T. 1987. *Römische Bildsprache als semantisches System*. Heidelberg: Winter.

Holsher, L. 1986. *The Reality of Mind: St. Augustine's Arguments for Human Soul as a Spiritual Substance*. London: Routledge.

Holum, K. G. 1982. *Theodosian Empresses*. Berkeley: University of California Press.

Honoré, T. 1979. "'Imperial' Rescripts A.D. 193–305: Authorship and Authenticity." *Journal of Roman Studies* 69: 51–64.

———. 1986. "The Making of the Theodosian Code." *Journal of the Savigny Foundation for Legal History, Roman Department* 103: 133–222.

Hood, F. C. 1987. *The Divine Politics: Literalism in the Philosophies of Hobbes, Locke, and Rousseau*. Ithaca, NY: Cornell University Press.

Hooke, S. H. 1963. *Babylonian and Assyrian Religion*. Norman: University of Oklahoma Press.

Hopkins, K. 1978. *Conquerors and Slaves: Sociological Studies in Roman History*. Vol. I. Cambridge: Cambridge University Press.

———. 1980. "Taxes and Trade in the Roman Empire (200 B.C.–A.D. 400)." *Journal of Roman Studies* 70: 101–125.

———. 1991a. "Conquest by Book." *Literacy in the Roman World*, 133–158. Humphrey, ed. Ann Arbor, MI: Journal of Roman Archaeology.

———. 1991b. "From Violence to Blessing: Symbols and Rituals in Ancient Rome." *City States in Classical Antiquity*, 479–498. Molho, Raaflaub, and Emlen, eds. Ann Arbor: University of Michigan Press.

Hopkinson, N. 1994. "Homeric Episodes in Nonnus." *Studies in the Dionysiaca of Nonnus*, 9–42. N. Hopkinson, ed. Cambridge: Cambridge University Press.

Houston, S. D. 2004. *The First Writing: Script Invention as History and Process*. Cambridge: Cambridge University Press.

Howgego, C. J. 1985. *Greek Imperial Countermarks*. Special Publication no. 17. London: Royal Numismatic Society.

_____. 1995. *Ancient History From Coins*. London: Routledge.

Hoyland, R. G. 2001. *Arabia and Arabs: From Bronze Age to the Coming of Islam*. London: Routledge.

_____. 2009. "Arab Kings and Arab Tribes and Beginning of Arab Historical Memory in Late Roman Epigraphy." *From Hellenism to Islam: Cultural and Linguistic Change in the Roman Near East*, 374–400. Cambridge: Cambridge University Press.

Humphrey, J. H., ed. 1991. *Literacy in the Roman World*. JRA Supplement 3. Ann Arbor, MI: Journal of Roman Archaeology.

Hunter, R. L. 1985. *The New Comedy of Greece and Rome*. Cambridge: Cambridge University Press.

Hurwit, J. M. 1999. *The Athenian Acropolis: History, Mythology, and Archaeology from the Neolithic Era to the Present*. Cambridge: Cambridge University Press.

Hutchinson, G. O. 1988. *Hellenistic Poetry*. Oxford: Oxford University Press.

Ibn Khaldun. 1958. *The Muqaddimah: An Introduction to History*, 3 vols. F. Rosenthal, trans. New York: Pantheon Books.

Immerman, R. H. 2010. *Empire for Liberty: A History of American Imperialism from Benjamin Franklin to Paul Wolfowitz*. Princeton, NJ: Princeton University Press.

Immerwahr, H. R. 1989. "Historiography." *The Cambridge History of Classical Literature*. P. E. Easterling and B. M. W. Knox, eds. Cambridge: Cambridge University Press.

_____. 1990. *Attic Scrip: A Survey*. Oxford: Clarendon Press.

Isaac, B. 1996. "Eusebius and the Geography of the Roman Provinces." *The Roman Army in the East*, 153–167. Ann Arbor, MI: Journal of Roman Archaeology.

Isbell, H. 1974. "Decimus Malgnis Ausonius: The Poet and His World." *Latin Literature of the Fourth Century*, 22–57. ed. J. W. Binns London: Routledge & K. Paul.

Jacobsen, T. 1976. *The Treasure of Darkness*. New Haven: Yale University Press.

Janson, T. 1964. *Latin Prose Prefaces: Studies in Literary Conventions*. Acta Universitatis Stockholmiensis, Studia Latina Stockholmiensia, 13. Stockholm: Almqvist and Wiksell.

Jastrow, M. 1905–12. *Die Religion Babyloniens und Assyriens*. Giessen: A. Topelmann.

Jeffery, L. H. 1961. *The Local Scripts of Archaic Greece: A Study of the Origin of the Greek Alphabet and its Development from the Eighth to the Fifth Centuries B.C.* Oxford: Clarendon Press.

Johns, C. H. W. 2000. *The Oldest Code of Laws in the World: The Code of Laws Promulgated by Hammurabi, King of Babylon, B.C. 2285–2242*. Union, NJ: Lawbook Exchange.

Johnson, R. 2003. *British Imperialism*. New York: Palgrave.

Johnston, D. 1984. *The Rhetoric of Leviathan*. Princeton, NJ: Princeton University Press.

Jolliffe, J. E. A. 1967. *The Constitutional History of Medieval England*. London: Adam and Charles Black.

Jolowicz, H. F. 1972. *Historical Introduction to the Studies of Roman Law*. Cambridge: Cambridge Unviersity Press.

Jones, A. H. M. 1960. *Studies in Roman Government and Law*. Oxford: Blackwell

_____. 1964. *The Later Roman Empire*. Oxford: Blackwell.

_____. 1971. *The Cities of the Eastern Roman Provinces*. Oxford: Clarendon Press.

_____. 1974. *The Roman Economy*. Oxford: Blackwell.

Jones, C. P. 1971. *Plutarch and Rome*. Oxford: Clarendon Press.

_____. 1978. *The Roman World of Dio Chrysostom*. Cambridge, MA: Harvard University Press.

Jones, C. P. 1984. "The Sacrae Litterae of 204: Two Colonial Copies." *Chiron* 14: 93–99.

Jones, C. P. 1986. *Culture and Society in Lucian*. Cambridge. MA: Harvard University Press.

Jones, C. P. 1996. "The Panhellenion." *Chiron* 26: 28–56.

Judge, E. A. 1974. "'Res publica restituta': A Modern Illusion?" *Polis and Imperium: Studies in Honour of Edward Togo Salmon*, 279–311. J. A. S. Evans, ed. Toronto: Hakkert.

Jussen, B. 1998. "Liturgie und Legitimation, oder: Wie die Gallo-Romanen das römische Reich beendeten." *Institutionen und Ereignis: Über historische Praktiken und Vorstellungen gesellschaftlichen Ordnens*, 75–136. eds. R. Blänker and B. Jussen. Göttingen: Vandenhoeck and Ruprecht.

Juynboll, G. H. A. 1969. *The Authenticity of the Tradition Literature: Discussions in Modern Egypt*. Leiden: Brill.

_____. 1996. *Studies on the Origins and Uses of Islamic Hadith*. Brookfield, VT: Variorum.

_____. 2008. *Muslim Tradition: Studies in Chronology, Provenance and Authorship of Early*

Hadith. Cambridge: Cambridge University Press.

Kagan, D. 1989. *The Outbreak of the Peloponnesian War*. Ithaca, NY: Cornell University Press.

_____. 1990. *The Archidamian War*. Ithaca, NY: Cornell University Press.

_____. 1991a. *The Peace of Nicias and the Sicilian Expedition*. Ithaca, NY: Cornell University Press.

_____. 1991b. *The Fall of the Athenian Empire*. Ithaca, NY: Cornell University Press.

_____. 2004. *The Peloponnesian War*. New York: Penguin.

Kallet, L. 2001. *Money and the Corrosion of Power in Thucydides: The Sicilian Expedition and its Aftermath*. Berkeley: University of California Press.

Kallet-Marx, L. 1995. "Money Talks: Rhetor, Demos and the Resources of the Athenian Empire." *Ritual, Finance, Politics*, 227–251. R. Osborne and S. Hornblower, eds. Oxford: Clarendon Press.

Kantorowicz, E. 1946. *Laudes Regiae: A Study in Liturgical Acclamations and Mediaeval Ruler Worship*. Berkeley: University of California Press.

_____. 1963. "Oriens Augusti — Lever du Roi." *Dumbarton Oaks Papers* 17: 119–177.

_____. 1965. *Selected Studies*. Locust Valley, NY: J. J. Augustin.

Karamer, M. P. 1992. *Imagining Language in America: From the Revolution to the Civil War*. Princeton, NJ: Princeton University Press.

Karayannopulos, I. 1956. "Konstantin der Grosse und der Kaiserkult." *Historia* 5: 341–357.

Karsh, E. 2006. *Islamic Imperialism: A History*. New Haven: Yale University Press.

Katzoff, R. 1972. "Precedents in the Courts of Roman Egypt." *Journal of the Savigny Foundation for Legal History, Roman Department* 89: 256 – 292.

_____. 1980. "Sources of Law in Roman Egypt: The Role of the Prefect." *Aufstieg und Niedergang der römische Welt* 2.13.807–844.

_____. 1981. "On the Intended Use of P. Col. 123." *Proceedings of the 16th International Congress of Papyrology. American Studies in Papyrology*, 23: 559–573. Chico, CA: Scholars Press.

Keel, O. 1978. *The Symbolism of the Biblical World: Ancient Near Eastern Iconography and the Book of Psalms*. New York: Seabury Press.

Kehoe, D. P. 1988. *The Economics of Agriculture on Roman Imperial Estates in North Africa*. Hypomnemata, 89. Göttingen: Vandenhoeck and Ruprecht.

Keller, M. 2007. *America's Three Regimes: A New Political History*. Oxford: Oxford University Press.

Kelling, J. K. 1992. *A Short History of Western Legal History*. Oxford: Oxford University Press.

Kelly, C., and S. Lovell. 2000. *Russian Literature, Modernism and the Visual Arts*. New York: Cambridge University Press.

Kelly, C. M. 1994. "Later Roman Bureaucracy: Going Through the Files." *Literacy and Power in the Ancient World*, 161–176. A. K. Bowman and G. Woolf, eds. Cambridge: Cambridge University Press.

Kelly, J. N. D. 1975. *Jerome: His Life, Writings and Controversies*. London: Duckworth.

Kelly, J. N. D. 1995. *Golden Mouth: The Story of John Chrysostom, Ascetic, Preacher, Bishop*. Ithaca, NY: Cornell University Press.

Kennedy, D. L., ed. 1996. *The Roman Army in the East. Journal of Roman Archaeology* Supplement 18. Ann Arbor, MI: Journal of Roman Archaeology.

Kennedy, G. A. 1989. "Language and Meaning in Archaic and Classic Greece." *The Cambridge History of Literary Criticism*, 1: 78–91. Kennedy, ed. Cambridge: Cambridge University Press.

Kenyon, J. P. 1986. *The Stuart Constitution 1603–1688*. Cambridge: Cambridge University Press.

Kerby-Fulton, K. 1990. *Reformist Apocalypticism and Piers Plowman*. Cambridge: Cambridge University Press.

_____, and D. L. Despres. 1999. *Iconography and the Professional Reader*. Minneapolis: University of Minnesota Press.

Kerenyi, K. 1975. *Zeus and Hera: Archetypal Image of Father, Husband, and Wife*. C. Holme, trans. London: Routledge & Kegan.

_____. 1980. *The Gods of the Greeks*. New York: Thames and Hudson.

Kern, F. 2006. *Kingship and Law in Middle Ages*. S. B. Chrimes, trans. New York: The Lawbook Exchange.

Kienast, D. 1982a. *Augustus: Prinzeps und Monarch*. Darmstadt: Wissenschaftliche Buchgesellschaft.

_____. 1982b. "Corpus imperii:" *Romanitas Christianitas: Untersuchungen zur Geschichte und Literatur der römischen Kaiserzeit*, 1–17. J. Straub et al., eds. Berlin: W. de Gruyter.

_____. 1990. *Römische Kaisertabelle*. Darmstadt: Wissenschaftliche Buchgesellschaft.

Kim, H. J. 2009. *Ethnicity and Foreigners in Ancient Greece and China*. London: Duckworth.

Kirk, G. S. 2008. "The Development of Ideas, 750–500 B.C." *The Cambridge Ancient History, 4, Persia, Greece and the Western Mediterranean C. 525 to 479 B.C.*, 32–56. Boardman, Bowman, Bury, and Cameron, eds. Cambridge: Cambridge University Press.

Kirk, G. S., M.W. Edwards, R. Janko, J. B. Hainsworth, and N. J. Richardson. 1985–1993. *The Iliad: A Commentary*. Cambridge: Cambridge University Press.

Kirk, G. S., J. E. Raven, and M. Schofield. 1983.

The Presocratic Philosophers. Cambridge: Cambridge University Press.

Klein, R. 1981. *Die Romrede des Aelius Aristides.* Darmstadt: Wissenschaftliche Buchgesellschaft.

Klein, R. 1986. "Die Romidee bei Symmachus, Claudian und Prudentius." *Colloque genevois sur Summaque,* 119–144. F. Paschoud, ed. Paris: Les Belles Lettres.

Klingner, F. 1927. "Rom als Idee." *Das Antike* 3: 17–34.

Kneissl, P. 1969. *Die Siegestitulatur der römischen Kaiser.* Hypomnemata, 23. Göttingen: Vandenhoeck and Ruprecht.

Knoche, U. 1952. "Die augusteische Ausprägung der Dea Roma." *Gymnasium* 59: 324–349.

Knohl, I. 2000. *The Messiah Before Jesus: The Suffering Servant of the Dead Sea Scrolls.* Berkeley: University of California Press.

Knysh, A. 2000. *Islamic Mysticism: A Short History.* Leiden: Brill.

Koenen, L. 1993. "The Ptolemaic King as a Religious Figure." *Images and Ideologies: Self-definition in the Hellenistic World,* 25–115. A. Bulloch et al., eds. Hellenistic Culture and Society, no. 12. Berkeley: University of California Press.

_____, and D. B. Thompson. 1984. "Gallus as Triptolemos on the Tazza Farnese." *The Bulletin of the American Society of Papyrologists* 21: 111–156.

König, I. 1987. *Origo Constantini, Anonymus Valesianus, Teil I: Text und Kommentar.* Trierer Historische Forschungen, 11. Trier: Trierer Historische Forschungen.

Konstan, D. 1983. *Roman Comedy.* Ithaca, NY: Cornell University Press.

Kramer, L. 1984. *Music and Poetry: The Nineteenth Century and After.* Berkeley: University of California Press.

Kramer, S. N. 1956. *Twenty-five Firsts in Man's Recorded History: From the Tablets of Sumer.* Indian Hills, CO: Falcon's Wing Press.

_____. 1969. *The Sacred Marriage Rite, Myth, and Ritual Aspects of Faith in Sumer.* Bloomington: Indiana University Press.

_____. 1981. *History Begins at Sumer.* Philadelphia: University of Pennsylvania Press.

_____. 1989. *Myth of Enki, the Crafty God.* Oxford: Oxford University Press.

_____. 1997. *Sumerian Mythology: A Study of Spiritual and Literary Achievement in the Third Millennium B.C.* Philadelphia: University of Pennsylvania Press.

Kraus, C. S. 1988. "Verba Tene: Form and Style in Livy." Dissertation, Harvard University.

_____, J. Marincola, and C. B. R. Pelling, eds. 2010. *Ancient Historiography and its Contexts: Studies in Honour of A.J. Woodman.* Oxford: Oxford University Press

Kretzmer, D. 1984. "Transformation of Tort Liability in the Nineteenth Century: The Visible Hand." *Oxford Journal of Legal Studies 4:* 46.

Kroll, J. H. 1997. "Coinage as an Index of Romanization." *The Romanization of Athens,* 135–150. Hoff and Rotroff, eds. Oxford: Oxbow.

Krostenko, B. A. 2001. *Cicero, Catullus, and Language of Social Performance.* Chicago: University of Chicago Press.

Kuhrt, A. 1995. *The Ancient Near East c. 3000–330 B.C.* London: Routledge.

Kuttner, A. 1995. *Dynasty and Empire in the Age of Augustus: The Case of the Boscoreale Cups.* Berkeley: University of California Press.

Laberius, D., and C. Panayotakis. 2010. *Decimus Laberius: the Fragments.* Cambridge: Cambridge University Press.

Lambert, W. G. 1960. *Babylonian Wisdom Literature.* Oxford: Clarendon Press.

_____, A. R. Millard, and M. Civil. 1999. *Atrahas-is: The Babylonian Story of the Flood.* Winona Lake, IN: Eisenbrauns.

Lamberton, R. 1986. *Homer the Theologian: Neoplatonist Allegorical Reading and the Growth of the Epic Tradition.* Berkeley: University of California Press.

Landels, J. G. 1999. *Music in Ancient Greece and Rome.* London: Routledge.

Landers, B. 2010. *Empires Apart: A History of American and Russian Imperialism.* New York: Pegasus Books and W. W. Norton.

Lane Fox, R. 1986. *Pagans and Christians.* New York: Knopf.

Langdon, S. 1919. *Sumerian Liturgies and Psalms.* Philadelphia: University of Pennsylvania Museum.

de Lange, N. R. M. 1978. "Jewish Attitudes to the Roman Empire." *Imperialism in the Ancient World,* 255–281. P. D. Garnsey and C. R. Whittaker, eds. Cambridge: Cambridge University Press.

Larrain, J. 1979. *The Concept of Ideology.* London: Hutchinson and Co.

Lassèrre, F. 1982. "Strabon devant l'empire romain." *Aufstieg und Niedergang der römische Welt* 2.30.1.867–896.

Latte, K. 1960. *Römische Religionsgeschichte.* Munich: Beck.

Lauffer, S. 1971. *Diokletians Preisedikt.* Berlin: de Gruyter.

Laurentin, R. 1965. *The Question of Mary.* New York: Holt, Rinehart and Winston.

Lawler, M. L. 1964. *The Dance of Ancient Greek Theatre.* Iowa City: University of Iowa Press.

Layton, S. 2005. *Russian Literature and Empire: Conquest of the Caucasus from Pushkin to Tolstoy.* Cambridge: Cambridge University Press.

Leask, N. 1992. *British Romantic Writers and the East: Anxieties of Empire.* Cambridge: Cambridge University Press.

_____, and P. Connell. 2009. *Romanticism and Popular Culture in Britain and Ireland.* Cambridge: New York: Cambridge University Press.

Leatherbarrow, W. J., and D. Offord. 2010. *A History of Russian Thought.* Cambridge: Cambridge University Press.

Lecker, M. 2000. "On the Brurial of Martyrs in Islam." *The Concept of Territory in Islamic law and Thought*, 34–49. Y. Hiroyuri, ed. London: Kegan Paul.

Lefkowitz, M. 2003. *Greek Gods, Human Lives: What We Can Learn from Myths.* New Haven: Yale University Press.

Lehman, W. 1985. "The First English Law." *The Journal of Legal History* 6 (19): 1–32.

Leishman, J. B. 1956. *Translating Horace: Thirty Odes Translated into the Original Metres with the Latin Text and an Introductiory and Critical Essay.* Oxford: Oxford University Press.

Lendon, J. E. 1990. "The Face on the Coins and Inflation in Roman Egypt." *Klio* 72: 106–134.

Lendon, J. E. 1997. *Empire of Honour: The Art of Government in the Roman World.* Oxford: Clarendon Press.

Lenhart, C. S. 1956. *Musical Influence on American Poetry.* Athens: University of Georgia Press.

Lerner, R. 1983. *The Power of Prophecy: The Cedar of Lebanon Vision from the Mongol Onslaught to the Dawn of the Enlightenment.* Berkeley: University of California Press.

Levick, B. 1967. *Roman Colonies in Southern Asia Minor.* Oxford: Clarendon Press.

_____. 1978. "Concordia at Rome." *Scripta Nummaria Romana: Essays Presented to Humphrey Sutherland*, 217–233. R. A. G. Carson and C. M. Kraay, eds. London: Spink and Son.

_____. 1982. "Propaganda and the Imperial Coinage." *Antichthon* 16: 104–116.

_____. 1983. "The *senatus consultum* from Larinum." *Journal of Roman Studies* 73: 97–115.

_____. 1986. "'Caesar omnia habet': Property and Politics under the Principate." *EntrHardt* 33: 187–218.

_____. 1990. *Claudius.* New Haven: Yale University Press.

Lewis, R. G. 1993. "Imperial Autobiography: Augustus to Hadrian." *Aufstieg und Niedergang der römische Welt* 2.34.1.629–706.

Ley, G. 2007. *The Theatricality of Greek Tragedy: Playing Space and Chorus.* Chicago: University of Chicago Press.

Leyser, H. 1984. *Hermits and the New Monasticism: A Study of Religious Communities in Western Europe 1000–1150.* New York: St. Martin's Press.

Lieberman, F. 1902–1916. *Die Gesetze der Angelsachsen.* 3 vols. Halle: S. Max Niemeyer.

Lieberman, S. 1944. "Roman Legal Institutions in Early Rabbinics and in the *Acta Martyrum.*" *Jewish Quarterly Review* 35: 1–57.

_____. 1946a. "Palestine in the Third and Fourth Centuries, I–II." *Jewish Quarterly Review* 36: 329–370.

_____. 1946b. "Palestine in the Third and Fourth Centuries, III." *Jewish Quarterly Review* 37: 31–54.

_____. 1962. *Hellenism in Jewish Palestine.* New York: Jewish Theological Seminary of America.

Liebeschuetz, J. H. W. G. 1979. *Continuity and Change in Roman Religion.* Oxford: Clarendon Press.

_____. 1989. *Barbarians and Bishops: Army, Church, and State in the Age of Arcadius and Chrysostom.* Oxford: Clarendon Press.

_____. 2001. *Decline and Fall of the Roman City.* Oxford: Oxford University Press.

_____. 2006. *Decline and Change in Late Antiquity: Religion, Barbarians and their Historiography.* Burlington, VT: Ashgate.

Lieu, S. N. C. 1986. *The Emperor Julian: Panegyric and Polemic.* Liverpool: Liverpool University Press.

Lintott, A. 1982. "The Roman Judiciary Law from Tarentum." *Zeitschrift für Papyrologie und Epigraphik* 45: 127–138.

Lintott, A. 1993. *Imperium Romanum.* London: Routledge.

Lippold, A. 1968. "Herrscherideal und Traditionsverbundenheit im Panegyricus des Pacatus." *Historia* 17: 228–250.

Livingstone, A. 1989. *Court Poetry and Literary Miscellanea.* Helsinki: Helsinki University Press.

Lloyd-Jones, H. 1971. *The Justice of Zeus.* Berkeley, University of California Press.

Llyne, R. A. M. 1989. *Words and the Poet: Characteristic Techniques of Style in Vergil's Aeneid.* Oxford: Oxford University Press.

Long, A. A. 1999. *The Cambridge Companion to Early Greek Philosophy.* Cambridge: Cambridge University Press.

Longfellow, B. 2011. *Roman Imperialism and Civic Patronage: Form, Meaning, and Ideology in Monumental Fountain Complexes.* New York: Cambridge University Press.

Low, P. 2008. *The Athenian Empire.* Edinburgh: Edinburgh University Press.

Lowe, N. J. 2007. *Comedy.* Cambridge: Cambridge University Press.

Luce, T. J. 1990. "Livy, Augustus, and the Forum Augustum." *Between Republic and Empire: Interpretations of Augustus and His Principate*, 123–138. Raaflaub and Toher, eds. Berkeley: University of California Press.

Lukaszewicz, A. 1981. "A Petition from Priests to Hadrian with His Subscription." *Proceedings of the 16th International Congress of Papyrology* (New York, 1980), *American Studies in Papyrology* 23, 357–361. Chico, CA: Scholars Press.

Lupoi, M. 2000. *The Origins of the European Legal Order*. A. Belton, trans. Cambridge: Cambridge University Press.

Lust, A. 2000. *From the Greek Mimes to Marcel Marceau and Beyond: Mimes, Actors, Pierrots, and Clowns: A Chronicle of the Many Visages of Mime in the Theatre*. Lanham, MD: Scarecrow Press.

Luttwak, E. 1976. *The Grand Strategy of the Roman Empire from the First Century A.D. to the Third*. Baltimore: Johns Hopkins University Press.

MacCormack, S. 1975a. "Latin Prose Panegyrics." *Empire and Aftermath*, 143–205. T. A. Dorey, ed. London: RKP.

_____. 1975b. "Roma, Constantinopolis, the Emperor, and his Genius." *Classical Quarterly* 25: 131–150.

_____. 1981. *Art and Ceremony in Late Antiquity. The Transformation of the Classical Heritage*, 1. Berkeley: University of California Press.

MacCoull, L. S. B. 1984. "The Panegyric on Justin II by Dioscorus of Aphrodite." *Byzantion* 54: 575–585.

_____. 1988. *Dioscorus of Aphrodito: His Work and His World*. Berkeley: University of California Press.

MacDonald, M. J. A. 2000. "Reflections on the Linguistic Map of pre–Islamic Arabia." *Arabian Archaeology and Epigraphy* ii: 28–79.

MacDonald, W.L. 1982. *The Architecture of the Roman Empire*. Vol. 1, *An Introductory Study*. 2d ed. New Haven: Yale University Press.

_____. 1986. *The Architecture of the Roman Empire*. Vol. 2, *An Urban Appraisal*. New Haven: Yale University Press.

MacDowell, D. M. 1978. *The Law in Classical Athens*. Ithaca, NY: Cornell University Press.

Mackay, E. A. 1999. *The Oral Tradition and Its Influence in the Greek and Roman World*. Leiden: Brill.

Mackenzie, J. M. 1986. *Imperialism and Popular Culture*. Manchester: Manchester University Press.

Macleod, C. 1982. *Homer, Iliad, Book 24*. Cambridge: Cambridge University Press.

MacMullen, R. 1981. *Paganism in Roman Empire*. New Haven: Yale University Press.

_____. 1982. "The Epigraphic Habit in the Roman Empire." *American Journal of Philology* 103: 233–246.

_____. 1990. *Changes in the Roman Empire*. Princeton, NJ: Princeton University Press.

Macready, S., and F. H. Thompson, eds. 1987. *Roman Architecture in the Greek World*. Society of Antiquaries of London, Occasional Papers, n.s., 10.

Magie, D. 1950. *Roman Rule in Asia Minor to the End of the Third Century after Christ*. Princeton, NJ: Princeton University Press.

Mahmassani, S. 1961. *Falsafat al-tashri fi al-Islam, The Philosophy of Jurisprudence in Islam*. Leiden: Brill.

Maitland, F. W. 1987. *Domesday Book and Beyond: Three Essays in the History of England*. Cambridge: Cambridge University Press.

_____. 1989. *The Forms of Action at Common Law*. Cambridge: Cambridge University Press.

_____. 1999. *The Collected Papers of Frederic William Maitland*. H. A. L. Fisher, ed. Holmes Beach, FL: Gaunt.

Majno, G. 1975. *The Healing Hand: Man and Wound in the Ancient World*. Cambridge, MA: Harvard University Press.

Makdisi, S. 1998. *Romantic Imperialism*. Cambridge: Cambridge University Press.

Malkin, I., and Z. W. Rubinsohn, eds. 1995. *Leaders and Masses in the Roman World: Studies in Honor of Z. Yavetz*. Leiden: Brill.

Margoliouth, J. P. 1909. *Extracts from the Ecclesiastical History of John, Bishop of Ephesus*. Semitic Studies Series, 13. Leiden: Brill.

Markensinis, B. S. 1990. *The German Law of Torts*. Oxford: Oxford University Press.

Markus, R. 1990. *The End of Ancient Christianity*. Cambridge: Cambridge University Press.

Marsh, R. J. 1986. *Soviet Fiction Since Stalin: Science, Literature and Politics*. London: Croom Helm.

_____. 1989. *Images of Dictatorship: Stalin in Literature*. London: Routledge.

_____. 2007. *Literature, History and Identity in Post-Soviet Russia, 1991–2006*. New York: Peter Lang.

Martindale, C. 1997. *Cambridge Companion to Virgil*. Cambridge: Cambridge University Press.

Mascush, M. 1998. *Origins of Individual Self-autobiography and Self-identity in England, 1591–1791*. Stanford: Stanford University Press.

Mason, H. J. 1974. *Greek Terms for Roman Institutions: A Lexicon and Analysis*. American Studies in Papyrology, 13. Toronto: Hakkert.

Matthews, G. B. 1992. *Thought's Ego in Augustine and Descartes*. Ithaca, NY: Cornell University Press.

_____. 1999. *The Augustinian Tradition*. Berkeley: University of California Press.

Matthews, J. F. 1974. "The Letters of Symmachus. *Latin Literature of the Fourth Century*, 58–99. J. W. Binns, ed. London: RKP.

_____. 1975. *Western Aristocracies and Imperial Court, A.D. 364–425*. Oxford: Clarendon Press.

_____. 1989. *The Roman Empire of Ammianus Marcellinus*. Baltimore: Johns Hopkins University Press.

_____. 1993. "The Making of the Text." *The Theodosian Code: Studies in the Imperial Law of Late Antiquity*, 19–44. J. Harries and I. Wood, eds. London: Duckworth.

Mathewson, R. 1975. *The Positive Hero in Russian Literature.* Stanford: Stanford University Press.

Mathiesen, T. J. 1999. *Apollo's Lyre, Greek Music and Music Theory in Antiquity and Middle Age.* Lincoln: University of Nebraska Press.

Mattingly, D. J. 1996. *The Athenian Empire Restored: Epigraphic and Historical Studies* Ann Arbor: University of Michigan Press.

_____. 1997. *Dialogues in Roman Imperialism: Power, Discourse, and Discrepant Experience in the Roman Empire.* Portsmouth, RI: Journal of Roman Archaeology.

Mattingly, H. B. 1996. "The Language of Athenian Imperialism." *The Athenian Empire Restored*, 361–85. Mattingly, ed. Ann Arbor: University of Michigan Press.

Mawer, I. 1960. *The Art of Mime: Its History and Technique in Education and Theater.* London: Methuen & Co.

McCarter, P. K. 1975. *The Antiquity of the Greek Alphabet and the Early Phoenician Scripts.* Cambridge, MA: Harvard University Press.

McCormick, M. 1986. *Eternal Victory.* Cambridge: Cambridge University Press.

McDonald, M. V. 1978. "Orally Transmitted Poetry in Pre-Islamic Arabia and Other Pre-Literate Societies." *Journal of Arabic Literature* 9: 14–31.

McGregor., M. F. 1987. *The Athenians and Their Empire.* Vancouver: University of British Columbia Press.

Megow, W.-R. 1987. *Kameen von Augustus bis Alexander Severus.* DAI, Antike Münzen und Geschnittene Steine, 11. Berlin: de Gruyter.

Meiggs, R. 1988. *A Selection of Greek Historical Inscriptions to the End of the Fifth Century B.C.* Oxford: Clarendon Press.

_____. 1972. *The Athenian Empire*: Oxford: Clarendon Press.

Mellor, R. 1975. Qea; JRwvmh: *The Worship of the Goddess Roma in the Greek World.* Göttingen: Vandenhoeck and Ruprecht.

Melville, H. 1967. *Moby Dick.* New York: W. W. Norton.

Melville, S. C., and A. L. Slotsky. 2010. *Opening the Tablet Box: Near Eastern Studies in Honor of Benjamin R. Foster.* Leiden: Brill.

Meyendorff, J. 1981. *Byzntium and the Rise of Russia.* Cambridge: Cambridge University Press.

Mierse, W. 1990. "Augustan Building Programs in the Western Provinces." *Between Republic and Empire: Interpretations of Augustus and his Principate*, 308–333. Raaflaub and Toher, eds. Berkeley: University of California Press.

Millar, F. G. B. 1964. *A Study of Cassius Dio.* Oxford: Clarendon Press.

_____. 1969. "P. Herennius Dexippus: The Greek World and the Third-century Invasions." *Journal of Roman Studies* 59: 12–29.

_____. 1971. "Paul of Samosata, Zenobia, and Aurelian: The Church, Local Culture, and Political Allegiance in Third-century Syria." *Journal of Roman Studies* 61: 1–17.

_____. 1977. *The Emperor in the Roman World.* Ithaca, NY: Cornell University Press.

_____. 1981a. *The Roman Empire and its Neighbors.* New York: Holmes and Meier.

_____. 1981b. "The World of *The Golden Ass.*" *Journal of Roman Studies* 71: 63–75.

_____. 1984. "State and Subject: The Impact of Monarchy." *Caesar Augustus: Seven Aspects*, 37–60. Millar and Segal, eds. Oxford: Clarendon Press.

_____. 1989. "'Senatorial' Provinces: An Institutionalized Ghost." *Ancient World* 20: 93–97.

_____. 1991. "Les congiaires à Rome et la monnaie." *Nourrir la plèbe: Actes du colloque tenu a Genève … en hommage à Denis van Berchem*, 143–159. A. Giovannini, ed. Basel: Freidrich Reinhardt.

_____. 1993a. "Ovid and the *Domus Augusta*: Rome Seen from Tomoi." *Journal of Roman Studies* 83: 1–17.

_____. 1993b. *The Roman Near East 31 B. C.–A. D. 337.* Cambridge, MA: Harvard University Press.

Millar, F., and E. Segal, eds. 1984. *Caesar Augustus: Seven Aspects.* Oxford: Clarendon Press.

Miller, M. C. 1997. *Athens and Persia in the Fifth Century B.C.: A study in Cultural Receptivity.* New York: Cambridge University Press.

Miller, P. D. 1994. *They Cried to the Lord: The Form and Theology of Biblical Prayer.* Minneapolis: Fortress Press.

Mills, S. 1997. *Theseus, Tragedy and the Athenian Empire.* Oxford: Clarendon Press.

Milne, H. J. M. 1934. *Greek Shorthand Manuals: Syllabary and Commentary.* London: Egypt Exploration Society.

Milsom, S. F. C. 1976. *The Legal Framework of English Feudalism: The Maitland Lectures Given in 1972.* Cambridge: Cambridge University Press.

_____. 1981. *Historical Foundations of the Common Law.* Toronto: Butterworths.

Minkova, D. 2003. *Alliteration and Sound Change in Early English.* Cambridge: Cambridge University Press.

Mitchell, S. 1976. "Requisitioned Transport in the Roman Empire: A New Inscription from Pisidia." *Journal of Roman Studies* 66: 106–131.

Mitchell, S. 1984. "The Greek City in the Roman World — The Case of Pontus and Bithynia." *Acts of the 8th International Congress of Greek and Latin Epigraphy, Athens, 1982* 1: 120–133. Athens: Hypourgeio Politismou kai Epistemon.

_____. 1987a. "Imperial Building in the Eastern

Provinces." *Harvard Studies in Classical Philology* 91: 333–365.

_____. 1988. "Maximinus and the Christians in A.D. 312: A New Latin Inscription." *Journal of Roman Studies* 78: 105–124.

_____. 1993. *Anatolia: Land, Men, and Gods in Asia Minor.* Oxford: Clarendon Press.

Mitford, T. B. 1991. "Inscriptiones Ponticae — Sebastopolis." *Zeitschrift für Papyrologie und Epigraphik* 87: 181–243.

Mitteis, L. 1891. *Reichsrecht und Volksrecht in den östlichen Provinzen des römischen Kaiserreichs.* Leipzig: Teubner.

Mitthof, F. 1993. "Vom: Die Ehrenprädikate in der Titulatur der Thronfolger des 3. Jh. n. Chr. nach den Papyri." *Zeitschrift für Papyrologie und Epigraphik* 99: 97–111.

Molho, A., K. Raaflaub, and J. Emlen, eds. 1991. *City States in Classical Antiquity and Medieval Italy.* Ann Arbor: University of Michigan Press.

Momigliano, A. 1986. "Some Preliminary Remarks on the 'Religious Opposition' to the Roman Empire." *EntrHardt* 33: 103–133.

_____. 1987. *On Pagans, Jews, and Christians.* Middletown: Wesleyan University Press.

Mondi, R. 1990. "Greek and Near Eastern Mythology." *Approaches to Greek Myth*, 141–98. L. Edmunds, ed. Baltimore: Johns Hopkins University Press.

Moosa, E. 2005. *Ghazali and the Poetics of Imagination.* Chapel Hill: University of North Carolina Press.

Morford M. P. O., and L. J. Lenardon. 2006. *Classical Mythology.* Oxford University Press.

Mornroe, J. T. 1972. "Oral Composition in Pre-Islamic Poetry." *Journal of Arabic Literature* 3: 1–53.

Morris, R. L. B. 1981. "Reflections of Citizen Attitudes in Petitions from Roman Oxyrhynchus." *Proceedings of the 16th International Congress of Papyrology* (New York, 1980), *American Studies in Papyrology* 23, 363–370. Chico, CA: Scholars Press.

Moser, C. A. 1992. *The Cambridge History of Russian Literature.* Cambridge: Cambridge University Press.

Muhly, J. D. 1970. "Homer and the Phoenicians: The Relations Between Greece and the Near East in the Late Bronze and Early Iron Ages." *Berytus* 19: 19–64.

Mullen, E. T. 1980. *The Divine Council in Canaanite and Early Hebrew Literature.* Chico, CA: Scholars Press.

Mullen, W. 1982. *Choreia: Pindar and Dance.* Princeton, NJ: Princeton University Press.

Müller-Rettig, B. 1990. *Der Panegyricus des Jahres 310 auf Konstantin den Grossen.* Stuttgart: Steiner.

Murray, R. 1975. *Symbols of Church and Kingdom: A Study in Early Syriac Tradition.* Cambridge: Cambridge University Press.

Musurillo, H. 1954. *The Acts of the Pagan Martyrs.* 2d ed. Oxford: Clarendon Press.

Myers, K. S. 1994. *Ovid's Causes Cosmogony and Aetiology in the Metamorphoses.* Ann Arbor: University of Michigan Press.

Neer, R. 1995. "The Lion's Eye: Imitation and Understanding in Attic Red-figure." *Representations* 51: 118–53.

Nelson, C. A. 1979. *Status Declarations in Roman Egypt. American Studies in Papyrology* 19. Amsterdam: Hakkert.

Neri, V. 1997. "L'usurpatore come tiranno nel lessico politico della tarda antichità." *Usurpationen in der Spätantike*, 71–86. F. Paschoud and J. Szidat, eds.. Stuttgart: Steiner.

Nicholson, R. A. 1969. *A Literary History of the Arabs.* London: Cambridge University Press.

Nicolet, C. 1991. *Space, Geography and Politics in the Early Roman Empire.* Ann Arbor: University of Michigan Press.

Nicolet, C. 1993. "Constantinus Oriens Imperator: Propaganda and Panegyric: On Reading Panegyric 7 (307)." *Historia* 24: 229–246.

Nicolet, C. 1995. "La Tabula Siarensis, la plèbe urbaine et les statues de Germanicus." *Leaders and Masses in the Roman World: Studies in Honor of Z. Yavetz*, 115–127. Malkin and Rubinsohn, eds. Leiden: Brill.

Nicolet, C. 1996. *Financial Documents and Geographical Knowledge in the Roman World.* Oxford: Leopard's Head Press.

Nilsson, M. P., and H. J. Rose. 1948. *Greek Piety.* Oxford: Clarendon Press.

Ninkovich, F. A. 2001. *The United States and Imperialism.* Malden, MA: Blackwell.

Nissen, H. 1988. *The Early History of the Ancient Near East, 9000–2000 B.C.* Chicago: University of Chicago Press.

Nixon, C. E. V. 1983. "Latin Panegyric in the Tetrarchic and Constantinian Period." *History and Historians in Late Antiquity*, 88–99. B. Croke and A. Emmett, eds. Sydney: Pergamon Press.

Nixon, C. E. V., and B. S. Rodgers. 1994. *In Praise of Later Roman Emperors: The Panegyrici Latini.* Berkeley: University of California Press.

Nock, A. D. 1972. *Essays on Religion and the Ancient World.* Z. Stewart, ed. Oxford: Clarendon Press.

Noll, K. L. 2001. *Canaan and Israel in Antiquity: An Introduction.* London: Sheffield Academic Press.

North, J. 1992. "The Development of Religious Pluralism." *The Jews Among Pagans and Christians in the Roman Empire*, 174–193. J. Lieu, et al., eds. London: Routledge.

Noy, D. 2000. *Foreigners at Rome: Citizens and Strangers*, London: Duckworth.

Nunn, J. F. 1996. *Ancient Egyptian Medicine.* Norman: University of Oklahoma Press.

Oakley, S. P. 1997. *A Commentary on Livy Book vi–x*, Oxford: Oxford University Press.

Ober, J. 1982. "Tiberius and the Political Testament of Augustus." *Historia* 31: 306 – 328.

Obeyesekere, G. 1996. *The Apotheosis of Captain Cook: European Mythmaking in the Pacific.* Princeton, NJ: Princeton University Press.

Obolensky, D. 1971. *Byzantine and Slaves: Collected Studies.* London: Variorum.

O'Brien, J. V., and W. Major. 1982. *In the Beginning: Creation Myths from Ancient Mesopotamia, Israel and Greece.* Chicago: Scholars Press.

O'Hara, J. J. 1996. *True Names. Vergil and the Alexandrian Tradition of Etymological Wordplay.* Ann Arbor: University of Micigan Press.

Oliensis, E. 1998. *Horace and the Rhetoric of Authority.* Cambridge: Cambridge University Press.

Oppeheim, A. L. 1964. *Ancient Mesopotamia.* Chicago: University of Chicago Press.

Osborne, R. 2000. *The Athenian Empire.* London: Association of Classical Teachers.

Ostrow, S. E. 1990. "The *Augustales* in the Augustan Scheme." *Between Republic and Empire: Interpretations of Augustus and his Principate*, 364–379. K. Raaflaub, M. Toher, G. W. Bowersock et al., eds. Berkeley: University of California Press.

Ostrowski, J. A. 1990. "*Simulacra Barbarorum:* Some Questions of Roman Personifications." *Akten des XIII. internationalen Kongresses für klassische Archäologie, Berlin, 1988*, 566–567. Mainz: von Zabern.

Ostrowski, J. A. 1996. "Personifications of Countries and Cities as a Symbol of Victory in Greek and Roman Art." *Griechenland und Rom*, 264–272. E. G. Schmidt, ed. Tbilissi: Univ. Verl; Erlangen: Jean Palm and Enke.

Ovid. 1998. *Metamorphoses, Book II.* A.D. Melville, ed. E. J. Kenney, trans. Oxford: Oxford University Press.

Oxford History of the British Empire, vol. 1–3. 1998. W. R. Louis, A. M. Low, and N. P. Canny, eds. Oxford: Oxford University Press, 1998.

Packman, Z. M. 1991. "Notes on Papyrus Texts with the Roman Imperial Oath." *Zeitschrift für Papyrologie und Epigraphik* 89: 91–102.

_____. 1992a. "Epithets with the Title *Despotes* in Regnal Formulas, in Document Dates, and in the Imperial Oath." *Zeitschrift für Papyrologie und Epigraphik* 90: 251–257.

_____. 1992b. "Further Notes on Texts with the Imperial Oath." *Zeitschrift für Papyrologie und Epigraphik* 90: 258.

_____. 1994. "Still Further Notes on Papyrus Documents with the Imperial Oath." *Zeitschrift für Papyrologie und Epigraphik* 100: 207–210.

Pagden, A. R. 1987. *The Languages of Political Theory in Early-modern Europe.* Cambridge: Cambridge University Press.

_____. 1995. *Lords of All the World: Ideologies of Empire in Spain, Britain and France, c. 1500– c. 1800.* New Haven: Yale University Press.

_____. 2000. *Facing Each Other: The World's Perception of Europe and Europe's Perception of the World.* Aldershot: Ashgate.

Page, D. L., and A. S. F. Gow., eds. 1965. *The Greek Anthology: Hellenistic Epigrams.* 2 vols. Cambridge: Cambridge University Press.

_____. 1981. *Further Greek Epigrams: Epigrams Before A.D. 50 from the Greek Anthology and Other Sources, Not Included in Hellenistic Epigrams or the Garland of Philip.* Cambridge: Cambridge University Press.

_____. 2008. *The Greek Anthology: The Garland of Philip and Some Contemporary Epigrams.* Cambridge: Cambridge University Press.

Paige, N. D. 2001. *Being Interior: Autobiography and the Contradictions of Modernity in Seventeenth-century France.* Philadelphia: University of Pennsylvania Press.

Paley, M. D. 1996. *Coleridge's Later Poetry.* Oxford: Oxford University Press.

Palm, J. 1959. *Rom, Römertum und Imperium in der griechischen Literatur der Kaiserzeit.* Lund: Gleerup.

Palmer, R. C. 1982. *County Courts of Medieval England.* Princeton, NJ: Princeton University Press.

Parfitt, G. 1992. *English Poetry of the Seventeenth Century.* Berkeley: University of California Press.

Parker, R. 1996. *Athenian Religion: A History.* Oxford: Clarendon Press.

Parker, R. 1983. *Miasma.* Oxford: Clarendon Press.

Parker, R. W. 1991. "Potamon of Mytilene and his Family." *Zeitschrift für Papyrologie und Epigraphik* 85: 115–129.

Parkinson, R. 1991. *Voices from Ancient Egypt: An Anthology of Middle Kingdom Writings.* London: British Museum.

Patai, R. 1990. *The Hebrew Goddess.* Detroit, MI: Wayne State University Press.

Patrides, C. A., and J. Wittreich, eds. 1984. *The Apocalypse in English Renaissance Thought and Literature.* Ithaca, NY: Cornell University Press.

Pattison, B. 1970. *Music and Poetry of English Renaissance.* London: Methuen.

Pattison, G., and D. O. Thompson. 2001. *Dostoevsky and the Christian Tradition.* Cambridge: Cambridge University Press.

Peachin, M. 1990. *Roman Imperial Titulature and Chronology, A.D. 235–284.* Amsterdam: Gieben.

Peachin, M. 1996. *Iudex vice Caesaris: Deputy Emperors and the Administration of Justice During the Principate.* Stuttgart: Steiner.

Penchansky, D. 2005. *Twilight of the Gods: Polytheism in the Hebrew Bible*. Louisville, KY: Westminster John Knox Press.

Pendergast, J. S. 2006. *Religion, Allegory, and Literacy in Early Modern England, 1560–1640: The Control of the Word*. Burlington, VT: Ashgate.

Peterson, R. 1993. *A History of Russian Symbolism*. Philadelphia: J. Benjamins.

Piehler, P. 1971. *The Visionary Landscape: A Study in Medieval Allegory*. London, Edward Arnold.

Pinch, G. 2004. *Egyptian Mythology: A Guide to the Gods, Goddesses, and Traditions of Ancient Egypt*. Oxford: Oxford University Press.

Plato. 2000. *The Republic*. G.R.F. Ferrari, Tom Griffith, eds. and trans. Cambridge: Cambridge University Press.

Platt, K. M. F. 1997. *History in a Grotesque Key: Russian Literature and the Idea of Revolution*. Stanford: Stanford University Press.

Plucknett, T. F. T. 1922. *Statutes and Their Interpretation in the First Half of the Fourteenth Century*. Cambridge: University Press.

_____. 1949. *Legislation of Edward I*. Oxford: Clarendon Press.

_____. 2001. *A Concise History of the Common Law*. Union, NJ: Lawbook Exchange.

Pocock, J. G. A. 1975. *The Machiavellian Moment* Princeton, NJ: Princeton University Press.

Pohlsander, H. A. 1964. *Metrical Studies in the Lyrics of Sophocles*. Leiden: Brill.

Pollock, F., and F. W. Maitland. 1968. *The History of English Law Before the Time of Edward I*. Cambridge: Cambridge University Press.

Portmann, W. 1988. *Geschichte in der spätantiken Panegyrik*. Frankfurt: Peter Lang.

Potter, D. S. 1990. *Prophecy and History in the Crisis of the Roman Empire*. Oxford: Clarendon Press.

_____. 1996a. "Emperors, Their Borders and Their Neighbors: The Scope of Imperial Mandata." *The Roman Army in the East*, 49–66. D. L. Kennedy, D. Braund, et al., eds. Ann Arbor, MI: Journal of Roman Archaeology.

_____. 1996b. "Palmyra and Rome: Odaenathus' Titulature and the Use of the *Imperium Maius*." *Zeitschrift für Papyrologie und Epigraphik* 113: 271–285.

_____. 1996c. "Performance, Power, and Justice in the High Empire." *Roman Theater and Society*, 129–159. W. J. Slater, ed. Ann Arbor: University of Michigan Press.

Powell, A. ed. 1992. *Roman Poetry and Propaganda in the age of Augustus*. London: Bristol Classical Press.

Powell, B.B. 1991. *Homer and the Origin of the Greek Alphabet*. Cambridge: Cambridge University Press.

Pratt, M. L. 1992. *Imperial Eyes: Travel Writing and Transculturation*. London: Routledge.

Price, J. J. 2001. *Thucydides and Internal War*. Cambridge: Cambridge University Press.

Price, S. R. F. 1984a. "Gods and Emperors: The Greek Language of the Roman Imperial Cult." *Journal of Hellenic Studies* 104: 79–95.

Price, S. R. F. 1984b. *Rituals and Power: The Roman Imperial Cult in Asia Minor*. Cambridge: Cambridge University Press.

Pritchard, J. B., ed. 1955. *The Ancient Near East in Pictures Relating to the Old Testament, Ancient Near Eastern Texts*. Princeton, NJ: Princeton University Press.

Pritchett, W. K. 1970. *The Choiseul Marble*. Berkeley: University of California Press.

_____. 1974. *The Greek State at War*. Berkeley: University of California Press.

_____. 1985. *Thucydides' Pentekontaetia and Other Essays*. Amsterdam: J.C. Gieben.

_____. 2002. *Ancient Greek Battle Speeches and a Palfrey*. Amsterdam: J.C. Gieben.

Pyman, A. 2006. *A History of Russian Symbolism*. Cambridge: Cambridge University Press.

Quirke, S. 1992. *Ancient Egyptian Religion*. London: British Museum Press.

Raaflaub, K. A., and L. J. Samons II. 1990. "Opposition to Augustus." *Between Republic and Empire: Interpretations of Augustus and his Principate*, 212–238. K. Raaflaub, M. Toher, G. W. Bowersock et al., eds. Berkeley: University of California Press.

Raeck, W. 1981. *Zum Barbarenbild in der Kunst Athens im 6. und 5. Jahrhundert*. Bonn: R. Habelt.

Ralston, W. R. S. 2005. *The Songs of the Russian People*. Whitefish, MT: Kessinger.

Ram, H. 2003. *The Imperial Sublime: A Russian Poetics of Empire*. Madison: University of Wisconsin Press.

Rapaczynski, A. 1987. *Nature and Politics: Liberalism in the Philosophies of Hobbes, Locke, and Rousseau*. Ithaca, NY: Cornell University Press.

Rasmussen, T., and N. J. Spivey. 1991. *Looking at Greek Vases*. Cambridge: Cambridge University Press.

Raven, S. 1993. *Rome in Africa*. 3d ed. London: Routledge.

Rawson, E. 1985. *Intellectual Life in the Late Roman Republic*. Baltimore: Johns Hopkins University Press.

Rawson, E. 1991. *Roman Culture and Society*. Oxford: Clarendon Press.

Redford, D. B. 2002. *The Ancient Gods Speak: A Guide to Egyptian Religion*. Oxford: Oxford University Press.

Reed, W. L. 1949. *The Asherah in the Old Testament*. Fort Worth, TX: Christian University Press.

Reeves, N. 1996. *The Complete Tutankhamun.* New York: Thames and Hudson.

Revell, L. 2009. *Roman Imperialism and Local Identities.* New York: Cambridge University Press.

Reynolds, J. 1980. "The Origins and Beginning of Imperial Cult at Aphrodisias." *Proceedings of the Cambridge Philological Society* 26: 70–84.

Reynolds, J. 1981. "New Evidence for the Imperial Cult in Julio-Claudian Aphrodisias." *Zeitschrift für Papyrologie und Epigraphik* 43: 317–327.

Reynolds, J. 1982. *Aphrodisias and Rome.* London: Society for the Promotion of Roman Studies.

_____, M. Beard, and C. Roueché. 1986. "Roman Inscriptions 1981–85." *Journal of Roman Studies* 76: 124–146.

Reynolds, L. J., and G. Hutner, eds. 2000. *National Imaginaries, American Identities.* Princeton, NJ: Princeton University Press.

Rhodes, P. J. 1985. *The Athenian Boule.* Oxford: Clarendon Press.

_____. 1981. *A Commentary on the Aristotelian Athenaion Politeia.* Oxford: Clarendon Press.

_____. 2004. *Athenian Democracy.* New York: Oxford University Press.

_____, and Robin Osborne. 2003. *Greek Historical Inscriptions: 404–323 B.C.* Oxford: Oxford University Press.

_____. 2006. *A History of the Classical Greek World: 478–323 B.C.* Malden, MA: Blackwell.

_____. 2007. "The Impact of Persian Wars on the Classical Greece." *Cultural Responses to the Persian Wars: Antiquity to the Third Millennium*, 31–46. E. Bridges, E. Hall and P. J. Rhodes, eds. Oxford: Oxford University Press.

Richardson, H. G., and G. O. Sayles. 1974. *The Governance of Mediaeval England from the Conquest to Magna Carta.* Edinburgh: Edinburgh University Press.

_____. 1964. *Governance of Medieval England.* Edinburgh: Edinburgh University Press.

Richardson, J. S. 1983. "The *Tabula Contrebiensis:* Roman Law in Spain in the Early First Century B.C." *Journal of Roman Studies* 73: 33–41.

Riche, P. 1976. *Education and Culture in the Barbarian West.* Columbia: University of South Carolina Press.

Richter, G. M. A. 1971. *The Engraved Gems of the Greeks, Etruscans and Romans.* Part 2, *Engraved Gems of the Romans.* London: Phaidon.

Riehle, W. 1981. *The Middle English Mystics.* London: Routledge and Kegan Paul.

Riepl, W. 1913. *Das Nachrichtenwesen des Altertums.* Leipzig: Teubner.

Rihll, T. E. 1999. *Greek Science.* New York: Oxford University Press.

Rist, J. M. 1994. *Augustine: Ancient Thought Baptized.* Cambridge: Cambridge University Press.

Rives, J. B. 1995. *Religion and Antiquity in Roman Carthage from Augustus to Constantine.* Oxford: Oxford University Press.

_____. 2007. *Religion in the Roman Empire.* Malden, MA: Blackwell.

Robbins, V. K. 1991. "Luke-Acts: A Mixed Population Seeks a Home in the Roman Empire." *Images of Empire*, 202–221. L. Alexander, ed. Sheffield, UK: Sheffield Academic Press.

Roberts, J. J. M. 1972. *The Earliest Semitic Pantheon: A Study of the Semitic Deities Attested in Mesopotamia Before Ur III.* Baltimore: Johns Hopkins University Press.

Robertson, A. J. 1925. *The Laws of the Kings of England from Edmund to Henry I.* Cambridge: Cambridge University Press.

_____, ed. 1956. *Anglo-Sexon Charters.* Cambridge: Cambridge University Press.

Rogers, G. M. 1991. *The Sacred Identity of Ephesos.* London: Routledge.

Romani, R. 2002. *National Character and Public Spirit in Britain and France, 1750–1914.* Cambridge: University Press.

Romm, J. 1998. *Herodotus.* New Haven: Yale University Press.

Rösch, G. 1978. "Onoma Basileias: Studien zum offiziellen Gebrach der Kaisertitel in spätantiker und frühbyzantinischer Zeit." *Byzantina Vindobonensia* 10. Vienna: Verlag der Österreichischen Akademie.

Rose, C. B. 1997a. *Dynastic Commemoration and Imperial Portraiture in the Julio Claudian Period.* Cambridge: Cambridge University Press.

Rose, C. B. 1997b. The Imperial Image in the Eastern Mediterranean." *Graecia Capta: The Landscapes of Roman Greece*, 108–120. S. Alcock, ed. Cambridge: Cambridge University Press.

Rosenstein, N. 1990. *Imperatores victi: Military Defeat and Aristocratic Competition in the Middle and Late Republic.* Berkeley: University of California Press.

Rosenthal, P. 2000. *The Poets' Jesus.* Oxford: Clarendon Press.

Ross, S. K. 1993. "The Last King of Edessa: New Evidence from the Middle Euphrates." *Zeitschrift für Papyrologie und Epigraphik* 97: 187–206.

Rostovtzeff, M. 1942. "*Vexillum* and Victory." *Journal of Roman Studies* 32: 92–106.

Roueché, C. 1984. "Acclamations in the Later Roman Empire: New Evidence from Aphrodisias." *Journal of Roman Studies* 74: 181–199.

Roueché, C. 1989. *Aphrodisias in Late Antiquity.* London: Society for the Promotion of Roman Studies.

Roussel, P., and F. de Visscher. 1942/43. "Les inscriptions du temple de Dmeir." *Syria* 23: 173–200.

Rowe, G. 1997. "*Omnis spes futura paternae stationis:* Public Responses to the Roman Imperial Succession." Doctoral thesis. The Queen's College, Oxford.

Rowling, J. T. 1989. *The Rise and Decline of Surgery in Dynastic Egypt.* Oxford: Antiquity Publications.

Roxan, M. M. 1978. *Roman Military Diplomas 1954–1977.* Institute of Archaeology, University of London.

Rubin, Z. 1980. *Civil-war Propaganda and Historiography.* Collection Latomus, 173. Brussels: Revue d'Études Latines.

Russell, L. 2001. *Colonial Frontiers: Indigenous-European Encounters in Settler Societies.* Manchester: Manchester University Press.

Russom, G. 1998. *Beowulf and Old Germanic Metre.* Cambridge: Cambridge University Press.

Ryan, R. M. 1997. *The Romantic Reformation, Religious Politics in English Literature, 1789–1824.* Cambridge: Cambridge University Press.

Sacchi, P. 2000. *The History of the Second Temple Period.* Sheffield, UK: Sheffield Academic Press.

Sachs, C. 1943. *The Rise of Music in the Ancient World, East and West.* New York: W. W. Norton.

Sacksteder, W. 1984. "Hobbes: Philosophical and Rhetorical Artifice." *Philosophy and Rhetoric* 17: 30–46.

Sa'd, Muhammad ibn. 1904–1940. *Kitab al-tabaqat al-kabir.* E. Sachau, ed. 9 vols. Leiden: Brill.

Said, E. 1978. *Orientalism.* New York: Penguin.

Salmon, E. T. 1982. *The Making of Roman Italy.* Ithaca, NY: Cornell University Press.

Sampson, G. 1985. *Writing Systems: A Linguistic Introduction.* Stanford: Stanford University Press.

Sandbach, F. H. 1977. *The Comic Theater of Greece and Rome.* New York: Norton.

Sanders, E. P. *The Historical Figure of Jesus.* London: Allen and Lane.

Schubert, F., ed. 1990. *Les archives de Marcus Lucretius Diogenes et textes apparentés.* Bonn: Habelt.

Schulz, F. 1936. *Principles of Roman Law.* Oxford: Clarendon Press.

_____. 1942. "Roman Registers of Births and Birth Certificates." *Journal of Roman Studies* 32: 78–91.

_____. 1943. "Roman Registers of Births and Birth Certificates, Part II." *Journal of Roman Studies* 33: 55–64.

Schurer, E. 1991. *The History of the Jewish People in the Age of Jesus Christ.* Edinburgh: Edinburgh University Press.

Schwartz, J. 1985. "Hobbes and the Two Kingdoms of God." *Polity* 18: 7–24.

Scott, W. C. 1984. *Musical Design in Aeschylean Theater.* Hanover, NH: Dartmouth College.

_____. 1996. *Musical Design in Sophoclean Theater.* Hanover, NH: Dartmouth College.

Sedley, D. 1998. *Lucretius and the Transformation of Greek Wisdom.* Cambridge: Cambridge University Press.

Segal, C. 1981. *Poetry and Myth in Ancient Pastoral: Essays on Theocritus and Virgil.* Princeton, NJ: Princeton University Press.

Segal, E. 1968. *Roman Laughter: The Comedy of Plautus.* Cambridge, MA: Harvard University Press.

Senner, W. M. 1991. *The Origins of Writing.* Lincoln: University of Nebraska Press.

Setton, K. M. 1941. *Christian Attitude Towards the Emperor in the Fourth Century.* New York: Columbia University Press.

Shacht, J. 1964. *An Introduction to Islamic Law.* Oxford: Clarendon Press.

_____. 1950. *The Origins of Mhuammadan Jurisprudence.* Oxford: Clarendon Press.

_____. 2004. "Pre-Islamic Background and Early Development of Jurisprudence." *Formation of Islamic Law,* 29–58. W. B. Hallaq, ed. Burlington: Ashgate.

Al-Shafi'I, M. B. I. 1961. *Kitab al-umm.* M. Au. al-Najjar, ed. 8 vols. Cairo: Maktabat al-Kulliyyat al-Azhariyya.

Shepherd, D. 1992. *Beyond Metafiction: Self-consciousness in Soviet Literature.* Oxford: Oxford University Press.

Sherbowitz-Wetzor, O. P., and S. H. Cross, eds. 1973. *The Russian Primary Chronicle: Laurentian Text.* Cambridge, MA: Mediaeval Academy of America.

Sherwin-White, A. N. 1966. *The Letters of Pliny: A Historical and Social Commentary.* Oxford: Clarendon Press.

_____. 1973a. *The Roman Citizenship.* Oxford: Oxford University Press.

_____. 1973b. "The *Tabula* of Banasa and the *Constitutio Antoniniana.*" *Journal of Roman Studies* 63: 86–98.

_____. 1982. "The *Lex Repetundarum* and the Political Ideas of Gaius Gracchus." *Journal of Roman Studies* 72: 18–31.

_____. 1984. *Roman Foreign Policy in the East, 168 B.C. to A.D. 1.* Norman: University of Oklahoma Press.

Siddiqi, M. Z. 1961. *Hadith Literature: Its Origin, Development, Special Features and Criticism.* Calcutta: Calcutta University Press.

Simon, D. 1994. "Legislation as Both a World Order and a Legal Order." *Law and Society in Byzantium: Ninth-Twelfth Centuries,* 1–25. A. E. Laiou and D. Simon, eds. Washington, DC: Dumbarton Oaks.

Simpson, A. W. B. 1986. *A History of the Land Law.* Oxford: Clarendon Press.

_____. 1987. *Legal Theory and Legal History: Es-*

says on the Common Law. Ronceverte, WV: Hambledon Press.

_____. 1981. "The Law of Ethelbert." *On the Laws and Customs of England*, 3–17. M. S. Arnold, et al., eds. Chapel Hill: University of North Carolina Press.

Sivan, H. 1991. "Eunapius and the West: Remarks on frg. 78 (Müller)." *Historia* 40: 95–104.

Slater, N. W. 1985. *Plautus in Performance*. Princeton, NJ: Princeton University Press.

Smallwood, E. M. 1970. *Philonis Alexandrini Legatio ad Gaium*. Leiden: Brill.

Smith, B. G. 2000. *Imperialism: A History in Documents*. Oxford: Oxford University Press.

Smith, M. 1995. *Early Mysticism in the Near and Middle East*. Oxford: Oxford University Press.

_____. 2001. *The Origins of Biblical Monotheism: Israel's Polytheistic Background and the Ugaritic Texts*. New York: Oxford University Press.

_____. 2002. *The Early History of God: Yahweh and Other Deities in Ancient Israel*. Grand Rapids, Mich.

Smith, R. R. R. 1987. "The Imperial Reliefs from the Sebasteion at Aphrodisias." *Journal of Roman Studies* 77: 88–138.

_____. 1988. "Simulacra Gentium: The Ethne from the Sebasteion at Aphrodisias." *Journal of Roman Studies* 78: 50–77.

_____. 1996. "Typology and Diversity in the Portraits of Augustus." *Journal of Roman Archaeology* 9: 30–47.

Snodgrass, A. M. 1971. *The Dark Age of Greece: An Archaeological Survey of the Eleventh to Eighth Century B.C.* Edinburgh: Edinburgh University Press.

Snyder, G. F. 1985. *Ante Pacem: Archaeological Evidence of Church Life Before Constantine*. Mercer: Mercer University Press.

Snyder, W. F. 1940. "Public Anniversaries in the Roman Empire." *Yale Classical Studies* 7: 223–317.

Spawforth, A. J. 1986. "The World of the Panhellenion, II: Three Dorian Cities." *Journal of Roman Studies* 76: 88–105.

Stack, F. 1985. *Pope and Horace*. Cambridge: Cambridge University Press.

Stadter, P. A. 1980. *Arrian of Nicomedia*. Chapel Hill: University of North Carolina Press.

Stahl, M. 1978. *Imperiale Herrschaft und provinziale Stadt: Strukturprobleme der römischen Reichsorganisation im 1.-3. Jh. der Kaiserzeit*. Hypomnemata 52. Göttingen: Vandenhoeck and Ruprecht.

Stein, P. 1966. *Regulae Iuris From Juristic Rules to Legal Maxims*. Edinburgh: Edinburgh University Press.

_____. 1988. *The Character and Influence of the Roman Civil Law*. London: Hambledon.

Steiner, D. T. 2001. *Images in Mind, Statues in Archaic and Classical Greek Literature and Thought*. Princeton, NJ: Princeton University Press.

Stemberger, G. 1996. *Introduction to the Talmud and Midrash*. M. Bockmuehl, trans. 2d ed. Edinburgh: T&T Clark.

Stanton, G. 1989. *The Gospels and Jesus*. Oxford: Oxford University Press.

Stern, M. 1987. "Josephus and the Roman Empire as Reflected in *The Jewish War*." In *Josephus, Judaism, and Christianity*, 71–80. L. H. Feldman and G. Hata, eds. Detroit: Wayne State University Press.

Stetkevych, S. P. 1983. "Structualist Interpretations of pre–Islamic Poetry." *Journal of Near Eastern Studies* 42 (2): 85–107.

_____. 1993. *The Mute Immortals Speak: Pre-Islamic Poetry and Poetics of Ritual (Myth and Poetics)*. Ithaca, NY: Cornell University Press.

_____. 2002. *The Poetics of Islamic Legitimacy: Myth, Gender, and Ceremony in the Classical Arabic Odes*. Bloomington: Indiana University Press.

_____. 2009. *Early Islamic Poetry and Poetics*. Burlington, VT: Ashgate.

_____. 2010. *The Mantle Odes: Arabic Praise Poems to the Prophet Muhammad*. Bloomington: Indiana University Press.

Stevenson, T. R. 1992. "The Ideal Benefactor and the Father Analogy in Greek and Roman Thought." *Classical Quarterly* 42: 421–436.

Stock, B. 1996. *The Reader: Meditation, Self-Knowledge, and the Ethics of Interpretation*. Cambridge, MA: Harvard University Press.

Stubbs, W. 1979. *The Constitutional History of England*. Chicago: University of Chicago Press.

Sullivan, Z. T. 1993. *Narratives of Empire: The Fictions of Rudyard Kipling*. Cambridge: Cambridge University Press.

Talbert, R. J. A. 1984. *The Senate of Imperial Rome*. Princeton, NJ: Princeton University Press.

_____. 1988. "Commodus as Diplomat in an Extract from the *Acta Aenatus*." *Zeitschrift für Papyrologie und Epigraphik* 71: 137–147.

Tambling, J. 2010. *Allegory*. New York: Routledge.

Taplin, 1992. *Homeric Soundings: The Shaping of the Iliad*. Oxford: Clarendon Press.

Tarn, W. W. 1948. *Alexander the Great*. Vol. 2, *Sources and Studies*. Cambridge: Cambridge University Press.

el-Tayib, Abdulla. 1983. *Pre-Islamic Poetry: Arabic Literature to the End of the Umayyad Period*, 27–113. A.F.L. Beeston, et al., eds. Cambridge: Cambridge University Press.

Taylor, J. H. 2001. *Death and the Afterlife in Ancient Egypt*. Chicago: University of Chicago Press.

Taylor, M. C. 2010. *Thucydides, Pericles, and the Idea of Athens in the Peloponnesian War*. Cambridge: Cambridge University Press.

Terras, V. 1991. *A History of Russian Literature.* New Haven: Yale University Press.

Thomas, N. 1994. *Colonialism's Culture: Anthropology, Travel and Government.* Cambridge: Cambridge University Press.

Thompson, J. B. 1990. *Ideology and Modern Culture: Critical Social Theory in the Era of Mass Communication.* Stanford: Stanford University Press.

Thorpe, B. 2002. *Ancient Laws and Institutes of England.* 2 vols. 1980. Reprint, Union, NJ: Law Book Exchange.

Tissol, G. 1988. "Narrative Style in Ovid's Metamorphoses and Influence of Callimachus." Ph.D. dissertation, University of California, Berkeley.

Toll, K. 1991. "The *Aeneid* as an Epic of National Identity: *Italiam laeto socii clamore salutant.*" *Helios* 18: 3–14.

_____. 1997. "Making Roman-ness and the *Aeneid.*" *Classical Antiquity* 16: 34–56.

Toynbee, A. J. 1973. *Constantine Porphyrogenitus and His World.* Oxford: Oxford University Press.

Toynbee, J. M. C. 1947. "*Roma* and *Constantinopolis* in Late-antique Art from 312 to 365." *Journal of Roman Studies* 37: 135–144.

_____. 1953. "*Roma* and *Constantinopolis* in Late-antique Art from 365 to Justin II." *Studies Presented to D. M. Robinson,* 261–277. G. E. Mylonas, ed. St. Louis: Washington University Press.

_____. 1986. *Roman Medallions.* Numismatic Studies 5. New York: American Numismatic Society. (Reprint, with bibliographic addenda by W. E. Metcalf.)

Tracy, S. V. 1990. *The Story of the Odyssey.* Princeton, NJ: Princeton University Press.

Tuplin, C. J. 1985. "Imperial Tyranny: Some Reflections on a Classical Greek Political Metaphor." *Crux: Essays in Greek History Presented to GEM de Ste Croix,* 348–75. P. A. Cartledge and F. D. Harvey, eds. London: Duckworth.

Turcan, R. 1996. *The Cults of the Roman Empire.* New York: Blackwell.

_____. 2000. *The Gods of Ancient Rome: Religion in Everyday Life from Archaic to Imperial Times.* London: Routledge.

Turner, V. 1974. *Dramas, Fields, and Metaphors.* Ithaca, NY: Cornell University Press.

_____. 1987. *The Anthropology of Performance.* New York: PAJ Publications.

Taylor, L. R. 1988. *The Divinity of the Roman Emperor.* Atlanta: Scholars Press.

van Berchem, D. 1939. *Les distributions de blé et d'argent à la plèbe romaine sous l'empire.* Geneva: Faculté des Lettres, Université de Genève.

Van Caenegem, R. C. 1959. *Royal Writs in England from the Conquest to Glanvill, Studies in*

the Early History of the Common Law. London: Selden Society, vol. 77.

_____. 1973. *The Birth of the English Common Law.* Cambridge: Cambridge University Press.

_____. 1987. *Judges, Legislators and Professors.* Cambridge: Cambridge University Press.

Van der Toorn, K. 1985. *Sin and Sanction in Israel and Mesopotamia: A Comparative Study.* Assen, Netherlands: Van Gorcum.

_____. 2007. *Scribal Culture and the Making of the Hebrew Bible.* Cambridge, MA: Harvard University Press.

Vandorpe, K. 1995. *Breaking the Seal of Secrecy: Sealing-practices in Graeco-Roman and Byzantine Egypt, Based on Greek, Demotic, and Latin Papyrological Evidence.* Leiden: Papyrologish Instituut.

Vermes, G. 1983. *Jesus the Jew: A Historian's Reading of the Gospels.* London: SCM Press.

_____. 1984. *Jesus and the World of Judaism.* Philadelphia: Fortress.

Veyne, P. 1962. "Les honneurs posthumes de Flavia Domitilla et les dédicaces grecques et latines." *Latomus* 21: 49–98.

_____. 1988. *Roman Erotic Elegy Love Poetry and the West.* Chicago: University of Chicago Press.

_____. 2003. *Seneca: The Life of a Stoic.* New York: Routledge.

Vidal-Naquet, P. 1986. *The Black Hunter: Forms of Thought and Forms of Society in the Greek World.* Baltimore: Johns Hopkins University Press.

Viljamaa, T. 1968. *Studies in Greek Encomiastic Poetry of the Early Byzantine Period.* Helsinki: Societas Scientiarum Fennica.

Vinokur, G. O. 1971. *The Russian Language: A Brief History.* Cambridge: Cambridge University Press.

Wachtel, A. 1994. *An Obsession with History: Russian Writers Confront the Past.* Stanford: Stanford University Press.

_____. 1998. *Intersections and Transpositions: Russian Music, Literature, and Society.* Evanston: Northwestern University Press.

_____. 2004. *The Cambridge Introduction to Russian Poetry.* Cambridge: Cambridge University Press.

_____. 2009. *Russian Literature.* Malden, MA: Polity.

Walbank, F. 1972. *Polybius.* Berkeley: University of California Press.

Walker, S. 1997. *Athens Under Augustus.* Hoff and Rotroff, 67–80.

Wallace, S. 1954. *A History of Speech Education in America.* New York: Appleton-Century-Crofts.

Wallace-Hadrill, A. 1990. "Roman Arches and Greek Honours: The Language of Power at Rome." *Proceedings of the Cambridge Philological Society* 36: 143–181.

Wallace-Hadrill, A. 1997. "*Mutatio Morum:* The Idea of a Cultural Revolution." *The Roman Cultural Revolution,* 3–22. T. Habinek and A. Schiesaro, eds. Cambridge: Cambridge University Press.

Walicki, A. 1979. *A History of Russian Thought from the Enlightenment to Marxism.* Stanford: Stanford University Press.

Warner, M. 1990. *The Letters of the Republic: Republication and the Public Sphere in Eighteenth Century America.* Cambridge, MA: Harvard University Press.

Warrior, V. M. 2006. *Roman Religion.* Cambridge: Cambridge University Press.

Watson, A. 1974. *Law Making in the Later Roman Republic.* Oxford: Clarendon Press.

_____. 1991. *Legal Origins and Legal Change.* London: Rio Grande.

Watt, M. 1956. *Muhammad in Medina.* Oxford: Oxford University Press.

_____. 1973. *The Formative Period of Islamic Thought.* Edinburgh: Edinburgh University Press.

Weber, M. 1968. *On Charisma and Institution Building.* S. N. Eisenstadt, ed. Chicago: University of Chicago Press.

Webster, J., and N. Cooper, eds. 1996. *Roman Imperialism: Post-colonial Perspectives.* Leicester: School of Archaeological Studies.

Weinstock, S. 1971. *Divus Julius.* Oxford: Clarendon Press.

Wellesley, K. 1989. *The Long Year A.D. 69.* Bristol: Bristol Classical Press.

Wenger, J. R. 1982. "Islamic and Talmudic Jurisprudence: The Four Roots of Islamic Law and Their Talmudic Counterparts." *The American Journal of Legal History* 26: 25–71.

West, D. 1966. *Reading Horace.* Edinburgh: University of Edinburgh Press.

West, F. J. 2005. *The Justiciarship in England, 1066–1232.* Cambridge: Cambridge University Press.

West, M. L. 1973. "Greek Poetry 2000–700 B.C." *Classical Quarterly* 23: 179–82.

_____. 1974. *Studies in Greek Elegy and Iambus.* Berlin.

_____. 1981. "The Singing of Homer." *Journal of Hellenic Studies* 101, 113–129.

_____. 1985. *The Hesiodic Catalogue of Women: Its Nature, Structure, and Origins.* Oxford: Clarendon Press.

_____. 1988. *Hesiod's "Theogony" and "Works and Days."* Oxford: Oxford University Press.

_____. 1993. *Greek Lyric Poetry.* Oxford: Oxford University Press.

_____. 1994a. *Ancient Greek Music.* Oxford: Clarendon Press.

_____. 1994b. "The Babylonian Musical Notation and the Hurrian Melodic Texts." *Music and Letters* 75: 161–179.

_____, ed. 1999. *Greek Lyric Poetry: The Poems and Fragments of the Greek Iambic Elegiac and Melic Poets (excluding Pindar and Bacchylides) Down to 450 B.C.* Oxford: Oxford University Press.

_____. 2007. *Indo-European Poetry and Myth.* Oxford: Oxford University Press.

_____, ed. 2003. *Greek Epic Fragments from the Seventh to the Fifth Centuries B.C.* Cambridge, MA: Harvard University Press.

_____, and E. Pöhlmann, eds. 2001. *Documents of Ancient Greek Music: The Extant Melodies and Fragments.* Oxford: Clarendon Press.

Westenholz, J. G. 1997. *Legends of the Kings of Akkade: The Texts.* Winona Lake, IN: Eisenbrauns.

Wetzel, J. 1992. *Augustine and the Limits of Virtue.* Cambridge: Cambridge University Press.

Wheeler, E. L. 1993. "Methodological Limits and the Mirage of Roman Strategy." *The Journal of Military History* 57: 7–41 and 215–240.

Whenlan, F. G. 1985. "Language and its Abuses in Hobbes's Political Philosophy." *American Polticial Science Review* 75: 59–75.

White, P. 1993. *Promised Verse: Poets in the Society of Augustan Rome.* Cambridge, MA: Harvard University Press.

_____. 1997. "Julius Caesar and the Publication of *Acta* in Late Republican Rome." *Chiron* 27: 73–84.

Whitby, M. 1985. "The Occasion of Paul in the Silentiary's Ekphrasis of S. Sophia." *Cambridge Quarterly* 36: 215–28.

Whittaker, C. R., ed. 1970. *Herodian.* Cambridge, MA: Harvard University Press.

Whittaker, C. R. 1994. *Frontiers of the Roman Empire: A Social and Economic Study.* Baltimore: Johns Hopkins University Press.

Whittaker, C. R. 1996. "Where are the Frontiers Now?" *The Roman Army in the East,* 24–41. D. L. Kennedy, ed. Ann Arbor, MI: Journal of Roman Archaeology.

Wigger, J. H. 1998. *Taking Heaven by Storm: Methodism and the Rise of Popular Christianity in America.* Oxford: Oxford University Press.

Wiggins, S. A. 2007. *A Reassessment of Asherah: With Further Considerations of the Goddess.* Piscataway, NJ: Gorgias Press.

Wiles, D. 1991. *The Masks of Menander Sign and Meaning in Greek and Roman Performance.* Cambridge: Cambridge University Press.

Wilkinson, R. H. 2003. *The Complete Gods and Goddesses of Ancient Egypt.* New York: Thames and Hudson.

Williams, M. 1983. *The Jazz Tradition New and Revised Edition.* Oxford: Oxford University Press.

Williams, S., and G. Friell. 1995. *Theodosius: The Empire at Bay.* New Haven: Yale University Press.

Wills, J. 1996. *Repetition in Latin Poetry: Figures of Allusion.* Oxford: Oxford University Press.

Wilson, P. 2003. *Sacred Signs: Hieroglyphs in Ancient Egypt.* Oxford: Oxford University Press.

Wilson, P. 2000. *The Athenian Institution of Khoregia: The Chorus, the City and the Stage.* Cambridge: Cambridge University Press.

Wilson, R. A. 1966. *Old Testament History and Religion.* New York.

Windeatt, B. 1994. *English Mystics of the Middle Ages.* Cambridge: Cambridge University Press.

Winnett, F. V., and W. L. Reed. 1970. *Ancient Records from North Arabia.* Toronto: University of Toronto Press.

Wiseman, T. P. 1995. *Remus: A Roman Myth.* Cambridge: Cambridge University Press.

Wilson, J. V. K. 1965. "An Introduction to Babylonian Psychiatry." *Assyriological Studies* 16: 289–98.

Wolf, E. 1969. "Society and Symbols in Latin Europe and in the Islamic Near East: Some Comparisons." *Anthropological Quarterly* 42 (3): 287–301.

Wolfe, E. 1988. *The Book Culture of a Colonial American City: Philadelphia Books, Bookmen, and Booksellers.* New York: Oxford University Press.

Woodard, R. D. 2007. *The Cambridge Companion to Greek Mythology.* Cambridge: Cambridge University Press.

Woodman, A. J. 1983. *Velleius Paterculus: The Caesarian and Augustan Narrative (2.41–93).* Cambridge: Cambridge University Press.

_____. 1988. *Rhetoric in Classical Historiography.* London: Croom Helm.

_____. 1993a. Amateur Dramatics at the Court of Nero: *Annals* 15: 48–74." *Tacitus and the Tacitean Tradition,* 104–128. T. J. Luce and A. J. Woodman, eds. Princeton, NJ: Princeton University Press.

_____. 2009. *The Cambridge Companion to Tacitus.* Cambridge: Cambridge University Press.

_____, and D. West, eds. 1984. *Poetry and Pol-* itics in the Age of Augustus. Cambridge: Cambridge University Press.

Woods, C., G. Emberling, and E. Teeter, eds. 2010. *Visible Language: Inventions of Writing in the Ancient Middle East and Beyond.* Chicago: Oriental Institute of the University of Chicago.

Woolf, G. 1997. "The Roman Urbanization of the East." *The Early Roman Empire in the East,* 1–14. S. Alcock, ed. Oxford: Oxbow.

_____. 1998. *Becoming Roman: The Origins of Provincial Civilization in Gaul.* Cambridge: Cambridge University Press.

Worp, K. A. 1982. "Byzantine Imperial Titulature in the Greek Documentary Papyri: The Oath Formulas." *Zeitschrift für Papyrologie und Epigraphi* 45: 199–223.

Wright, J. 1974. *Dancing in Chains: The Stylistic Unity of the Comoedia Palliata.* Rome: American Academy.

Wyke, W. 2002. *The Roman Mistress.* Oxford: Oxford University Press.

Youtie, H. C. 1971b. Between Literacy and Illiteracy." *Greek, Roman, and Byzantine Studies* 12: 239–261.

_____. 1975a. "Because They Do Not Know Letters." *Zeitschrift für Papyrologie und Epigraphik* 19: 101–108.

_____. 1975b. "Upografeus: The Social Impact of Illiteracy in Graeco-Roman Egypt." *Zeitschrift für Papyrologie und Epigraphik* 17: 201–221.

Zayadine, F. 1989. "Peintures et mosaiques mythologiques en Jordanie." *Iconographic Classique et Identities Regionales,* 406–32. L. Kahil and C. Auge, eds. Paris: Flammarion.

Ziff, L. 1997. *Writing in the New Nation: Prose, Print, and Politics in the Early United States.* New Haven: Yale University Press.

Zimmermann, R. 1990. *The Law of Obligations: Roman Founation of the Civilian Tradition,* Capetown: Juta.

Index